Bias in
Psychotherapy

Bias in Psychotherapy

Edited by

JOAN MURRAY

and

PAUL R. ABRAMSON

PRAEGER

PRAEGER SPECIAL STUDIES • PRAEGER SCIENTIFIC

616.8914
B 579

Library of Congress Cataloging in Publication Data

Main entry under title:

Bias in psychotherapy.

"Praeger special studies."
"Praeger scientific."
Bibliography: p.
Includes index.
1. Psychotherapist and patient.   2. Counter-transference (Psychology)   3. Sex (Psychology)
4. Race—Psychological aspects.   I. Murray,
Joan, Ph. D.   II. Abramson, Paul R.   [DNLM:
1. Psychotherapy.   2. Identification (Psychology)
3. Prejudice.   4. Attitude of health personnel.
5. Professional-patient relations.   WM 420 B579]
RC480.8.B5   1983   616.89′14   82-22315
ISBN 0-03-063226-9

Published in 1983 by Praeger Publishers
CBS Educational and Professional Publishing
a Division of CBS Inc.
521 Fifth Avenue, New York, New York 10175 U.S.A.

3456789   052   987654321

Printed in the United States of America

Contents

v

Introduction

PAUL R. ABRAMSON

In writing about the history of psychotherapy, Zilboorg (1941) stressed the importance of circumspection. It was all too easy, he felt, to ignore the limitations and inconsistencies in favor of the achievements. Unfortunately, this perspective gives a jaundiced representation of the field of psychotherapy. Vital details and factors are frequently disregarded because we minimize their importance—or because we remember them with "quaint" regard.

Bias in psychotherapy is one such factor. In the original medical model, bias was unconscionable, because the psychotherapist was merely an instrument in the treatment process. Freud suggested that the therapist should be like the "surgeon who puts aside all of his own feelings, including that of human sympathy, and concentrates his mind on one single purpose, that of performing the operation as skillfully as possible" (Freud, 1910/1924). Freud later recanted this position and introduced the notion of *countertransference* to refer to feelings that the psychotherapist experiences as a result of the patient's influence on his or her (the psychotherapist's) unconscious feelings. Freud also noted that every psychotherapist's achievements were limited by his or her own "complexes and resistances" (Freud, 1912/1924). As an alternative, psychotherapists were then urged to be honest and human (Fenichel, 1945; Menninger, 1958), with the added belief that countertransference would continue to provoke constructive intrapsychic changes within the patient (Whitaker & Malone, 1953).

To ignore the fact that Freud drew an analogy between the psychotherapist and the surgeon would be to certainly misrepresent the spirit of psychotherapy in the beginning of the 20th century. For whatever reason, it is clear that psychotherapy was originally conceptualized as a mechanistic process. When substantial evidence indicated that it was not, the conception changed. Now we can look back with quaint amusement at the attempt to liken the psychotherapist and surgeon as equally dispassionate operators.

Although the focus has shifted, psychotherapists are once again expressing

vii

concerns about bias in psychotherapy. Now the issue is the extent to which cultural expectations, stereotypes, and prejudices influence the therapeutic process. The specific concerns generally include the perpetuation of traditional sex roles, differential treatment for white and nonwhite patients, sexualization of the treatment process, and heterosexual bias of treatment orientations. The present volume is addressed to these later concerns. As a guiding premise, the editors have collected chapters that either provide a foundation for research on bias, examine experimental literature on bias in psychotherapy, or provide alternative conceptualizations for bias in psychotherapy. As a whole, the book has been edited in the spirit of a productive challenge to psychotherapists—not in condemnation of the practice of psychotherapy. As such, the heuristic objective is to encourage psychotherapists to evaluate examples of the current literature on bias in psychotherapy. In this manner, the editors are striving to maintain what Zilboorg (1941) has called the "spirit of humanism":

> The whole course of the history of medical psychology is punctuated by the medical man's struggle to rise above the prejudices of all ages in order to identify himself with the psychological realities of his patients. Every time such an identification was achieved the medical man became a psychiatrist. The history of psychiatry is essentially the history of humanism. Every time humanism has diminished or degenerated into mere philanthropic sentimentality, psychiatry has entered a new ebb. Every time the spirit of humanism has arisen, a new contribution to psychiatry has been made. (pp. 524–525)

ORGANIZATION OF THE VOLUME

This book is intended for clinicians who practice psychotherapy and for students who are in training. Although much of the material presented herein involves experimental literature, it addresses issues that all clinicians must consider. However, the literature is presented in the experimental mode because it is still subject to debate. Thus, the clinician can evaluate the substance or merits of the original sources (or reviews of the original literature). Since the literature is still equivocal, a number of different perspectives have been included. Consequently, the reader is confronted with chapters that raise considerable concerns about prejudice and bias in psychotherapy, and with other chapters that attempt to dispel such concerns. In addition to these contrasting points of view, chapters have also been included on the history of bias in psychotherapy, the social psychology of bias, experimental research on bias in psychotherapy, treatment issues in bias in psychotherapy, and practical alternatives to bias in psychotherapy.

This book has five sections. Section I, "Historical Perspective," includes two chapters: Joan Murray's "Sex Bias in Psychotherapy: A Historical Perspective" (Chapter 1), and "A Summary of Phyllis Chesler's *Women and Madness*" (Chapter 2). These two chapters provide a historical overview of the issue of gender bias in psychotherapy. Chapter 1 reviews material on social factors and the traditional female role, the representation of women in psychological theory, and the practice of psychotherapy. Chapter 2 presents a provocative statement concerning the relationship of the traditional female sex role to female psychopathology and treatment.

Section II of this volume is entitled "Social-Psychological Issues in Bias." Three chapters are included: Elaine Hatfield and Morton S. Perlmutter's "Social-Psychological Issues in Bias: Physical Attractiveness" (Chapter 3); Robert Rosenthal's "Experimenter Effects in Laboratories, Classrooms, and Clinics" (Chapter 4); and David L. Hamilton's "Effects of Bias on Attribution and Information Processing: A Cognitive-Attributional Analysis of Stereotyping" (Chapter 5). These chapters have been incorporated in the present volume to provide theoretical underpinnings for the clinical literature and to suggest processes through which bias may occur. For instance, Hatfield and Perlmutter's review of the social-psychological literature on bias and physical attractiveness presents persuasive evidence that most people (including psychotherapists) believe that beauty is sanity, character, and competence. Furthermore, Hatfield and Perlmutter review evidence suggesting that beautiful people are treated more compassionately and that they are more popular, have better self-concepts, and are often better adjusted and mentally healthier than their unattractive peers. Also of significance is Robert Rosenthal's review of the literature on experimenter effects in laboratories, classrooms, and clinics. The well-documented phenomenon of expectancy effects has considerable relevance to the therapeutic process, especially in terms of the consequences of interpersonal self-fulfilling prophecies. Finally, Hamilton's chapter on bias in attribution has considerable relevance for how psychotherapists generate causal explanations of behavior.

Section III of this volume is entitled "Research on Bias in Therapy." Seven chapters are included, covering three separate issues: gender, race, and sexuality. For gender, three chapters are included: Joan Murray and Paul R. Abramson's "An Investigation of the Effects of Client Gender and Attractiveness on Psychotherapists' Judgments" (Chapter 6); Christine V. Davidson's "Making the Conceptual Leap from Sex Bias to Countertransference: A Closer Look at the Patient-Therapist Dyad" (Chapter 7); and George Stricker and Robin Shafran's "Gender and Psychotherapy: A Review of the Empirical Literature" (Chapter 8). For race, a comprehensive review of the literature is included, Stephen I. Abramowitz and Joan Murray's "Race Effects in Psychotherapy" (Chapter 9). And, finally, for sexuality, three chapters are included:

Leslie R. Schover's "Psychotherapists' Responses to Client Sexuality: A Source of Bias in Treatment?" (Chapter 10); Jean C. Holroyd's "Erotic Contact as an Instance of Sex-Biased Therapy" (Chapter 11); and Stephen F. Morin and Kenneth A. Charles' "Heterosexual Bias in Psychotherapy" (Chapter 12).

The chapters within Section III consist of original research and/or reviews of the experimental literature. In the gender subsection, Murray and Abramson's chapter describes an experiment that examined the extent to which a client's gender and/or physical attractiveness influenced the course of that client's therapy. Subjects were drawn from a nationwide sample of practicing psychotherapists. Davidson's chapter, which is quite different in conceptualization, suggests the possibility that the issue of sex bias in psychotherapy might be more fruitfully examined if it were conceptualized as a form of countertransference. The last gender chapter, by Stricker and Shafran, addresses the concern that gender bias may be overemphasized in relation to the complexity of the psychotherapeutic process.

In the race subsection of Section III, Abramowitz and Murray provide a critical overview of the experimental and clinical literature on bias effects attributable to race. As their chapter indicates, the conclusions are far from being straightforward, with complications arising from limited methodology and unqualified generalizations.

Finally, in the sexuality subsection, Schover's chapter describes a unique experiment (using an analogue methodology) that examined therapists' reactions to client sexual material. Holroyd's chapter is an extensive review of the literature on erotic contact between psychotherapists and their clients. This literature is discussed in terms of prevalence, gender differences, ethical standards, transference and countertransference, sex therapy, the reasons why therapists have sex with patients, consequences for clients, and remedies. Lastly, Morin and Charles's chapter addresses the issue of heterosexual bias in psychotherapy with lesbian and gay male clients. Suggestions that are offered include affirmative psychotherapies, consciousness raising for mental health professionals, and consumer awareness.

The last two sections of this book (Sections IV and V) each include one chapter. Section IV, "Reducing Bias In Therapy," presents a chapter by Elizabeth Cooley and Joan Murray entitled "What Can Be Done about Bias in Therapy?" Section V, "Conclusions and Future Directions," presents a chapter by Steven López entitled "The Study of Psychotherapy Bias: Some Conceptual Issues and Some Concluding Remarks." Cooley and Murray outline a variety of practical alternatives in the areas of therapist training, continuing education programs, and professional and consumer awareness. The López chapter, which is the final one in this book, presents an overview of the conceptual issues within the field of clinical judgment bias, with reference to all of the previous chapters. López concludes his chapter with recommendations for future research.

REFERENCES

Fenichel, O. *The psychoanalytic theory of neurosis.* New York: Norton, 1945.

Freud, S. The future prospects of psychoanalytic therapy. In J. Strachey (Ed.), *Collected papers.* London: Hogarth Press, 1924. (Originally published, 1910.)

Freud, S. Recommendations for physicians on the psychoanalytic method of treatment. In J. Strachey, (Ed.), *Collected papers.* London: Hogarth Press, 1924. (Originally published, 1912.)

Menninger, K. *Theory of psychoanalytic technique.* New York: Basic Books, 1958.

Whitaker, C. A., & Malone, T. P. *The roots of psychotherapy.* New York: McGraw-Hill, 1953.

Zilboorg, G. *A history of medical psychology.* New York: Norton, 1941.

I Historical Perspective

Chapter 1 discusses the emergence of interest in gender bias in psychotherapy, why gender bias might be expected to occur there, and how the various concerns developed into research investigating the occurrence of sex bias in psychotherapy. The strong demands placed on a woman to stay within the traditional female role of wife and mother, the fact that expectations about women had been incorporated into psychological theory and equated with normal behavior, and the existence of widely shared stereotypes of women gave early investigators good reason to expect gender bias to occur in therapy. The kinds of research that they developed to explore whether and how bias occurs can be broadly classified into investigations of whether therapists believe in a double standard of mental health paralleling traditional sex roles and investigations of whether they treat men and women differently (e.g., by fostering traditional sex-role behavior in their clients).

Unfortunately, this research has been plagued with methodological problems, many of which have biased the research against finding gender effects. These problems are discussed, with an eye toward improving research in this area.

Chapter 2 summarizes the work that was largely responsible for generating interest in sex bias in psychotherapy—Phyllis Chesler's *Women and Madness* (1972). Before its publication, the existence of sex bias in psychotherapy was seldom mentioned, even less often researched. Since 1972, research in this area has grown tremendously; some researchers have been motivated by a desire to disprove Chesler's claims, others by a desire to validate them.

In addition, Chesler's work has served to stimulate discussion of the issue of sex bias in therapy among clinicians and clinicians-in-training. Such discussion has made increasingly greater numbers of therapists conscious of the

1

possibility of sex bias in therapy, and perhaps this awareness has already led to a diminution of sex bias in psychotherapeutic practice.

The major thrust of *Women and Madness* is the contention that traditional psychotherapy is based on an acceptance of the traditional female role as the only "normal" role for women. In order to be considered "normal" in the eyes of clinicians, a woman must be passive, dependent, and helpless; must marry, bear children, and raise them; and must be content with herself in this role. Even though the traditional female role is seen as less socially desirable than the traditional male role, it is the only acceptable role for a woman.

This split in the behaviors that clinicians consider mentally healthy for men and for women constitutes a double standard of mental health. That is, psychotherapists hold one standard for men and another for women, and both standards parallel the traditional sex-role stereotypes. Consequently, the behaviors diagnosed as abnormal in women are different from those so diagnosed in men. Generally, the behaviors considered pathological are exaggerations of the respective male and female sex roles (e.g., extremes of passivity in women, extremes of aggressiveness in men) or rejections of those roles (e.g., aggressiveness in women, passivity in men).

Chesler reinterprets "female" mental illnesses as symptoms of female oppression, which is the fact of women's being powerless, being discriminated against, and believing in their own inferiority (i.e., women's position in society today). She draws parallels between women's position in contemporary society relative to men and the position of slaves in their society relative to the slave owners. By taking this view, Chesler shifts the emphasis from pathology in the individual woman to pathology in the society. What is now necessary is a similar shift in the focus of treatment—from the sick patient to the sick society. When clinicians encourage women to accept the traditional female role, they are ignoring the oppression of women and, in effect, are telling women to accept their oppression as normal and natural. This is the great injustice perpetrated by the institution of psychotherapy.

1 Sex Bias in Psychotherapy: A Historical Perspective

JOAN MURRAY

A new area of psychotherapy research has emerged within the past 10 years—the examination of sex bias in psychotherapy. Why did this area of interest emerge? What led investigators to suspect that sex bias was occurring in the practice of psychotherapy? These questions are addressed in this chapter.

THE EMERGENCE OF INTEREST IN SEX BIAS IN PSYCHOTHERAPY

The possibility of sex bias in psychotherapy was given little or no attention before 1970, even though psychotherapy research had flourished for decades. Then in the early 1970s concern with sex bias in therapy appeared and blossomed. The rather sudden interest in this area was sparked by Phyllis Chesler's book *Women and Madness*,[1] which presented a totally new perspective on women in therapy—a perspective that viewed therapy as having various negative effects on women. Foremost among these was a tendency among therapists to encourage women to conform to the traditional female role by branding nontraditional behaviors in women as "sick" or "neurotic." Within the receptive climate of growing feminism, many others became interested in this point of view. Within a relatively short time, there was a literature on why bias in therapy might be *expected*, based on conceptions of woman's role in society, views of women in psychological theories, and present stereotypes of the sexes. By 1980, sex bias in psychotherapy had become es-

3

tablished as an area of research inquiry, with its own burgeoning literature. Each of these facets of the emergence of interest in sex bias in psychotherapy —and others—is discussed below, beginning with writings on the possibly pernicious effects of psychotherapy.

PSYCHOTHERAPY: A WOLF IN SHEEP'S CLOTHING?

During the 1970s, numerous writers claimed that, under the guise of healing the sick, the institution of psychotherapy had been performing more pernicious functions—namely, exercising social control in order to maintain the status quo and thereby to keep women in restrictive traditional roles. Psychotherapy was believed to act as a mechanism for social control (Chesler, 1971a; Kirsh, 1974), to serve to shore up society's institutions (e.g., marriage; Chesler, 1971a), and to reinforce socially approved behavior patterns (e.g., passivity and compliance in women) in order to achieve social conformity (Howard & Howard, 1974). As a result, psychotherapy was seen to bolster the status quo (Agel, 1971; London, 1964), one that was seen as oppressive to women (Brown, 1971; Chesler, 1971a; Kunnes, 1971; A Redstockings Sister, 1971). The situation of women was viewed as oppressive because women were forced into restrictive sex roles (Kirsh, 1974; Pollock, 1972; Steiner, 1971); their behavioral options were limited to those encompassed by women's traditional role, which was assumed to be their proper role (Kirsh, 1974). Phyllis Chesler (1971b) acridly portrayed the view that psychotherapy bolsters the traditional role of women when she maintained that psychotherapy views woman's fulfillment as coming "with marriage, children, and the vaginal orgasm" (p. 27). This picture of women was elaborated by Mintz (1974), who enumerated four assumptions that she believed many psychotherapists held. These were as follows: (1) a woman should wish to get married; (2) a woman should wish to have children; (3) lack of ambition is normal and healthy in a woman (but is a psychological problem in a man); and (4) in male-female relationships and sexual encounters, the man should take the initiative. Such a conception of women had been called "a minority group stereotype" (Weisstein, 1969).

WOMAN'S ROLE

To explain why sex bias might exist in psychotherapy, many turned their attention to women's role. Before describing the contemporary role seen for women in the United States in the 1970s, it is helpful to examine just what the term *sex role* means. The female sex role reflects the part that society reserves for women. It describes the behavior that is ideally desirable for them (Keller, 1974). The woman's role is complementary to the roles of others; the social structure is made up of organizations of roles (Kirsh, 1974). In essence, the role describes the type of behavior that is expected from women (Keller, 1974).

The role of women was viewed as having three central themes—namely, maternal, wifely, and erotic functions, with primary emphasis on the maternal and wifely aspects. As Keller explained, the core aspects of the female role included the following:

1. A concentration on marriage, home, and children as the primary focus of feminine concern.
2. A reliance on a male provider for sustenance and status. This important component of the wife role is symbolized by the woman taking her husband's name and sharing her husband's income.
3. An expectation that women will emphasize nurturance and life-preserving activities, both literally as in the creation of life and symbolically, in taking care of, healing, and ministering to the helpless, the unfortunate, the ill. Preeminent qualities of character stressed for women include sympathy, care, love, and compassion, seemingly best realized in the roles of mother, teacher, and nurse.
4. An injunction that women live through and for others rather than for the self. Ideally, a woman is enjoined to lead a vicarious existence—feeling pride or dismay about her husband's achievements and failures or about her children's competitive standing.
5. A stress on beauty, personal adornment, and eroticism, which, though a general feature of the female role, is most marked for the glamour girl.
6. A ban on the expression of direct assertion, aggression, and power strivings except in areas clearly marked woman's domain—as in the defense of hearth and home. There is a similar ban on women taking the direct (but not indirect) sexual initiative. (Keller, 1974, pp. 417–418)

It is true that this analysis was not applied to all American women. In the black community, the ideal woman had different qualities—being strong, responsible, autonomous, maternal, and sensual (Keller, 1974). Still, since most of the theorizing and experimentation on psychotherapy has concerned mainstream America, the foregoing analysis is probably representative of the expectations held about women in the United States at the time, as they relate to the present analysis.

The often-cited research of Steinmann and her colleagues (Steinmann & Fox, 1966; Steinmann, Levi, & Fox, 1964) painted a somewhat different picture of the role of American women. These researchers found that college women described themselves as equally balanced between active (seeing their own satifactions as just as important as their families') and passive (seeing their families' satisfactions as taking precedence over their own satisfactions and any occupation) orientations. Furthermore, these women described the ideal woman as more active than themselves (Steinmann, Levi, & Fox, 1964). And college men described the ideal woman as relatively balanced between passive and active elements (Steinmann & Fox, 1966).

Even though these formulations of the woman's role presented a picture more active than the one described by Keller, they still retained a partially home-oriented picture of women. More important, it must be remembered that the subjects in these studies were all college students, who were certainly not a representative sample of American society. They were, importantly, at an age where their attitudes were still in flux and also tended to be more liberal (nontraditional) than they would be later in life. So, their description of woman's role could not be extrapolated to the whole of American society, but only to a small portion of it (i.e., young college students).

Other research clearly suggested that society placed very strong demands on women to be wives and mothers. Zellman (1976) went so far as to say that there is a "cultural mandate to bear children" (p. 35). After reviewing the literature, Russo (1976) concluded:

> There has generally been consensus that the major goal of a woman's life is to raise well-adjusted children. A woman can spend time working—as long as she keeps the house clean and her husband and children well tended. (p. 144)

Not having any children "is still viewed as a deficient condition" (Russo, 1976, p. 149).

The primacy of the mother role for women was seen as tied to the following commonly held beliefs:

1. Mother is the center of the family.
2. Mother is responsible for the family's happiness.
3. Mother is responsible for the emotional well-being (or lack thereof) of her children.
4. Maternal deprivation is dangerous, and consequently,
5. Working or professional mothers run the risk of neglecting or damaging their children's psychic integrity. (Baum, Grotstein, & Wolfson, 1977, p. 2)

These views had been reinforced—if not encouraged—by the scientific community. For many years, child development and mental health professionals encouraged women to find total fulfillment in the role of mother. Many professionals viewed the woman who did not want children as "sick" (Baum et al., 1977).

The mother was further tied to her home and children by the belief that she must *personally* care for her children. This belief was based "scientifically" on the studies of maternal deprivation conducted in the early 20th century by such researchers as Bowlby and Spitz. Their findings were wrongly generalized from a small number of institutionalized children to the population at large; even so, they had a great impact on authors of parenting books, and in turn, on mothers. Such widely read authors as Spock and Ginott warned mothers not to be separated from their children for any length of time. In fact, Ginott saw the need for maternal care as biologically determined, and thus viewed the lack of maternal care as threatening an infant's mental health and even its survival. As a consequence of such writings, working mothers were seen as depriving their children of needed maternal attention and were viewed with disapproval (Baum et al., 1977). All in all, women were and are faced with strong pressure to be mothers, and to have careers only to the extent that their responsibilities as mothers were not disrupted.

Another force that would tend to keep women in the traditional role was the fear of negative consequences for out-of-role behavior. One such consequence was being seen as less attractive by men. Schlossberg and Pietrofesa (1973) reported a 1971 dissertation by Naffziger in which male counselors, counselor educators, and teachers found career women less attractive to men than more traditional women. Horner (1970) and others documented the strong negative consequences that are associated with out-of-role behavior for women in the case where the out-of-role behavior is successful achievement. Women were found to hold the expectation that success in achievement situations would be followed by negative consequences, including social rejection and loss of femininity.

The resulting pressure on women to stay within their traditional role might lead to untoward effects. For instance, if a woman became educated and had the skills to pursue a career, she might experience conflict because of the pressure not to deviate from acceptable sex-role behavior. Howard and Howard (1974) concluded from an examination of psychiatric admissions in 1970 that for women the possession of education made discomfort more likely, whereas for men, the lack of education presented difficulties in coping with society.

Given that there was strong pressure on women to conform to the female sex role, what were the consequences of conforming? Phyllis Chesler (1971a, 1972) believed that one consequence was an increased incidence of mental illness, as a result of trying to fit into a role that was "too tight." She claimed that since mental illness could be seen as a departure from expected sex-role behavior, then women, who have fewer roles available than men do, would suffer more mental illness than men. Chesler argued that the female sex role was, in fact, so narrow that women were viewed as mentally ill as often if they rejected the role (lesbians, aggressive women) as if they accepted the role (depression, lack of self-confidence).

And, in fact, there was a higher incidence of mental illness among women than among men. Women are twice as likely as men to be admitted and readmitted to psychiatric hospitals or private psychotherapy. According to National Institute of Mental Health (NIMH) statistics, 223,268 more women than men were hospitalized in state and county hospitals between 1950 and 1968 (Chesler, 1971b). Women were also overrepresented among psychiatric outpatients (Chesler, 1972). In addition, women reported more symptoms of mental illness than did men. One reason for this higher incidence of mental illness in women might be a direct result of conformity to the female role. The woman who devotes herself to the care of her children has little left to fill her life after they leave home. Bart (1970, 1972) claimed that depression in middle-aged women was often related to this loss of the mother role.

Lastly, this female sex role, which was viewed as severely restricting women's behavioral options and possibly even contributing to mental illness among them, was very widely held and was buttressed by religion, family, peers, teachers, the mass media, textbooks (e.g., by overemphasis on fertility technology, as compared to contraceptive technology), and even elementary-school books (where working mothers were rarely found; see Bem & Bem, 1970; Bernard, 1974). In fact, Bem and Bem (1970) believed that there existed a "nonconscious ideology" about women in American society—a set of beliefs and attitudes that individuals accepted implicitly because they were not aware of any alternative conceptions. The Bems made an instructive analogy regarding the nonconcious ideology about women. They asked whether a "fish is aware that his environment is wet. After all, what else could it be?" (p. 89) The fish has no alternative conception of its world; individuals in our society had no alternative conception of women. This ideology was so pervasive that the individual was not aware of it at all. The woman's role was seen as natural, and therefore was not questioned. Such a pervasive and unseen influence was liable to affect nearly everyone—even psychotherapists.

PSYCHOLOGICAL THEORIES
OF WOMEN

The conception of women in psychological theories was seen as another source of sex bias in therapy. Because psychotherapists study psychological theories and often base their treatments on them, psychological theories of personality functioning in women would be expected to have a strong influence on how psychotherapists behave toward women in psychotherapy. Accordingly, this section surveys the various theories concerning women's psychological development and personality functioning. The oldest and most influential of the theoretical formulations are the psychoanalytic theories. Consequently, these are discussed in some detail, beginning with the founder of the psychoanalytic movement, Freud. It is important to keep in mind that Freud's views have become the basis of much of psychotherapy as it is currently practiced (Osmond, Franks, & Burtle, 1974).

Freud based his theory of personality development in females on the anatomical difference between males and females. He *assumed that this anatomical difference must have psychological consequences* (Buytendijk, 1968). Specifically, Freud theorized that the girl at some time discovers that the boy has a penis and she does not. She feels inferior to the boy and develops "penis envy." Later, her penis envy changes to a desire to be impregnated by her father. This desire persists into adult life in the form of maternal urges. Because the female chooses a *passive* approach to acquiring a penis (i.e., being impregnated), Freud believed that she develops a generally passive approach to life, a pervasive tendency "to be done to, not to do" (Hyde & Rosenberg, 1976, p. 34). This passive attitude persists throughout her life (Hyde & Rosenberg, 1976).

From the same developmental formulation, Freud deduced that the woman's approach to life is also masochistic. The desire to be impregnated was considered masochistic because intercourse and childbirth were considered painful for the woman. Woman was believed to be passive and masochistic also because the ovum awaits (passivity) being penetrated (masochism) (Hyde & Rosenberg, 1976).

Because the woman is never able to accept her lack of a penis, the theory goes, she can never identify with her mother as completely as the boy can with his father; that is, she cannot resolve her Oedipal complex as fully as the boy can. According to Freud, the girl's inability to resolve her Oedipal complex fully results in lifelong feelings of inferiority, a predisposition to jealousy, and intense maternal desires. Because her resolution of the complex is not complete, the woman retains an immature superego—she remains dependent on her parents for her values and therefore has a less mature sense of morality than the man has (Chesler, 1972; Hyde & Rosenberg, 1976).

In summary, Freud's theory pictured women as passive, masochistic, and immature in their morality (Mitchell, 1974). It is important to note that these qualities were viewed as natural and *normal* in a woman. The theory was based on men, and women's personality was elaborated on the basis of their differences from men. Women were seen only in relation to men (Koedt, 1971).[2] It is also important to realize that Freud regarded women as essentially and inherently inferior to men (Kupers, 1971; Mintz, 1974). In his thinking, he showed a *double standard* of mental health or normality—he had one standard for men and another for women. This difference in standards was based on the differences that he believed to occur in male and female development. As Freud wrote,

> We say also of women that their social interests are weaker than those of men and that their capacity for the sublimation of their interests is less . . . the difficult development which leads to femininity [seems to] exhaust all the possibilities of the individual. (Quoted by Chesler, 1972, p. 76)

He stood firm on his belief in the basic inequality of the sexes in his paper "Some Psychological Consequences of the Anatomical Distinction between Sexes":

> [Women] refuse to accept the fact of being castrated and have the hope someday of obtaining a penis in spite of everything . . . I cannot escape the notion (though I hesitate to give it expression) that for woman the level of what is ethically normal is different from what it is in man. We must not allow ourselves to be deflected from such conclusions by the denials of the feminists who are anxious to force us to regard the two sexes as completely equal in position and worth. (Quoted by Chesler, 1972, p. 76)

Even though Freud's ideas were not based on proven fact but only on assumptions and deductions from assumptions, they had a great influence on the practice of psychotherapy.[3]

Although their theories may have differed in some ways from Freud's, many influential psychoanalytic writers after him maintained the basic features of his theory and elaborated other aspects. One very important aspect that became more clear with later theorists was the central importance of motherhood in the lives of women. Motherhood was seen as normal for all women; the woman who did not want children was seen as deviant. This belief was especially critical in the analysis of the effects of psychoanalytic theory and practice on women because once the primacy of motherhood for women was assumed, roles other than mother were seen as deviant or even pathological (Bernard, 1974). The equation of woman with mother can be seen in the writings of Joseph Rheingold:

> Woman is nurturance . . . anatomy decrees the life of a woman . . . when women grow up without dread of their biological functions, without subversion by feminist doctrines, and therefore enter upon motherhood with a sense of fulfillment and altruistic sentiment we shall attain the goal of a good life and a secure world in which to live. (Quoted by Chesler, 1971b)

Karen Horney (1967) summarized early psychoanalytic literature as portraying that "the specific satisfactions sought and found in female sex life and motherhood are of a masochistic nature" (p. 215) and viewing "feminine masochism as one psychic consequence of anatomical sex differences" (p. 214). She noted that the possibility of social conditioning's contributing to masochism in women had not been considered. In another summary, Julia Sherman (1976) concluded that the psychoanalytic literature insists that women need to be passive and dependent to function sexually and as mothers.[4]

Helene Deutsch (1944) was typical of these psychoanalysts. She emphasized passivity and masochism as prominent characteristics of a normal woman:

> The theory that I have long supported—according to which feminity [sic] is largely associated with passivity and masochism—has been confirmed in the course of years by clinical observations. (p. 220)

She also shared Freud's biological determinism, basing female passivity on vaginal functioning (Fabrikant, 1974) and attributing female masochism to a genetic factor (Horney, 1967). Deutsch also agreed that all women experienced penis envy: "There is no doubt that penis envy exists in woman's psyche and has a great influence on the development of her personality" (p. 26). In addition, she introduced the term *masculinity complex* to refer to the expression of a woman's "dissatisfaction with her own constitution . . . combined with attempts to remedy it" (p. 226)—that is, the active and/or aggressive women (e.g., a woman who wants a career). Further, narcissism was seen as characteristic of female personality, to which instinct and intuition made important contributions. And the most critical feature of woman's development was held to be motherhood (Hyde & Rosenberg, 1976).

More recently, Erik Erikson (1968) reiterated the importance of motherhood for women, writing that the core of female identity was "a biological, psychological, and ethical commitment to take care of human infancy" (Bernard, 1974). "Inner space"—for bearing offspring—was the basis of femininity (Doherty, 1973; Hyde & Rosenberg, 1976).

> Am I saying, then, that "anatomy is destiny"? Yes, it is destiny, insofar as it determines not only the range and configuration of physiological functioning and its limitation but also, to an extent, personality configurations. (Erikson, 1968, p. 185)

Erikson emphasized dependency in female development and conceived female identity in relation to men (Bernard, 1974):

> . . . the stage of life crucial for the emergence of an integrated female identity is the step from youth to maturity, the state when the young woman, whatever her work career, relinquishes the care received from the parental family in order to commit herself to the love of a stranger and to the care to be given to his and her offspring. (Erikson, 1968, p. 265)

Other areas of psychoanalytic theorizing included the role of work and the importance of domination of women. Writing in 1967, Fine discussed how the role of work varied for men and women. He viewed work as far more crucial for a man's self-image and relatedness to the world than for a woman's. Her "primary area of functioning is usually that of wife and mother" (p. 84). Work can enter into her life in two ways. One, when her children are grown, she wants more to do with her time, and so work becomes an adjunct to her life.

> Or the woman may fail to find real satisfaction in the traditional feminine roles, and then seeks compensation in work. Here the neurotic conflicts as a rule go deeper, since even when she is successful, work still covers up other frustrations. (Fine, 1967, p. 84)

Psychoanalytic writers often recommended that a woman learn to adjust to her role as wife and mother. Akin to this formulation was the belief that a woman is to be dominated and will become neurotic if she is not dominated. To be mentally healthy, a woman must be dominated. The dominance-submission relationship in marriage was considered mentally healthy (Seidenberg, 1971).

To summarize, throughout the bulk of the psychoanalytic theories there was (and is) a pervasive double standard of mental health—men should be active, women passive; men should dominate, women should be dominated; men's lives are strongly influenced by their work, women's are not. The psychoanalysts not only believed that this was the present situation of mankind and womankind; they also believed that this was their *natural* state and was to be desired. The latter belief created a strong pressure to maintain the status quo—that is, to encourage women to be satisfied with the traditional female role.

Of course, not all existing psychotherapies shared this traditional view of women. Even a few analytic writers strayed from the fold. For instance, Alfred Adler contended that women feel inferior to men not because of an anatomical deficiency but because men have greater political and economic power than they do. The importance of penis envy was also questioned by Karen Horney, who rejected it as the critical factor in female development. She believed that the male's envy of the female, especially of her ability to reproduce, was much more important (Hyde & Rosenberg, 1976). Even Erikson later foresaw a change in the personalities of men and women so that both sexes could enjoy both nurturance and strength (Bernard, 1974).

Some modern schools of psychotherapy diverged drastically from the orthodox Freudians. Several relatively new psychological technologies concerning child rearing (behavior modification, Parent Effectiveness Training, and Individual Psychology Associations) encouraged a much less traditional role for mothers by relaxing the child care demands on them (Bernard, 1974). A number of more recent theories of psychotherapy completely relinquished the double standard of mental health for males and females. Gestalt theory, for example, viewed the same set of qualities as desirable in a man as in a woman. And some Gestalt writers even saw psychotherapy as a force that should move the person beyond stereotypes of man or woman (Polster, 1974). Behavior therapy, too, emerged with no double standard of health. For instance, behavioral therapists valued assertive behavior over unassertive behavior for both sexes. In addition, the theory behind behavior therapy added the concept—in direct opposition to the emphasis on innate character-istics of psychoanalytic theory—that the environment is important in shaping and maintaining the problems of individuals (Lazarus, 1974). The conscious-ness-raising groups went a step further in conceptualizing the goals of thera-py as the promotion of change in the individual and in the culture (Kirsh, 1974).

Even though such innovations have occurred in recent times, the influence of the older, psychoanalytic thinking cannot be dismissed. Because such thinking permeated the early theories, it has remained the basis of much cur-rently practiced psychotherapy. Moreover, many practicing psychothera-pists were trained when psychoanalytic theory was the only theory available —or the only one taught. Even in the 1970s, psychoanalytic theory was often emphasized in medical training. Consequently, the early psychoanalytic the-ories, with their emphasis on the anatomical determination of women's per-sonality, could be expected to have a great influence on the psychotherapy that clients received.

More broadly, a traditional view of women and a tendency to generalize from men to women without empirical justification has characterized much of Western scientific theorizing and experimentation. For instance, Kohlberg's theory of sex-role identification included the idea that it is morally wrong to deviate from one's sex-role stereotype (Fodor, 1974). Also, females were gen-erally neglected as subjects for research and conceptualization (Brodsky & Holroyd, 1975). Consequently, it was not unusual for experimental work to have been done on men and then for the conclusions to have been generalized to women. Such was largely the case in work on alcoholism and homosexual-ity, for example, where theories were formulated on data collected from men and then were applied to women (Franks & Burtle, 1974). Of Western psy-chological theories in general, Doherty (1973) concluded that they (1) view the male as the prototype of humanity and understand the female in relation to him; and (2) assign the cognitive aspects of human functioning to men and the affective aspects to women. With this, there is a positive valuation of cog-nitive or rational behavior and a less positive—or negative—valuation of affective or sensual behavior. Thus, there is a positive valuation of man over woman (Doherty, 1973).

And all this was done without establishing any basis in fact by means of ex-perimentation. Assumption was regarded as a sufficient foundation for theo-rizing. Why? Probably because the assumptions—that women had to be as they had traditionally been—were so strongly and implicitly believed to be true. This "nonconscious ideology" required no experimental test because it was so *pervasive*. Considering this, as well as the strong and clear role de-mands placed on women and the traditional view of women taken in influen-tial psychological theories, it was reasonable to expect that individuals in our society—including psychotherapists—would have strong, definite, and traditional expectations about what women should be like. Let us now consider how the practice of psychotherapy might be affected if psychotherapists did indeed share these expectations.

For one thing, psychotherapists' expectations could influence how they define *normal* and *abnormal*, as well as how they diagnose specific individuals. This is to be expected, because the behavior that is considered "abnormal" varies with the social context and because social values influence diagnosis (Frank, 1974; Hollingshead & Redlich, 1958; Ullmann & Krasner, 1969). Similarly, many writers have argued that psychotherapists' values affect their definition of mental health and their choice of goals in psychotherapy (Buhler, 1962; Frank, 1974; London, 1964; Parloff, 1967).

Even more germane to the present discussion is the experimental literature demonstrating that the expectations of experimenters or psychotherapists can and do affect the behavior of their subjects or patients. The array of experiments is varied and quite impressive. Rosenthal (1966) presents a number of studies with human subjects that show effects of experimenter expectations on subject behavior.[5] Such effects have been found in studies in survey research, as well as in experimental research in psychology, education, medicine, and psychotherapy (Goldstein, 1962b; Rosenthal, 1970; Weisstein, 1971). Specifically in the area of research on psychotherapy, evidence suggests that therapist prognostic expectancies influence patient improvement (Goldstein, 1962b); and that both subtle and explicit therapist behaviors can function as reinforcement for the patient, and hence alter the patient's verbal behavior in the direction of the psychotherapist's expectations (Goldstein, 1962a). For instance, in a study involving therapists who favored increased independence in their clients, Heller and Goldstein (reported in Rosenthal, 1966) found that after 15 sessions clients' self-descriptions were of more independent behavior than their pretherapy descriptions had been.

It is apparent, then, that whatever psychotherapists' expectations concerning women are, these expectations are liable to affect their practice of psychotherapy with female clients. Before evaluating the research on just what the effects of being a woman are in the psychotherapeutic situation, let us first take a look at the experimental research on expectations about women in order to establish just what these expectations are. Since such expectations are delineated in the content of stereotypes of women, research on the content of stereotypes of women is presented in some detail.

STEREOTYPES OF WOMEN

Sherriffs and McKee (1957) found distinct stereotypes of males and females, and found these to be shared by subjects of both sexes. The stereotype of men involved three general notions: frank and straightforward in social relations; intellectually rational and competent; and active, bold, and effective in dealing with the environment. Women were seen, generally, as socially skillful; emotionally warm and supportive; and concerned with the spiritual. In a later study (McKee & Sherriffs, 1959), these investigators found, in addition, that men desired such sex-role stereotyping in women. Men were concerned that women not be aggressive, courageous, daring, deliberate, dominant, dynamic, forceful, independent, rugged, and sharp-witted. Moreover, these stereotypes were quite inclusive, as Sherriffs and Jarrett (1953) concluded; almost no behavior or quality was not included in either the male or the female stereotpye.

A decade later, Rosenkrantz, Vogel, Bee, Broverman, and Broverman (1968) discovered very similar sex-role stereotypes. Men were seen, in relation to women, as possessing competence and lacking warmth and expressiveness; women were seen as possessing warmth and expressiveness but lacking competence. Adjectives in the "competence" cluster included *ambitious, independent, objective,* and *active;* adjectives in the "warmth-expressiveness" cluster included *gentle, sensitive to the feelings of others, quiet,* and *able to express tender feelings.* These stereotypes were found to be shared by subjects differing in socioeconomic class, religion, age, education, and marital status (Broverman, Vogel, Broverman, Clarkson, & Rosenkrantz, 1972). In addition, when beliefs about *ideal* men and women were investigated, it was shown that greater competence in men than in women and greater warmth and expressiveness in women than in men were seen as desirable (Elman, Press, & Rosenkrantz, 1970).

In a more recent study (Clifton, McGrath, & Wick, 1976), the traditional stereotype of women still appeared. Although Clifton et al. found some evidence for the existence of more than one stereotype of women ("housewife" and "bunny" stereotypes), a close examination of their methodology shows that the "housewife" stereotype parallels the stereotype of women found in earlier studies—and this may be the only realistic stereotype of the two found in the study. For Clifton et al. elecited a consistent description of a "bunny," but how many women—in reality—would be seen as fitting this description? Few, this author would venture. It is interesting to note that women who were portrayed as relatively independent of men ("club woman," "career woman," and "woman athlete") were seen as having lost their femininity.

Furthermore, the characteristics attributed to women were generally seen as less positive, less valued, or less socially desirable than the characteristics attributed to men were (McKee & Sherriffs, 1959; Rosenkrantz et al., 1968; Sherriffs & McKee, 1957). The effect of this relatively negative evaluation of women reached into the evaluation of achievements of women. A number of investigations demonstrated that when the identical production (an article, a painting, etc.) was presented as the work of a man or a woman (and the quality of the production was not already established), it was evaluated as of lower quality when presented as the work of a woman than when presented as the work of a man (Feldman-Summers & Kiesler, 1974; Goldberg, 1968;

Mischel, 1974; Pheterson, Kiesler, & Goldberg, 1971). Merely knowing that a woman was the creator caused the work to be evaluated more negatively.

So, we have seen that there were broad, definite, and widely shared stereotypes of women—expectations about what women are like. Moreover, these stereotypes were considered desirable—women should be warm and expressive but not competent. At the same time, female characteristics were seen as less valued than male characteristics. Even further, what women produced, whether professional articles or paintings, was evaluated as of lower quality than what men produced. This last belief was especially insidious, because if a society believes that women cannot produce work of as good quality as that of men, then that society is likely to discourage women from working, or at least to discourage women from working at a professional level. And, in fact, there is plentiful evidence that our society did—and still does—just this. Numerous studies have found that women's qualifications are downgraded solely on the basis of sex, and that men are hired in preference to women with identical credentials (Nieva & Gutek, 1981). These studies have involved college students, as well as managers who actually do hiring—university chairpersons hiring psychologists, as well as business people hiring managers. In a representative study, Rosen, Jerdee, and Prestwich (reported in Nieva & Gutek, 1981) found that in a personnel selection task, managers (all male) rated male candidates as more acceptable and more suitable for the available job than equally qualified female candidates. After reviewing the literature on personnel selection, Nieva and Gutek (1981) concluded that where equally qualified men and women were evaluated, men were more likely to be judged competent and qualified, and were more likely to be selected for hiring, training, and promotion. So widespread and powerful are the effects of expectations of women.

Since the stereotypes of women seem so pervasive, psychotherapists might be expected to share them. In order to determine whether psychotherapists actually did hold traditional sex-role stereotypes, some reseachers directly investigated the stereotypes held by psychotherapists. Fabrikant (1974) elicited descriptions of the male and female sex roles from psychotherapists. He found that some characteristics attributed to males only or females only in previous stereotype research were attributed to both males and females; therapists saw both sexes as *animalistic, dependent, devoted, hesitant, intellectual, manipulative, nurturant, tempermental, virtuous,* and *wise*. Previous research had found *animalistic, intellectual,* and *wise* to be associated with males and the rest of these characteristics with females. A number of positive characteristics previously seen as typical of women were now seen as typical of men (i.e., *faithful, kind,* and *loving*). What adjectives were seen as descriptive of females? Women were seen as *assertive, castrating, chatterer, decorative, dizzy, exploitative, fragile,* and *generous* by male and female therapists; but as *devoted, slave,* and *subordinate* by female therapists only. Although this picture of women differed somewhat from earlier findings, it did retain some aspects of the traditional view of women. Moreover, it strongly retained a *negative* view of women. Male characteristics were generally seen as positive, female characteristics as strongly negative. In fact, 83 % of male characteristics were seen as positive by male therapists, 86 % by female therapists; whereas only 31 % of female characteristics were seen as positive by male therapists, and 33 % by female therapists. Fabrikant concluded that women were seen as "neurotic," just as they had been in earlier studies. Delk and Ryan (1975) also found sex-role stereotyping by some therapists, to the disparagement of females.

In the same study, Fabrikant (1974) also assessed therapists' attitudes toward men's and women's roles. Since these attitudes were investigated by means of direct questions requiring "yes" or "no" answers, the results could not be viewed as conclusive, because there was no control over social desirability effects. It is likely that the therapists were generally aware that at the time of the study it was not socially desirable to take the stand that "a woman's place is in the home." Fabrikant found that male and female therapists said that neither men nor women needed to be married to experience full and satisfying lives; that male therapists agreed—and female therapists disagreed—that most women can be satisfied and fulfilled in the wife/mother role; that female therapists said that bringing up children is the mother's responsibility, whereas the male therapists said this should be a joint responsibility; and that male therapists saw the male as the provider of most of the family's income, whereas female therapists were more flexible. These results showed some departure from traditional role expectations, but it is possible that social desirability effects were responsible for this deviation.

In a study designed to control for social desirability effects, Drapkin and Ansel (Note 1) presented therapists with an excerpt from a bogus initial therapy interview and asked for ratings on a scale similar to that used by Broverman, Broverman, Clarkson, Rosenkrantz, and Vogel (1970) (the Broverman et al. study is described in the next section). Their findings lent some support to the contention that therapists maintain sex-role stereotypes. Female therapists were more prone to sex-role stereotyping than male therapists. Older women therapists were the group most concerned with having women retain traditional feminine characteristics. Younger women therapists were most committed to traditional characteristics in males.

DO THERAPISTS EMPLOY A DOUBLE STANDARD OF MENTAL HEALTH?

Research interest in whether psychotherapists hold a double standard of mental health grew from a belief that if psychotherapists hold strong, implicit beliefs about what men and women are like, then these expectations about the character of men and women might have come to be seen as not only typical but also *normal*. That is, the differing conceptions of men and women might have been transformed into differing standards of health for the two sexes, with the result that different behaviors would be encouraged for men than for women. Moreover, therapists might remember stereotypic characteristics of women clients more than they might remember other characteristics. Hamilton (Note 2) has shown that individuals recall traits that are consistent with their prior expectations, especially if those traits confirm a stereotype.

In the earliest investigation of whether there was a double standard of mental health among therapists, Neulinger (1968) presented a group of psychiatrists, psychologists, and social workers with 20 paragraphs, each of which described one of Murray's manifest needs (e.g., need for affiliation, need for achievement, need for aggression), and asked therapists to rank order them according to how descriptive they were first of the optimally integrated male and then of the optimally integrated female. Mean ranks of each need were compared for males and females, and differences were found on 18 of the 20 needs. Women were ranked higher in socioemotional needs (such as affiliation and nurturance), while men were ranked higher in needs such as dominance and achievement (these were tied for third rank for men, and were ranked ninth and eighth for women). Neulinger concluded that the conception of mental health was different for a male than for a female in the United States; the healthy male was seen as more dominant than the healthy female, who was seen as more submissive.

The conclusions of this study were criticized by Stricker (1977). He contended that even though "some absolute differences in the needs were demonstrated, the relative ordering of the needs was highly similar" (p. 16). He based this contention on the finding that the rank-ordering of the needs for males correlated .91 with the rank-ordering for females. This, he believed, suggested that mental health personnel actually saw optimally integrated males and females as very similar. He further supported this belief with a later study by Neulinger and his colleagues, in which therapists' rankings of optimally integrated males and females were again found to be highly correlated (correlation of .91 for male and .90 for female therapists).

Stricker's viewpoint can be challenged. Calling differences on 18 out of 20 needs "some" differences seems highly inaccurate. After thus minimizing the significant differences that Neulinger did find, Stricker then proceeded to treat them as unimportant. In fact, he did not even make an interpretation of what such differences might mean. It seems that such differences as the finding that dominance was ranked ninth for women and third for men suggests that therapists did indeed see optimally integrated men as different from optimally integrated women. The finding of a high correlation between the rankings of needs for males and females does certainly suggest that many needs were ranked similarly for the two sexes, as Stricker argued. However, the fact that a few needs were ranked quite differently and, more important, that these differences paralleled the stereotypic conceptions of males and females, suggests that psychotherapists' conceptions of mental health may differ, and differ in a way that reflects an influence of the beliefs about men and women typically found in our society.

The most widely cited study on the question of a double standard of mental health was conducted by Broverman et al. (1970). Their subjects were 79 clinically trained, practicing psychotherapists, including psychologists, psychiatrists, and social workers. Of these, 49 held Ph.D. or M.D. degrees. The therapists' experience ranged from internship to "extensive professional experience," and their ages varied between 23 and 55 years. All subjects responded to a Sex-Role Stereotype Questionnaire (developed by Rosenkrantz et al., 1968), which consisted of 122 bipolar items, each of which described a behavioral trait or characteristic, as in these examples:

Very aggressive   Not at all aggressive
Doesn't hide emotions at all Always hides emotions

Each clinician was given *one* of three sets of instructions—"male," "female," or "adult." The "male" instructions stated, "Think of normal, adult men and then indicate on each item the pole to which a mature, healthy, socially competent adult man would be closer." Subjects were asked to look at the poles of the items in terms of directions rather than extremes of behavior. The "female" instructions substituted the word "woman" for "man," and the "adult" instructions substituted the word "person." Only data on the 38 items that had been seen as typically masculine or typically feminine in prior research (called "stereotypic items") were analyzed. Data from male and female clinicians were pooled because these two groups were in strong agreement (in fact, they did not differ on any of the *t* tests conducted). There was also strong agreement among clinicians about which behaviors and attributes characterized a healthy man, a healthy woman, and a healthy adult. The therapists' conception of a healthy man was different from their conception of a healthy woman, and the differences paralleled sex-role stereotypes. Healthy women were seen as differing from healthy men by, for instance, being more submissive, less independent, less adventurous, more easily influenced, less aggressive, less competitive, and more excitable in minor crises; by having their feelings more easily hurt; by being more emotional, more conceited about their appearance, and less objective; and by disliking math and science. Moreover, it was found that the concept of health for a sex-unspecified adult (representing ideal health) did not differ significantly from the concept of health for a man, but *did* differ significantly from the concept of health for a woman. That is, healthy women were seen as less healthy than healthy men.

Broverman and her colleagues speculated that these results were due to clinicians' employing an adjustment notion of health (i.e., health consisted of fulfilling one's sex role). Since men and women have different sex roles, there would be different standards of health for the two sexes. A healthy woman would have to conform to standards of health that are not considered as healthy as the standards to which the healthy man would have to conform. In addition, Broverman et al. saw the differences in the conception of health for males and females as reflecting the sex-role stereotypes, and the lower evaluation of the female stereotype, prevalent in our society. Using the Sex-Role Stereotype Questionnaire and a semantic differential scale, Nowacki and Poe (1973) found a double standard of mental health among college students. Employing a similar methodology, Maslin and Davis (1975) found such a double standard among male—but not among female—counselors-in-training.

The Broverman et al. (1970) study was broadly criticized by Stricker (1977). He attacked Broverman et al.'s semantics, their methodology, and their conclusions. He stated that they jumped from their data to "pejorative labels," and that they concluded that a woman was seen as illogical when their data supported only the conclusion that a woman was seen as less logical than a man. But even in the quote that Stricker gave to support his contention, Broverman et al. did not state what he said they did. They said that *"relative to men*, women are perceived to be . . . illogical" (italics added). This aspect of Stricker's discussion is merely a game of semantics (one could say that if there are two individuals and individual A is less logical than individual B, then individual A is more illogical than individual B), and Stricker made much too much of it in order to detract from the substantive findings of the study.

When discussing Broverman et al.'s finding that males were seen as healthier than females, Stricker claimed that this conclusion is not justified because no analyses of individual items were presented. He stated:

> An overall *t* test did suggest that male health scores are higher, but this may well have been an artifact, because both males and females were rated on a set of items that contained a greater number of stereotypic masculine items than stereotypic feminine items. (p. 18)

But actually, the *t* test was on the *means* of the health scores of all the items. So the statistical procedure would not have yielded an artifact simply because of the greater number of male stereotypic items. The only way the procedure could yield an "artifact" would be if there were very few items on which the pole seen as healthy for a woman corresponded with the pole seen as healthy for an adult. In fact, this is probably what occurred—but it is certainly not an artifact. Rather, it is more likely a telling reflection on the evaluation of women in our society. The procedure by which Broverman et al.'s 38 stereotypic characteristics were found (reported in Rosenkrantz et al., 1968) was an extremely exhaustive one; so it is likely that women *are actually seen* as characterized by a smaller number of traits than men are, few of which are seen as healthy.

Stricker disputed that the Broverman et al. (1970) study *actually found* a double standard. He argued that instead of interpreting their results as indicating a double standard, it would be "more parsimonious" to explain the finding of a difference between the conception of health for a woman and the conception of health for an adult by realizing that "a judge presented with the task of rating an adult *would think of a male* and thus produce a rating more consistent with ratings of males than of females" (p. 18; italics added). On the contrary, it seems that if judges *would* have assumed that "adult" meant "male," it was likely that Broverman et al.'s finding that healthy males were more likely healthy adults than healthy females were was accurate. Moreover, by his use of the phrase "more consistent with ratings of males than females," Stricker was *assuming* that there were in reality differences between the characteristics considered healthy for males and females. Stricker was implying that the judges based their ratings of a healthy adult on their conception of a healthy male—which was of course different from the conception of a healthy female. Then he concluded that the study did not support a double standard of health after he had assumed a double standard of health to show just this.

To bolster his case further, Stricker presented a 1976 unpublished study by Maxfield, in which approximately 250 experienced therapists responded to the Sex-Role Stereotype Questionnaire, read specially constructed vignettes, and responded to 11 questions regarding diagnostic and therapeutic implications for each of the people described in the vignettes. Each therapist completed the questionnaire for a healthy male or female and for a therapy patient of the same sex. Like Broverman et al. (1970), Maxfield found that there were virtually no differences between the responses of male and female therapists.

> When the data were analyzed by chi-square techniques in a manner similar to that employed by Broverman et al., Maxfield found that when the masculine and socially desirable poles corresponded, males were closer to that pole than females on only 30 of the 53 items, a finding that was not significant. When the feminine and socially desirable poles corresponded, females were closer to the pole than males on 23 of the 25 items, a finding that *was* significant. When individual means were compared, fewer than half of them differentiated healthy males and females, and of these, approximately half favored females. Further, on over 90% of the items, the means for healthy males and females were on the same side of the neutral point, so that any differences were quantitative rather than qualitative. (Stricker, 1977, p. 19)

There are a number of problems here. First of all, it is unclear that Maxfield did indeed use the Sex-Role Stereotype Questionnaire, because it has 41 items which are seen as either masculine or feminine, whereas the questionnaire used in the above study had to have at least 25 items that were seen as feminine and 53 that were seen as masculine. Also, how could the 53 masculine items *be* masculine items if males were closer to the masculine pole than females on only 30 of them? A masculine item, according to Broverman et al. (1970), is one where one sex is seen as characterized by one pole more than by the other. Aside from the question of just what methodology Maxfield did use, it seems that Stricker was again overlooking some indications of sex bias. He did not try to explain—or even to mention—why male characteristics were more often seen as socially desirable than female characteristics (53 characteristics for males and 25 for females were seen as socially desirable). Of greater consequence, "fewer than half" of the individual means differentiated healthy males from healthy females. If nearly half of the means differentiated the sexes as to the level of that characteristic considered healthy, this would seem a strong indication that there *was* a double standard of mental health. Further, just because the means were "on the same side of the neutral point" does not negate the existence of such a double standard; there were significant differences between many of the means, so they were not too close together. If men needed to be, for example, more aggressive than women to be seen as healthy, then there was a different standard of health for men than for women.

Looking at the data on the vignettes, the only item that differentiated males and females was an item concerning expected income: Therapists expected men to earn more money than women. And even this, Stricker argued, was probably merely a veridical reflection of reality. But what were the other items? What did they assess? Without knowing the answers to these questions, it is impossible to assess the meaning of the finding that only one item differentiated males and females.

Stricker reported that Maxfield did find "striking differences" between patients and healthy people, so we can conclude that the therapists answered the questions carefully. We might also conclude something else—that there was a very subtle bias in Maxfield's study. By asking each therapist to describe a healthy person and a therapy patient, Maxfield may have suggested that the therapists consider *extremes* of behavior (i.e., healthy vs. unhealthy). This is just what Broverman et al. (1970) instructed their therapist/subjects *not* to do. So, for this reason and because of the uncertainty about what questionnaire Maxfield actually used, the Maxfield and Broverman et al. studies may not have really been comparable.

In another study using the Sex-Role Stereotype Questionnaire, Cowan (Note 3) asked a small sample of therapists to consider the average male and female client, and indicate the extent to which they thought one of the poles represented a greater problem for female than for male clients. Cowan found that female clients were seen as too feminine (e.g., too gentle, too unaggressive), while male clients' problems were not conceptualized in terms of sex-role stereotypes. Cowan concluded that these results were contrary to the idea that therapists bolster sex-role-stereotypic characteristics in women. To the contrary, this author would argue that since therapists did indicate for a number of characteristics that one pole of the characteristic represented a greater problem for females than males, they were *employing a double standard of mental health.* So Cowan's data could support the existence of such a double standard.

Similar to Cowan, Fabrikant (1974) argued that his results indicated that therapists did not perpetuate the female role. He had psychotherapists agree or disagree with statements such as "Women need not be married to have a full life" (p. 90). We do not know, however, whether therapists believed that a woman needed to be married to be mentally healthy. Also, asking the questions as openly as Fabrikant did maximizes social desirability effects. So we do not know how the therapists would behave in practice.

This problem of investigators' employing methodologies that were subject to social desirability effects was common in this area. After research on sex bias in therapy got started and became known, few therapists were probably so naive that they did not realize what an investigator was interested in when he or she asked them to describe a "healthy female." The validity of any study whose purpose was so obvious is certainly questionable. Consequently, emphasis in the remainder of this chapter is on studies where the experimenter's intentions were somewhat more veiled.

Closely related to the issue of a double standard of health was the research on whether out-of-role behavior was viewed as sicker than in-role behavior. Judging the same behavior as sicker in a woman than in a man because it is closer to acceptable male behavior than to acceptable female behavior demonstrates the existence of a double standard of health. For instance, Gomberg (1974) noted that the alcoholic female is seen as sicker than the alcoholic male. The influence of sex-role expectations also manifests itself when one woman is judged sicker than another because she behaves in a sex-role-inappropriate manner. A number of studies suggested that individuals who exhibit sex-role-inappropriate behavior were seen as less psychologically healthy. McClelland and Watt (1968) found that women hospitalized as schizophrenic were more aggressive and men hospitalized as schizophrenic were more withdrawn than were same-sex normals (aggression being out-of-role for a woman and withdrawal being out-of-role for a man). When rating a defendant in a murder trial (who was clearly accused of a violent crime, which would be seen as more out-of-role for a woman), undergraduates perceived a female defendant as sicker than a male defendant (McGlynn, Megas, & Benson, 1976).

Coie, Pennington, and Buckley (1974) investigated the effects of in-role versus out-of-role behavior in two ways. In the materials that they presented to their subjects, they varied both the type of situation in which stress occurred (oral examination vs. interpersonal rejection) and the individual's reaction to the stress (aggressive behavior vs. somatic complaints). They reasoned that males would be expected to react more extremely to a stress related to career and females to a stress related to social relationships, because sex roles carry with them differential tolerances for reactions to the same situation (e.g., a woman is expected to react to the loss of a social relationship more strongly than to a career stress). And further, a male's reacting strongly to a career stress would be seen as more normal than such a reaction to a social stress would be. As for types of reactions, aggressive behavior was role-appropriate for a male but not for a female; somatic complaints were role-appropriate for a female but not for a male. In-role reactions were expected to be judged as less sick than out-of-role reactions were.

The responses of college students acting as judges conformed to this analysis. In the pressure of oral-examination-stress condition, less psychological disorder was attributed to males than to females for identical behavior. Hospitalization was seen as more appropriate (i.e., the individual was viewed as sicker) for a male than for a female who was reacting to a social rejection. Also, greater psychological disorder was attributed to females than to males for aggressive behavior, and greater disorder was attributed to males than to females for somatic complaints. So the type of stress and the reaction to it may have been important determinants of evaluation; out-of-role behavior was likely to be viewed as sicker than in-role behavior.

Two related studies were conducted with children as the stimulus persons. Meyer and Sobieszek (1972) showed adults videotapes of 17-month-old children playing. A specific child was identified as a boy for some observers and as a girl for others. For the group of adults who had had previous experience with children, behaviors were noticed more if they ran counter to sex-role stereotypes (e.g., an exuberant behavior was more likely to be labeled as "aggressive" if the adult believed the child was a girl than if the adult believed the child was a boy). In a 1976 study, Feinblatt and Gold concluded that a child exhibiting sex-role-inappropriate behavior was seen as more severely disturbed, as more in need of treatment, and as having a less successful future than a child exhibiting sex-role-appropriate behavior was seen as having. These conclusions were based on two kinds of data: (1) reactions of parents, clinical psychology graduate students, and school psychology graduate students to hypothetical case studies in which identical behavior problems were attributed to a boy or a girl; and (2) the finding that at an outpatient clinic more boys than girls were referred for being emotional or passive, while more girls than boys were referred for being defiant and verbally aggressive. This issue of the effect of out-of-role behavior on evaluation is discussed further in the section on experimental analogues of the therapy situation. Next, let us address other types of experimental evidence that bear on the question of whether women are treated differently than men are by therapists and counselors. Indirect evidence is presented first, and then more direct evidence.

DO THERAPISTS TREAT MEN AND WOMEN DIFFERENTLY?

Indirect Evidence

Some evidence has been found that therapists—especially male therapists—treat female patients differently than they do male patients due to sexual curiosity. In the extreme form, male therapists may "exploit" female patients by having sexual relationships with them (Asher, 1975; Holroyd & Brodsky, 1977; Kardener, Fuller, & Mensh, 1973; Masling & Harris, 1969; Perry, 1976).[6] In milder forms, the therapists' sexual curiosity is said to show itself in voyeuristic fashion. For instance, Brodey and Detre (1972) found that the therapists (almost all male psychiatric residents and social workers) in their study tended to recommend individual therapy with the interviewer (as opposed to other options) for women they had seen in intake interviews more than they did for men. Also, patients recommended for individual therapy were 14 times more likely to be viewed as having sexual problems than were patients recommended for group therapy. However, this study was far from conclusive, because the sample of therapists was a very small one (nine therapists).

Further evidence for voyeurism among therapists was offered by S. I. Abramowitz, Roback, Schwartz, Yasuna, Abramowitz, and Gomes (1976). They asked experienced male and female group therapists what option they would use in group therapy with a bogus outpatient, who was identified as either male or female in the case materials presented, and found a tendency toward the use of role playing with an opposite-sex patient. Another study by the same group of investigators (S. I. Abramowitz, Abramowitz, Roback, Corney, & McKee, 1976) showed that male, but not female, therapists tended to see female clients for a greater number of sessions than they tended to see male clients.

There has also been suggestive evidence of voyeurism in testing. Masling and Harris (1969) noted that male, but not female, graduate students gave more Thematic Apperception Test (TAT) cards with sexual and/or romantic themes to females than to males. Similarly, Siskind (1973) reported that male interns, but not male staff members, gave more sexual and/or romantic TAT cards to women than to men. However, the results of these last two studies were clearly not generalizable, because of the inexperience of the testers and the suggestion that the effect might disappear with experienced testers.

Other evidence, too, has suggested that sex effects occur in testing. Lewittes, Moselle, and Simmons (1973) found that in evaluating a Rorschach protocol, both male and female psychologists judged protocols of same-sex individuals as less pathological than they did protocols of opposite-sex individuals. Also, career interest inventories have been criticized for being biased against women. White (1975) pointed out that many career interest inventories are based on the assumption that having traits similar to individuals in a specific occupation is a good predicator of satisfaction in that occupation. To construct such inventories, a set of items is administered to persons in various job categories. The scales of the interest inventories are then constructed based on the responses of these individuals. Because many jobs are held predominantly by men, such a procedure may be biased against women because it maintains the status quo (i.e., on jobs held mainly by men, a woman would have to have interests similar to men to appear interested in the jobs). Since these interest inventories are used to help women choose a career, such bias could have the effect of discouraging women from entering predominantly male occupations. White added that five of the major inventories use such empirically developed occupational scales, often using only one sex in the criterion group during test development.

More Direct Evidence

The evidence presented thus far has *suggested* that sex bias may occur in therapy. However, the studies cited generally did not directly test whether a therapist would treat a patient differently simply because that patient was female. The investigations to be presented next more closely approximate direct tests of whether sex bias exists in the therapy situation, beginning with studies that tested more general hypotheses and proceeding to those that tested more specific ones.

To investigate whether counselors reacted differently to male than female clients, Hill (1975) asked a sample of counselors to record their second session with one male and one female client. In an analysis of specific types of verbal behavior, it was found that the counselors generally did react differently to the two sexes. For instance, experienced counselors gave more advice to female than to male clients.

Oppedisano-Reich (reported in Stricker, 1977) presented mental health professionals (including psychiatrists, psychologists, and social workers) with vignettes about patients and asked for various diagnostic and prognostic judgements. There were no main effects of sex, and interactions involving sex generally showed bias toward females. It is difficult to evaluate this study, because it was not presented in detail. For instance, the reader does not know *what* diagnostic and prognostic judgments were requested.

A pair of investigations examined large pools of actual treatment records and assessed whether males and females received different types of therapy. Hollingshead and Redlich (1958) found no association between sex and the type of treatement (psychotherapy, organic therapy, or custodial care) administered in a large sample drawn from the New Haven, Connecticut area. After reviewing records of 2400 clients in 17 community mental health centers in the Seattle area, Sue (1976) concluded that there was no effect of client sex on services received (i.e., inpatient vs. outpatient, professional vs. nonprofessional therapist, individual vs. group therapy, and number of sessions). Even though both samples were large and no effect of sex was found, it is important to note that the measures used in both studies were very broad (e.g., psychotherapy vs. custodial care, inpatient vs. outpatient treatment).

Do Therapists View Women as Less Mentally Healthy than Men?

Moving to those comparatively direct studies that have more specific areas of interest, some have evaluated whether therapists viewed women as less mentally healthy than men. Concerned by their finding that female college students described women as less psychologically well adjusted than men, S. I. Abramowitz and Abramowitz (1973) asked male and female professionals in mental health and education to rate a bogus case in terms of psychological adjustment. The identical case history was presented, with the individual described portrayed as either male or female. They found that the woman was rated as more maladjusted than the man, but only by women professionals. The authors noted that there were problems with their study— the sample was regional; it consisted of counseling center personnel; and most subjects were B.A.s or M.A.s, not Ph.D.s.

Three studies reported finding no bias against women. S. I. Abramowitz, Roback, Schwartz, Yasuna, Abramowitz, and Gomes (1976) presented a clinical profile and a description of a "representative therapy incident" to experienced group therapists. The same materials were described as belonging to a man or a woman. Few effects of the patient's sex were found, and these favored the woman (e.g., the woman received a better prognosis than the man did). However, these results do not clearly indicate bias in favor of women, for the patient began to cry in the therapy incident given to the subjects. Such behavior may have indicated to the therapists that the man was sicker than the female, because it is less common—and is out-of-role—for a man to cry. In one of two studies by Zeldow (1975), college undergraduates evaluated statements that were supposedly made by psychiatric patients, but were actually Minnesota Multiphasic Personality Inventory (MMPI) items, on a scale of maladjustment. There was no effect of sex of patient. In Zeldow's second study, college students, social workers, medical students, and mental health paraprofessionals judged degree of maladjustment, need for therapy, and prognosis in therapy from case descriptions (which were taken from textbooks). There was again no effect of sex of patient. Zeldow's studies share a major problem. In both of them, the patients presented clear-cut and well-defined pathology. In the first, a typical item was "[the patient] says that someone has it in for her"; and in the second, "textbook examples" of, for instance, suicidal depression and paranoid schizophrenia were used. So, it was unlikely that the subjects would need to invoke sex and sex-role expectations to provide the information needed to make the required judgments; they already had all the information that was necessary.

Bias in judgments of women's psychological adjustment may be moderated by knowledge of the individual's political convictions. When they varied both a student's sex and political inclination (left- or right-oriented) in bogus protocols, and asked counselors for judgments of psychological comfort, S. I. Abramowitz, Abramowitz, Jackson, and Gomes (1973) found no main effect of the sex of the student, but they did find that the less liberal subjects judged the left-oriented female student more harshly than they did the left-oriented male student. However, the finding of no main effect of the student's sex is inconclusive, because the experimenters made a strong suggestion about the student's psychological comfort in the protocols, all of which shared statements saying that the student scored low on three tests of psychological adjustment. If the subjects knew that the student was poorly psychologically adjusted, their evaluation of his or her psychological comfort would probably be strongly determined by this information. And, in fact, the various students described in the protocols were generally rated as being average or below average in psychological comfort. This strong effect of the student's poor psychological adjustment could have outweighed effects of other variables (e.g., sex of student) for some judges.

Do Therapists Foster Traditional Sex Roles?

The review of the early research on whether therapists tend to encourage women to stay within the traditional female role again proceeds from general studies to studies with more narrow foci. A few years ago, the American Psychological Association (APA) Task Force on Sex Bias and Sex-Role Stereotyping in Psychotherapeutic Practice sent out open-ended questionnaires to 2000 women psychologists asking them to describe any sexist practices that they had encountered in the therapeutic situation. The results of this survey were of limited generalizability, because only 320 replies (16%) were received; so small a return rate may have biased the sample. Among these, the largest number of comments concerned therapists' fostering traditional sex roles; that is, "advocating marriage or perfecting the role of wife, depreciating the importance of a woman's career, using a client's attitude toward child bearing/rearing as an index of emotional maturity" (Asher, 1975, p. 4). Also, many respondents gave examples of therapists who criticized female clients' assertiveness (Asher, 1975).

In a more empirical investigation, Gomes and Abramowitz (1976) mailed clinical protocols to APA members (30% return rate). The patient's presenting problem was identified within a cluster of either stereotypic masculine (dominant) or stereotypic feminine (submissive) traits, and the patient's sex was varied in the protocols. The therapists made a number of broad, general assessments—for example, of emotional maturity and social adjustment. The clinicians' attitudes toward sex roles were also evaluated, and the sample was found to be skewed toward the liberal. Their responses showed an evaluation of females, especially the sex-role-deviant females, as more mature. In general, the findings suggested that women elicited more favorable impressions than men did. Overall, there was no consistent bias found due to patient sex, sex-role appropriateness, therapist sex, or therapist traditionalism. However, the generalizability of these results is questionable, because the sample of therapists was skewed toward the liberal and because of inclusion of a measure of sex-role traditionalism (specifically, five items from the Spence and Helmreich Attitudes Toward Women Scale) may have alerted the subjects to be wary of expressing any traditional attitudes about sex roles. In addition, it is possible that broad, general dependent measures such as the ones used in this study are not specific enough to be sensitive to any existing biases. It is interesting to note that even though the dominant woman was judged as more mature than the submissive woman was, she was *liked* less. Liking may be a more sensitive indicator of the therapists' biases than the other measures, because it more strongly reflects their emotional reactions and personal values.

In a very well-designed study, Billingsley (1977) investigated the effects of therapist sex, client sex, and client pathology on the formulation of treatment goals. She presented practicing psychotherapists with one of two case histories. In one, the client (designated as male or female) was described as seriously disturbed (psychotic)—that is, as experiencing serious difficulties in all areas of living, as being on job probation because of "idiosyncratic" behavior, and as cognitively disorganized and potentially explosive. In the other history, the client was described as having a specific phobia of recent origin (no previous psychological problems). Therapists selected therapy goals for the client from a list of items taken from the Sex-Role Stereotype Questionnaire (e.g., "increase in ability to think logically"), which consisted half of items considered desirable for females and half of items considered desirable for males; and made judgments of prognosis, diagnosis, and severity of difficulty. Analysis of the clinicians' responses indicated that there was no main effect of client sex, nor did this variable interact with any other variable. There were main effects of therapist sex and of client pathology. Female therapists chose more masculine goals and male therapists chose more feminine goals, regardless of client sex. In this study, the therapists responded to the client's pathology, not his or her sex. Billingsley concluded that a client's sex does not influence treatment goals when a client's pathology is well defined. Indeed, when pathology is so clearly defined, therapists need not invoke sex to infer in what areas the client needs help.

A more focused area of research on therapists' fostering traditionalism concerns whether the mother is considered responsible for psychopathology in her child. It will be remembered that early theories and child-rearing manuals view improper mothering as the cause of a host of problems in the child. Traditionally, the mother's role has been stressed in formulations about personality development and psychopathology. To explore whether these attitudes affect current clinical practice, C. V. Abramowitz (in press) asked family-oriented clinicians who were attending a workshop in Nashville to read case reports and to assess the mother's and father's contribution to the child's pathology (i.e., to allocate blame) and the need for treatment of the mother and father (another measure of responsibility). There was a trend toward blaming the mother and a tendency to focus treatment efforts on the mother when the child had certain problems. These effects may have been more robust if the sample had been more representative. As it was, the subjects were self-selected (because they chose to attend the workshop on family therapy) and were generally untraditional. So the sample was probably less likely to show sex bias than a more representative sample would have been. An extension of this study by C. V. Abramowitz, Abramowitz, Weitz, and Tittler (1976) reported only a slight tendency to view the mother as more involved in the child's psychopathology than the father. But, again, the sample was not representative. The subjects were attending a workshop and were, in general, inexperienced.

A very relevant area of research on whether therapists bolster traditional sex roles in women concerns clinicians' reactions to in-role and out-of-role career aspirations. Schlossberg and Pietrofesa (1973) have presented two studies that investigated whether counselors restrict their female clients' occupational choices. In the first, a 1969 unpublished study by Friedersdorf, male and female secondary school counselors responded to students who were role-playing college-bound and non-college-bound girls. It was found that male counselors associated college-bound girls with traditionally feminine occupations at the semiskilled level, but that female counselors saw them as interested in occupations that required a college education. Male counselors did not consider occupations traditionally engaged in by men as occupations that college-bound girls would like as careers. Schlossberg and Pietrofesa note that such counselor attitudes might affect the goals favored for female clients in counseling sessions.

In the second study, conducted by Pietrofesa and Schlossberg in 1970, interviews were arranged between counselor trainees and a coached female counselee at an urban university. In the interviews, the counselee said that she was entering her junior year of college and could not decide whether to choose engineering (a "masculine" occupation) or education (a "feminine" occupation) as a career. Analysis of the recordings of the interviews revealed counselor bias against a woman entering a masculine occupation among both male and female counselors. In their remarks, the counselors generally mentioned that engineering was a masculine field. This investigation suggests that counselors may encourage women to go into traditional careers, but it is only suggestive because of the inexperience of the counselors and the small size of the sample ($n = 29$).

A similar tendency among counselors was reported by Thomas and Stewart (1971). They played audiotapes of interviews with high-school girls (clients) for groups of secondary-school counselors. Each group heard two clients, one with a deviate career choice (engineering) and one with a conforming career choice (home economics). The same tape was presented for some groups as being of a client with a deviate career choice and for others as being of a client with a conforming career choice. Then the counselors made ratings of the client to provide indicators of acceptance of the client, appropriateness of career choice, and need for further counseling. Male and female counselors saw the conforming career goal as more appropriate than they did the deviate career goal. In making their ratings of appropriateness, they expressed concerns about realism, practicality, interests, and chances for satisfaction. Girls with a deviate goal were seen as needing further counseling more than girls with a conforming career goal were; however, this effect was due to the ratings of inexperienced female counselors only. This subgroup felt that the further counseling of girls with deviate career choices should focus on "choice of career," "reevaluation of present career goal," "interests," and "understanding of self."

Contradictory results were reported by Smith (1974), who conducted an investigation of the responses of junior-high-school and high-school counselors. They were given materials concerning a hypothetical case and asked to choose the most and least appropriate careers for the client from a list of six careers. The sex of the client was found not to affect which occupation was judged as best or worst. However, this study is difficult to evaluate, because what the six occupations were is not stated. A study by S. I. Abramowitz, Weitz, Schwartz, Amira, Gomes, and Abramowitz (1975) explored the reactions of counselors to sex-role-transgressing females, but was inconclusive because role-abiding females were not included in the design.

SUMMARY

Available evidence strongly suggests that the demands on a woman to stay within the traditional female role of wife and mother are strong, being reinforced by seemingly omnipresent influences—child care manuals, religious institutions, family, peers, the mass media, teachers, textbooks, and even elementary-school readers. The concomitant expectations about women—that they be passive, dependent, supportive, and so forth—have been incorporated into influential psychological theories that view mental health in women as acceptance of and compliance with the traditional female role. In light of the pervasiveness of the traditional view of women in our society and the strong influence of this view on psychological theorizing, we would expect psychotherapists not only to share this traditional image of women, but also to encourage women to conform to this stereotypic form. And indeed, there is some evidence that therapists do share traditional expectations of women and that such expectations manifest themselves in psychotherapeutic practice in the form of a double standard of mental health. Since therapists view a healthy woman as different from a healthy man, we would expect to find that therapists treat men and women differently.

However, differential treatment of men and women by therapists has not been conclusively demonstrated. Differences in the treatment accorded males and females have been found in research on counselors' occupational guidance. It appears that counselors tend to direct women into traditionally female careers. At the same time, studies of psychotherapy have yielded mixed results. As Davidson and Abramowitz conclude in their recent review (1980), recent studies of sex bias in clinical judgment have proven as inconclusive as earlier studies have. Results appear to be related to the methodology employed, analogues yielding findings of no sex bias, and naturalistic investigations yielding findings consistent with sex bias formulations. The picture is further confused by the fact that investigations of sex bias in psychotherapy have been replete with methodological problems. For example, many have employed very broad dependent measures of treatment variables—for instance, psychotherapy versus custodial care, or inpatient versus outpatient treatment. Such procedures are, very likely, not specific enough to detect any existing sex effects.

METHODOLOGICAL PROBLEMS IN THE EXPERIMENTAL LITERATURE ON SEX BIAS IN THERAPY

Many investigations of differential treatment of men and women in therapy have employed procedures that are *biased against* finding an effect of sex. One strong and common form of bias has been the use of methodologies that are subject to social desirability effects. That is, the experimenter's concern with sex effects has been so obvious (e.g., through inclusion of a traditionalism scale in the experimental materials) that the therapist/subject is aware of the purpose of the study and therefore likely to respond in a manner that obscures the very effects that are being investigated. Sex effects may have also been hidden by designs in which a client's pathology is clearly defined in the case materials given to the subjects, and/or hints as to the appropriate responses to the dependent measures are given in the materials. In both cases, the therapists' responses are likely to have been completely determined by the information given, and the subjects do not need to invoke sex and sex-role expectations to make the required judgments (e.g., Billingsley's study). Studies have also been subject to bias because of their use of nonrepresentative samples, which may be skewed to the nontraditional. Samples have typically been small and/or regional and/or made up of inexperienced practitioners. In addition, investigations where subjects have been led to consider extremes of behavior or where the design has omitted a crucial cell are similarly inconclusive.

A most serious, and very prevalent, methodological bias toward the finding of no sex effect is the use of broad, general dependent measures—for example, having therapists rate "social adjustment" or "emotional maturity." Studies employing such measures do not provide a fair test of whether sex bias exists in psychotherapeutic practice because these dependent variables are not tied to sex-role expectations. More specific measures that are related to sex roles need to be employed. One study that employed specific sex-role-related measures, Coie et al. (1974), did find strong evidence of sex effects. The investigators varied both type of stress (related to career or social life) and the type of reaction to that stress (aggressive behavior or somatic complaints) and were able to show that these interacted with client sex, and did so in a manner suggesting a strong influence of sex-role expectations on the judgments made.

CONCLUSION

There is certainly good reason to expect sex bias in psychotherapy. However, research in the area has yielded inconclusive findings. It may be hoped that refinements in methodology will one day uncloud the picture. Researchers have only begun to refine their measures so that they will be sensitive to sex effects, and to consider moderator variables[7] that may provide the clue to discovering whether—and where—sex bias exists in the practice of psychotherapy.

NOTES

[1]For a synopsis of *Women and Madness*, see Chapter 2.

[2]This process of viewing women in relation to men can be clearly seen in Freud's theorizing about sexual orgasm in women. He believed that the only normal kind of orgasm was the vaginal (as opposed to clitoral) orgasm. This belief was not based on an anatomical study of women (which, in fact, would have shown that the only type of orgasm women have is a clitoral one), but on

women's relation to men. Because men derive pleasure and have orgasm through friction with the vagina, it was assumed that women should have orgasm in the vagina (Koedt, 1971).

[3]After decades of research on the personality of females, there was still no evidence to support the psychoanalytic conception of women as passive and dependent (Maccoby & Jacklin, 1974; Weisstein, 1971). Even Maccoby and Jacklin's exhaustive review (1974) of the experimental literature did not find support for the belief that women are more passive or dependent than men are.

[4]Sherman also noted that the contrary may actually be closer to the truth: Research indicates that meeting the ideal of stereotypic femininity (i.e., a woman's being passive, dependent, etc.) is not salutory for mental health, motherhood, or intellectual development.

[5]See Chapter 4 for a more detailed presentation on expectancy effects.

[6]See Chapter 11 for a more detailed discussion of client-therapist sex.

[7]One moderator variable that promises to be important is physical attractiveness. See Chapter 3 for a discussion of attractiveness effects, and Chapter 6 for a review of literature on attractiveness effects in psychotherapy and some interesting new results demonstrating how potent attractiveness effects may be in the psychotherapeutic situation.

REFERENCE NOTES

1. Drapkin, R., & Anzel, A. *Sex-role bias in clinical judgments.* Manuscript in preparation, 1977.

2. Hamilton, D. *Contextual factors in stereotyping.* Paper presented at University of California at Los Angeles, October 1977.

3. Cowan, G. *Therapists' judgments of sex-role problems of clients.* Paper presented at the meeting of the Western Psychological Association, San Francisco, April 1975.

REFERENCES

Abramowitz, C. V. Blaming the mother: An experimental investigation of sex-role bias in countertransference. *Psychology of Women Quarterly,* in press.

Abramowitz, C. V., Abramowitz, S. I., Weitz, L. J., & Tittler, B. Sex-related effects on clinicians' attributions of parental involvement in child psychopathology. *Journal of Abnormal Child Psychology,* 1976, 4, 129–138.

Abramowitz, S. I., & Abramowitz, C. V. Should prospective women clients seek out women practitioners? Intimations of a "dingbat" effect in clinical evaluation. *Proceedings of the 81st Annual Convention of the American Psychological Association,* 1973, 8, 503–504. (Summary)

Abramowitz, S. I., Abramowitz, C. V., Jackson, C., & Gomes, B. The politics of clinical judgment: What nonliberal examiners infer about women who do not stifle themselves. *Journal of Consulting and Clinical Psychology,* 1973, 41, 385–391.

Abramowitz, S. I., Abramowitz, C. V., Roback, H., Corney, R., & McKee, E. Sex-role-related countertransference in psychotherapy. *Archives of General Psychiatry,* 1976, 33, 71–73.

Abramowitz, S. I., Roback, H. B., Schwartz, J. M., Yasuna, A., Abramowitz, C. V., & Gomes, B. Sex bias in psychotherapy: A failure to confirm. *American Journal of Psychiatry,* 1976, 133, 706–709.

Abramowitz, S. I., Weitz, L. J., Schwartz, J. M., Amira, S., Gomes, B., & Abramowitz, C. V. Comparative counselor inferences toward women with medical school aspirations. *Journal of College Student Personnel,* 1975, 16, 128–130.

Agel, J. Manifesto. In J. Agel (Ed.), *The radical therapist.* New York: Ballantine, 1971.

Asher, J. Sex bias found in therapy. *APA Monitor,* April, 1975, pp. 1, 4.

Bart, P. Mother Portnoy's complaints. *Trans-Action,* 1970, *8,* 60–74.

Bart, P. Depression in middle-aged women. In J. M. Bardwick (Ed.), *Reading on the psychology of women.* New York: Harper & Row, 1972.

Baum, C. L., Grotstein, S. E., & Wolfson, J. P. *Value inconsistencies in therapists' attitudes toward mothers.* Unpublished master's thesis, University of California at Los Angeles, 1977.

Bem, S. L., & Bem, D. J. Case study of a nonconscious ideology: Training the woman to know her place. In D. J. Bem (Ed.), *Beliefs, attitudes, and human affairs.* Belmont, Calif.: Brooks/Cole, 1970.

Bernard, J. *The future of motherhood.* New York: Dial Press, 1974.

Billingsley, D. Sex bias in psychotherapy: An examination of the effects of client sex, client pathology, and therapist sex on treatment planning. *Journal of Consulting and Clinical Psychology,* 1977, *45,* 250–256.

Brodey, J. F., & Detre, T. Criteria used by clinicians in referring patients to individual or group therapy. *American Journal of Psychotherapy,* 1972, *26,* 176–184.

Brodsky, A., & Holroyd, J. *Report of the Task Force on Sex Bias and Sex-Role Stereotyping in Psychotherapeutic Practice.* Washington, D.C.: American Psychological Association, 1975.

Broverman, I., Broverman, D., Clarkson, F., Rosenkrantz, P., & Vogel, S. Sex-role stereotypes and clinical judgments of mental health. *Journal of Consulting and Clinical Psychology,* 1970, *34,* 1–7.

Broverman, I., Vogel, S., Broverman, D., Clarkson, F., & Rosenkrantz, S. Sex-role stereotypes: A current appraisal. *Journal of Social Issues,* 1972, *28,* 59–78.

Brown, J. Editorial. In J. Agel (Ed.), *The radical therapist.* New York: Ballantine, 1971.

Buhler, C. *Values in psychotherapy.* New York: The Free Press, of Glencoe, 1962.

Buytendijk, F. J. J. *[Woman: A contemporary view]* (D. J. Barrett, trans.). New York: Newman Press, 1963.

Chesler, P. Marriage and psychotherapy. In J. Agel (Ed.), *The radical therapist.* New York: Ballantine, 1971. (a)

Chesler, P. Men drive women crazy. *Psychology Today,* July 1971, pp. 18, 22, 26–27, 97–98. (b)

Chesler, P. *Women and madness.* New York: Doubleday, 1972.

Clifton, A. K., McGrath, D., & Wick, B. Stereotypes of women: A single category? *Sex Roles,* 1976, *2,* 135–148.

Coie, J. D., Pennington, B. F., & Buckley, H. H. Effects of situational stress and sex roles on the attribution of psychological disorder. *Journal of Consulting and Clinical Psychology,* 1974, *42,* 559–568.

Davidson, C. V., & Abramowitz, S. I. Sex bias in clinical judgment: Later empirical returns. *Psychology of Women Quarterly,* 1980, *4,* 377–395.

Delk, J. L., & Ryan, T. L. Sex role stereotyping and A-B therapist status: Who is more chauvinistic? *Journal of Consulting and Clinical Psychology,* 1975, *43,* 589.

Deutsch, H. *The psychology of women: A psychoanalytic interpretation.* New York: Grune & Stratton, 1944.

Doherty, M. A. Sexual bias in personality theory. *Counseling Psychologist,* 1973, *4,* 67–75.

Elman, J., Press, A., & Rosenkrantz, P. Sex roles and self-concepts: Real and ideal. *Proceedings of the 78th Annual Convention of the American Psychological Association,* 1970, *5,* 455–456. (Summary)

Erikson, E. H. *Identity, youth, and crisis.* New York: Norton, 1968.

Fabrikant, B. The psychotherapist and the female patient: Perceptions, misperceptions, and change. In V. Franks & V. Burtle (Eds.), *Women in therapy.* New York: Brunner/Mazel, 1974.

Feinblatt, J. A., & Gold, A. E. Sex roles and the psychiatric referral process. *Sex Roles*, 1976, 2, 109–121.

Feldman-Summers, S., & Kiesler, S. Those who are number two try harder: The effect of sex on attributions of causality. *Journal of Personality and Social Psychology*, 1974, 30, 846–855.

Fine, R. The goals of psychoanalysis. In A. R. Maher (Ed.), *The goals of psychotherapy*. New York: Appleton-Century-Crofts, 1967.

Fodor, I. G. The phobic syndrome in women: Implications for treatment. In V. Franks & V. Burtle (Eds.), *Women in therapy*. New York: Brunner/Mazel, 1974.

Frank, J. D. *Persuasion and healing*. New York: Schocken, 1974.

Franks, V., & Burtle, V. Preface. In V. Franks & V. Burtle (Eds.), *Women in therapy*. New York: Brunner/Mazel, 1974.

Goldberg, P. Are women prejudiced against women? *Transaction*, 1968, 5, 28–30.

Goldstein, A. P. Participant expectancies in psychotherapy. *Psychiatry*, 1962, 25, 72–79. (a)

Goldstein, A. P. *Therapist-patient expectancies in psychotherapy*. Oxford: Pergamon Press, 1962. (b)

Gomberg, E. Women and alcoholism. In V. Franks & V. Burtle (Eds.), *Women in therapy*. New York: Brunner/Mazel, 1974.

Gomes, B., & Abramowitz, S. Sex-related patient and therapist effects on clinical judgment. *Sex Roles*, 1976, 2, 1–13.

Hill, C. E. Sex of client and sex and experience level of counselor. *Journal of Counseling Psychology*, 1975, 22, 6–11.

Hollingshead, A., & Redlich, F. C. *Social class and mental illness: A community study*. New York: Wiley, 1958.

Holroyd, J., & Brodsky, A. Psychologists' attitudes and practices regarding erotic and nonerotic physical contact with patients. *American Psychologist*, 1977, 32, 843–849.

Horner, M. S. Femininity and successful achievement: A basic inconsistency. In J. M. Bardwick, E. Douvan, M. S. Horner, & D. Gutmann (Eds.), *Feminine personality and conflict*. Belmont, Calif.: Brooks/Cole, 1970.

Horney, K. *Feminine psychology*. New York: Norton, 1967.

Howard, E. M., & Howard, J. L. Women in institutions: Treatment in prisons and mental hospitals. In V. Franks & V. Burtle (Eds.), *Women in therapy*. New York: Brunner/Mazel, 1974.

Hyde, J. S., & Rosenberg, B. G. *Half the human experience: The psychology of women*. Lexington, Mass.: Heath, 1976.

Kardener, S., Fuller, M., & Mensh, I. A survey of physician's attitudes and practices regarding erotic and nonerotic contact with patients. *American Journal of Psychiatry*, 1973, 10, 1077–1081.

Keller, S. The female role: Constants and change. In V. Franks & V. Burtle (Eds.), *Women in therapy*. New York: Brunner/Mazel, 1974.

Kirsh, B. Consciousness-raising groups as therapy for women. In V. Franks & V. Burtle (Eds.), *Women in therapy*. New York: Brunner/Mazel, 1974.

Koedt, A. The myth of the vaginal orgasm. In J. Agel (Ed.), *The radical therapist*. New York: Ballantine, 1971.

Kunnes, R. How to be a radical therapist. In J. Agel (Ed.), *The radical therapist*. New York: Ballantine, 1971.

Kupers, T. Radical therapy needs revolutionary theory. In J. Agel (Ed.), *The radical therapist*. New York: Ballantine, 1971.

Lazarus, A. A. Women in behavior therapy. In V. Franks & V. Burtle (Eds.), *Women in therapy*. New York: Brunner/Mazel, 1974.

Lewittes, D. J., Moselle, J. A., & Simmons, W. L. Sex-role bias in clinical judgments based on

Rorschach interpretations. *Proceedings of the 81st Annual Convention of the American Psychological Association,* 1973, *8,* 495–496. (Summary)

London, P. *The modes and morals of psychotherapy.* New York: Holt, Rinehart & Winston, 1964.

Maccoby, E. E., & Jacklin, C. N. *The psychology of sex differences.* Stanford, Calif.: Stanford University Press, 1974.

Maslin, A., & Davis, J. Sex-role stereotyping as a factor in mental health standards among counselors-in-training. *Journal of Counseling Psychology,* 1975, *22,* 87–91.

Masling, J., & Harris, S. Sexual aspects of TAT administration. *Journal of Consulting and Clinical Psychology,* 1969, *33,* 166–169.

McClelland, D. C., & Watt, N. F. Sex-role alienation in schizophrenia. *Journal of Abnormal Psychology,* 1968, *73,* 226–239.

McGlynn, R. P., Megas, J. C., & Benson, D. H. Sex and race as factors affecting the attribution of insanity in a murder trial. *Journal of Psychology,* 1976, *93,* 93–99.

McKee, J., & Sherriffs, A. Men's and women's beliefs, ideals, and self-concepts. *American Journal of Sociology,* 1959, *64,* 356–363.

Meyer, J. W., & Sobieszek, B. J. The effect of a child's sex on adult interpretations of its behavior. *Developmental Psychology,* 1972, *6,* 42–48.

Mintz, E. E. What do we owe today's woman? *International Journal of Group Psychotherapy,* 1974, *24,* 273–280.

Mischel, H. Sex bias in the evaluation of professional articles. *Journal of Educational Psychology,* 1974, *66,* 157–166.

Mitchell, J. *Psychoanalysis and feminism.* New York: Pantheon, 1974.

Neulinger, J. Perceptions of the optimally integrated person: A redefinition of mental health. *Proceedings of the 76th Annual Convention of the American Psychological Association,* 1968, *3,* 553–554. (Summary)

Nieva, V. F., & Gutek, B. A. *Women and work: A psychological perspective.* New York: Praeger, 1981.

Nowacki, C. M., & Poe, C. A. The concept of mental health as related to sex of person perceived. *Journal of Consulting and Clinical Psychology,* 1973, *40,* 160.

Osmond, H., Franks, V., & Burtle, V. Changing views of women and therapeutic approaches: Some historical considerations. In V. Franks & V. Burtle (Eds.), *Women in therapy.* New York: Brunner/Mazel, 1974.

Parloff, M. B. Goals in psychotherapy: Mediating and ultimate. In A. R. Maher (Ed.), *The goals of psychotherapy.* New York: Appleton-Century-Crofts, 1967.

Perry, J. Physicians' erotic and nonerotic physical involvement with patients. *American Journal of Psychiatry,* 1976, *33,* 838–840.

Pheterson, G., Kiesler, S., & Goldberg, P. Evaluation of the performance of women as a function of their sex, achievement, and personal history. *Journal of Personality and Social Psychology,* 1971, *19,* 114–118.

Pollock, M. J. Changing the role of women. In H. Wortis & C. Rabinowitz (Eds.), *The women's movement: Social and psychological perspectives.* New York: Wiley, 1972.

Polster, M. Women in therapy: A Gestalt therapist's view. In V. Franks & V. Burtle (Eds.), *Women in therapy.* New York: Brunner/Mazel, 1974.

A Redstockings Sister. Brainwashing and women. In J. Agel (Ed.), *The radical therapist.* New York: Ballantine, 1971.

Rosenkrantz, P., Vogel, S., Bee, H., Broverman, I., & Broverman, D. Sex-role stereotypes and self-concepts in college students. *Journal of Consulting and Clinical Psychology,* 1968, *32,* 287–295.

Rosenthal, R. *Experimenter effects in behavioral research.* New York: Appleton-Century-Crofts, 1966.

Rosenthal, R. Experimenter outcome-orientation and the results of the psychological experiment. In P. Badia, A. Haber, & R. Runyon (Eds.), *Research problems in psychotherapy*. Reading, Mass.: Addison-Wesley, 1970.

Russo, N. F. The motherhood mandate. *Journal of Social Issues*, 1976, *32*, 143–153.

Schlossberg, N. K., & Pietrofesa, J. J. Perspectives on counseling bias: Implications for counselor education. *Counseling Psychologist*, 1973, *4*, 44–54.

Seidenberg, R. Oedipus and male supremacy. In J. Agel (Ed.), *The radical therapist*. New York: Ballantine, 1971.

Sherman, J. Social values, femininity, and the development of female competence. *Journal of Social Issues*, 1976, *32*, 181–195.

Sherriffs, A., & Jarrett, R. Sex differences in attitudes about sex differences. *Journal of Psychology*, 1953, *35*, 161–168.

Sherriffs, A., & McKee, J. Qualitative aspects of beliefs about men and women. *Journal of Personality*, 1957, *25*, 451–464.

Siskind, G. Sexual aspects of Thematic Apperception Test administration. *Journal of Consulting and Clinical Psychology*, 1973, *40*, 20–21.

Smith, M. L. Influence of client sex and ethnic group on counselor judgments. *Journal of Counseling Psychology*, 1974, *21*, 516–521.

Steiner, C. Radical psychiatry: Principles. In J. Agel (Ed.), *The radical therapist*. New York: Ballantine, 1971.

Steinmann, A., & Fox, D. J. Male-female perceptions of the female role in the United States. *Journal of Psychology*, 1966, *64*, 265–276.

Steinmann, A., Levi, J., & Fox, D. J. Self-concept of college women compared with their concept of ideal woman and men's ideal woman. *Journal of Counseling Psychology*, 1964, *11*, 370–374.

Stricker, G. Implications of research for psychotherapeutic treatment of women. *American Psychologist*, 1977, *32*, 14–22.

Sue, S. Clients' demographic characteristics and therapeutic treatment: Differences that make a difference. *Journal of Consulting and Clinical Psychology*, 1976, *44*, 864.

Thomas, A. H., & Stewart, N. R. Counselor response to female clients with deviate and conforming career goals. *Journal of Counseling Psychology*, 1971, *18*, 352–357.

Ullmann, L. P., & Krasner, L. *A psychological approach to abnormal behavior*. Englewood Cliffs, N.J.: Prentice-Hall, 1969.

Weisstein, N. Woman as nigger. *Psychology Today*, October 1969, pp. 20, 22, 58.

Weisstein, N. Psychology constructs the female. In V. Gornick & B. K. Moran (Eds.), *Woman in sexist society*. New York: Basic Books, 1971.

White, W. Career interest inventories: NIE issues test guidelines for detecting sex bias. *APA Monitor*, March 1975, p. 14.

Zeldow, P. B. Search for sex differences in clinical judgment. *Psychological Reports*, 1975, *37*, 1135–1142.

Zellmann, G. L. The role of structural factors in limiting women's institutional participation. *Journal of Social Issues*, 1976, *32*, 33–46.

2   A Summary of Phyllis Chesler's *Women & Madness*

JOAN MURRAY

THE DOUBLE STANDARD OF MENTAL HEALTH

. . . female reproductive biology, patriarchal culture, and the modern parent-daughter relationship have combined to insure such characteristically female behaviors—and ideals—as self-sacrifice, masochism, reproductive narcissism, compassionate "maternality," dependency, sexual timidity and unhappiness, father-worship—and the overwhelming dislike and devaluation of women. (p. xxi)

Adjustment to this female sex role is viewed as healthy for a woman (p. 68). Even though behavior fitting this description "is pitied, disliked, and diagnosed by society and its clinicians, any other kind of behavior is unacceptable in women!" (p. 69). Both acting out the female role (e.g., depression—an exaggeration of passivity; suicide attempts—an exaggeration of helplessness) and total or partial rejection of the female role (e.g., aggressiveness, promiscuity) are viewed as abnormal (p. 56). In attempting to bring the woman patient to terms with the female role, the traditional therapist is ignoring the oppression of women, the oppression involved in imposing the female role on women (p. 110).

Why is therapists' encouraging women to accept the female role a form of oppression? It is oppression because in viewing the traditional female role as the only normal role for women, the therapist is confining women to a role that keeps them in an oppressed position—oppressed because fully accepting the female role requires a woman to believe that women are inferior to men and to confine herself to a lower status position in society relative to men.

Because normality (as defined by psychotherapists) amounts to acceptance of the female role for women, there exists a *double standard of mental health* —one standard for men and another for women. And this double standard is enforced by clinicians. Both female and male clinicians, "whether they are disciples of a particular psychoanalytic or psychological theory or not, currently share and act upon traditional myths about abnormality, sex-role stereotypes, and female inferiority." Moreover, "most traditional psychoanalytic and therapeutic theories and practices perpetrate certain misogynistic views of women and of sex-role stereotypes as 'scientific' or 'curative'" (p. 61).

What is labeled "crazy" is "role rejection" or "sex-role alienation"—for example, the overactive dominating female and the underactive passive male (p. 53). This double standard of mental health has been documented by Inge K. Broverman and her colleagues.

Seventy-nine clinicians (forty-six male and thirty-three female psychiatrists, psychologists, and social workers) completed a sex-role stereotype questionnaire. The questionnaire consisted of 122 bipolar items, each of which described a particular behavior or trait. For example:

very subjective _____ very objective
not at all aggressive_____very aggressive

The clinicians were instructed to check off those traits that represent healthy male, healthy female, or healthy adult (sex unspecified) behavior. The results were as follows:

1. There was high agreement among clinicians as to the attributes characterizing healthy adult men, healthy adult women, and healthy adults, sex unspecified.
2. There were no differences among men and women clinicians.
3. Clinicians had different standards of health for men and women. Their concepts of healthy mature men did not differ significantly from their concepts of healthy mature adults, but their concepts of healthy mature women did differ significantly from those for men and for adults. Clinicians were likely to suggest that women differ from healthy men by being more submissive, less independent, less adventurous, more easily influenced, less aggressive, less competitive, more excitable in minor crises, more easily hurt, more emotional, more conceited about their appearances, less objective, and less interested in math and science.

Finally, what was judged healthy for adults, sex unspecified, and for adult males, was in general highly correlated with previous studies of social desirability as perceived by non-professional subjects.

It is clear that for a woman to be healthy she must "adjust" to and accept the behavioral norms for her sex even though these kinds of behavior are generally regarded as less socially desirable. As the authors themselves remark, "This constellation seems a most unusual way of describing any mature, healthy individual." (pp. 67–69)

In a 1971 study by Dr. Nathan Rickel, entitled "The Angry Woman Syndrome," husbands who "put up" with their middle-aged wives' "angry" and malelike behavior are described as suffering from a "Job complex." The author notes that while the reverse is often seen, namely, "where men are the angry protagonists and women the passive recipients . . . our society is so geared that it more readily accepts this as only an exaggeration of the expected masculine-feminine roles." Rickel's "angry" women are all highly successful professionally and are "neurotic" because they exhibit "male" behaviors such as

> an inability to brook criticism or competition; bursts of uncontrollable temper; the use of foul language; possessiveness or jealousy; the use of alcohol or drugs; and consorting with spouses who accept such behaviour.

If such "male" behavior is "neurotic" or "self-destructive," then it should be seen as such for both sexes. (Of course, when women do the very same things as men, it always has a completely different meaning and set of consequences: even here, it is the *wives* who are seeking treatment—the husbands, for all their "female"-like suffering, are not.) (pp. 69–70)

Another aspect of the double standard of mental health is the idea among clinicians that "women need to be mothers and that children need intensive and exclusive female mothering in order for both to be mentally 'healthy' " (p. 73). Men do not need to be fathers, and intensive father-child contact is not seen as necessary for the mental health of the child.

PSYCHOANALYTIC THEORY

There is much in the psychoanalytic literature in which we can see this double standard of mental health. The following quotes are illustrative:

Sigmund Freud:

> [Women] refuse to accept the fact of being castrated and have the hope of someday obtaining a penis in spite of everything. . . . I cannot escape the notion (though I hesitate to give it expression) that for woman the level of what is ethically normal is different from what is in man. We must not allow ourselves to be deflected

from such conclusions by the denials of the feminists who are anxious to force us to regard the two sexes as completely equal in position and worth.

We say also of women that their social interests are weaker than those of men and that their capacity for the sublimation of their interests is less . . . the difficult development which leads to femininity [seems to] exhaust all the possibilities of the individual.

Erik Erikson:

For the student of development and practitioner of psychoanalysis, the stage of life crucial for the understanding of womanhood is the step from youth to maturity, the state when the young woman relinquishes the care received from the parental family and the extended care of institutions of education, in order to commit herself to the love of a stranger and to the care to be given to his or her offspring . . . young women often ask, whether they can "have an identity" before they know whom they will marry and for whom they will make a home. Granted that something in the young woman's identity must keep itself open for the peculiarities of the man to be joined and of the children to be brought up, I think that much of a young woman's identity is already defined in her kind of attractiveness and in the selectivity of her search for the man (or men) by whom she wishes to be sought.

Bruno Bettelheim:

. . . as much as women want to be good scientists and engineers, they want, first and foremost, to be womanly companions of men and to be mothers.

Joseph Rheingold:

. . . woman is nurturance . . . anatomy decrees the life of a woman. . . . When women grow up without dread of their biological functions and without subversion by feminist doctrines and therefore enter upon motherhood with a sense of fulfillment and altruistic sentiment we shall attain the goal of a good life and a secure world in which to live.[1]

Carl G. Jung:

"But no one can evade the fact, that in taking up a masculine calling, studying, and working in a man's way, woman is doing something not wholly in agreement with, if not directly injurious to, her feminine nature." . . . [Female] psychology is founded on the principle of Eros, the great binder and deliverer; while age-old wisdom has ascribed Logos to man as his ruling principle.

These are all familiar, prescribed, and therefore extremely seductive views of women. Their affirmation by experts has indirectly strengthened such views among men and more directly tyrannized women: events such as childbirth and marriage which, in other centuries, was [sic] unavoidable, common, and unromanticized, are here being touted by experts as spiritual luxuries, which women must *strive for*. The unchosen necessities of the past (perhaps no different from poverty, disease, or early death) were revived as salvation myths for twentieth-century women by the major psychoanalytic theorists. American middle-class women were also "seduced and abandoned" by the institution of psychotherapy and the tyranny of published "expert" opinion which stressed the mother's importance (and deadly responsibility) for healthy child development. Most child development research, like most birth control research, has centered around women, not men: for this is "woman's work," for which she is totally responsible, which is "never done," and for which, in a wage-labor economy, she is never directly paid. She does it for love and is amply rewarded—in the writings of Freud et al.

Freud's views and self-professed confusion about women have been embraced, often romantically and devotedly, by female theoreticians, such as Freud's analysand and disciple Helene Deutsch, and by Marie Bonaparte, Marie Robinson, and Marynia Farnham, and by male theoreticians such as Frederick Lundberg, Erik Erikson, Bruno Bettelheim, and Joseph Rheingold. Freud's views have been more subtly supported by C. G. Jung and his disciple, Esther Harding, whose approach to human psychology is more "spiritual" and anthropological than Freud's.[2]

The "Freudian" vision beholds women as essentially "breeders and bearers," as potentially warmhearted creatures, but more often as cranky children with uteruses, forever mourning the loss of male organs and male identity. The headaches, fatigue, chronic depression, frigidity, paranoia, and overwhelming sense of inferiority that Freud recorded so accurately about his many female patients was never *interpreted* in any remotely accurate terms. Female "symptoms" were certainly not viewed by Freud as the indirect communications characteristic of slave psychologies. Instead, such symptoms were viewed as "hysterical" and neurotic productions, as underhanded domestic tyrannies manufactured by spiteful, self-pitying, and generally unpleasant women whose *inability to be happy as women* stems from unresolved penis envy, unresolved Electra (or female Oedipal) complexes, or from general, intractable, and mysterious female stubbornness. (pp. 76–79)

SEX-TYPED PSYCHIATRIC CATEGORIES

The types of behaviors that are considered "mentally ill" are sex-typed. So are psychiatric categories.

Typically "female" and "male" symptomatology appear early in life. Studies of childhood behavior problems have indicated that boys are most often referred to child guidance clinics for aggressive, destructive (anti-social), and competitive behavior; girls are referred (if they are referred at all), for personality problems, such as excessive fears and worries, shyness, timidity, lack of self-confidence, and feelings of inferiority.[3] Similar, sex-typed symptoms exist in adults also:

> ... the symptoms of men are also much more likely to reflect a destructive hostility toward others, as well as a pathological self-indulgence. ... Women's symp-

toms, on the other hand, express a harsh, self-critical, self-depriving and often self-destructive set of attitudes.

A study by E. Zigler and L. Phillips, comparing the symptoms of male and female mental hospital patients, found male patients significantly more assaultive than females and more prone to indulge their impulses in socially deviant ways like "robbery, rape, drinking, and homosexuality." Female patients were often found to be "self-deprecatory, depressed, perplexed, suffering from suicidal thoughts, or making actual suicidal attempts."

Most women display "female" psychiatric symptoms such as depression, frigidity, paranoia, psychoneurosis, suicide attempts, and anxiety. Men display "male" diseases such as alcoholism, drug addiction, personality disorders, and brain diseases.[4] . . . Typically female symptoms all share a "dread of happiness" —a phrase coined by Thomas Szasz to describe the "indirect forms of communication" that characterize "slave psychology."

> In general, the open acknowledgement of satisfaction is feared only in situations of relative oppression (e.g. all suffering wife vis-a-vis domineering husband). The experiences of satisfaction (joy, contentment) are inhibited lest they lead to an augmentation of one's burden . . . *the fear of acknowledging satisfaction is a characteristic feature of slave psychology.* The "properly exploited" slave is forced to labor until he shows signs of fatigue or exhaustion. Completion of his task does not signify that his work is finished and that he may rest. At the same time, even though his task is unfinished, he may be able to influence his master to stop driving him—and to let him rest—if he exhibits signs of imminent collapse. Such signs may be genuine or contrived. Exhibiting signs of fatigue or exhaustion—irrespective of whether they are genuine or contrived (e.g. "being on strike" against one's boss)—is likely to induce a feeling of fatigue or exhaustion in the actor. I believe that this is the mechanism responsible for the great majority of so-called chronic fatigue states. Most of these were formerly called "neurasthenia," a term rarely used nowadays. Chronic fatigue or a feeling of lifelessness and exhaustion are still frequently encountered in clinical practice.
>
> Psychoanalytically, they are considered "character symptoms." Many of these patients are unconsciously "on strike" against persons (actual or internal) to whom they relate with subservience and against whom they wage an unending and unsuccessful covert rebellion.

The analogy between "slave" and "woman" is by no means a perfect one. However, there is some theoretical justification for viewing women, or the sex-caste system, as the *prototype* for all subsequent class and race slavery. Women were probably the first group of human beings to be enslaved by another group. In a sense, "woman's work," or woman's psychological identity, consists in exhibiting the signs and "symptoms" of slavery—as well as, or instead of, working around the clock in the kitchen, the nursery, the bedroom, and the factory. (pp. 39–41)

"Female" diseases such as depression and frigidity constitute female role rituals, enacted by many women.

Depression

Women become "depressed" long before menopausal chemistry becomes the standard explanation for the disease. National statistics and research studies all document a much higher female to male ratio of depression or manic-depression at all ages. Perhaps more women *do* get "depressed" as they grow older—when their already limited opportunities for sexual, emotional, and intellectual growth decrease even further. Dr. Pauline Bart studied depression in middle-aged women and found that such women had completely accepted their "feminine" role—and were "depressed" because that role was no longer possible or needed. (pp. 41, 44)

It is important to note that "depressed" women are (like women in general) only *verbally* hostile; unlike most men, they do not express their hostility physically —either directly, to the "significant others" in their lives, or indirectly, through physical and athletic prowess. It is safer for women to become "depressed" than physically violent. (p. 45)

Frigidity

. . . most clinicians have tried hard to help their female patients "achieve" heterosexual orgasms—usually by counseling a joyous and/or philosophical acceptance of the female role as envisioned and enforced by men: as Madonna-housewife and mother, or as Magdalene Earth Goddess. Even sexual liberationist pioneers, such as Wilhelm Reich, have posited the primary of vaginal eroticism, and viewed bisexuality and lesbianism as "regressive" or "infantile." Most clinicians have not thought deeply about the sociopolitical—*or* the psychological—conditions that are necessary for female sexual self-definition. Women can never be sexually actualized as long as men control the means of production and reproduction. Women have had to barter their sexuality (or their capacity for sexual pleasure) for economic survival and maternity. Female frigidity *as we know it* will cease only when such bartering ceases. Most women cannot be "sexual" as long as prostitution, rape, and patriarchal marriage exist, with such attendant concepts and practices as "illegitimate" pregnancies, enforced maternity, "non-maternal" paternity, and the sexual deprivation of "aging" women. (p. 47)

Schizophrenia

During the last decade three psychologists have discussed "schizophrenia" in terms of sex-role alienation or sex-role rejection. In 1961, Dr. Shirley Angrist compared female ex-mental patients who were returned to asylums with those who weren't. She found that the rehospitalized women had refused to function "domestically" in terms of cleaning, cooking, child care, and shopping. The re-hospitalized women were no different from the ex-mental patients in terms of their willingness to participate in "leisure" activities, such as traveling, socializing, or enjoying themselves. The rehospitalized women were, in Angrist's terms, slightly more "middle class and more frequently married than their non-returned counterparts." Further, the husbands who readmitted their wives expressed significantly lower expectations for their total human functioning. They seemed more willing to tolerate extremely childlike and dependent behavior in their wives—such as incessant complaining and incoherence—as long as the dishes were washed. . . . Ex-patients, whether they were rehospitalized or not, swore more often, attempted aggressive acts more frequently, got drunk, did not want to "see" people, and "misbehaved sexually"—behaviors considered more "masculine" than "feminine." (pp. 50–51)

In 1964, Dr. Frances Cheek published a study entitled "A Serendipitous Finding: Sex Role and Schizophrenia." She compared male and female "schizophrenics" between the ages of fifteen and twenty-six with their "normal" counterparts, expecting to find a classic profile of schizophrenic passivity, withdrawal, and emotionally constrained behavior. Instead she found that female schizophrenics were more dominant and aggressive with their parents than were female—or male—normals or male schizophrenics. The male schizophrenics presented a more "feminine" (or schizophrenic) pattern of passivity, more so than schizophrenic females and normal males.

It is important to note that the male schizophrenics were still very similar to normal males in the expression of negative social-emotional behavior, such as expression of hostility and disagreement. The female schizophrenics were less "negative" emotionally than were female or male normals or male schizophrenics. Nevertheless, female schizophrenics were perceived by both their parents as the "least conforming" of all the groups. Their parents remembered them as unusually "active" (for girls?) during childhood. This reference to "activeness" may not refer as much to physical or aggressive behavior as to perceptual, intellectual, or verbal behavior. Perhaps it was this rather specific rejection of one aspect of the female role that caused family conflict, and ultimately led to psychiatric labeling and incarceration.

Dr. Cheek refers to an earlier study done by Letailleur, in which he suggests that "the overactive dominating female and the underactive passive male are cultural anomalies and are therefore hospitalized." (pp. 52–53)

CONCLUSION

The traditional psychoanalytic method is "based on the illusion of individual freedom." Therefore, it cannot "cure" a patient as long as the major social institutions remain "uncured" (p. 96). Society places restrictions on a woman. And these restrictions play a large part in causing mental and emotional distress in women.

NOTES

[1]Chesler's footnote: "Anatomy, like the bubonic plague, is history, not destiny. Of course, there are bio-anatomical differences between the sexes. The question now is whether these differences —or the cultural conclusions drawn from them—are either necessary or desirable."

[2]Chesler's footnote: "However, their female ideal is essentially a chivalrous one. Women are biologically and therefore psychologically different from men and *vive la difference!* Woman's real problems stem from a resistance to her very unique and glorious capacity for a life of love, feeling, and maternity. Of course, modern society devalues such a life, but then, more's the pity. Women, preferably well-educated and wealthy women, like Jung's female disciples, should, as individuals, transcend such devaluing."

[3]Chesler's footnote: "Self-destructive or 'loser' behavior, from suicide attempts to a fearful narrowing of life experience, is only fully punished as the female grows older. The female child is usually praised for the 'maturity' of her submissiveness, obedience, and unadventurousness."

[4]Chesler's footnote: "There are still fewer men hospitalized for 'male' diseases than women hospitalized for 'female' diseases."

II Social-Psychological Issues in Bias

How do our stereotypes and other biases affect our perceptions, expectations, and behavior? This question is the subject of the next three chapters. In Chapter 3, Hatfield and Perlmutter discuss how physical attractiveness influences the perceiver's expectations and behavior—even when the perceiver is a therapist. In Chapter 4, Rosenthal reviews the literature on expectancy effects—an area of research with great relevance for psychotherapy; consider the huge impact that self-fulfilling prophecies could have in therapy. And in Chapter 5, Hamilton discusses how the way we process information reinforces our biases and hinders the disconfirmation of stereotypes and expectations. Such a process is important to consider in psychotherapy, for a therapist's expectations about a client could remain unchanged, even though the client presents information contrary to the expectations.

Chapter 3 focuses on the effects of physical attractiveness. Hatfield and Perlmutter examine how a person's physical attractiveness influences our reactions to him or her, pointing out that we can "hardly avoid judging others by their physical appearance—physical attractiveness (or its lack) is immediately apparent in every social encounter." The authors also present evidence that "most people, most of the time, treat the beautiful more compassionately than they treat the ugly."

Psychotherapists are not immune; they are influenced by beauty too. Implications for psychotherapy are discussed, and some interesting findings reported concerning psychotherapists' reactions to beautiful women clients. Hatfield and Perlmutter conclude that although attractive patients sometimes receive more and better treatment than do their unattractive counterparts, they may also receive "pseudo-help" instead of real treatment.

In Chapter 4, Rosenthal reviews the research on interpersonal expectancy effects and how they can lead to self-fulfilling prophecies. The existence of

49

these well-documented, widely occurring effects is important for psychotherapy, because a therapist's expectations about a client could influence his or her behavior toward that client and could ultimately affect the course of that client's therapy. For instance, if a therapist saw a client as having a good prognosis, that therapist might behave in therapy in such a way as to promote improvement in the client more than he or she would if the client's prognosis was seen to be poor.

In Chapter 5, Hamilton discusses how stereotypes affect perception and behavior. He describes research demonstrating that an individual's stereotypes about a group (e.g., women, blacks) can affect (1) the causal attributions that the individual makes about the behavior of members of that group; (2) the individual's interpretations of the behavior of group members; (3) what the individual remembers of group members' behavior; and (4) the individual's own behavior toward group members—behavior that can result in "self-fulfilling prophecies." He convincingly shows that stereotypic expectations influence our perception of others, our interpretation of information about others, and our behavior toward them. People consistently "see" evidence that confirms their stereotypes—even when such evidence is not there.

The operation of such cognitive processes has direct relevance to bias in psychotherapy. For example, let us consider the finding that people tend to attribute success in men to ability but attribute success in women to luck or effort (which are not stable characteristics like ability). A therapist might attribute a woman client's successful performance in her first year of college to luck or great effort, rather than ability, with the result that he believes that she does not have the ability to complete college and so encourages her to accept a proposal of marriage and quit school.

A therapist's retaining information consistent with his or her stereotypes of men and women could have detrimental effects on a woman client. Let us say that a woman has shown both passive and active, both dependent and independent behavior during the course of therapy. But the therapist remembers much more of the passive/dependent behavior than he or she does of the active/independent behavior, and so counsels the client to avoid situations where she would have to be active and independent (e.g., medical school, work, divorce).

Similarly, if the therapist treats the woman client in such a way that she eventually confirms his or her beliefs about what women are like, the client's alternatives would be severely reduced. For instance, if the therapist believes that women are dependent and need husbands to take care of them, he or she might encourage a woman client to turn down a fellowship and get married.

It is important to note that the operation of such cognitive processes in the minds of therapists can not only confine women to the limited options defined by the female sex role, but can also confine men to the limited options encompassed in the male sex role. For instance, a man with a desire to keep house and raise a family might be encouraged to go to professional school simply because he is a male.

Similarly, a therapist's belief that blacks are intellectually inferior to whites could lead him or her to dissuade a black person from going to college, perhaps drastically changing that client's life. There are other cases, too; any time a group stereotype exists, there is a danger that some therapist's treatment of members of that group could be unconsciously influenced by stereotypic expectations, most likely to the detriment of the client involved.

3 Social-Psychological Issues in Bias: Physical Attractiveness

ELAINE HATFIELD AND
MORTON S. PERLMUTTER

In even the briefest of social interactions, people's physical appearance—their beauty (or lack of it), their carriage, their dress—is obvious to others. And, according to folklore, people's appearance telegraphs information about their intelligence, personalities, and characters. From flame-colored hair through flat feet, appearance is reputed to provide kernels of folk insight into others' natures. What stereotypes do people hold about the beautiful or the homely? Are they accurate? Do we really treat the beautiful and the homely so differently?

For many years, social psychologists displayed a studied lack of professional interest in these and related questions. Recently, however, there has been a surge of interest in such topics. In their 1974 review of physical-attractiveness research, Berscheid and Walster (1974) cited only 42 studies dealing with "physical attractiveness." From 1974 to 1978, *Psychological Abstracts* listed more than 250 publications on this topic. This chapter is an attempt to review what social psychologists know about physical attractiveness as a biasing factor in interpersonal encounters—including psychotherapy.

The research reported in this chapter was funded, in part, by a National Institutes of Health Biomedical Grant to the University of Wisconsin. The authors would like to thank Carol T. Miller (1978) for her review of the physical-attractiveness research that has been conducted since Berscheid and Walster's review (1974). Miller's review alerted the authors to a number of studies they would have otherwise missed.

A note: In late 1975, family therapist Morton Perlmutter interviewed 67 therapeutic nurses, social workers, psychologists, and psychiatrists in Madison and Milwaukee, Wisconsin, and the surrounding areas. At that time, he was interested in sexism in therapy and the differences, if any, in the way psychotherapists treated male versus female patients. Again and again, however, he found the conversations taking an unexpected turn. The therapists (mostly men) began by discussing how they treated men versus women, but they *ended up* talking about their encounters with beautiful women patients. In this chapter, Perlmutter's interviews with psychotherapists are used as a frame for the discussion of the biasing effects of beauty, both in psychotherapy and in day-to-day encounters.

The first section of this chapter asks, "What is beauty?" The second section asks what people *expect* beautiful people to be like. The third section asks to what extent perception is translated into action: Do the beautiful *really* have an advantage in life? The fourth section reviews the impact that such differential treatment has on the beautiful: What are they *really* like? Finally, the fifth section suggests some directions that future research on the biasing effect of beauty in psychotherapy might take.

WHO IS PHYSICALLY ATTRACTIVE?

Intellectually, from psychotherapists to the person in the street, people may all agree, glibly, that "beauty is in the eye of the beholder"; however, they don't really believe it. For example, Perlmutter assumed that psychotherapists would be sensitive to the fact that their perceptions of who was beautiful and who was not must be shaped by their own histories. Yet Perlmutter found that psychotherapists inevitably talked as if beauty was "out there"; they assumed that everyone would share their perceptions. In their research, Berscheid and Hatfield found that judges hired to rate the physical attractiveness of various stimuli had exactly the same response. They assumed that everyone *must* share their opinions. When they found others did not, they were incredulous. Even then, it did not occur to them that the differences were *real*. They'd say: "Look—look—at her eyes—her nose," or "Can't you see?" to them, beauty was very real.

The data suggest that the truth lies somewhere between—to some extent, people can agree as to what is beautiful. Yet, ultimately, beauty is always in the eye of the beholder. Researchers have found that there is reasonable concensus as to what is beautiful or homely, but only that. (Typically, in such studies, interrater reliabilities range from .70 to .95; see Cavior & Dokecki, Note 1; Darwin, 1872; Ford & Beach, 1951; Kopera, Maier, & Johnson, Note 2; and Murstein, 1972.)

Given the fact that there is only partial agreement as to what is beautiful and what is not, the question becomes this: What do most people, most of the time, perceive to be beautiful?

Characteristics of Attractive Stimuli

The question of who is physically attractive, and why, is one that has fascinated novelists, poets, and street-corner pundits for centuries. Unfortunately, the popularity of the question is not reflected in the definitiveness of the available answers.

It has been said that "Except for some arbitrary beauty-contest conventions about 'ideal' female dimensions, we know *less* about attractive stimuli for people than we do about those for fish" (Hochberg, 1964). A few intrepid analysts (e.g., Bain, 1868) attempted to order the chaos and to advance theories of beauty in humans, but without conspicuous success. Darwin (1872) surveyed the beauty standards of various tribes throughout the world, and sadly concluded that there is no universal standard of beauty. Modern analysts agree (see Berscheid & Walster, 1974). Authors of serious treatises on beauty are inevitably reduced to gaping at the dazzling variety of characteristics that some people, somewhere, sometime have considered to be beautiful or sexually appealing. Let us review what little *is* known about the traits that are considered to be physically attractive.

Cross-Cultural Data

Ford and Beach (1951) examined more than 200 primitive societies. They were unable to find *any* universal standards of sexual attractiveness. They found enormous cultural differences as to the particular characteristics that are considered critically important. For some peoples, the shape and color of the eyes is important; for others, it is height and weight. In still others, what really matters is the size and shape of the sexual organs—the penis and the labia majora and minora. To complicate things still further, even if two societies do agree as to which bodily parts are important, they rarely agree as to what constitutes beauty in that feature. In some societies, like our own, a thin woman is assumed to be more attractive than a plump one; in most others, the reverse is true.

Western Society

Within a given society, however, there is a reasonable consensus as to what is beautiful or sexy. For example, Europeans and Americans show considerable agreement in their perception of beauty. For example, Iliffe (1960) conducted a study in Great Britain. A national daily newspaper asked readers to rank the "prettiness" of 12 photographs of women's faces. Iliffe found that the thousands of readers who responded—and readers were from markedly different social classes and regions and ranged in age from 8 to 80— had similar ideas as to what was beautiful. (Cross & Cross, 1971, and Kopera et al., Note 2, found similar results.)

What specific traits are beautiful or sexy?   Americans agree as to what constitutes good looks, on the whole. What happens when they focus preferences on specific aspects of beauty? What *is* a "good-looking" man or woman?

Terry and Davis (1976) asked college students how important a variety of various facial features were in determining attractiveness. Most people felt the most critical features were the mouth, eyes, structure of the face, hair, and nose (in that order). Similar results have been secured by Kleck, Richardson, and Ronald (1974), McCullers and Staat (1974), and Terry (1977).

Wiggins, Wiggins, and Conger (1968) conducted the best systematic study of what *men* think is beautiful and sexy. The psychologists prepared 105 nude silhouettes of women. One woman had a "golden mean" figure—she had average-sized breasts, buttocks, and legs. In the remaining silhouettes, the models' breasts, buttocks, and legs were systematically varied in size. For example, various silhouettes had large ($+2$), moderately large ($+1$) standard (0), moderately small (-1), or small (-2) breasts. The silhouettes' legs and buttocks were varied in the same way. College men were asked to look at the figures, two at a time, and indicate which they liked best. Most men judged the women with medium-sized breasts, buttocks, and legs to be far more attractive than they did those who possessed unusually small or large ones. The most popular figure had medium legs, medium to slightly small buttocks, and slightly large breasts.

What about women? What do they think is beautiful or sexy in men? Lavrakas (1975) constructed 19 different male figures, combining the same-size head with different-size arms, legs and torsos. He then paired the figures in all possible ways. He asked 70 women from the ages of 18 to 30 to rate each pair. Overall, women preferred men with a medium to wide upper trunk, a medium to thin lower trunk, and thin legs—a look that has been labeled the "Robert Redford tapered V-look." The most disliked build was either a thin upper trunk or a wide lower trunk—the "Alfred Hitchcock pear-shaped look."

One other characteristic that is critically important for men is height. Feldman (Note 3) contends that "American society is a society with a heightist premise: To be tall is to be good and to be short is to be stigmatized" (p. 1). Experimental evidence that he is right comes from Berkowitz, Nebel, and Reitman (Note 4), Dannenmaier and Thumin (1964), Kassarjian (1963), Koulack and Tuthill (1972), Ward (1967), and P. R. Wilson (1968).

Can men and women even agree on anything?   According to the folklore, men and women are supposed to have markedly different standards of beauty—and of everything else. For example, women are supposed to prefer delicate, ladylike women, while men are supposed to prefer earthy, sexy ones. And, the folklore continues, women are supposed to be a pushover for pretty boys, while men value rugged good looks. The existing research indicates that this stereotype is not true. Men and women show surprising agreement as to what is good-looking and what is not (Berscheid, Dion, Walster, and Walster, 1971; Cavior & Dokecki, Note 1; Kopera et al., Note 2; Murstein, 1972; and Walster, Aronson, Abrahams, & Rottman, 1966).

Luckily, for the vast majority of us, although there is substantial agreement as to what is beautiful or ugly, there is not *complete* agreement. The poetic hope that anyone will be found beautiful by someone also seems to be true. For example, Cross and Cross (1971) report,

> The most popular face in the sample was chosen as best of this group of 6 by 207 judges but there was no face that was never chosen, and even the least popular face was picked as *best* of its group (of six portraits similar in age, sex, and race) by four subjects. (p. 438)

Conclusion. The data suggest that men and women show substantial agreement as to what is beautiful or ugly.

THE OPERATION OF BIAS: WHAT DO PEOPLE *THINK* BEAUTIFUL PEOPLE ARE LIKE?

Berscheid and Walster (1974) found that most of us possess very definite stereotypes as to what beautiful or ugly people are like.

What Is Beautiful Is Good; What Is Ugly Is Bad

According to folk psychology, people's appearance tells us a great deal about their personality and character. "What is beautiful is good" (Sappho, 1965); "Physical beauty is a sign of an interior beauty, a spiritual and moral beauty" (Schiller, 1882). There is considerable evidence that most people assume that highly attractive individuals possess a wide variety of socially desired traits, while unattractive people possess an equal complement of unappealing traits. (Let us review a *sprinkling* of these studies. There are, it may be recalled, more than 200 such studies in existence.)

The data suggest that prejudice begins early. Children have very different expectations as to how unattractive and attractive children they have not yet met will *probably* behave (see Dion, 1973; Styczynski & Langlois, 1977).

What happens when children become acquainted? Several studies indicate that even when children know one another, they are biased in favor of the beautiful. Dion and Berscheid (Note 5) asked nursery-school children to look at photographs of their classmates and to tell them something about their classmates' social behaviors. They found that, as early as nursery school, children's perceptions were influenced by their peers' physical attractiveness. The children believed, for example, that unattractive boys were the most likely to engage in aggressive, antisocial behavior. They were accused of fighting a lot, hitting and yelling at their teachers, and saying angry things. When children were asked to nominate "someone who scares you," they generally chose their unattractive classmates (male and female). At the same time, however, when children were asked to nominate "someone who's afraid of lots of things," it was unattractive *girls* who were identified. The unattractive were thus seen as both frightening and frightened. Attractive boys and girls, in contrast, were perceived to be more independent than their unattractive peers—they were perceived as enjoying doing things alone, as not needing help from anyone, and as not afraid of anything. (Similar results were secured by Lerner & Lerner, 1977.)

How can we account for the children's biased perceptions of their attractive and unattractive peers? The preceeding evaluations could have been due to either of two factors: (1) prejudice, and/or (2) the operation of self-fulfilling prophecies. It is possible that unattractive children are caught in a vicious cycle of stereotyped expectations and self-fulfilling prophecies. Other children expect them to be unpleasant and therefore remember behaviors that confirm their expectancies and ignore those that do not. In reacting to their status as social outcasts, unattractive children begin to behave in ways that confirm this stereotype. (See Adams, 1977; Berscheid & Walster, 1974; Styczynski & Langlois, 1977.)

By adulthood, bias based on beauty is firmly entrenched. Experiments make it clear that the beautiful and the ugly are *perceived* to be very different, even when observers know nothing about their behavior, or when the behavior of the beautiful and the ugly is identical. Let us consider some of this research.

Dion, Berscheid, and Walster (1972) asked men and women to examine a collection of photographs. They were asked to attempt to guess what the people in the photographs, who differed markedly in appearance, were like. (Raters were told that their inferences would be scored for accuracy.) Dion et al. found that men and women assumed that attractive people possess almost every socially desirable personality trait possible. For example, physically attractive people were assumed to be more sexually warm and responsive, sensitive, kind, interesting, strong, poised, modest, sociable, and outgoing than persons of lesser physical attractiveness were assumed to be. Attractive people were also assumed to be more "exciting dates," to be more "nurturant" individuals, and to have "better characters" than others.

The raters were asked not only to estimate the current personality characteristics of people simply from their appearance, but to guess what fate held
in store for them. They predicted that physically attractive individuals would
have happier marriages and more prestigious occupations than would the less
attractive. All in all, attractive people were expected to lead far more fulfilling lives than the unattractive were. (Similar results were secured by Smits &
Cherhoniak, 1976.)

In general, then, it appears that most people assume that what is beautiful
is good; what is ugly is bad. Scientists have explored people's stereotypes
about the beautiful and the ugly in more detail.

Beauty Is Sanity

There is considerable evidence that the beautiful are assumed to be
more mentally healthy than are the ugly. Cash, Kehr, Polyson, and Freeman
(1977) asked college students to listen to a male psychologist interview a
"well-adjusted" or a "poorly adjusted" college woman. They were led to believe that the woman was attractive or unattractive, or they were given no
idea as to what she looked like. The students' ratings of the woman's mental
health, degree of disturbance, and prognosis for future happiness showed the
following: When the woman described herself as maladjusted, students rated
the physically attractive woman more favorably on all dimensions than they
rated the unseen woman or the unattractive interviewee. When the woman
described herself as well-adjusted, the students rated the attractive woman or
the unseen woman more positively than they rated the unattractive woman.

Psychotherapists' perceptions of clients.   Are psychotherapists less swayed
by physical appearance than is the person on the street? The data suggest,
"Probably not."

There is some evidence that men's judgments of whether or not a woman
has "something to live for" may depend on her beauty. Pavlos and Newcomb
(1974) asked men to read background information about an attractive or unattractive woman who learned that she had treatable or incurable cancer.
Shortly thereafter, she tried to kill herself. Was she justified? The attractive
woman was perceived as quite unjustified in attempting suicide, especially
when her cancer was treatable. In contrast, unattractive women were perceived as more justified in their desperate act. (Startlingly, the men's feelings
about whether or not the *unattractive* woman was justified in attempting to
commit suicide was *not* influenced by the prognosis of the disease. Apparently, the men assumed that unattractive women have little to live for, with or
without cancer.)

Muirhead (Note 6) conducted an experiment to determine whether clinicians shared society's bias against the homely. Muirhead interviewed two
types of therapists: (1) Freudians—those who described themselves as disciples of Freud or one of Freud's followers (Adler, Sullivan, or Rogers); (2)

"eclectic" therapists—those who described themselves as "without any particular philosophy of therapy." Half of the therapists were men, half were women. The therapists had various levels of academic attainment and a variety of experience (most had maintained personal caseloads for a year or more).

Muirhead asked the therapists to examine a patient's background information. (This background information included a picture of an attractive or unattractive male or female client.) The biographical sketch described the client as an academically talented college junior, from an intact, five-member middle-class family, with no known history of mental illness.

Then the theapists listened to a tape of a therapy session. Interwoven in the dialogue were a number of symptom statements taken from the Minnesota Multiphasic Personality Inventory (MMPI), such as: "I don't like someone watching me when I work," and so on. The therapists were asked to (1) diagnose the client's problem, and (2) make treatment recommendations.

The study found, unexpectedly, that therapists' philosophical orientation had a substantial impact on their evaluations. Regardless of their theoretical orientation, therapists rated attractive versus unattractive men about the same. However, Freudian therapists rated attractive women as better adjusted than unattractive clients. Freudians judged attractive women more favorably on a number of dimensions: need for support, sexual adjustment, intellectual functioning, verbal fluency, how relaxed versus nervous they felt, and how self-revealing versus defensive they were. In contrast, eclectic therapists did not rate attractive and unattractive women any differently.

This study is consistent with several others that have found that attractive clients receive more favorable clinical ratings than unattractive clients do (Barocas & Black, 1974; Barocas & Vance, 1974; Katz & Zimbardo, 1977). The study suggests that therapists are no more immune to the halo effect cast by physical beauty than are lay persons.

Clients' perceptions of psychotherapists.   Of course, bias is a two-way street. If counselors are biased, so are patients. There is some evidence that clinicians' physical attractiveness influences their clients' expectations. Cash, Begley, McCown, and Weise (1975) found that men and women expected an attractive psychologist to be more helpful than they did an unattractive psychologist in dealing with general anxiety, inferiority feelings, parent problems, dating problems, and drug addiction.

Beauty Is Character

Judgments about potential wrongdoers.   If people do assume that "beauty is good," they might be expected to give the physically attractive the benefit of the doubt when it seems possible that they might be guilty of wrongdoing. Even when the attractive are clearly guilty, people may be inclined to find excuses for their actions. As a result, the physically attractive may be punished less severely than unattractive people may be. There is *some* evidence that these hypotheses are correct.

Dion and Berscheid (Note 5) studied women's reactions to the transgression of beautiful or ugly children. Women were asked to review some teachers' reports. These reports contained each child's name, age, and photograph (attractive or unattractive), and some rudimentary background information. In each report, the teacher described a mild or severe transgression that the 7-year-old had committed.

The women were asked how they thought the child usually behaved on a typical day. (These free descriptions were categorized by judges as being predominantly "prosocial," "mixed," or "antisocial.") Dion found that the attractive child does seem to have a big advantage. When the child's transgression was very mild in nature, there were no differences in how the act was perceived. When the transgression was severe, the women attributed significantly more antisocial behavioral dispositions to unattractive boys and girls than to attractive children. For example, when the severe transgression was attributed to an attractive child, one of the women said,

> She appears to be a perfectly charming little girl, well-mannered, basically unselfish. It seems that she can adapt well among children her age and make a good impression . . . she plays well with everyone, but like anyone else, a bad day can occur. Her cruelty . . . need not be taken too seriously.

When the same act was committed by a physically unattractive child, another woman inferred,

> I think the child would be quite bratty and would be a problem to teachers . . . she would probably try to pick a fight with other children her own age . . . she would be a brat at home . . . all in all, she would be a real problem.

When asked to estimate how likely it was that a child would commit a similar transgression in the future, the attractive and unattractive children were both given the benefit of the doubt, when transgression had been *slight*. When the transgression had been *severe*, however, the women judged the attractive children's characters to be more positive than the unattractive children's.

The authors found no support for the speculation that women would feel that the unattractive child should be punished more severely than the attractive one. Regardless of the crime, the women generally thought the transgression should be discussed with the child; physical punishment, withdrawal of love, and other alternatives were eminently unpopular. Nevertheless, one wonders whether a child who is perceived to be a chronic troublemaker, and likely to commit the same transgression in the future, would not be "reasoned with" more swiftly than would the attractive child, and if perhaps the discussion would not proceed along somewhat different lines.

Other researchers have explored the importance of physical attractiveness in influencing people's perceptions of adults' characters. Some studies have found that the beautiful have a distinct advantage in simulated jury settings (see Efran, 1974; Leventhal & Krate, 1977). Others have found that they do not, or that "it depends" (Jacobson & Berger, 1974; Piehl, 1977; Sigall & Ostrove, 1975; D. W. Wilson & Donnerstein, 1977).

Judgments about victims. What about victims? Do the beautiful receive more compassion than the ugly? Perhaps. Seligman, Brickman, and Koulack (1977) and Thornton (1977) asked students for their opinions about a rape case involving an attractive or an unattractive woman. Seligman et al. found that students made quite different attributions as to why each of the women was raped. If the woman was beautiful, that seemed to "explain" the rape. If the woman was not, the students felt she must have done *something* to provoke her attack. Regardless of *what* the woman looked like, and regardless of *why* students thought the attack had occurred, they were equally convinced of the defendant's guilt, however. Thornton found that students recommended a longer sentence for a man who raped an attractive woman than for one who attacked an unattractive woman.

What can we conclude from the preceding evidence? Sometimes, the physical attractiveness of the accused or the victim is important; when it is, the beautiful person almost always has the advantage. Often, however, justice does appear to be "blind."

Beauty Is Competence

There is considerable evidence that physical attractiveness affects parents', teachers', employers', and peers' perception of how competent others are. Let us review a sprinkling of this evidence.

Clifford and Walster (1973) asked 400 fifth-grade teachers to examine students' academic files and to give their professional evaluations of the students' intellectual ability. The files contained a good deal of information about the students. The students' pictures were pasted in one corner of the report. The report cards reported the students' absences during the school year; grades in the content areas of reading, language, arithmetic, social studies, science, art, music, and physical education; and grades in the three personal trait areas of "healthful living," "personal development," and "work habits and attitudes." The teachers were asked to estimate the children's parents' attitudes toward school, the children's IQs, and their probable future educational accomplishments. As predicted, the children's physical attractiveness had a strong impact on the teacher's expectations of their intellectual potential.

In another study, Ross and Salvia (1975) asked teachers to evaluate attractive or unattractive children who were *identical* in maturity, intelligence, and behavior problems. Once again, teachers showed a strong bias: They assumed that the unattractive children's IQs were really lower than the scores indicated, and they were more likely to recommend that an unattractive child be placed in a class for the mentally retarded. They also predicted that the unattractive children would have more serious social difficulties.

A variety of other studies have indicated that teachers *expect* beauty and brains to go together, and they grade accordingly. For example, beauty is related to teacher expectations of academic ability (Clifford, 1975; Lerner & Lerner, 1977) and to actual report-card grades (Clifford, 1975; Lerner & Lerner, 1977; Salvia, Algozzine, & Sheare, 1977). These biases are especially ominous in light of the fact that physical attractiveness is *not* related to students' scores on *objective* tests (Clifford, 1975).

The attractive and the unattractive are likely to confront such biases through life. For example, college students rate essays (Landy & Sigall, 1974) and paintings (Murphy & Hellkamp, 1976) more positively when they are attributed to attractive individuals than to unattractive ones. Similarly, personnel managers (Cash et al., 1977; Dipboye, Arvey, & Terpstra, 1977) evaluate attractive job applicants more favorably than they do equally qualified but unattractive candidates.

Sex × Beauty Interactions

Do people see handsome *men* and beautiful *women* any differently? There is some evidence that they do. Berscheid and Walster (1974) observed that gender may be important in determining people's reactions to beauty, for two different reasons: (1) It may be more *important* to be a beautiful woman than to be a handsome man or (2) the *content* of the physical-attractiveness stereotype may differ for men and women.

There is evidence in support of both contentions. (1) Several researchers have found that physical attractiveness *is* a more important determinant of how women are evaluated than of how men are evaluated (see Bar-Tal & Saxe, 1976a, 1976b). (2) People do seem to have gender-specific stereotypes. They expect physically attractive women to be more feminine, and to conform more to feminine sex-role stereotypes, than would their unattractive peers (see Hill & Lando, 1976). They expect attractive men to be more masculine and to conform more to masculine sex-role stereotypes (see Cash et al., 1977).

Conclusion

People can hardly avoid judging others by their physical appearance—physical attractiveness (or its lack) is immediately apparent in every social encounter. People might know full well that a host of other things—

IQ, personality, character, socioeconomic status, or genetic background—
are more "important" than mere beauty, but they have no way to assess another's standing in these areas. People do not wear their IQs tattooed on their
foreheads; people's financial status is a private matter among themselves,
their bankers, and the Internal Revenue Service; most persons would not
know how to interpret people's genes, even after examining a photomicro-
graphic print of them. Small wonder, then, that most people search for a link
between appearance and the more elusive realities. In this section we have
seen that most people are biased in favor of the beautiful and against the
homely. They simply assume that beauty is good—that beauty is sanity,
character, and competence—even in the face of evidence to the contrary.

THE OPERATION OF BIAS:
DO PEOPLE *TREAT* THE BEAUTIFUL
AND THE NONBEAUTIFUL
DIFFERENTLY?

A given *individual* may or may not share others' stereotypes
about what the beautiful are like. For most people, beauty and goodness are
virtually synonymous. For Jack the Ripper, "sexiness" was evil. If people
think differently about the beautiful and the ugly and *feel* differently about
them, their biases *must* inevitably be reflected in their actions. Not surprisingly, there is some evidence that they are: Most people, most of the time,
treat the beautiful more compassionately than they treat the ugly. Let us consider some examples of this research.

Behavior in Intimate Settings

According to Perlmutter and Hatfield (1980), people communicate their feelings about their relationships with others via a panoply of
"metamessages." It is by paralinguistic and kinesic signals—which include
changes of facial expression, hesitations, shifts in tempo of speech or movement, overtones of the voice, irregularities of respiration, and so forth—that
people signal the limits of their relationships. The evidence indicates that people send very different metamessages, as well as different objective messages,
to the attractive and the ugly.
Barocas and Karoly (1972) asked college men to listen to a tape of a woman
describing her college experiences. The "speaker's" picture was either attractive or unattractive. The men were told to press a button each time they felt
like signaling their responsiveness to the woman, trying to increase their rap-

port with her, or approving of what she was saying. As expected, men were more responsive when they thought the speaker was attractive than when she was not.

Snyder, Tanke, and Berscheid (1977), too, found that observers treat physically attractive and unattractive women very differently. The authors showed men a picture of an attractive or an unattractive woman and asked them (1) to give their first impression of her; (2) to have a brief conversation with her; (3) finally, to rate her again, now that they were better acquainted. (In fact, the woman in each case was simply a randomly selected college student who had agreed to participate in the experiment.)

What were men's first impressions of the "beautiful" or the "unattractive" woman? As one might expect, they *expected* the attractive woman to be more poised, sociable, warm, and outgoing than they did the unattractive one.

Then they actually had a chance to talk with this woman, who they *belived* was unusually attractive or unattractive. How did these conversations go? In order to find out, the experimenters separately recorded the men's and women's portions of the conversation and, later, asked raters to give their impressions of them. How "sociable" were the men and women? How sexy were they? And so on.

According to the raters, when men thought they were conversing with an attractive woman, they used their voices with unusual effectiveness. They were unusually sociable, sexually warm, interesting, independent, sexually permissive, bold, outgoing, humorous, obvious, and socially adept. The raters also judged men to be more comfortable, more attracted to their partners, and more attractive to their partners when they thought she was attractive then when they thought she was not. Somehow, men conveyed a very different metamessage to an "attractive" partner than to an "unappealing" one.

What about women? Do they respond differently to attractive men than to unattractive ones? Of course. For example, Brundage, Derlega, and Cash (1977) found that women were willing to reveal far more about themselves to attractive men than to unattractive ones.

Of course, it is not only in our intimate relations that beauty counts; it is critically important in our day-to-day encounters as well.

Helping Behavior

In old fairy tales, the "damsel in distress" was inevitably beautiful. It's lucky for her that she was. A number of experiments document that beautiful damsels—and ruggedly handsome knights—are more likely to get help when they need it than are their less appealing peers.

In one study, Benson, Karabenick, and Lerner (1976) "misplaced" completed graduate-school applications in stamped envelopes in airport phone booths. Attached to the applications was a picture of an attractive or unattractive man or woman. The Good Samaritans who found the envelope were more likely to mail the envelope if the candidate was attractive than if he or she was not. When the applicant was attractive, 47% of the envelopes were mailed. When the applicant was not, only 35% were returned.

In a variety of other settings, researchers have documented that (regardless of race, gender, or age) people are far more eager to help physically attractive people than they are to help their unattractive counterparts. (See Athanasiou & Greene, 1973; Sroufe, Chaikin, Cook, & Freeman, 1977; West & Brown, 1975.)

Help-Seeking Behavior

What about the opposite side of the coin? When people in general need help, who are they most likely to ask for aid—a beautiful person or an unattractive one? Stokes and Bickman (1974) argued that men and women should be unusually hesitant to ask attractive people for aid. It is hard to ask *anyone* for help; it threatens one's self-esteem and public image. If others are attractive, and help seekers value their esteem, it should be almost impossible to ask them for aid. The authors found support for their notion: People are less willing to ask attractive people than to ask unattractive people for aid.

Summary

It comes as no surprise to discover that most people react very differently to the beautiful and to the homely. It appears that because most people believe that "beautiful is good," they make it "good to be beautiful."

THE OPERATION OF BIAS: WHAT ARE PHYSICALLY ATTRACTIVE PEOPLE *REALLY* LIKE?

In the preceding section, we reviewed evidence that people perceive attractive and unattractive people very differently and treat them very differently. In these studies, social psychologists carefully arranged things so that the beautiful and the homely would be identical in all other traits. But, in nature, all things are rarely equal. What are the beautiful really like?

The Origin of Possible Differences:
Genetics or a Self-Fulfilling Prophecy?

Recently, researchers have begun to collect information as to what attractive and unattractive people are *really* like. The evidence confirms what many have suspected all along: Attractive and unattractive people *are* different in a variety of ways.

Of course, these differences may be caused by two very different factors:

1. *Nature.* There may be a genetic link between attractiveness and a host of other variables.
2. *Nurture.* Or, as seems more likely, the existence of preconceived notions about what physically attractive and unattractive individuals are probably like sets the stage for people to assess the beautiful and the ugly's behavior in biased ways and to treat them in very different ways. Naturally, the beautiful and the nonbeautiful are molded by these experiences. In the end, they become what everyone "knew" they were from the start.

Regardless of why the beautiful and the homely are different, there is evidence that people's stereotypes about beauty do have a kernel of truth. There is considerable evidence that—even by nursery-school age—the beautiful and the ugly are very different indeed.

Self-Concept

Only a few researchers have tried to determine whether or not self-esteem and physical attractiveness are related. Adams (1977) found that physically attractive men and women do have unusually high self-esteem. There is also some evidence that attractive men and women are unusually self-accepting. Glasgow and Arkowitz (1975) found that after a brief encounter with another person, physically attractive people perceived themselves as more socially skillful than did their unattractive peers.

Personality

Do physically attractive people have "better" personalities than those of their unattractive peers? We really do not know. Only a few researchers have studied the beautiful's personality profiles. A few scattered studies indicate that the physically attractive may be more internal in their locus of control (Cash et al., 1975), more assertive (Jackson & Huston, 1975), and more independent, ambitious and sociable (Krebs & Adinolfi, 1975) than unattractive people.

The data on attractiveness-personality links are, however, surprisingly sparse. As Miller (1978) has observed, "disinterest in personality differences between attractive and unattractive people has continued unabated to the present" (p. 83).

Popularity

Dion and Berscheid (Note 5) found some evidence that, as early as nursery school, physical attractiveness and popularity are related. They found that at all ages attractive nursery-school boys were more popular than their less attractive peers. For nursery-school girls, however, the relationship between beauty and popularity was more complex. At very young ages, unattractive girls were the *most* popular. As the girls got older, however, the attractive girls became more and more popular, while the unattractive girls' popularity declined.

By adulthood, there is no doubt that beautiful men and women are more popular than their peers are. In a series of studies, social psychologists randomly assigned college students to dates. Again and again, researchers found that the more physically attractive the dates were, the more they were liked. Physical attractiveness has proved to be more important than intelligence, shared opinions, income, and other factors in determining who likes whom (see Berscheid et al., 1971; Curran & Lippold, 1975; Huston, 1973; Mathes, 1975; and Walster et al., 1966).

There is also compelling evidence that our liking for same-sex peers is similarly influenced by physical attractiveness (see Krebs & Adinolfi, 1975).

Sociability

In the third section of this chapter, we have established that people *expect* attractive people to be unusually sociable, outgoing, and warm (Dermer & Thiel, 1975; Dion et al., 1972; Snyder et al., 1977). Research indicates that these perceptions may be correct. A number of researchers have found that the beautiful are more sociable and more socially skilled than are their unattractive peers. In one study, Goldman and Lewis (1977) asked college students to have a conversation with an *unseen* member of the opposite sex. Students whose *unseen* partner was in fact physically attractive rated their partner as more desirable, likable, and socially skilled than did men who spoke with *unseen* partners who happened in fact to be very unattractive.

In a study of men and women's conversations, Snyder et al. (1977) provided some information as to the process by which a "self-fulfilling prophecy"— in which the beautiful become charming and the homely become awkward and shy—might develop. As reported earlier in this chapter, Snyder et al.

found that men talked quite differently when they *believed* their telephone partners were attractive than when they believed they were not. Men presented themselves far more positively when they believed they were speaking to attractive women than when they did not. How did their randomly assigned partners (who, of course, did not differ in beauty on the average) respond to this differential treatment? According to the naive observers, the supposedly "attractive" partners responded by becoming unusually confident, animated, enthusiastic, and positive. The women who were treated as if they were unattractive did just the reverse.

This experiment demonstrates rather clearly how our stereotyped expectations can bias and subtly shape our behavior—and, in reaction, our partner's. The authors pointed out that participants in *their* experiment conversed for only 10 minutes. The cumulative effects of a lifetime of such differential treatment should prove powerful indeed.

Happiness

From our discussion thus far, it seems evident that physically attractive men and women *should* feel happier and more fulfilled than do their less fortunate peers. In terms of acceptance by peers and by adults, in terms of opportunities to select a compatible mate, and in terms of the increased educational and employment opportunities, it is clear that attractive people *ought* to be happier than the unattractive.

But the bluebird of happiness is an elusive fowl, whose habits have not been fully identified. Often, people's personal feelings of satisfaction with their lot do not show a one-to-one correspondence with the "objective" goodness of that lot. Happiness may follow "adaptation" rules (cf. Crespi, 1942; Helson, 1964). For example, Thibaut and Kelley (1965) pointed out that individuals' happiness in any given relationship is a function of the outcomes they receive in that relationship, compared to all the outcomes they have known in other relationships.

Brickman and Campbell (1971) argue, then, that we all may be on a sort of "hedonic treadmill." The more we get, the more we expect, and the more we expect, the less happy we are with what we have. The best and the worst one can hope for, they argue, is to be happy and miserable about half the time each. Thus, it is *not* a foregone conclusion that attractive people should be happier than the unattractive.

There is almost no evidence available concerning the possible relationship between physical attractiveness and happiness. The data that do exist suggest that beautiful people probably *are* happier than unattractive ones, but the data are far from clear (see Berscheid, Walster, & Bohrnstedt, 1973; Cash & Burns, 1977; and Dion et al., 1972).

Mental Illness

A number of researchers have attempted to determine whether or not physical attractiveness or ugliness is related to mental and emotional health.

In a classic study, Farina, Fischer, Sherman, Smith, Groh, and Mermin (1977) observed that in our society, "beautiful people are greatly valued and well-treated while those who are unattractive receive a most regrettable reception." Farina et al. reviewed the remarkable number of ways in which the beautiful are advantaged and the unattractive are disadvantaged, and concluded:

> Evidently, the environment is quite a different place for physically attractive people than it is for those who are homely. The former have a nicer, more forgiving, supportive, and pliable social world and it should be easier to adapt to it than to the conditions faced by the latter group. Hence the long-term adjustment of unattractive people ought to be relatively poor, and more of them should be mentally ill than good-looking persons. (p. 510)

The authors found that this was so. They asked raters to evaluate the physical attractiveness—both from photographs and from face-to-face interviews—of psychiatric patients and normal women in the community. They found considerable evidence that beauty *is* related to social adjustment and mental health:

1. Psychiatric patients *were* less attractive than normal women.
2. When psychiatric patients were asked about their early lives, it appeared that physical attractiveness and mental illness *were* linked early on. The better-looking a patient was, the better adjusted she felt she was as a child.
3. Physical attractiveness also seemed to be linked to *current* adjustment. The more attractive the patient was, the better she reported her current adjustment to be. There was a tendency for aides to agree. So did the psychotherapist. The more attractive the patient was, the *less* likely she was to receive a diagnosis indicative of severe maladjustment (schizophrenia).

What about more "objective indicators" of adjustment? Those also seem to suggest that the more attractive the patient was, the "less maladjusted" she was. Women's interpersonal adjustment was assessed via the Minimal Social Behavior Scale (MSBS). (The MSBS was administered in the guise of an interview. It measures such things as "Do women sit in a chair when asked to?" "Do they respond to questions?") Attractive patients received unusually high scores on this scale.

Finally, the more attractive the patient, the shorter a time she estimated she would have to remain in the hospital; the shorter her current stay in the hospital had been already; and the shorter the length of time she had been in a mental hospital in her lifetime.

Of course, in Farina et al.'s study, it was not possible to tell for sure which came first: Did unattractiveness generate mental illness, or are the mentally ill simply unable to maintain their appearance?

Since then, other researchers, assessing beauty earlier in patients' lives (i.e., from childhood snapshots, yearbook photos, etc.), have attempted to disentangle this riddle (see Napoleon, Chassin, & Young, Note 7). Their results suggest that probably both factors were operating in Farina et al.'s study.

Cavior (1970) has argued that there are implications for psychotherapy research and practice in these results.

> Psychotherapists might do well to consider plastic surgery (reconstructive and cosmetic) as an alternative or adjunct to psychotherapy. Anecdotal reports by plastic surgeons and interdisciplinary research by psychologists, sociologists, and plastic surgeons (e.g., Kurtzberg, Safar, & Cavior, 1968) have suggested that plastic surgery can result in marked changes in self-concept, behavior, and the responses of others. For example, if an unattractive girl requests psychotherapy because she feels lonely and rejected and cannot find a husband, it might be more advantageous in terms of time and expense to consider plastic surgery. Rather than have the girl spend months or years in expensive therapy trying to discover her intrapsychic difficulties, it might be better to help her integrate and adjust to the changes which might result from plastic surgery. (p. 97)

Cavior goes on to note that some progressive mental hospitals have recently employed professional cosmetologists to help patients become more attractive.

Kurtzberg et al. (1968) have provided some evidence that Cavior's arguments may be correct. They proposed that if prison inmates' physical disfigurements were surgically corrected in prison, inmates should develop better self-concepts and better social relations. After release, the inmates should show improved psychological adjustment, less prison recidivism, and have more job success.

To test their hypotheses, Kurtzberg et al. assigned disfigured inmates of the New York City jail system to one of four experimental groups: surgery alone; surgery and social and vocational services; social and vocational services without surgery; and a no-treatment control group. (These prisoners' disfigurements ranged from knife and burn scars to lopped ears, needle tracks from drug usage, and tattoos.)

Data from follow-ups on all inmates, conducted 1 year following surgery or release from prison, revealed that the recidivism rate of nonaddicts receiving surgery was significantly less (36% less) than that of disfigured nonaddicts and control subjects. Nonaddict subjects receiving only social and vocational services, but not surgery, had a recidivism rate 33 % *higher* than that of control subjects. This group also appeared to show poorer social relations and a tendency to become further alienated from society during the 1-year follow-up period.

They report that with regard to specific disfigurements, "plastic surgery appeared to help those with facial disfigurements to a greater extent than those with disfigurements on their bodies" (p. 650). Kurtzberg et al. concluded that although the cost of plastic surgery in the rehabilitation of adult offenders is relatively high, it "can be considered negligible if the offender is helped to remain out of prison for even 1 year" (p. 649).

SUGGESTIONS FOR FUTURE RESEARCH

Is beauty an advantage or a disadvantage? Earlier, we observed that in any *individual* case, beauty may be either an asset or a liability. There will always be some people (say, a movie star's brutalized child) who equate beauty with insensitivity and cruelty, and who react to the beautiful with anger and resentment. In earlier sections of this chapter, however, we have established that most people, in most settings, most of the time, are biased in favor of the beautiful: In general, it is a distinct advantage to be beautiful. But what about therapy? Is beauty an asset *there*? That is not at all clear.

Perlmutter's interviews (in press) with psychotherapists provide some suggestions as to how beauty might affect therapists' initial impression of patients, their eventual diagnosis, and the course and eventual outcome of psychotherapy.

In his interviews, Perlmutter found that psychotherapists were acutely aware that, when they were dealing with beautiful clients,[1] they had mixed motives. For many therapists, the therapist–beautiful woman interaction became the focus of their struggle with self-definition. On the one hand, therapists were concerned about professional and ethical standards. They tried to be objective. On the other hand, consciously or unconsciously, they were attracted to the beautiful patients, and they hoped their patients were attracted to them.

Perlmutter observes that, in systems terms (see Bateson, 1972; Watzlawick & Weakland, 1977), therapists and patients are bound by the rules constructed from their individual, and jointly negotiated, metastructures. The jointly negotiated metastructure contains aspects of their individual socialization (which includes a sense of the ethical, commitment to mates, fairness, acquisitiveness, shame, and guilt). It is this metastructure that guides the negotiations in the early therapeutic interactions and allows each therapist and patient as a system, to develop (implicit) rules for how they will conduct themselves in the context of their highly sexually charged relationship. Psycho-analysts label this as *transference* and *countertransference*. It is the ideational and affectional state that therapist and client possess as a frame of reference in regarding the other. Since the beautiful client is "different" from other patients, there is no way that therapists can fail to recognize this difference and react to it. (To perceive a difference and not to acknowledge it is rarely possible between two relatively cognitively and emotionally functional humans.) How, then, do therapists differ in the ways they perceive and treat beautiful and homely people? How do the beautiful and the homely react to such treatment? Perlmutter argues that psychotherapists' biases affect their initial impressions of patients, their eventual diagnoses, their interactions, and the outcome of therapy.[2]

Therapists' Sensitivity to Issues of Beauty

The psychotherapists were well aware that the patients' beauty or ugliness was a critical issue for them. They joked a great deal about the problem. However, they focused almost entirely on the problems of dealing with women who were *beautiful and sexy*. Only rarely did they mention the difficulty of dealing with patients who were unattractive. (There were only two references to *this* problem in Perlmutter's tapescripts. One therapist decribed a patient as "a dog." Another said, "I've had some real pigs.")

Therapists' case records substantiated their concern with their patients' appearance. For example, several therapists had clients who were beautiful *and* possessed other socially desirable characteristics (e.g., they were graphic artists, were gymnasts, had Ph.D.s, played with the Milwaukee Philharmonic). The therapists' reports often noted beauty-related issues; however, they rarely contained any reference to such women's artistic or professional lives.

Diagnosis and Course of Therapy

Perlmutter concluded that therapists are biased in their diagnoses of the beautiful and the ugly's problems.

1. When dealing with most patients, therapists were fairly certain as to what their goals were. When dealing with beautiful women, however, therapists were far more uncertain about their goals. Sometimes they would start out with clear-cut objectives, but as therapy progressed, they continually revised them. Frequently their diagnoses were complex and mixed. (Does this reflect the therapists' ambivalences?)

2. Therapists tended to settle upon *intrapsychic* interpretations of beautiful women's personal, marital, or familial problems. Since the women were

defined as the real patients, it was "unnecessary" or "useless" to deal with the husbands. (Sometimes husbands were described as "less amenable" to therapy than their wives or "intractable.") An example: One psychiatrist reported his experiences with a 43-year-old university graduate. She was "very beautiful . . . very sexy." She complained that her husband abused her physically. On the basis of the intake interview, the psychiatrist concluded that the problem was hers—she was "probably invitational" and had "managed to seduce her husband into beating her." He concluded that the husband was probably *not* an abusive husband, and, thus, it was not necessary to see *him*.

3. When the patient was beautiful, most therapists chose to engage in verbal therapies—even when the therapist *usually* relied heavily on the behavioral/learning approaches. (According to Schofield, 1964, attractive men and women *are* more likely to obtain individual psychotherapy than are unattractive clients.)

Length of Therapy

Perlmutter found that therapists' initial *expectations* as to how long therapy would probably last differed markedly from reality. If the patient was beautiful, the male therapists reported that they had initially expected therapy to take an unusually long time. (Did therapists hope that they would have to spend a great deal of time with the women? Perhaps. One therapist, treating a beautiful woman, reported that he was tempted to "keep her in therapy as long as [he] possibly could.")

What *actually* happened, however, was a little more complicated than this.

1. Traditionally, in therapy, both the beginning and the end of sessions are social times. Often therapist and patient engage in small talk before getting down to business or terminating the interview. Many therapists reported that when their patients were beautiful women, they had a tendency to prolong the social time at both the outset and the terminus of each session.

2. In addition, therapists observed that when the patient was beautiful, *each individual session* tended to last somewhat longer than usual. (Are therapists especially reluctant to terminate the therapeutic hour?) Barocas and Black (1974) and Katz and Zimbardo (1977) provide some support for Perlmutter's observation. They found that attractive psychiatric patients received qualitatively better and quantitatively more treatment than did their unattractive counterparts.

3. In the end, however, therapists found that beautiful women actually ended up spending *less total time* in therapy than other women. Farina et al. (1977) reported similar results. (Do therapists do a better job? Or do they find, in the end, that it makes them *nervous* to confront so much tempting beauty day after day?)

Therapist-Patient Interactions

Therapists' Self-Presentations

Many therapists were aware that beauty served as a nexus, about which a male-female sexual power struggle ensued. Therapists wished to help their clients, to rescue them. At the same time, much of male role socialization attaches to acquisitiveness; they longed to possess the beautiful patient. The paradox, possession without possession, frequently continued throughout the duration of therapy.

Therapists were often aware that they became very concerned about their image when dealing with beautiful patients. They wanted to seem charming, masculine, desirable. They had a hidden (or not so hidden) desire to become more intimate with their patients. Therapists observed that they found themselves trying to "seduce" their patients in a variety of ways.

Many therapists found themselves acting in an unusually "macho" way with their striking patients. For example, some therapists who regularly served tea or coffee to their patients found themselves gruffly barking out, "Get it yourself," when an attractive woman was the patient. Another therapist caught himself acting "puffed up" in front of his good-looking patients. For example, he would pompously give orders to his secretary in such a patient's presence.

Other therapists noticed that they had a tendency to be more fatherly or more charming than usual when the patient was a beautiful woman. For example, some therapists admitted that they tended to be better dressed on the days that a beautiful woman was due. Some tried to behave more suavely — for example, offering tea or coffee (and serving it) to beautiful women, while expecting their other patients to serve themselves. Many therapists reported that they tended to be more humorous and light when dealing with beautiful women.

Finally, some therapists reported that when their patients were beautiful women, they had a tendency to try to act not just as therapists, but as physicians and lawyers, too. For example, one therapist found himself giving his patient quasi-legal advice, even though he was not qualified (by his own admission) to do so.

An example: A strikingly beautiful woman, who was suffering from a mild agitated depression, came in. Although she couldn't quite put her finger on *how* she knew, she knew that her husband was having an affair. Her husband insisted that there was no truth to her accusations.

What the client secretly hoped for was that the therapist would recognize how upset, frightened, and enraged she was at her husband's infidelity; that he would lure her husband in; and that he would force a reconciliation. She wanted to *threaten* her husband with a divorce, but that was really all. The therapist empathized with her greatly; he became very angry at her husband.

He began to play the "macho" adviser, urging her to file for divorce and instructing her on exactly what kind of divorce to file, how to go about it, and so on. Of course, this advice made her panic. She did not want a divorce. She simply wanted some way to bludgeon her husband into loving her more. The therapist's "advice" precipitated full-fledged terror. He was a poor therapist and a worse lawyer.

Perlmutter speculates that all of these reactions really represent the same process: Therapists are trying to play out stereotyped sex roles—the cowboy or the playboy—rather than responding professionally or honestly. Perlmutter's observations are in accord with the research reported earlier, which has found that men and women try to appear at their best—and "at their best" generally means conforming to traditional sex roles—when confronting beautiful people (see Shaw & Wagner, 1975).

Seating

Many therapists reported that seating was a problem with *any* woman—beautiful or not. If they sat too far away, they appeared to be cool and distant. If they sat too close, they semed to be conveying a sexual invitation. The problems were intensified when the client was a beautiful woman. Many therapists reported that the therapist-client seating arrangement did depend on whether the client was a beautiful woman as opposed to an average or homely one. Generally therapists sat closer to beautiful women than to others. Many therapists acknowledged that an intimate seating arrangement was *their* idea. One therapist, who described himself as "somewhat sexually assertive," admitted that he enjoyed sitting so that he could look under his clients' skirts or obtain a view of their breasts, or both. "That," he reported, "is one of the fringe benefits of being a therapist." A few other therapists made similar comments. Other therapists acknowledged that there were problems involved in seating, but they insisted it was the *client's* fault; she was seductive. These therapists insisted that beautiful women sit in provocative ways. For example, one therapist reported, "It is interesting to note how beautiful women sit so that one can look up their skirt and see their genitalia . . . or at least the outline of their genitalia. They are seductive . . . manipulative." In spite of the fact that the beautiful women were "at fault," the therapists acknowledged that they enjoyed "the performance."

The Outcome of Therapy

According to Perlmutter's interviewees, then, therapist-client relationships are very different when patients are beautiful than when they are not. How does this work out? As always, it depends.

Sometimes the therapists' biases worked to the patients' advantage. One therapist provided an example. The husband was an "average-looking" physician; he earned over $100,000 a year. The wife was a very beautiful housewife. The therapist diagnosed the woman's problem as chronic dependency; she was unable to express anger. (When upset, she became incapable of speaking; she signaled her distress by "psychotically" waving her arms.) The therapist took an enormous interest in the wife; he increased her number of visits to three or four times a week. He helped *her* a great deal. The husband, however, was ignored. He became more and more depressed. Finally he saw a second therapist, who gave him some attention. (Barocas & Black, 1974, and Katz & Zimbardo, 1977, insist that such cases are typical; patients receive quantitatively more and qualitatively better treatment than do their unattractive counterparts.)

In other cases, however, being beautiful did *not* seem to be an advantage. Instead of receiving the help they needed, beautiful women received "pseudo-help." (In citing these cases, Perlmutter takes issue with the Barocas & Black, 1974, and Katz & Zimbardo, 1977, conclusion.)

Therapists reported that they were unusually concerned about doing well when their patients were beautiful. Human relations inevitably involve an exchange (see Walster, Walster, & Berscheid, 1978). In a therapeutic give-and-take, therapists trade their training, skill, and attention for the patients' attention, effort, money, and gratitude. Patients are supposed to get their "money's worth." The therapists reported that when dealing with beautiful women, they kept having the uneasy feeling that they must be at their best. They began to try harder—often too hard.

Perlmutter argues, as noted, that such therapists tended to give their patients "pseudo-help"—help that had more to do with the therapists' needs than the patients'. According to Perlmutter, the therapist and patients generally entered a collusory relationship: He pretended to help; she pretended she was being helped (see Perlmutter, in press). The beautiful woman often found herself in a bind. She was afraid to intentionally metacommunicate her dissatisfaction with her treatment. Should she confront her therapist, she would run the risk of openly escalating the latent intimate relationship and all of its sexual implications (see Perlmutter & Hatfield, 1980). Should she continue to act as if all was well, she risked getting no help at all.

How does this all end? According to Perlmutter, "Not well." Let us consider two examples:

One couple—Jane and Ted—came in for marriage counseling. Ted was "an ugly pock-marked man"; Jane was extremely beautiful. They had multiple problems: Their son had cancer; they drank heavily; they fought constantly. The therapist concluded that the wife was "pathologically dependent" on her husband. He concluded that she needed to have an affair to free herself. She did. During therapy, she was encouraged to devote a large portion of the hour to recounting her sexual experiences. (The therapist admitted that he found this very exciting.) Soon, the husband, a very "macho" personality, became depressed. He withdrew even fruther from his family and his business. In retrospect, the therapist realized he had neglected the husband. Eventually, the husband became desperate. He was unable to handle his wife's affairs; eventually he tracked her to a hotel and took pictures of her engaged in a sexual act with another man. He threatened to use these pictures to divorce her and take custody of his son. The outcome of therapy was not good.

In a second case, two therapists reported difficulties in dealing with the same woman patient. The woman was a handsome woman who had lost the musculature in her calves as a result of adolescent poliomyelitis. The first therapist saw her for a few sessions, but soon realized it was impossible to go on. He couldn't distinguish between his pity and his physical attraction to her. (He found himself thinking obsessively along these lines: "How can it be that anyone so beautiful is so maimed?" "Ah, but she is still beautiful." "Ah, but the beauty has a poignant quality.") Eventually Therapist 1 referred her to Therapist 2, suggesting that what she needed was quick symptom relief. (She was phobic; she worried that she'd fall over in her wheelchair and be hurt. She was worried that people would invade her house and injure her. She was suicidal.) He recommended a combination of hypnosis and behavior therapy. Once these symptoms were ameliorated, he thought that more therapy could be done if she needed it.

Therapist 2 had problems identical to Therapist 1's. *He* decided to persevere in therapy, however. In retrospect, Therapist 2 realized that he, too, had become so personally involved with her that he had failed as a therapist. He never attempted quick symptom relief. He plunged into insight-oriented therapy. He had insisted on denying that his patient had any real problems. When she would talk about the problem of being handicapped, he would say such things as, "Don't give me that bullshit. You're as capable at getting around as the rest of us." What he really needed to do was to acknowledge her limitations—to consult with an expert in such handicaps who could acknowledge her limitations and teach her to deal with them. After 3 years of therapy, she showed no improvement; if anything, she was worse.

SUMMARY

In the first section of this chapter, we begin by asking "What is beauty?" The question of who is physically attractive, and why, is one that has fascinated men and women for centuries. Unfortunately, the popularity of the question is not reflected in the definitiveness of the available answers. Ford and Beach (1951) surveyed more than 200 primitive societies. They were unable to find *any* universal standards of sexual attractiveness. Researchers find, however, that within a given society, however, there *is* reasonable consensus as to what is beautiful and/or sexy and what is not.

In the second section, we begin to explore the operation of bias. We ask: "What do people *think* beautiful people are like?" There is considerable evidence that, generally, most people assume that the beautiful possess a wide variety of socially desirable traits, while the unattractive possess an equal compliment of unappealing characteristics. Specifically, most people—including psychotherapists—seem to believe that beauty is sanity, character, and competence—even in the face of hard evidence to the contrary.

In the third section, we ask to what extent perception is translated into action. Do people *treat* the beautiful and the nonbeautiful differently? Do the beautiful *really* have an advantage in life? The evidence suggests that most people, most of the time, *do* treat the beautiful more compassionately than they treat the ugly. They send "metamessages" indicating their willingness to become intimate more quickly; they are quicker to offer help and less quick to demand help in return.

In the first three sections, in short, we review evidence that people perceive attractive and unattractive people very differently and treat them very differently. What impact does such differential treatment have on the beautiful? In the fourth section, we review the sparse evidence as to what the attractive and the unattractive are really like. There is some evidence that people's stereotypes about beauty *do* have a kernel of truth. There is considerable evidence that, by nursery school, the beautiful and the ugly are different indeed. For example, the beautiful have a more positive self-concept; may differ in personality; are more popular (from late nursery school on); and, not surprisingly in light of all this, are more sociable. Whether or not the beautiful and the nonbeautiful differ in happiness is open to question. There is considerable evidence, in any case, that the beautiful are better adjusted and mentally healthier than their unattractive peers.

Finally, in the fifth section, we close by suggesting some directions that future research on the biasing effect of beauty in psychotherapy might take.

NOTES

[1]Since nearly all of the therapists were men, one can really substitute "strikingly beautiful *women*" here.

[2]Perlmutter's impressions have not yet been tested experimentally. They remain "suggestions for research."

REFERENCE NOTES

1. Cavior, N., & Dokecki, P. R. *Physical-attractiveness self-concept: A test of Mead's hypothesis.* Paper presented at the 79th Annual Convention of the American Psychological Association, 1971.

2. Kopera, A. A., Maier, R. A., & Johnson, J. E. *Perception of physical attractiveness:*

The influence of group interaction and group coaction on ratings of the attractiveness of photographs of women. Paper presented at the 79th Annual Convention of the American Psychological Association, 1971.

   3. Feldman, S. D. *The presentation of shortness in everyday life—height and heightism in American society: Toward a sociology of stature.* Paper presented at the meeting of the American Sociological Association, Denver, 1971.

   4. Berkowitz, W. R., Nebel, J. C., & Reitman, J. W. *Height and interpersonal attraction: The 1969 mayoral election in New York City.* Paper presented at the 79th Annual Convention of the American Psychological Association, 1971.

   5. Dion, K., & Berscheid, E. *Physical attractiveness and social perception of peers in preschool children.* Unpublished manuscript, 1972. (Available from the authors.)

   6. Muirhead, S. *Therapists' sex, clients' sex, and client attractiveness in psychodiagnostic assessments.* Paper presented at the 87th Annual Meeting of the American Psychological Association, New York, September 1979.

   7. Napoleon, T., Chassin, L., & Young, R. D. *A replication and extension of physical attractiveness and mental illness.* Manuscript submitted for publication, 1979.

REFERENCES

Adams, G. R. Physical-attractiveness research: Toward a developmental social psychology of beauty. *Human Development, 1977, 10,* 217–239.

Athanasiou, R., & Greene, P. Physical attractiveness and helping behavior. *Proceedings of the 81st Annual Convention of the American Psychological Association, 1973, 8,* 289–290.

Bain, A. *John Stuart Mill: A criticism, with personal recollections.* New York: Holt, 1868.

Barocas, R., & Black, H. K. Referral rate and physical attractiveness in third-grade children. *Perceptual and Motor Skills, 1974, 39,* 731–734.

Barocas, R., & Karoly, P. Effects of physical appearance on social responsiveness. *Psychological Reports, 1972, 31,* 495–500.

Barocas, R., & Vance, F. L. Physical appearance and personal adjustment counseling. *Journal of Counseling Psychology, 1974, 21,* 96–100.

Bar-Tal, D., & Saxe, L. Perceptions of similarly and dissimilarly attractive couples and individuals. *Journal of Personality and Social Psychology, 1976, 33,* 772–781. (a)

Bar-Tal, D., & Saxe, L. Physical attractiveness and its relationship to sex-role stereotyping. *Sex Roles, 1976, 2,* 123–133. (b)

Bateson, G. *Steps to an ecology of mind.* New York: Ballantine, 1972.

Benson, P. L., Karabenick, S. A., & Lerner, R. M. Pretty please: The effects of physical attractiveness, race, and sex on receiving help. *Journal of Experimental Social Psychology, 1976, 12,* 409–415.

Berscheid, E., Dion, K., Walster, E., & Walster, G. W. Physical attractiveness and dating choice: A test of the matching hypothesis: *Journal of Experimental Social Psychology, 1971, 7,* 173–189.

Berscheid, E., & Walster, E. Physical attractiveness. In L. Berkowitz (Ed.), *Advances in experimental social psychology* (Vol. 7). New York: Academic Press, 1974.

Berscheid, E., Walster, E., & Bohrnstedt, G. The happy American body: A survey report. *Psychology Today,* November 1973, pp. 119–131.

Brickman, P., & Campbell, D. T. Hedonic relativism and planning the good society. In M. H. Appley (Ed.), *Adaptation-level theory: A symposium.* New York: Academic Press, 1971.

Brundage, L. E., Derlega, V. J., & Cash, T. F. The effects of physical attractiveness and need for approval on self-disclosure. *Personality and Social Psychology Bulletin, 1977, 3,* 63–66.

Cash, T. F., Begley, P. J., McCown, D. A., & Weise, B. C. When counselors are heard but not seen: Initial impact of physical attractiveness. *Journal of Counseling Psychology*, 1975, *22*, 273-279.

Cash, T. F., & Burns, D. S. The occurrence of reinforcing activities in relation to locus of control, success-failure expectancies, and physical attractiveness. *Journal of Personality Assessment*, 1977, *41*, 387-391.

Cash, T. F., Kehr, J., Polyson, J., & Freeman, V. Role of physical attractiveness in peer attribution of psychological disturbance. *Journal of Consulting and Clinical Psychology*, 1977, *45*, 987-993.

Cavior, N. *Physical attractiveness, perceived attitude similarity, and interpersonal attraction among fifth- and eleventh-grade boys and girls*. Unpublished doctoral dissertation, University of Houston, 1970.

Clifford, M. M. Physical attractiveness and academic performance. *Child Study Journal*, 1975, *5*, 201-209.

Clifford, M. M., & Walster, E. Research note: The effect of physical attractiveness on teacher expectation. *Sociology of Education*, 1973, *46*, 248-258.

Crespi, L. P. Quantitative variation in incentive and performance in the white rat. *American Journal of Psychology*, 1942, *55*, 467-517.

Cross, J. F., & Cross, J. Age, sex, race, and the perception of facial beauty. *Developmental Psychology*, 1971, *5*, 433-439.

Curran, J. P., & Lippold, S. The effects of physical attraction and attitude similarity in dating dyads. *Journal of Personality*, 1975, *43*, 528-539.

Dannenmaier, W. D., and Thumin, F. J. Authority status as a factor in perceptual distortion of size. *Journal of Social Psychology*, 1964, *63*, 361-365.

Darwin, C. *The expression of the emotions in man and animals*. London: Murray, 1872.

Dermer, M., & Thiel, D. L. When beauty may fail. *Journal of Personality and Social Psychology*, 1975, *31*, 1168-1176.

Dion, K. K. Young children's stereotyping of facial attractiveness. *Developmental Psychology*, 1973, *9*, 183-188.

Dion, K. K., Berscheid, E., & Walster, E. What is beautiful is good. *Journal of Personality and Social Psychology*, 1972, *24*, 285-290.

Dipboye, R. L., Arvey, R. D., & Terpstra, D. E. Sex and physical attractiveness of raters and applicants as determinants of resume evaluations. *Journal of Applied Psychology*, 1977, *62*, 288-294.

Efran, M. G. The effect of physical appearance on the judgment of guilt, interpersonal attraction, and severity of recommended punishment in a simulated jury task. *Journal of Research in Personality*, 1974, *8*, 45-54.

Farina, F., Fischer, E. H., Sherman, S., Smith, W. T., Groh, T., & Mermin, P. Physical attractiveness and mental illness. *Journal of Abnormal Psychology*, 1977, *86*, 510-517.

Ford, C. S., & Beach, F. A. *Patterns of sexual behavior*. New York: Harper & Row, 1951.

Glasgow, R. E., & Arkowitz, H. The behavioral assessment of male and female social competence in dyadic heterosexual interactions. *Behavior Therapy*, 1975, *6*, 488-498.

Goldman, W., & Lewis, P. Beautiful is good: Evidence that the physically attractive are more socially skillful. *Journal of Experimental Social Psychology*, 1977, *13*, 125-130.

Helson, H. *Adaptation-level theory: An experimental and systematic approach to behavior*. New York: Harper & Row, 1964.

Hill, M. K., & Lando, H. A. Physical attractiveness and sex-role stereotypes in impression formation. *Perceptual and Motor Skills*, 1976, *43*, 1251-1255.

Hochberg, J. E. *Perception*. Englewood Cliffs, N.J.: Prentice-Hall, 1964.

Huston, T. L. Ambiguity of acceptance, social desirability, and dating choices. *Journal of Experimental Social Psychology*, 1973, *9*, 32-42.

Iliffe, A. H. A study of preferences in feminine beauty. *British Journal of Psychology*, 1960, *51*, 267–273.

Jackson, D. J., & Huston, T. L. Physical attractiveness and assertiveness. *Journal of Social Psychology*, 1975, *96*, 79–84.

Jacobson, S. K., & Berger, C. R. Communication and justice: Defendant attributes and their effects on the severity of his sentence. *Speech Monographs*, 1974, *41*, 282–286.

Kassarjian, H. H. Voting intentions and political perception. *Journal of Psychology*, 1963, *56*, 85–88.

Katz, M., & Zimbardo, P. Making it as a mental patient. *Psychology Today*, April 1977, pp. 122–126.

Kleck, R. E., Richardson, S. A., & Ronald, L. Physical appearance cues and interpersonal attraction in children. *Child Development*, 1974, *45*, 305–310.

Koulack, D., & Tuthill, J. A. Height perception: A function of social distance. *Canadian Journal of Behavioural Science*, 1972, *4*(1), 50–53.

Krebs, D., & Adinolfi, A. A. Physical attractiveness, social relations, and personality style. *Journal of Personality and Social Psychology*, 1975, *31*, 245–253.

Kurtzberg, R. L., Safar, H., & Cavior, N. Surgical and social rehabilitation on adult offenders. *Proceedings of the 76th Annual Convention of the American Psychological Association*, 1968, *3*, 649–650.

Landy, D., & Sigall, H. Beauty is talent: Task evaluation as a function of the performer's physical attractiveness. *Journal of Personality and Social Psychology*, 1974, *29*, 299–304.

Lavrakas, P. J. Female preferences for male physiques. *Journal of Research in Personality*, 1975, *9*, 324–344.

Lerner, R. M., & Lerner, J. V. Effects of age, sex, and physical attractiveness on child-peer relations, academic performance, and elementary-school adjustment. *Developmental Psychology*, 1977, *13*, 585–590.

Leventhal, G., & Krate, R. Physical attractiveness and severity of sentencing. *Psychological Reports*, 1977, *40*, 315–318.

Mathes, E. W. The effects of physical attractiveness and anxiety on heterosexual attraction over a series of five encounters. *Journal of Marriage and the Family*, 1975, *37*, 769–772.

McCullers, J. C., & Staat, J. Draw an ugly man: An inquiry into the dimensions of physical attractiveness. *Personality and Social Psychology Bulletin*, 1974, *1*, 33–35.

Miller, C. T. *Physical attractiveness: Issues and evidence.* Unpublished doctoral dissertation, Purdue University, 1978.

Murphy, M. J., & Hellkamp, D. T. Attractiveness and personality warmth: Evaluations of paintings rated by college men and women. *Perceptual and Motor Skills*, 1976, *43*, 1163–1166.

Murstein, B. I. Physical attractiveness and marital choice. *Journal of Personality and Social Psychology*, 1972, *22*(1), 8–12.

Pavlos, A. J., & Newcomb, J. D. Effects of physical attractiveness and severity of physical illness on justification seen for attempting suicide. *Personality and Social Psychology Bulletin*, 1974, *1*, 36–38.

Perlmutter, M. S. The frail male syndrome. In *Resources for rehabilitation practitioners: Sexuality of physical disability.* Minneapolis: Program in Medical School, University of Minnesota, in press.

Perlmutter, M., & Hatfield, E. Intimacy, intentional metacommunication, and second-order change. *American Journal of Family Therapy*, 1980, *8*, 17–23.

Piehl, J. Integration of information in the courts: Influence of physical attractiveness on amount of punishment for a traffic offender. *Psychological Reports*, 1977, *41*, 551–556.

Ross, M. B., & Salvia, J. Attractiveness as a biasing factor in teacher judgments. *American Journal of Mental Deficiency*, 1975, *80*, 96–98.

Salvia, J., Algozzine, R., & Sheare, J. B. Attractiveness and school adjustment. *Journal of School Psychology*, 1977, *15*, 60–67.

Sappho. [*Poems and fragments*] (G. Davenport, Ed. and trans.). Ann Arbor: University of Michigan Press, 1965.

Schiller, J. C. F. *Essays, esthetical and philosophical, including the dissertation on the "Connexions between the animals and the spiritual in man."* London: G. Bell & Sons, 1882.

Schofield, W. *Psychotherapy: The purchase of friendship.* Englewood Cliffs, N.J.: Prentice-Hall, 1964.

Seligman, C., Brickman, J., & Koulack, D. Rape and physical attractiveness: Assigning responsibility to victims. *Journal of Personality*, 1977, *45*, 554–563.

Shaw, M. E., & Wagner, P. J. Role selection in the service of self-presentation. *Memory and Cognition*, 1975, *3*, 481–484.

Sigall, H., & Ostrove, N. Beautiful but dangerous: Effects of offender attractiveness and nature of crime on juridic judgment. *Journal of Personality and Social Psychology*, 1975, *31*, 410–414.

Smits, G. J., & Cherhoniak, I. M. Physical attractiveness and friendliness in interpersonal attraction. *Psychological Reports*, 1976, *39*, 171–174.

Snyder, M., Tanke, E. D., & Berscheid, E. Social perception and interpersonal behavior: On the self-fulfilling nature of social stereotypes. *Journal of Personality and Social Psychology*, 1977, *35*, 656–666.

Sroufe, R., Chaikin, A., Cook, R., & Freeman, V. The effects of physical attractiveness on honesty: A socially desirable response. *Personality and Social Psychology Bulletin*, 1977, *3*, 59–62.

Stokes, S. J., & Bickman, L. The effect of physical attractiveness and role of the helper on help seeking. *Journal of Applied Social Psychology*, 1974, *4*, 286–294.

Styczynski, L. E., & Langlois, J. H. The effects of familiarity on behavioral stereotypes associated with physical attractiveness in young children. *Child Development*, 1977, *48*, 1137–1141.

Terry, R. L. Further evidence on components of facial attractiveness. *Perceptual and Motor Skills*, 1977, *45*, 130.

Terry, R. L., & Davis, J. S. Components of facial attractiveness. *Perceptual and Motor Skills*, 1976, *42*, 918.

Thibaut, J. W., & Kelley, H. H. *The social psychology of groups.* New York: Wiley, 1965.

Thornton, B. Effect of rape victim's attractiveness on jury simulation. *Personality and Social Psychology Bulletin*, 1977, *3*, 666–669.

Walster, E., Aronson, V., Abrahams, D., & Rottmann, L. Importance of physical attractiveness in dating behavior. *Journal of Personality and Social Psychology*, 1966, *4*(5), 508–516.

Walster, E., Walster, G. W., & Berscheid, E. *Equity: Theory and research.* New York: Allyn & Bacon, 1978.

Ward, C. Own height, sex, and liking in the judgment of the heights of others. *Journal of Personality*, 1967, *35*, 381–401.

Watzlawick, P., & Weakland, J. H. *The interactional view: Studies at Mental Research Institute, Palo Alto, 1965–1974.* New York: Norton, 1977.

West, S. G., & Brown, T. J. Physical attractiveness, the severity of the emergency, and helping: A field experiment and interpersonal simulation. *Journal of Experimental Social Psychology*, 1975, *11*, 531–538.

Wiggins, J. S., Wiggins, N., & Conger, J. C. Correlates of heterosexual somatic preference. *Journal of Personality and Social Psychology*, 1968, *10*, 82–90.

Wilson, D. W., & Donnerstein, E. Guilty or not guilty?: A look at the "simulated" jury paradigm. *Journal of Applied Social Psychology*, 1977, *7*, 175–190.

Wilson, P. R. Perceptual distortion of height as a function of ascribed academic status. *Journal of Social Psychology*, 1968, *74*, 97–102.

4 Experimenter Effects in Laboratories, Classrooms, and Clinics

ROBERT ROSENTHAL

The effort to understand human behavior must itself be one of the oldest of human behaviors. But for all the centuries of effort, there is no compelling evidence to convince us that we do understand human behavior very well. The application of that reasoning and of those procedures that together we call "the scientific method" to the understanding of human behavior is of relatively very recent origin. What we have learned about human behavior in the short period—let us say from the founding of Wundt's laboratory in Leipzig in 1879 until now—is out of all proportion to what we learned in preceding centuries. The success of the application of scientific method to the study of human behavior has given us new hope for an accelerating return of knowledge on our investment of time and effort. But most of what we want to know is still unknown. The application of scientific method has not simplified human behavior; it has perhaps shown us more precisely just how complex it really is.

In the contemporary behavioral science experiment, it is the reseach subjects we try to understand. They serve as our model of people in general, or at least of a certain kind of person. We know that human behavior is complex. We know it because no subject behaves exactly as any other subject does. We know it because sometimes we change the subject's world ever so slightly and observe that the resulting behavior changes enormously. We know it because sometimes we change the subject's world greatly and observe that the result-

Preparation of this chapter was facilitated by support from the National Science Foundation.

ing behavior changes only minutely. We know it because the "same" careful experiment conducted in one place at one time yields results very different from one conducted in another place at another time. We know our subjects' complexity because they are so often able to surprise us with their behavior.

Most of this complexity of human behavior may be in the nature of the organism. But some of this complexity may derive from the social nature of the behavioral experiment itself. Some of the complexity of people as we know it from their model, the research subject, resides not in the subject per se, but rather in the particular experimenter and in the particular interaction between subject and experimenter.

The portion of the complexity of human behavior that can be attributed to the experimenter as another person and to his or her interaction with the subject is the focus of this chapter. Whatever we can learn about experimenters and their interaction with their subjects becomes uniquely important to us as behavioral scientists. To the extent that we hope for dependable knowledge in the behavioral sciences generally, and to the extent that we rely on the methods of empirical research, we must have dependable knowledge about the researcher and the research situation. In this sense, the study of the behavioral scientist as experimenter is crucial. It will have important implications for how we conduct and how we asses our research.

But there is also another sense in which the study of the experimenter and his or her interaction with the research subject is important. In this sense, it is not at all crucial that the experimenter happens to be the collector of scientific data. Experimenters might as well be teachers interacting with their students, employers interacting with their employees, therapists interacting with their patients, or any other type of person interacting with any other. In this sense, experimenters serve as a model of people or of one kind of person. Subjects also serve as models, and the interaction between them, the situation arising from their encounter, serves as a model of other more or less analogous situations. From the behavior of the experimenter, we may learn something of consequence about human behavior in general.

EXPERIMENTER EFFECTS

It is useful to think of two major types of effects, usually unintentional, that psychologists or other behavioral researchers can have upon the results of their research. The first type operates, so to speak, in the mind, in the eye, or in the hand of the scientist. It operates without affecting the actual response of the human or animal subjects of the experiment. It is not interactional. The second type of experimenter effect is interactional. It operates by affecting the actual response of the subject of the experiment. It is a subtype of this latter type of effect—the effects of the investigators' expectancy or hypothesis on the results of their research—that occupies most of the present discussion. First, however, some examples of other effects of behavioral researchers on their research are mentioned.

Observer Effects

In any science, the experimenter must make provision for the careful observation and recording of the events under study. It is not always so easy to be sure that one has, in fact, made an accurate observation. That lesson was learned by the psychologists, who needed to know it, but it was not the psychologists who focused our attention on it originally. It was the astronomers.

Just near the end of the 18th century, the royal astronomer at the Greenwich Observatory, a man called Maskelyne, discovered that his assistant, Kinnebrook, was consistently "too slow" in his observations of the movement of stars across the sky. Maskelyne cautioned Kinnebrook about his "errors," but the errors continued for months. Kinnebrook was fired.

The man who might have saved that job was Bessel, the astronomer at Königsberg, but he was 20 years too late. It was not until then that he arrived at the conclusion that Kinnebrook's "error" was probably not willful. Bessel studied the observations of stellar transits made by a number of senior astronomers. Differences in observation, he discovered, were the rule, not the exception (Boring, 1950).

That early observation of the effects of the scientist on the observations of science made Bessel perhaps the first student of the psychology of scientists. More contemporary research on the psychology of scientists has shown that while observer errors are not necessarily serious, they tend to occur in a biased manner. By that is meant that, more often than we would expect by chance, when errors of observation do occur they tend to give results more in the direction of the investigator's hypothesis (Rosenthal, 1976, 1978b).

To make the matter more concrete and to illustrate the probable rate at which observer or recording errors are made in the behavioral sciences, Table 1 has been prepared. On the basis of 21 studies involving 314 observers recording a total of 139,000 observations, we find that about 1% of the observations are in error. The last column of Table 1 shows that about two-thirds of the time, errors are in the direction of the observer's hypothesis (Rosenthal, 1969a, 1978b).

Interpreter Effects

The interpretation of the data collected is part of the research process, and a glance at any of the technical journals of contemporary behavioral science suggests strongly that while researchers only rarely debate each other's observations they often debate the interpretation of those observations. It is as difficult to state the rules for accurate interpretation of data as it is to state those for accurate observation of data, but the variety of interpretations offered in explanation of the same data imply that many of us must turn out to be wrong. The history of science generally, and the history of psychology more specifically, suggest that more of us are wrong longer than we need to be because we hold our theories not quite lightly enough. The common practice of "theory monogamy" has its advantages, however. It does keep us motivated to make more crucial observations. In any case, interpreter effects seem less serious than observer effects do. The reason is that the former are public, while the latter are private. Given a set of observations, their interpretations become generally available to the scientific community. We are free to agree or disagree with any specific interpretation. This is not so with the case of the observations themselves: Often these are made by a single investigator, so that we are not free to agree or disagree. We can only hope that no observer errors have occurred, and we can, and should, repeat the observations.

Some kinds of common interpreter effects in the behavioral sciences may be reducible by means of improved research and data-analytic methodology. For example, the interpretations by Eysenck (1952, 1960) of the literature on psychotherapy outcome—namely, that psychotherapy does not work—held sway for a long time until Glass (Note 1; in press), Smith (in press), and Smith and Glass (1977) showed on the basis of quantitative, comprehensive analyses of all the literature that the Eysenck interpretation was not only in error but in error to a large and specifiable degree.

Until recently, bodies of literature were little more than massive inkblots upon which the interpreter could impose a wide range of interpretations. Now, however, a variety of procedures are evolving to make more objective, more systematic, and more quantitative, the summarizing of entire research domains (Rosenthal, in press-b). Thus, Glass (in press) has recently summarized work on estimation of the size of the effect under investigation; Rosenthal (1978a; 1979a; in press-c) has summarized work on the combining of significance levels across a set of studies; Rosenthal and Rubin (1979a) have shown how to compare significance levels from different studies; and Pillemer and Light (in press) have emphasized the scientific benefits to be derived from the careful analysis of the variation to be found in a run of studies.

Recent examples of quantitative summaries of research domains include those of (1) Glass and Smith (cited above), showing that psychotherapy is clearly and nontrivially effective; (2) Hall (1979; in press), showing that women are more effective than men at encoding and decoding nonverbal cues; and (3) Rosenthal and Rubin (1978; in press), showing that interpersonal expectancy effects not only occur but are of substantial magnitude. As more behavioral researchers employ these newer techniques of analysis of en-

TABLE 1
Recording Errors in 21 Experiments

STUDY	OBSERVERS	RECORDINGS	ERRORS	ERROR %	BIAS %
1. Kennedy & Uphoff, 1939	28	11,125	126	1.13	68
2. Rosenthal, Freidman, Johnson, Fode, Schill, White, & Vikan-Kline, 1964	30	3,000	20	.67	75
3. Weiss, 1967	34	1,770	30	1.69	85
4. Persinger, Knutson, & Rosenthal, 1968	11	828	6	.72	67
5. Jacob, 1969	36	1,260	40	3.17	60
6. Todd, 1971	6	864	2	.23	50
7. Glass, 1971	4	96	4	4.17	33
8. Hawthorne, 1972	18	1,009	16	1.59	19
9. Rosenthal & Hall, 1968	5	5,012	41	.82	—
10. Doctor, 1968	15	9,600	39	.41	—

11. Compton, 1970	9	3,794	36	.95	—
12. Howland, 1970	9	360	9	2.50	—
13. Mayo, 1972	15	688	0	.00	—
14. Eisner, Kosick, & Thomas, 1974	12	9,600	66	.69	—
15. Fleming & Anttonen, 1971	—	89,980	558	.62	—
16. Johnson & Adair, 1970	12	—	—	—	62
17. Johnson & Adair, 1972	12	—	—	—	58
18. Ennis, 1974	42	—	—	—	74
19. Rusch, 1974	2	—	—	—	36
20. Johnson & Ryan, 1976	6	—	—	—	91
21. Johnson & Ryan, 1976	8	—	—	—	65
Combined	314	138,986	993	.71[a]	67[b]

Note. From "How Often Are Our Numbers Wrong?" by R. Rosenthal, American Psychologist, 1978, 33, 1005–1008.
[a]Weighted by number of recordings; 1.41 when weighted by number of observers.
[b]Weighted by number of recordings; 66 when weighted by number of observers.

tire research domains, our rate of overlooking real effects (i.e., committing Type II errors) should drop noticeably (Cooper & Rosenthal, 1980).

Intentional Effects

It happens sometimes in undergraduate laboratory science courses that students "collect" and report data too beautiful to be true. (That probably happens most often when students are taught to be scientists by being told what results they must get to do well in the course rather than being taught the logic of scientific inquiry and the value of being completely open-eyed and open-minded.) Unfortunately, the history of science tells us that not only undergraduates have been dishonest in science. Fortunately, such instances are rare; nevertheless, intentional effects must be regarded as part of the inventory of the effects of investigators themselves. Four recent reports on important cases of scientific error that were very likely to have been intentional have been presented by Hearnshaw (1979), Hixson (1976), Koestler (1971), and Wade (1976). The first and the last of these, of greatest relevance to behavioral researchers, describe the case of the late Cyril Burt, who, in three separate reports of over 20, over 30, and over 50 pairs of twins, reported a correlation coefficient between IQ scores of these twins (who had been raised apart) of exactly .771 for all three studies! Such consistency of correlation would bespeak a statistical miracle if it were real, and Wade credits Leon Kamin for having made this discovery on what must surely have been the first careful reading of Burt.

Although the evidence is strong that Burt's errors were intentional, we cannot be sure of the matter. That is often the case also in instances where fabrication of data is not the issue, but where there are massive self-serving errors of citation of the literature, such as have been documented recently in the work of Jensen (1980) (Rosenthal, in press-a).

Intentional effects, interpreter effects, and observer effects all operate without experimenters' affecting their subjects' responses to the experimental task. In those effects of the experimenters themselves to be described next, we see that the subject's response to the experimental task is affected.

Biosocial Effects

The sex, age, and race of the investigator have all been found to affect the results of his or her research. What we do not know and what we need to learn is whether subjects respond differently simply to the presence of experimenters varying in these biosocial attributes, or whether experimenters varying in these attributes behave differently toward their subjects, and therefore obtain different responses from them because they have, in effect, altered the experimental situation for their subjects. So far, the evidence suggests that male and female experimenters, for example, conduct the "same" experiment quite differently, so that the different results they obtain may well be due to the fact that they unintentionally conducted different experiments. Male experimenters, for instance, were found in two experiments to be more friendly to their subjects. Biosocial attributes of the subject can also affect the experimenter's behavior, which in turn affects the subject's responses. In one study, for example, the interactions between experimenters and their subjects were recorded on sound films. In that study it was found that only 12 % of the experimenters ever smiled at their male subjects, while 70 % of the experimenters smiled at their female subjects. Smiling by the experimenters, it was found, affected the results of the experiment. The moral is clear. Before claiming a sex difference in the results of behavioral research, we must first be sure that males and females were treated identically by the experimenter. If they were not, then sex differences may be due not to genic, constitutional, enculturational, or other factors, but simply to the fact that males and females were not really in the same experiment (Rosenthal, 1967).

Psychosocial Effects

The personality of the experimenter has also been found to affect the results of his or her research. Experimenters who differ in anxiety, need for approval, hostility, authoritarianism, status, and warmth tend to obtain different responses from their experimental subjects. Experimenters higher in status, for example, tend to obtain more conforming responses from their subjects, and experimenters who are warmer in their interaction with their subjects tend to obtain more pleasant responses from their subjects. Warmer examiners administering standardized tests of intelligence are likely to obtain better intellectual performance than are cooler examiners, or examiners who are more threatening or more strange to their examinees (Rosenthal, 1969b).

Situational Effects

Experimenters who are more experienced at conducting a given experiment obtain different responses from their subjects than do their less experienced colleagues. Experimenters who are acquainted with their subjects obtain different responses than do their colleagues who have never met their subjects before. The things that happen to experimenters during the course of their experiment, including the responses they obtain from their first few subjects, can all influence the experimenters' behavior, and changes in their behavior can lead to changes in their subjects' responses. When the first few subjects of an experiment tend to respond as they are expected to respond, the behavior of the experimenter changes in such a way as to influence the subsequent subjects to respond too often in the direction of the experimenter's hypothesis (Rosenthal, 1976).

Modeling Effects

It sometimes happens that before experimenters conduct their study, they try out the task they will later have their research subjects perform. Though the evidence on this point is not all that clear, it would seem that, at least sometimes, the investigators' own performance becomes a factor in their subjects' performance. When the experimental stimuli are ambiguous, for example, subjects' interpretations of their meaning may too often agree with the investigator's own interpretations of the stimuli.

Expectancy Effects

Some expectation of how the research will turn out is virtually a constant in science. Psychologists, like other scientists generally, conduct research specifically to test hypotheses or expectations about the nature of things. In the behavioral sciences, the hypotheses held by investigators can lead them unintentionally to alter their behavior toward their subjects in such a way as to increase the likelihood that subjects will respond so as to confirm the investigators' hypotheses or expectations. We are speaking, then, of the investigators' hypotheses as self-fulfilling prophecies. One prophesies an event, and the expectation of the event then changes the behavior of the prophet in such a way as to make the prophesied event more likely. The history of science documents the occurrence of this phenomenon, with the case of Clever Hans as the prime example (Pfungst, 1911/1965).

Hans was the horse of von Osten, a German mathematics instructor. By tapping his foot, Hans was able to perform difficult mathematical calculations, and he could also spell, read, and solve problems of musical harmony. A distinguished panel of scientists and experts on animals ruled that no fraud was involved. There were no cues given to Hans to tell him when to start and when to stop the tapping of his foot. But of course there were such cues, though it remained for Pfungst to demonstrate that fact. Pfungst, in a series of brilliant experiments, showed that Hans could answer questions only when the questioner or experimenter personally knew the answer and was within Hans' view. Finally, Pfungst learned that a tiny forward movement of the experimenter's head was the signal for Hans to start tapping. A tiny upward movement of the head of the questioner or a raising of the eyebrows was the signal to Hans to stop his tapping. Hans' questioners expected Hans to give correct answers, and this expectation was reflected in their unwitting signal to Hans that the time had come for him to stop his tapping. Thus the questioner's expectation became the reason for Hans' amazing abilities. We turn now to a consideration of more recent experiments showing that an investigator's expectation can come to serve as a self-fulfilling prophecy.

RECENT STUDIES OF EXPECTANCY EFFECTS

To demonstrate the effects of the investigators' expectancies on the results of their research, at least two groups of experimenters are needed, each group with a different hypothesis or expectancy as to the outcome of its research. One approach might be to do a kind of census or poll of actual or potential experimenters in a given area of research in which opinions as to relationships between variables were divided. Some experimenters expecting one type of result and some experimenters expecting the opposite type of result might then be asked to conduct a standard experiment. If each group of experimenters obtained the results expected—results opposite to those expected by the other group of experimenters—we could conclude that the expectations of experimenters do indeed affect the results of their research. Or could we? Perhaps not. The problem would be that experimenters who differ in their theories, hypotheses, or expectations might very well differ in a number of important related ways as well. The differences in the data they obtained from their subjects might be due, then, not to the differences in expectations about the results, but to other variables correlated with expectancies.

A better strategy, therefore, than trying to find two groups of experimenters differing in their hypotheses would be to "create" two groups of experimenters differing only in the hypotheses or expectations they held about the results of a particular experiment. That was the plan employed in the following research.

Twelve experimenters were each given five rats who were to be taught to run a maze with the aid of visual cues. Half the experimenters were told that their rats had been specially bred for "maze brightness"; half the experimenters were told their rats had been bred for "maze dullness." Actually, of course, there were no differences between the rats assigned to each of the two groups. At the end of the experiment, the results were clear. Rats who had been run by experimenters expecting brighter behavior showed significantly superior learning compared to rats run by experimenters expecting dull behavior (Rosenthal & Fode, 1963). The experiment was repeated, this time employing a series of learning experiments each conducted in Skinner boxes. Half the experimenters were led to believe their rats were bred for "Skinner box brightness" and half were led to believe their animals were bred for

"Skinner box dullness." Once again there were not really any differences in the two groups of rats, at least not until the end of the experiment. Then the allegedly brighter animals really were brighter; the alleged dullards were really duller (Rosenthal & Lawson, 1964).

If rats became more bright when they were expected by their experimenter to be bright, it seemed possible that children might become more bright if they were expected by their teacher to be bright. Educational theorists had, after all, been saying for a long time that culturally disadvantaged children were unable to learn because their teachers expected them to be unable to learn. True, there was no experimental evidence for that theory, but the two studies employing rats suggested that these theorists might be correct. The following experiment was therefore conducted (Rosenthal & Jacobson, 1968).

The Pygmalion Experiment

All of the children in an elementary school were administered a nonverbal test of intelligence, which was disguised as a test that would predict intellectual "blooming." There were 18 classrooms in the school, three at each of the six grade levels. Within each grade level, the three classrooms were composed of children with above-average ability, average ability, and below-average ability, respectively. Within each of the 18 classrooms, approximately 20% of the children were chosen at random to form the experimental group. Each teacher was given the names of the children from his or her class who were in the experimental condition. The teacher was told that these children had scored on the "test for intellectual blooming" such that they would show remarkable gains in intellectual competence during the next 8 months of school. The only difference between the experimental-group and the control-group children, then, was in the mind of the teacher.

At the end of the school year, 8 months later, all the children were retested with the same IQ test. Considering the school as a whole, these children from whom the teachers had been led to expect greater intellectual gain showed a significantly greater gain in IQ than did the children of the control group.

An Unexpected Finding in Pygmalion

At the time the Pygmalion experiment was conducted, there was already considerable evidence that interpersonal self-fulfilling prophecies could occur, at least in laboratory settings. As the mathematical statisticians might put it, there were already some more than gentle prior probabilities that self-fulfilling prophecies could occur in the classroom (Mosteller & Tukey, 1968). It should not then have come as such a great surprise that teachers' expectations might affect pupils' intellectual development. For those well acquainted with the prior research, the surprise value was, in fact, not all so great. There was, however, a surprise in the Pygmalion research. For this surprise there was no great prior probability, at least not in terms of many formal research studies.

At the end of the school year of the Pygmalion study, all teachers were asked to describe the classroom behavior of their pupils. Those children in whom intellectual growth was expected were described as having a significantly better chance of becoming successful in the future, as well as significantly more interesting, curious, and happy. There was a tendency, too, for these children to be seen as more appealing, adjusted, and affectionate, and as less in need of social approval. In short, the children in whom intellectual growth was expected became more intellectually alive and autonomous, or at least were so perceived by their teachers.

But we already know that the children of the experimental group gained more intellectually, so that perhaps it was the fact of such gaining that accounted for the more favorable ratings of these children's behavior and aptitude. But a great many of the control-group children also gained in IQ during the course of the year. We might expect that those who gained more intellectually among these undesignated children would also be rated more favorably by their teachers. Such was not the case. The more the control-group children gained in IQ, the more they were regarded as *less* well adjusted, as *less* interesting, and as *less* affectionate. From these results, it would seem that when children who are expected to grow intellectually do so, they are benefited in other ways as well. When children who are not specifically expected to develop intellectually do so, they seem to show accompanying undesirable behavior, or at least are perceived by their teachers as showing such undesirable behavior. If children are to show intellectual gain, it seems to be better for their real or perceived intellectual vitality and for their real or perceived mental health if their teachers have been expecting them to grow intellectually. It appears worthwhile to investigate further the proposition that there may be hazards to unpredicted intellectual growth (Rosenthal, 1974).

THE GENERALITY OF INTERPERSONAL EXPECTANCY EFFECTS

In this chapter, there has been space to describe only a few experiments designed to test the hypothesis that one person's expectation can come to serve as a self-fulfilling prophecy for the behavior of another person. However, the basic issue is no longer in doubt. There are now well over 300 experiments investigating this phenomenon, and the cumulative results of all show an essentially zero probability that these results could have been obtained if there were no such phenomenon as interpersonal expectancy effects (Rosenthal, 1976; Rosenthal & Rubin, 1978).

The first column of Table 2 lists eight areas of behavioral research that have been investigated for the operation of interpersonal expectancy effects. The second column of Table 2 shows the number of studies that were conducted in each area up to the time of this analysis. The third column shows the proportion of studies reaching statistical significance for each area. Even for the least frequently significant research areas, the proportion of significant results was more than four times greater than would have been expected if there were really no such phenomenon as interpersonal expectancy effects. The last column of Table 2 shows for each area the estimated average size of the effect of the interpersonal expectation. The measure of effect size is a standard deviation unit. Thus, if we were dealing with commonly used IQ tests, the average size of the effect of interpersonal expectations would be on the order of 10 or more IQ points.

Effect Size, r, r^2, and the Binomial Effect Size Display (BESD)

The measure of effect size employed above is called d by Cohen (1977), and it tells the importance or magnitude of an experimental effect by taking the difference between the mean scores of the experimental and control groups and dividing this difference by the standard deviation common to both groups. Probably the most common alternative to d for presenting the size of an experimental effect is to report r, the product moment correlation between the independent and dependent variable. However, there is a prob-

TABLE 2

Expectancy Effects in Eight Research Areas

RESEARCH AREA	NUMBER OF STUDIES	PROPORTION OF STUDIES REACH- ING $p < .05$	ESTIMATED MEAN EFFECT SIZE (σ)
Reaction time	9	.22	.17
Inkblot tests	9	.44	.84
Animal learning	15	.73	1.73
Laboratory interviews	29	.38	.14
Psychophysical judgments	23	.43	1.05
Learning and ability	34	.29	.54
Person perception	119	.27	.55
Everyday situations	112	.40	.88
Median	26	.39[a]	.70

[a]The value expected is .05 if there were no such process as interpersonal expectancy effects.

lem in interpreting r (and its next of kin, r^2); the typical use of these indexes may lead to a widespread tendency to underestimate the importance of the effects of behavioral and biomedical interventions (Rosenthal & Rubin, 1979b, Note 2). This tendency to underestimate the importance of effects was found not only among experienced behavioral researchers, but among experienced statisticians as well. Accordingly, Rosenthal and Rubin have proposed an intuitively appealing general purpose effect size display whose interpretation is far more transparent: the Binomial Effect Size Display (BESD).

The question addressed by BESD is this: What is the effect on the success rate (e.g., survival rate, cure rate, improvement rate, selection rate, etc.) of the institution of a new treatment procedure? It therefore displays the change in outcome attributable to the new treatment procedure. An example shows the appeal of this procedure.

In their meta-analysis of psychotherapy outcome studies, Smith and Glass (1977) summarized the results of some 400 studies. An eminent critic stated that the results of their analysis sounded the "death knell" for psychotherapy because of the modest size of the effect (Rimland, 1979). This modest effect size was calculated to be equivalent to an r of .32, accounting for "only 10% of the variance" (p. 192).

Table 3 shows the BESD corresponding to an r of .32 or an r^2 of .10. The table shows clearly that it is absurd to label as "modest indeed" (p. 192) an effect size equivalent to reducing a death rate from 66% to 34%.

Table 4 shows systematically the increase in success rates associated with various values of r^2 and r. Even so "small" an r as .20, accounting for "only 4% of the variance," is associated with an increase in success rate from 40% to 60% (e.g., a reduction in death rate from 60% to 40%). The last column of Table 4 shows that the difference in success rates is identical to r. Consequently, the experimental success rate in the BESD is computed as $.50 + r/2$, whereas the control-group success rate is computed as $.50 - r/2$. Friedman (1968) has a useful discussion of computing the r associated with a variety of test statistics, and Table 5 gives the three most frequently used equivalences.

Rosenthal and Rubin (Note 2) have proposed that the reporting of effect sizes can be made more intuitive and more informative by using the BESD. It is their belief that the use of the BESD to display the increase in success rate due to treatment would more clearly convey the real-world importance of treatment effects than would the commonly used descriptions of effect size based on "the proportion of variance accounted for."

FUTURE RESEARCH

Much is known about the phenomenon of interpersonal expectancy effects, but much, much more is yet unknown. What are the factors increasing or decreasing the effects of interpersonal expectations (i.e., what are

TABLE 3
The Binomial Effect Size Display (BESD): An Example "Accounting for Only 10% of the Variance"

| | TREATMENT OUTCOME | | |
CONDITION	DEAD	ALIVE	Σ
Control condition	66	34	100
Treatment condition	34	66	100
Σ	100	100	200

TABLE 4
Binomial Effect Size Displays Corresponding to Various Values of r^2 and r

| | | SUCCESS RATE INCREASED | | DIFFERENCE IN SUCCESS |
r^2	r	FROM	TO	RATES
.01	.10	.450	.550	.10
.02	.15	.425	.575	.15
.04	.20	.400	.600	.20
.06	.25	.375	.625	.25
.09	.30	.350	.650	.30
.12	.35	.325	.675	.35
.16	.40	.300	.700	.40
.20	.45	.275	.725	.45
.25	.50	.250	.750	.50
.30	.55	.225	.775	.55
.36	.60	.200	.800	.60
.42	.65	.175	.825	.65
.49	.70	.150	.850	.70
.56	.75	.125	.875	.75
.64	.80	.100	.900	.80
.72	.85	.075	.925	.85
.81	.90	.050	.950	.90
.90	.95	.025	.975	.95
1.00	1.00	.000	1.000	1.00

TABLE 5
Computation of r from t, F, and χ^2

IF THE TEST STATISTIC IS	THEN r IS GIVEN BY
t	$\sqrt{\dfrac{t^2}{t^2+df}}$
F^a	$\sqrt{\dfrac{F}{F+df\,(\text{error})}}$
χ^{2b}	$\sqrt{\dfrac{\chi^2}{n}}$

Note. The sign of r should be positive if the experimental group is superior to the control group and negative if the control group is superior to the experimental group.

[a]Used only when df for numerator $=1$, as in the comparison of two group means or any other contrast.

[b]Used only when df for $\chi^2=1$.

the moderating variables)? What are the variables serving to mediate the effects of interpersonal self-fulfilling prophecies? Only some bare beginnings have been made to address these questions. The role of moderating variables has been considered elsewhere and is being actively surveyed at the present time (Rosenthal, 1969a). The variables serving to mediate the effects of interpersonal expectancies have also been considered elsewhere, and for the teacher-pupil interaction a four-factor "theory" has been proposed (Rosenthal, 1969a, 1974). This "theory" suggests that teachers, counselors, and supervisors who have been led to expect superior performance from some of their pupils, clients, or trainees appear to treat these "special" persons differently than they treat the remaining not-so-special persons in roughly four ways:

1. *Climate.* Teachers appear to create a warmer socioemotional climate for their "special" students.
2. *Feedback.* Teachers appear to give their "special" students more differentiated feedback as to how they have been performing.
3. *Input.* Teachers appear to teach more material and more difficult material to their "special" students.
4. *Output.* Teachers appear to give their "special" students greater opportunities for responding.

Work on this four-factor theory is currently in progress.

Much of the research on interpersonal expectancies has suggested that mediation of these expectancies depends to some important degree on various processes of nonverbal communication (Rosenthal, 1969a, 1974). Moreover, there appear to be important differences among experimenters, teachers, psychotherapists, and people generally in the clarity of their communication through different channels of nonverbal communication. In addition, there appear to be important differences among research subjects, pupils, patients, and people generally in their sensitivity to nonverbal communications transmitted through different nonverbal channels. If we knew a great deal more about differential sending and receiving abilities, we might be in a much better position to address the general question of what kind of person (in terms of sending abilities) can most effectively influence covertly what kind of other person (in terms of receiving abilities). Thus, for example, if those therapists who best communicate their expectations for patients' functioning in the auditory channel were assigned patients whose best channels of reception were also auditory, we might predict greater effects of therapist expectation than we would if those same therapists were assigned patients less sensitive to auditory-channel nonverbal communication.

Ultimately, then, what we would want would be a series of accurate measurements for each person, describing his or her relative ability to send and to receive in each of a variety of channels of nonverbal communication. It seems reasonable to suppose that if we had this information for two or more people, we would be better able to predict the outcome of their interaction, regardless of whether the focus of the analysis were on the mediation of interpersonal expectations or on some other interpersonal transaction.

As a start toward the goal of more completely specifying accuracy of sending and receiving nonverbal cues in dyadic interaction, this author and his colleagues have been developing instruments designed to measure differential sensitivity to various channels of nonverbal communication (e.g., the Profile of Nonverbal Sensitivity, or PONS) (Rosenthal, Hall, DiMatteo, Rogers, & Archer, 1979). It is the group's hope that research employing the PONS and related measures of skill at sending and receiving messages in various channels of nonverbal communication, along with related research, will help to unravel the mystery of the mediation of interpersonal expectancy effects (e.g., Rosenthal, 1979b). That is the hope; but the work lies ahead, and there is a great deal of it yet to be done.

REFERENCE NOTES

1. Glass, G. V. *Primary, secondary, and meta-analysis of research.* Paper presented at the meeting of the American Educational Research Association, San Francisco, April 1976.
2. Rosenthal, R., & Rubin, D. B. *A simple, general-purpose display of magnitude of experimental effect.* Unpublished manuscript, Harvard University, 1980.

REFERENCES

Boring, E. G. *A history of experimental psychology* (2nd ed.). New York: Appleton-Century-Crofts, 1950.

Cohen, J. *Statistical power analysis for the behavioral sciences* (Rev. ed.). New York: Academic Press, 1977.

Cooper, H. M., & Rosenthal, R. Statistical versus traditional procedures for summarizing research findings. *Psychological Bulletin,* 1980, *87,* 442–449.

Eysenck, H. J. The effects of psychotherapy: An evaluation. *Journal of Consulting Psychology,* 1952, *16,* 319–324.

Eysenck, H. J. The effects of psychotherapy. In H. J. Eysenck (Ed.), *Handbook of abnormal psychology.* New York: Basic Books, 1960.

Friedman, H. Magnitude of experimental effect and a table for its rapid estimation. *Psychological Bulletin,* 1968, *70,* 245–251.

Glass, G. V. Summarizing effect sizes. In R. Rosenthal (Ed.), *New directions for methodology of behavioral science: Quantitative assessment of research domains.* San Francisco: Jossey-Bass, in press.

Hall, J. A. Gender, gender roles, and nonverbal communication skills. In R. Rosenthal (Ed.), *Skill in nonverbal communication.* Cambridge, Mass.: Oelgeschlager, Gunn & Hain, 1979.

Hall, J. A. Gender differences in nonverbal communication skills. In R. Rosenthal (Ed.), *New directions for methodology of behavioral science: Quantitative assessment of research domains.* San Francisco: Jossey-Bass, in press.

Hearnshaw, L. S. *Cyril Burt: Psychologist.* Ithaca, N.Y.: Cornell University Press, 1979.

Hixson, J. *The patchwork mouse.* Garden City, N.Y.: Doubleday/Anchor, 1976.

Jensen, A. R. *Bias in mental testing.* New York: Free Press, 1980.

Koestler, A. *The case of the midwife toad.* New York: Random House, 1971.

Mosteller, F., & Tukey, J. W. Data analysis, including statistics. In G. Lindzey & E. Aronson (Eds.), *The handbook of social psychology* (2nd ed., Vol. 2). Reading, Mass.: Addison-Wesley, 1968.

Pfungst, O. *[Clever Hans]* (C. L. Rahn, trans.). New York: Holt, Rinehart & Winston, 1965. (Originally published, 1911.)

Pillemer, D. B., & Light, R. J. Benefiting from variation in study outcomes. In R. Rosenthal (Ed.), *New directions for methodology of behavioral science: Quantitative assessment of research domains.* San Francisco: Jossey-Bass, in press.

Rimland, B. Death knell for psychotherapy? *American Psychologist,* 1979, *34,* 192.

Rosenthal, R. Covert communication in the psychological experiment. *Psychological Bulletin,* 1967, *67,* 356–367.

Rosenthal, R. Interpersonal expectations. In R. Rosenthal & R. L. Rosnow (Eds.), *Artifact in behavioral research.* New York: Academic Press, 1969. (a)

Rosenthal, R. Unintended effects of the clinician in clinical interaction: A taxonomy and a review of clinician expectancy effects. *Australian Journal of Psychology,* 1969, *21,* 1–20. (b)

Rosenthal, R. On the social psychology of the self-fulfilling prophecy: Further evidence for Pygmalion effects and their mediating mechanisms (Module 53). New York: MSS Modular Publications, 1974.

Rosenthal, R. *Experimenter effects in behavioral research: Enlarged edition.* New York: Irvington, 1976.

Rosenthal, R. Combining results of independent studies. *Psychological Bulletin,* 1978, *85,* 185–193. (a)

Rosenthal, R. How often are our numbers wrong? *American Psychologist,* 1978, *33,* 1005–1008. (b)

Rosenthal, R. The "file drawer problem" and tolerance for null results. *Psychological Bulletin,* 1979, *86,* 638–641. (a)

Rosenthal, R. (Ed.). *Skill in nonverbal communication.* Cambridge, Mass.: Oelgeschlager, Gunn & Hain, 1979. (b)

Rosenthal, R. Error and bias in the selection of data. *The Behavioral and Brain Sciences,* in press. (a)

Rosenthal, R. (Ed.). *New directions for methodology of behavioral science: Quantitative assessment of research domains.* San Francisco: Jossey-Bass, in press. (b)

Rosenthal, R. Summarizing significance levels. In R. Rosenthal (Ed.), *New directions for methodology of behavioral science: Quantitative assessment of research domains.* San Francisco: Jossey-Bass, in press. (c)

Rosenthal, R., & Fode, K. L. The effect of experimenter bias on the performance of the albino rat. *Behavioral Science,* 1963, *8,* 183–189.

Rosenthal, R., Hall, J. A., DiMatteo, M. R., Rogers, P. L., & Archer, D. *Sensitivity to nonverbal communication: The PONS test.* Baltimore: Johns Hopkins University Press, 1979.

Rosenthal, R., & Jacobson, L. *Pygmalion in the classroom.* New York: Holt, Rinehart & Winston, 1968.

Rosenthal, R., & Lawson, R. A longitudinal study of the effects of experimenter bias on the operant learning of laboratory rats. *Journal of Psychiatric Research,* 1964, *2,* 61–72.

Rosenthal, R., & Rubin, D. B. Interpersonal expectancy effects: The first 345 studies. *The Behavioral and Brain Sciences,* 1978, *3,* 377–386.

Rosenthal, R., & Rubin, D. B. Comparing significance levels of independent studies. *Psychological Bulletin,* 1979, *86,* 1165–1168. (a)

Rosenthal, R., & Rubin, D. B. A note on percent variance explained as a measure of the importance of effects. *Journal of Applied Social Psychology,* 1979, *9,* 395–396. (b)

Rosenthal, R., & Rubin, D. B. Summarizing 345 studies of interpersonal expectancy effects. In R. Rosenthal (Ed.), *New directions for methodology of behavioral science: Quantitative assessment of research domains.* San Francisco: Jossey-Bass, in press.

Smith, M. L. Integrating studies of psychotherapy outcomes. In R. Rosenthal (Ed.), *New directions for methodology of behavioral science: Quantitative assessment of research domains.* San Francisco: Jossey-Bass, in press.

Smith, M. L., & Glass, G. V. Meta-analysis of psychotherapy outcome studies. *American Psychologist,* 1977, *32,* 752–760.

Wade, N. IQ and heredity: Suspicion of fraud beclouds classic experiment. *Science,* 1976, *194,* 916–919.

5 Effects of Bias on Attribution and Information Processing: A Cognitive-Attributional Analysis of Stereotyping

DAVID L. HAMILTON

INTRODUCTION

Attribution theory is concerned with the cognitive processes involved in how perceivers generate causal explanations for behavior. For the last decade, it has been the primary area of research activity within the broader domain of person perception. More recently, it has been a major contributing factor to the currently developing interest in *social cognition*, the direct and explicit study of the cognitive processes involved in social-psychological phenomena, such as person perception. This chapter attempts to bring this literature to bear on a topic in person perception that has considerable social significance, namely, stereotyping. The chapter attempts to show that an analysis of this topic from an attributional and social cognition perspective can greatly facilitate our understanding of the processes involved in stereotyping.

Reprinted, in part, from *Advances in Experimental Social Psychology*, 1979, 12, 53–84. Copyright 1979 by Academic Press, Inc. Reprinted by permission. Preparation of this chapter was supported in part by NIMH Grant 29418 and was completed while the author was a visiting Research Associate at Harvard University. The author expresses his appreciation to Shelley Taylor and Mark Zanna for their comments on an earlier version of the manuscript.

103

Since the early writing of Heider on attribution processes, a major distinction has been drawn between *internal attributions*, or explanations of behavior in terms of the actor's dispositions, abilities, and motivational states, and *external attributions*, which explain behavior in terms of the situational forces influencing the actor. This distinction has played a central role in a number of theoretical accounts regarding attribution processes (e.g., Jones & Davis, 1965; Jones & Nisbett, 1972; Kelley, 1967; Weiner, Frieze, Kukla, Reed, Rest, & Rosenbaum, 1972). One of Heider's early insights was that perceivers appeared to be more heavily influenced, in making their attributions, by the behavior they observed an actor perform than by the situational and interpersonal constraints under which the behavior was performed. This tendency, which Heider referred to as "behavior engulfing the field" (Heider, 1958), results in the overattribution of behavior to internal, dispositional causes, even when quite reasonable explanations in terms of situational factors are readily available. Empirical support for this phenomenon has been obtained in a number of studies (e.g., Jones & Harris, 1967). Thus perceivers seem prone to making internal attributions.

At present, we do not have a thorough knowledge of the conditions under which perceivers make internal as opposed to external attributions, although research testing the propositions of correspondent inference theory (Jones & Davis, 1965; Jones & McGillis, 1976) and actor-observer differences (e.g., Jones & Nisbett, 1972) has provided some understanding of this issue. For example, internal attributions and/or stronger dispositional inferences have been shown to be likely when the actor's behavior is out of role (e.g., Jones, Davis, & Gergen, 1961), or otherwise violates normative expectations (e.g., Jones & Harris, 1967), or is highly salient to the perceiver (e.g., S. E. Taylor & Fiske, 1975).

Stereotyping is said to occur when a perceiver makes inferences about a person because of that person's membership in some group. Thus, when a person's ethnicity serves as a cue that increases the likelihood of the perceiver making certain internal attributions about the person, then stereotyping has occurred. Until recently, relatively little was known about the cognitive processes involved in stereotyping. The recent surge of interest in a cognitive analysis of person perception has resulted in a number of studies that have increased our understanding of this issue.

COGNITIVE BIASES *RESULTING FROM* STEREOTYPIC CONCEPTIONS

Regardless of their origins, it is clear that by the onset of adulthood all of us hold a diversity of stereotypic beliefs about various social groups. This section examines the consequences, for attributional and cognitive representational processes, of a perceiver's having a stereotypic conception of a particular group. It is obvious that the stereotypes we hold influence our perceptions of members of the stereotyped groups; indeed, this seems almost inherent in the concept of stereotype itself. The questions of importance for understanding the nature of stereotyping are how this influence comes about and how it is maintained.

The term *stereotype* is in essence a cognitive structural concept, referring to a set of expectations held by the perceiver regarding members of a social group. It is, then, similar to an implicit personality theory, in this case one's group membership being the stimulus cue on which a number of inferences about the person are based (Schneider, 1973). A stereotype can also be thought of as a structural framework in terms of which information about another is processed and hence has the properties of a *schema*, a concept of importance in recent research on attribution processes (e.g., Kelley, 1972) and related topics (e.g., Cantor & Mischel, 1977; Markus, 1977; S. E. Taylor & Crocker, 1981). The discussion that follows reviews some of the research that has investigated these processes.

Influence of Stereotypes on Causal Attributions

If stereotypes bias the way in which we perceive members of social groups, it seems likely that such an influence would be manifested in our causal attributions regarding the behavior of such persons. As noted in the introduction to this chapter, attribution researchers have made a basic differentiation between *internal attributions*, in which an actor's behavior is explained in terms of his or her dispositional characteristics, and *external attributions*, in which situational influences are perceived as causing the actor's behavior. It seems highly plausible that our stereotypic evaluations of and expectations about others influence the way in which we interpret such behavioral "evidence," and, if so, this would have implications for the maintenance and change of stereotypes. Consider, for example, the possibility that behaviors confirming stereotypic expectations are attributed to the actor's dispositional characteristics, but that behaviors inconsistent with a stereotype tend to be attributed to external factors. Since the stereotype reflects the perceiver's assumptions about the dispositional attributes of members of a particular group, this attributional bias would essentially prevent the perceiver from having to confront and cope with disconfirming evidence; after all, according to this attribution scheme, such behaviors are due to situational influences and do not reflect anything about the person. If such a perceptual distortion were present, as intuitively seems likely, the extreme persistence of stereotypes would be understandable.

A few studies investigating the attributional bias have been reported, although their number is surprisingly small. D. M. Taylor and Jaggi (1974), in an experiment conducted in India, investigated the effect of stereotype-based evaluative biases on causal attributions. Their subjects, all of whom were of the Hindu religion, rated the concepts "Hindu" and "Muslim" on a set of trait scales. These ratings showed that the subjects had much higher evaluations of their own group than of the Muslims. Subjects were then given a series of stimulus paragraphs, each of which described an actor performing some behavior in a social context. In these descriptions, the ethnic identification of the actor (Hindu or Muslim) and the desirability of his or her behavior were systematically varied, making four possible combinations, which were represented an equal number of times in the stimulus series. For each descriptive paragraph, several possible reasons were presented for the actor's behavior, and subjects were asked to choose the best alternative. Analysis of the subjects' responses indicated that these Hindu subjects attributed the desirable behavior of Hindu actors to internal factors and their undesirable acts to external causes. In contrast, when the actor was identified as a Muslim, the opposite pattern of attributions occurred. Thus, salient ingroup-outgroup distinctions can influence one's attributions regarding the behavior of members of these groups.

The influence of stereotypic expectations on causal attributions has been further investigated in studies of sex stereotypes. Recently Deaux (1976) has discussed such effects in terms of a model formulated by Weiner et al. (1972). According to this framework, causal attributions vary in terms of two major dimensions—an internal-external dimension and a temporary-stable dimension. The type of causal attribution likely to be made is a function of the nature of the information available, in terms of these two dimensions. Combining the two dimensions into a 2×2 table yields four major categories of attribution, as shown in Table 1. For example, behavior that is viewed as relatively stable and as due to internal factors tends to be explained in terms of the actor's ability; performance that is considered unstable (inconsistent) and influ-

TABLE 1
Classification of Causal Attributions
According to Stability and Internality-
Externality

	INTERNAL	EXTERNAL
Stable	Ability	Task difficulty
Unstable	Effort	Luck

enced by internal causes tends to be viewed as reflecting the actor's effort or motivation; and so forth. This model has proved quite useful in research investigating achievement behavior (Weiner et al., 1972).

Building on this framework, Deaux (1976) has proposed that the successful or unsuccessful performance of an actor is evaluated by the perceiver in terms of the expectancies held by the perceiver regarding males and females, and that these combine in influencing the perceiver's attribution regarding that behavior. Specifically, she has proposed that behavior consistent with expectations (success by a male on a masculinity-related task, such as one requiring mechanical skills) will be attributed to a stable rather than a temporary cause (usually ability). In contrast, performance inconsistent with stereotypic expectations will be attributed to a temporary cause (luck or effort). Results of several studies (e.g., Deaux & Emswiller, 1974; Feldman-Summers & Kiesler, 1974), summarized by Deaux (1976), have provided partial support for this interpretation, and the model warrants further investigation.

Ashmore and Del Boca (1976) have suggested an interesting interpretation of recent changes in stereotypic conceptions of blacks, an interpretation that is also easily understood in terms of the framework represented in Table 1. Historically, the fact that disproportionate numbers of blacks are found at the lower socioeconomic levels (i.e., they fail to succeed) has commonly been interpreted as due to their innate intellectual inferiority. Public opinion surveys and studies of stereotypes, conducted over the past several decades, have shown that the number of whites subscribing to this belief in the innate inferiority of blacks has decreased considerably. However, since blacks continue to be overrepresented at the bottom of the socioeconomic ladder, among the unemployed, on welfare rolls, and so on, the same behavioral fact remains and, according to attribution theory, needs to be "explained." In terms of the model shown in Table 1, two options seem to be available to the naive theorist. One may recognize that, in order to achieve socioeconomic success, blacks face greater "task difficulty" than do whites—a quite plausible assumption in view of the discriminatory barriers, educational disadvantages, and poor "starting position" that are commonly experienced by blacks. This explanation emphasizes the role of relatively stable, external factors that can make success difficult to achieve. Alternatively, one may maintain the belief that the failure of blacks to rise socioeconomically is due to internal factors, but that these factors are of a motivational rather than an intellectual nature. According to this view, black poverty would not be viewed as a consequence of any innate difference from whites in their capability, or as a consequence of discriminatory practices that blacks face, but would be attributed to their lack of effort and the low aspirations they set for themselves. Since perceivers are inclined to make internal, dispositional attributions, even when credible situational explanations are readily available, it is perhaps not surprising that the belief that "blacks are lazy" continues to be a prominent characteristic in stereotypes of blacks. While this intuitive analysis within the framework of this model of causal attributions seems quite plausible, the author knows of no studies that have empirically tested this line of reasoning.

The concepts and findings discussed in this section suggest that stereotypic expectations about social groups may bias considerably the perceiver's attributions regarding the causes of a person's behavior when his or her membership in a particular group has been made salient. If, as some of these findings indicate, perceivers are more likely to make dispositional inferences (and less likely to make situational attributions) when the observed behavior is consistent with stereotypic expectations, this bias would in the long run result in subjective confirmation of those expectancies, even in the absence of actual support in the observed behavior. This, in turn, would contribute to the maintenance and persistence of the stereotype.

A full understanding of this relationship requires empirical investigation of the cognitive mediating processes that might underlie this effect; that is, if the schema-based expectancies do bias the perceiver's use of the information available to him or her, then it is important to determine at what point(s) in the cognitive processing system this bias is occurring. Recently, social psychologists have begun to investigate these mediating processes directly, adapting the techniques and methodologies of cognitive psychology in studying these cognitive mediators. Despite the "newness" of this research in social cognition, a number of recent findings bear directly on this issue, and the next two subsections examine this emerging literature.

Influence of Stereotypes on Processing Information about Persons

Stereotypic schemata conceivably could influence the processing of information about an individual member of a social group in any of several possible ways. For example, such expectancies may focus one's attention on a particular aspect of the person's behavior, thereby making that aspect of the stimulus field more salient; or they may lead the perceiver to interpret certain behaviors in a biased manner; or they may result in a selective retrieval of information from what is stored in memory. Any of these is a reasonable possibility, as is any combination of them; such effects need not be limited to one stage of the process.

In addition to these influences on the processing of the information per se, stereotypic schemata may also lead the perceiver to go beyond that information in certain specifiable ways. As "prototypes" called up in response to certain stimulus cues, well-developed stereotypes may result in the perceiver's "seeing" certain things that were not a part of the stimulus configuration, "filling in the gaps" in terms of the schema-based expectancies.

The notion that cognitive schemata can influence the learning and retention of the available material is far from new. Bartlett's early work (1932) was concerned specifically with this question. The current interest in social cognition has resulted in renewed investigation of these issues.

A number of recent studies have been concerned with the kinds of processes enumerated above. Some of them have focused on how such biases can influence the perception of members of stereotyped groups; other studies have not dealt specifically with this content, but have reported findings that have clear implications for the effect of stereotypes on these processes. This section attempts to bring together these studies and evaluate their significance for understanding how stereotypes function.

The potentially important role of stereotypic schemata in the encoding process is suggested in an experiment by Duncan (1976). In this study, white college-student subjects watched a videotape in which two males discussed possible solutions to a problem. The subjects were led to believe that they were observing, over closed-circuit television, a "live" interaction taking place in another room. They were told that their job was to code, each time the experimenter gave a signal, the behavior that had just occurred according to a Bales-like category system. Several such signals were given during the interaction, the last one coming immediately after the discussion had become heated and one actor had given an "ambiguous shove" to the other. At that point the television screen went blank and the experiment was terminated.

The major independent variables were the race—black or white—of the two actors in the videotape, the protagonist and the victim. Four coding categories were used in categorizing the "shoving" incident—"playing around," "dramatizes," "aggressive behavior," and "violent behavior." How this behavior was interpreted by the observers was almost totally a function of the race of the protagonist: If he was white, the shove was viewed as playfulness or dramatization; if he was black, it was interpreted as aggressive or violent behavior. If these results are valid,[1] they have considerable significance for understanding the important influence of stereotypes on information processing. Stereotypic expectations influenced the manner in which the same behavior was interpreted. However, once a behavior has been interpreted and encoded in a particular way, its meaning for the perceiver is determined, the stereotypic expectation has been "confirmed," and the perceiver has received "evidence" that would support and maintain the preexisting conception of the stereotyped group.

While Duncan's research (1976) suggests a biasing effect of stereotypes on the encoding of information about others, other studies have focused on the influence that stereotypic schemata can have on what is retained about others. Cohen (Note 1) had subjects view a videotape of a woman, whom they had been told was either a waitress or a librarian, having dinner with her husband. Several characteristics stereotypic of librarians and of waitresses (e.g., appearance and clothing, food preferences) were incorporated into the stimulus tape. For example, according to previously obtained data regarding stereotypic expectations, perceivers expect a librarian to be more likely than a waitress to wear glasses, but they consider waitresses more likely than librarians to drink beer with a meal. Following the videotape, subjects were asked a number of factual questions regarding the content of the tape. For example, one item asked what the woman had to drink with her dinner, and subjects were to choose between two options, wine and beer. In each case, one of the two choices was stereotypic of librarians, the other of waitresses; and of course, only one was correct. Cohen predicted that subjects would be more likely to be accurate if the correct alternative was also stereotypic of the "occupational set" they had been given (i.e., instructions that the woman was a librarian or a waitress). The results provided partial support for the hypothesis. The predicted effect was quite strong for subjects given the "waitress" set, and this memory bias persisted for up to 1 week. Unexpectedly, subjects who were told that the woman was a librarian showed no differential recognition accuracy in an immediate test, although the results for subjects who were not tested until 1 week later followed the predicted pattern. While Cohen's predictions received only partial support, the findings are nevertheless suggestive and, like Duncan's study, indicate that further research investigating stereotype-based biases in the observation of ongoing behavior is warranted.

Though not concerned with stereotyping per se, a series of studies by Zadney and Gerard (1974) is quite germane to this issue. In these experiments, subjects were shown a videotape in which a number of the behaviors enacted and statements made by the participants could be readily interpreted in terms of several possible intentions that might be attributed to the actors. Different groups of subjects were given instructions that attributed one or another of the possible intentions to the actors. The results of these studies showed a tendency for intent-related information to be recalled better than behaviors and statements that were relevant to the other possible interpretations. One of the experiments demonstrated that this effect was observed only when the intention-inducing instructions were given prior to viewing the videotape; when this manipulation followed presentation of the tape, there was little evidence of biased recall. This pattern of findings suggests that the biasing effect of attributed intentions occurred primarily during the encoding phase rather than during the retrieval of information from memory.

Several recent papers have discussed the manner in which cognitive schemata influence the processing of information about persons. While these studies have not been concerned with stereotyping per se, they have straightforward implications for this topic, since the cognitive structures investigated in them are conceptually similar to stereotypes. These studies have to do with the effect of "prototypes" (e.g., Cantor & Mischel, 1977, 1979a), "schemata" (e.g., Markus, 1977; S. E. Taylor & Crocker, 1981), or "scripts" (e.g., Abelson, 1976) on the processing of information about others.

Cantor and Mischel (1977, 1979a, 1979b) have suggested that people hold well-developed conceptions of certain personality types (such as "extraverts"), which they refer to as "prototypes." A *prototype* consists of a network of traits and behavior patterns characteristic of that type, as well as situations in which that type of person is likely to manifest those behaviors. Cantor and Mischel argue that information acquired about others is coded, structured, and stored in terms of these prototypes, with the consequence that information consistent with a prototype is most likely to be remembered, while information inconsistent with these prior expectations is least likely to be retained. Results from their experiments support this notion. On a free-recall task, subjects recalled more information consistent with the prototype (Cantor & Mischel, 1979b); and on a recognition-memory task, subjects made more errors in the "recognition" of items that were prototypic but that had not been presented (Cantor & Mischel, 1977). Findings similar to these reflecting the role of self-schemata in processing information about oneself have been reported by Markus (1977).

If we recognize that a prototype of, for example, extraverts is conceptually the same as a stereotype of an ethnic group, then the implications of these findings for stereotyping becomes clear. As was true in Cohen's research (1977), the prototype biased the perceiver's cognitive representation of a person in a direction consistent with the prior expectations based on that prototype. As a result, the perceiver has gained subjective "evidence" for the validity of the prototype.

The exact locus of the effects reported in these studies remains unclear. To mention just two of the possibilities cited earlier, stereotypes may bias the encoding process, such that the information that "fits" with the prototypic conception is more likely to enter the cognitive system. This suggests that some information is not being attended to or acquired. Alternatively, it may be that all of the information is registered, but that a stereotype has its primary influence on the retrieval of information—a process that would also bias recall and judgment measures. Of course, both processes may occur.

While most discussions imply the former process (e.g., Duncan, 1976; Zadney & Gerard, 1974), there is also some evidence that the latter bias may also exist. Kanungo and Dutta (Dutta, Kanungo, & Freibergs, 1972; Kanungo & Dutta, 1966) have shown that subjects are more likely to remember desirable information about their own group and undesirable information about an outgroup. They report evidence suggesting that this bias occurs during retrieval of information from memory. In a more direct examination of a retrieval bias, Snyder and Uranowitz (1978) had subjects read an extensive "case history" of a female character named Betty. The case history spanned Betty's childhood, education, and adult career and included material regarding her home life, relations with her parents, social life, and so on. Subjects returned a week later and were given a recognition-memory test on various details of the character description. Before this test was given, half of the subjects were told that Betty was now living a lesbian lifestyle, while the other half were told that she was living a heterosexual lifestyle. This information had a significant effect on subjects' performance on the recognition-memory task. Subjects' memories for the details of Betty's life were biased in the direction consistent with this instruction. Assuming that subjects had differing stereotypic conceptions of lesbian versus heterosexual females, it appeared that subjects reconstructed the information they had received in a manner consistent with the prototype that had been activated prior to this task. This evidence indicates that retrieval processes can be biased in the same manner as the initial processing of information.

Influence of Stereotypes on Processing Information about Groups

The research described in the preceding two sections was concerned with how a stereotype about a particular group could influence a perceiver's cognitive representation of and attributions about individual members of that group. A question of obvious importance for understanding stereotyping concerns how stereotypes influence the cognitive processes involved in making judgments about groups. That is, one might observe or acquire information about a number of individuals who belong to a particular social group. If one has certain stereotypic expectations about that group, does that conception of the group influence the processing of the information about individual group members in such a way that subsequent judgments are biased? The findings of some recent studies suggest an affirmative answer to this question.

Hamilton and Rose (Hamilton, Note 2; Hamilton & Rose, Note 3) have reported evidence bearing on this issue. This work was based on research on illusory correlations in judgment processes, and as such, focused on processes that result in errors in an observer's perception of the degree of relationship between two variables. Hamilton and Rose have investigated the role of associative relationships between variables as a basis for an illusory correlation.

Several studies have shown that subjects tend to overestimate the frequency with which associatively linked stimulus pairs have occurred in a stimulus list (e.g., Chapman, 1967; Chapman & Chapman, 1967, 1969; Tversky & Kahneman, 1973). For example, in a study in which each pair in a series of word pairs was shown to subjects an equal number of times, subjects consistently estimated that pairs having a meaningful or associative relationship (e.g., "bacon-eggs") had occurred more frequently than unrelated pairs (Chapman, 1967). Hamilton and Rose (Note 3) suggest that this pattern is conceptually the same as the effects of stereotypic associations on processing information about members of social groups (see also Hamilton, 1981). That is, if one has acquired the belief that blacks are more likely than whites to be lazy, then information consistent with that expectation is likely to be salient and hence be more available (Tversky & Kahneman, 1973) for recall and therefore influential in judgment processes. Thus, even in the absence of any actual difference between blacks and whites in the extent to which laziness is manifested in their behavior, the perceiver would "see" a relationship between race and this category of behavior.

To investigate this possibility, Hamilton and Rose (Note 3) showed subjects a series of sentences, each of which described a person, identified by first name and occupation, as having two personality attributes; for example, "Sue, a waitress, is attractive and loud." On the basis of pretesting, traits rated as highly descriptive of one occupational group but not of the others included in the sentences could be identified. In one study, the 24 sentences described members of three groups (e.g., librarians, stewardesses, and waitresses). Within the set of sentences, each group occurred eight times, and each of eight traits described a member of each group twice. Thus, in the stimulus materials there were no actual relationships between trait characteristics and group membership. Among the eight trait words, two had been rated as highly characteristic of librarians, two as characteristic of stewardesses, two as characteristic of waitresses, and two as unrelated to any of the three groups. After they had viewed the sentences, subjects were given a questionnaire asking how many times each trait adjective had described each group. The results, shown in Table 2, indicate that stereotypic expectations signifi-

TABLE 2

Mean Frequency Estimates of Occupation-Associated Traits for Each Occupational Group

OCCUPATIONAL GROUP	OCCUPATION-ASSOCIATED TRAITS			
Replication 1: Female Occupations	LIBRARIAN	STEWARDESS	WAITRESS	NONE
Librarians	2.83	2.01	2.39	2.24
Stewardesses	2.13	2.65	2.42	2.08
Waitresses	2.13	2.42	2.81	2.03
Replication 2: Male Occupations	ACCOUNTANT	DOCTOR	SALESMAN	NONE
Accountants	2.50	1.96	2.18	2.44
Doctors	2.29	2.67	2.40	2.11
Salesmen	1.75	1.82	3.07	2.58

cantly influenced these frequency estimates. In this table, the rows represent the three occupational groups, and the columns represent the grouping of adjectives according to their stereotypic association. The data are collapsed across the two traits of each type. The values shown are the mean number of times an adjective of each type was estimated to have described a particular group. The correct answer for every cell in the table is 2.00. Hamilton and Rose's prediction was that the italicized entries would be the largest values in that row and column; that is, that subjects would overestimate the frequency with which stereotypically expected descriptions had occurred. The results provide strong support for this hypothesis.

As noted above, the trait characteristics were totally uncorrelated with group membership in the stimulus sentences used in this study, a situation that probably is rare in "real" social information. Would this bias also be observed if some attributes were in fact related to the group membership variable? To answer this question, Hamilton and Rose (Note 3) conducted a second experiment in which the trait descriptors were correlated with group membership. The findings show that when an attribute describes one group more frequently than another, subjects are much more likely to recognize that relationship if that attribute is consistent with stereotypic expectations than if the trait is unrelated to the group stereotype. Thus, while the preceding study shows that stereotypes can lead a perceiver to "see" a nonexistent relationship, this study indicates that when an actual relationship exists, it will be perceived as stronger if it confirms stereotypic expectations. Finally, results of a third experiment showed that, at least under some conditions, subjects underestmated the frequency with which information incongruent with a group stereotype occurred in a stimulus set, relative to attributes unrelated to the stereotype.

Similar findings have been reported by Rothbart, Evans, and Fulero (1979). Rather than utilizing groups about whom subjects would likely share stereotypic expectancies, Rothbart et al. induced specific expectancies in subjects by telling them that the members of the stimulus group were either "more intellectual than average" or "more friendly and sociable than average." Subjects then read a series of sentences describing members of the group. In the set of sentences, "intelligent" and "friendly" behaviors were equally frequent. Similar to Hamilton and Rose's findings, subjects given the "intelligent" set estimated that more "intelligent" than "friendly" behaviors had described group members, while the opposite pattern was shown by subjects given the "friendly" instructions. In addition, on a free-recall task, subjects were able to remember more sentences congruent with the instruction-based expectations. Thus, this rather simple "set" manipulation resulted in substantial differences in the subjects' conceptions of the group, despite the fact that both groups of subjects read the identical set of descriptive sentences.

Taken together, the findings of these experiments by Hamilton and Rose and by Rothbart et al. clearly reveal the extent to which a group stereotype can bias the processing of information about members of that group. Subjects overestimated the frequency with which the information they received confirmed their stereotypic expectations and underestimated the frequency of occurrence of disconfirming evidence. Thus, as in other studies described earlier, these subjects were "seeing" evidence that would confirm their stereotypes and "not seeing" incongruent information, even when there was no relationship between the pattern of trait descriptions and the group memberships.

An interesting study by Gurwitz and Dodge (1977) indicates that the pattern of confirming and disconfirming information received about group members can influence its impact on stereotypic inferences. Subjects in this experiment learned information about three friends of a target person, about whom they were then asked to make inferences. The four persons were members of a stereotyped group. Some of the information describing the target persons' friends either confirmed or disconfirmed the stereotype, and that information was either distributed across the descriptions of the three friends or was confined to the description of one of the friends. The extent to which subjects made stereotypic attributions about the target person was determined. Confirming evidence increased stereotyping more when it was dispersed across the three descriptions, but disconfirming evidence had greater impact (i.e., reduced stereotypic inferences) when it was concentrated in one of the descriptions. Thus, the pattern of information, as well as its confirming or disconfirming nature, can influence the extent to which perceivers make stereotypic attributions.

Conclusion

This section has summarized research evidence elucidating a number of cognitive biases in our processing of information that result from the stereotypic schemata we hold about significant social groups. In this review of studies concerned with causal attributions, processing information about individuals, and making judgments about groups, evidence has consistently indicated that stereotypic expectations bias the processing and interpretation of information in the direction of confirming those expectations. The consistency of this finding across numerous studies focusing on different processes is impressive and suggests that stereotypic schemata can have powerful and widespread consequences.

Yet, it would be unwise to conclude that information is always bent, folded, and spindled in the direction of schematic confirmation. Behavioral evidence that is not congruent with expectations cannot always be ignored or dismissed; in fact, under some conditions the very incongruency of information with expectancies may increase its salience and hence its impact, resulting in a change in one's cognitive structure.

Such an interpretation was proposed by Hamilton and Bishop (1976) to account for the reactions of white suburban home owners to the integration of their neighborhoods. In this study, residents of white neighborhoods into which a new family (in some cases black, in other cases white) had just moved were interviewed at various times over the course of a year. A variety of attitudinal and behavioral measures obtained from the interviews indicated that an initial negative reaction to new black neighbors changed over time into an acceptance of this family's living in their area and more favorable racial attitudes. Since the extent of actual interracial interaction was unrelated to attitude change, the contact hypothesis could not account for these findings. Hamilton and Bishop (1976) suggested that the observed changes over time were due to a disconfirmation of expectancies:

> This interpretation would hold that white suburban residents oppose the integration of their neighborhoods and expect and fear such integration to have undesirable consequences. Many of their expectations are probably stereotypic in nature and based on widely shared myths—that blacks will not take care of their property, that their yards will be messy, that they pose a threat to personal safety, that their children will be "rough," that property values will decline, etc. Over time, the experience of having black neighbors serves to disconfirm many of these expectations—the appearance of the neighborhood has not changed, physical assault and other forms of violence have not occurred, real estate prices have continued to climb as in similar neighborhoods, etc. The disconfirmation of these negative expectancies thus results in a change in the residents' beliefs about and attitudes towards blacks and towards neighborhood integration. (p. 66)

A pattern of findings based on a variety of dependent measures supported this interpretation.

While the Hamilton and Bishop study (1976) was not concerned with stereotypes per se, its findings are useful in demonstrating that information inconsistent with expectancies can have rather dramatic effects on one's cognitions. Thus, disconfirming evidence will have differing effects, depending on the circumstances. A delineation of the conditions under which we can expect stereotype-incongruent information to have lesser and greater influences on our cognitive representations is an important issue that future research needs to address.

BEHAVIORAL CONSEQUENCES OF STEREOTYPES

The discussion to this point has focused almost exclusively on processes and phenomena that function or reside in the head of the perceiver. In the picture drawn so far, the human being has been portrayed as a busy, if not totally accurate, cognizer of the stimulus world around him or her. Little has been said about interpersonal behavior, yet an issue that obviously is of crucial importance concerns the relationship of these cognitions to real-world behavior. In their enthusiasm for studying the cognitive dynamics which underly the attribution process, social psychologists have perhaps been too willing simply to assume that these cognitive contortions do in fact have behavioral consequences. As a result, cognitive social psychologists have been open to criticism (e.g., Thorngate, 1976), and the reader will note the relative paucity of research described in this, compared to the two preceding sections. Nevertheless, several recent experiments clearly illustrate some processes by which stereotypic attributions are translated into significant behavioral consequences.

The notion that a person's expectancies can unintentionally influence one's behavior is not new and has been the subject of a considerable amount of research in recent years (e.g., Rosenthal, 1966; Rosenthal & Jacobson, 1968). The possibility that expectancies based on racial stereotypes can result in differential behavior toward blacks and whites was investigated by Rubovits and Maehr (1973). They had female undergraduates enrolled in a teacher training course teach a lesson to four junior-high-school students of comparable ability. Immediately prior to the session, each teacher was given a seating chart which provided each student's first name and IQ score and indicated whether the student was from the school's gifted program or from the regular track. Each session included two black and two white students, and one student of each race was randomly assigned a high IQ score and the "gifted" label. During the 40-minute teaching session, an observer coded the teacher's behavior according to several categories of student-teacher interaction. Analyses of these codings indicated that "black students were given less attention, ignored more, praised less, and criticized more" (Rubovits & Maehr, 1973, p. 217). Moreover, these effects were somewhat augmented in the case of the gifted black student. The results of this field experiment provide rather dramatic evidence of the effect of racial cues on interpersonal behavior.

Three recent experiments provide compelling evidence of how stereotypes can be maintained through the self-fulfilling nature of their influence on social interaction. In a study by Word, Zanna, and Cooper (1974), white college students acted as job interviewers, with either black or white confederates as job applicants. They found that the nonverbal behavior of the interviewer/subjects reflected less positive affect and friendliness in the presence of the black than the white confederates. That is, in comparison to the white-confederate condition, subjects interacting with a black applicant maintained greater interpersonal distance, made more speech errors, and terminated the interview sooner. In a follow-up experiment, white confederates were trained to act as interviewers and to reproduce the nonverbal behavior patterns that in the first study had been expressed toward the black and the white applicants. Subjects in this experiment, all of whom were white, played the role of job applicants and were videotaped during the interview sessions. From these videotapes, judges later rated the adequacy of the subject/applicant's performance and composure during the interview. Subjects who received the less positive pattern of nonverbal behavior from the interviewer (as had the black applicants in the first experiment) received significantly lower ratings of both performance and demeanor from the naive judges. Taken together, these experiments nicely demonstrate that the differential nonverbal behavior of whites in the presence of black and white others can produce behavior in those others that results in lower evaluations of the blacks. In other words, the nonverbal behavior of the white interviewer would itself produce reciprocal behavior in the black, which would confirm the white's stereotypic expectancies.

More recently, Snyder, Tanke, and Berscheid (1977) have reported a similar demonstration of the self-fulfilling nature of stereotypes. They had male subjects interact with female target persons in a study purportedly concerned with the acquaintance process. One male and one female subject reported to separate experimental rooms. The male was given a snapshot of either an attractive or an unattractive female and was told that it was a picture of the other subject. In actuality, the same pictures were used throughout the experiment. Consistent with a considerable amount of research showing perceivers assume that "beautiful people are good people" (cf. Berscheid & Walster, 1974), the male subjects given the picture of an attractive female made much more favorable trait ratings of their partner than did those given the picture of an unattractive female. Thus, differing patterns of stereotypic expectations were created by this manipulation. The two subjects then carried on a "get acquainted" conversation over the telephone, during which each participant's voice was separately recorded on a tape recorder. Independent judges, unaware of the hypotheses or manipulations, rated the conversational behavior of the female on a variety of scales. Female targets whom their male partners had been led to believe were physically attractive were rated as having manifested more animation, confidence, and enjoyment in their conversation and greater liking for their male partners than did women whose perceivers believed they were unattractive. They were also rated as more sociable, poised, sexually warm, and outgoing than were the targets whose male partners perceived them to be unattractive. Thus the females behaved in such a way that would confirm the artificially induced expectations of their male partners. Subsequent analyses suggested that the males' expectations about their partners (based on physical-attractiveness stereotypes) influenced their own behavior (i.e., males who thought they were talking with an attractive female were more animated, sociable, etc.), and that this in turn produced in the targets the very behaviors that would be expected from the males' stereotypic conceptions.

A somewhat different self-fulfilling mechanism has been demonstrated by

Zanna and Pack (1975). In this experiment, female subjects expected to inter-act with a male subject in a study of impression formation. From information provided about their partner, subjects were led to believe that he would be either desirable or undesirable as a potential date, and that he held either a traditional or a nontraditional stereotype of the "ideal woman." On both atti-tudinal and behavioral indicators of self-presentation, when the partner was desirable, subjects portrayed themselves as being conventional or unconven-tional with regard to sex roles, depending on whether the males' stereotype of women was traditional or not. Thus, as in the Word et al. (1974) and Snyder et al. (1977) studies, the behavior of one person has been indirectly influenced in such a way as to confirm a stereotype held by another person.

There is, however, a difference between Zanna and Pack's and the two previous demonstrations of the self-fulfilling nature of social stereotypes. In the Word et al. and Snyder et al. experiments, the stereotype holder's expec-tations presumably influenced his own behavior, which in turn created the stereotype-confirming behavior in the target person. In contrast, subjects in the Zanna and Pack (1975) study modified their own behavior in accordance with their perceptions of the stereotypic beliefs of a valued other.

Of course, it is not always the case that a person's expectancies will bring about confirming behavior in another person. There are instances when an-other's behavior clearly violates our stereotypic beliefs. How the perceiver re-acts in these circumstances has not been extensively investigated. Earlier this author suggested that disconfirmation of stereotypic expectancies might, under some conditions, result in a revision of one's beliefs (Gurwitz & Dodge, 1977; Hamilton & Bishop, 1976). A quite different possibility is suggested by the research of Costrich, Feinstein, Kidder, Marecek, and Pascale (1975). They report a series of three experiments in which subjects interacted with, listened to a tape of, or read about a male or a female stimulus person who acted in a passive or an aggressive manner. They reasoned that the passive male and the aggressive female represented instances of sex-role reversals and hence violated the stereotypic expectancies of the subjects. Costrich et al. (1975) report evidence showing that these stimulus persons were liked less, judged less popular, and rated as more likely to need therapeutic help than those whose behavior conformed to sex-role stereotypes. Thus, the person whose behavior does not "fit" into well-established, and therefore expected, patterns can receive rather harsh judgment from the typical perceiver.

The studies summarized in this section have shown that stereotypic beliefs can have an effect on social interaction in several ways. Stereotypic expecta-tions can influence the perceiver's own behavior toward a member of the stereotyped group (Rubovits & Maehr, 1973; Snyder et al., 1977; Word et al., 1974); that behavior, which has been affected by stereotypic beliefs, can have an influence on the nature of the behavior manifested by the target person (Snyder et al., 1977; Word et al., 1974); and the target's behavior can be modified by his or her perception of the stereotypic expectations held by the perceiver (Zanna & Pack, 1975). Finally, one's stereotypes, when used as a basis for judging others, can result in negative evaluations of one who manifests counterstereotypic behavior (Costrich et al., 1975).

SUMMARY

The cognitive-attributional analysis of stereotyping presented in this chapter has revealed the significant role of cognitive mechanisms at several possible points in the overall attribution process. We have seen that stereotypes, as cognitive schemata, can influence the encoding, interpretation, retention, and retrieval of subsequently obtained information about members of stereotyped groups, as well as the perceiver's causal attributions regarding the target person's behavior. The cognitive biases evidenced in these processes were consistently of such a nature that the perceiver would "see" evidence that confirmed his or her stereotypic expectations, even in the total absence of such confirming evidence. And finally, we have seen that the perceiver's stereotypic conceptions of another person can bring about behavior in the other that in fact confirms his expectations based on that stereotype.

One of the primary characteristics of stereotypes is their rigidity, persistence over time, and resistance to change (Ashmore & Del Boca, 1981; Brigham, 1971). As construed from the psychodynamic perspective, this rigidity can be understood in terms of the functional value of the stereotypic beliefs for the perceiver. To the extent that they provide gratification for unconscious needs or reflect the ego-defensive processing of the perceiver, they are likely to be highly resistant to change. According to the sociocultural approach this persistence is understood in terms of the cultural basis of the stereotypic beliefs. As long as the stereotype remains a part of the person's culture or subculture, the individual is reinforced for holding those beliefs. Since cultural mores are slow in changing, it is not surprising that stereotypes are so stable.

The cognitive orientation presented in this chapter provides a new perspective for understanding why stereotypes are so persistent over time and resistant to change. Throughout this chapter, a number of cognitive biases that have bearing on the stereotyping process have been discussed. In virtually every case the nature of these biases has been such that their effect is to maintain the stereotypic belief; that is, the perceiver "sees" or creates evidence that seemingly indicates that the stereotypic schema employed is indeed useful and appropriate. Thus, use of the stereotype serves to reinforce its apparent usefulness. A stereotype's persistence, then, is a natural consequence of the biases inherent in its employment.

The cognitive viewpoint is a functional viewpoint. That is, the cognitive mechanisms we use continue to be employed because, in some sense, they work. The biases discussed here help to reduce the complexity of a stimulus world that may otherwise be overwhelming and hence are in many circumstances quite adaptive. Recognition of this fact presents a rather depressing dilemma: If these biases are so functionally useful in the sense just noted, how will we be able to change them in those instances when they have undesirable consequences, as in stereotyping? A cognitive mechanism that in general has adaptive value would seem to be extremely resistant to change. This is an obviously important issue for which there is no answer at present. The major reason for our inability to address this question lies, this author believes, in the newness of this field of research. The development of social cognition as an area of investigation has, to this point, focused on demonstrations of the kind of biases that characterize us as information processors. One of the primary challenges facing researchers in this field is the question of how these biases can be altered or modified in those cases where they yield consequences that reduce, rather than facilitate, our effectiveness as social beings. It may be hoped that this question will receive the research attention it warrants in the near future.

NOTES

[1]There is, unfortunately, a serious problem in the interpretation of these findings. It is difficult to guarantee that the behaviors portrayed in different stimulus tapes are equivalent in all important respects. The possibility remains, for example, that the "shove" given by the white actors was in fact more timid than that given by the black actors. In that case, the subjects' judgments might simply reflect actual behavior differences. To assure that the results are due to interpretational processes, evidence that the crucial behaviors were equivalent in all stimulus tapes is essential. Since none is provided, these results provide only tentative support for the hypothesis.

REFERENCE NOTES

1. Cohen, C. *Cognitive basis of stereotyping*. Paper presented at the meeting of the American Psychological Association, San Francisco, August 1977.
2. Hamilton, D. L. *Illusory correlation as a basis for social stereotypes*. Paper presented at the meeting of the American Psychological Association, San Francisco, August 1977.
3. Hamilton, D. L., & Rose, T. *Illusory correlation and the maintenance of stereotypic beliefs*. Unpublished manuscript, University of California at Santa Barbara, 1978.

REFERENCES

Abelson, R. P. Script processing in attitude formation and decision making. In J. S. Carroll & J. W. Payne (Eds.), *Cognition and social behavior*. Hillsdale, N.J.: Erlbaum, 1976.
Ashmore, R. D., & Del Boca, F. K. Psychological approaches to understanding intergroup conflict. In P. A. Katz (Eds.), *Towards the elimination of racism*. New York: Pergamon, 1976.

Ashmore, R. D., & Del Boca, F. K. Conceptual approaches to stereotypes and stereotyping. In D. L. Hamilton (Ed.), *Cognitive processes in stereotyping and intergroup behavior.* Hillsdale, N.J.: Erlbaum, 1981.

Bartlett, F. C. *Remembering.* Cambridge, England: Cambridge University Press, 1932.

Berscheid, E., & Walster, E. Physical attractiveness. In L. Berkowitz (Ed.), *Advances in experimental social psychology* (Vol. 7). New York: Academic Press, 1974.

Brigham, J. C. Ethnic stereotypes. *Psychological Bulletin,* 1971, *76,* 15–38.

Cantor, N., & Mischel, W. Traits as prototypes: Effects on recognition memory. *Journal of Personality and Social Psychology,* 1977, *35,* 38–48.

Cantor, N., & Mischel, W. Prototypes in person perception. In L. Berkowitz (Ed.), *Advances in experimental social psychology* (Vol. 12). New York: Academic Press, 1979. (a)

Cantor, N., & Mischel, W. Prototypicality and personality: Effects on free recall and personality impressions. *Journal of Research in Personality,* 1979, *13,* 187–205. (b)

Chapman, L. J. Illusory correlation in observational report. *Journal of Verbal Learning and Verbal Behavior,* 1967, *6,* 151–155.

Chapman, L. J., & Chapman, J. P. Genesis of popular but erroneous psychodiagnostic observations. *Journal of Abnormal Psychology,* 1967, *72,* 193–204.

Chapman, L. J., & Chapman, J. P. Illusory correlation as an obstacle to the use of valid psychodiagnostic signs. *Journal of Abnormal Psychology,* 1969, *74,* 271–280.

Costrich, N., Feintein, J., Kidder, L., Maracek, J., & Pascale, L. When stereotypes hurt: Three studies of penalties for sex-role reversals. *Journal of Experimental Social Psychology,* 1975, *11,* 520–530.

Deaux, K. Sex: A perspective on the attribution process. In J. H. Harvey, W. J. Ickes, & R. F. Kidd (Eds.), *New directions in attribution research* (Vol. 1). Hillsdale, N.J.: Erlbaum, 1976.

Deaux, K., & Emswiller, T. Explanation of successful performance on sex-linked tasks: What is skill for the male is luck for the female. *Journal of Personality and Social Psychology,* 1974, *29,* 80–85.

Duncan, B. L. Differential social perception and attribution of intergroup violence: Testing the lower limits of stereotyping of blacks. *Journal of Personality and Social Psychology,* 1976, *34,* 590–598.

Dutta, S., Kanungo, R. N., & Freibergs, V. Retention of affective material: Effects of intensity of affect on retrieval. *Journal of Personality and Social Psychology,* 1972, *23,* 64–80.

Feldman-Summers, S., & Kiesler, S. B. Those who are number two try harder: The effect of sex on attributions of causality. *Journal of Personality and Social Psychology,* 1974, *30,* 846–855.

Gurwitz, S. B., & Dodge, K. A. Effects of confirmations and disconfirmations on stereotype-based attributions. *Journal of Personality and Social Psychology,* 1977, *35,* 495–500.

Hamilton, D. L. The role of illusory correlation in the development and maintenance of stereotypes. In D. L. Hamilton (Ed.), *Cognitive processes in stereotyping and intergroup behavior.* Hillsdale, N.J.: Erlbaum, 1981.

Hamilton, D. L., & Bishop, G. D. Attitudinal and behavioral effects of initial integration of white suburban neighborhoods. *Journal of Social Issues,* 1976, *32*(2), 47–67.

Heider, F. *The psychology of interpersonal relations.* New York: Wiley, 1958.

Jones, E. E., & Davis, K. E. From acts to dispositions: The attribution process in person perception. In L. Berkowitz (Ed.), *Advances in experimental social psychology* (Vol. 2). New York: Academic Press, 1965.

Jones, E. E., Davis, K. E., & Gergen, K. J. Role playing variations and their informational value for person perception. *Journal of Abnormal and Social Psychology,* 1961, *63,* 302–310.

Jones, E. E., & Harris, V. A. The attribution of attitudes. *Journal of Experimental Social Psychology,* 1967, *3,* 1–24.

Jones, E. E., & McGillis, D. Correspondent inferences and the attribution cube: A comparative reappraisal. In J. H. Harvey, W. J. Ickes, & R. F. Kidd (Eds.), *New directions in attribu-*

tion research (Vol. 1). Hillsdale, N.J.: Erlbaum, 1976.

Jones, E. E., & Nisbett, R. E. The actor and the observer: Divergent perceptions of the causes of behavior. In E. E. Jones, D. E. Kanouse, H. H. Kelley, R. E. Nisbett, S. Valins, & B. Weiner (Eds.), *Attribution: Perceiving the causes of behavior.* Morristown, N.J.: General Learning Press, 1972.

Kanungo, R. N., & Dutta, S. Retention of affective material: Frame of reference or intensity? *Journal of Personality and Social Psychology,* 1966, *4,* 27–35.

Kelley, H. H. Attribution theory in social psychology. In D. Levine (Ed.), *Nebraska Symposium on Motivation* (Vol. 15). Lincoln: University of Nebraska Press, 1967.

Kelley, H. H. Causal schemata and the attribution process. In E. E. Jones, D. E. Kanouse, H. H. Kelley, R. E. Nisbett, S. Valins, & B. Weiner (Eds.), *Attribution: Perceiving the causes of behavior.* Morristown, N.J.: General Learning Press, 1972.

Markus, H. Self-schemata and processing information about the self. *Journal of Personality and Social Psychology,* 1977, *35,* 63–78.

Rosenthal, R. *Experimenter effects in behavioral research.* New York: Appleton-Century-Crofts, 1966.

Rosenthal, R., & Jacobson, L. *Pygmalion in the classroom: Teacher expectation and pupils' intellectual development.* New York: Holt, Rinehart & Winston, 1968.

Rothbart, M., Evans, M., & Fulero, S. Recall for confirming events: Memory processes and the maintenance of social stereotypes. *Journal of Experimental Social Psychology,* 1979, *15,* 343–355.

Rubovits, P. C., & Maehr, M. L. Pygmalion black and white. *Journal of Personality and Social Psychology,* 1973, *25,* 210–218.

Schneider, D. J. Implicit personality theory: A review. *Psychological Bulletin,* 1973, *79,* 294–309.

Snyder, M., Tanke, E. D., & Berscheid, E. Social perception and interpersonal behavior: On the self-fulfilling nature of social stereotypes. *Journal of Personality and Social Psychology,* 1977, *35,* 656–666.

Snyder, M., & Uranowitz, S. Reconstructing the past: Some cognitive consequences of person perception. *Journal of Personality and Social Psychology,* 1978, *36,* 941–950.

Taylor, D. M., & Jaggi, V. Ethnocentrism and causal attribution in a South Indian context. *Journal of Cross-Cultural Psychology,* 1974, *5,* 162–171.

Taylor, S. E., & Crocker, J. Schematic bases of social information processing. In E. T. Higgins, C. P. Herman, & M. P. Zanna (Eds.), *Social cognition: The Ontario Symposium on Personality and Social Psychology* (Vol. 1). Hillsdale, N.J.: Erlbaum, 1981.

Taylor, S. E., & Fiske, S. T. Point of view and perceptions of causality. *Journal of Personality and Social Psychology,* 1975, *32,* 439–445.

Thorngate, W. Must we always think before we act? *Personality and Social Psychology Bulletin,* 1976, *2,* 31–35.

Tversky, A., & Kahneman, D. Availability: A heuristic for judging frequency and probability. *Cognitive Psychology,* 1973, *5,* 207–232.

Weiner, B., Frieze, I., Kukla, A., Reed, L., Rest, S., & Rosenbaum, R. M. Perceiving the causes of success and failure. In E. E. Jones, D. E. Kanouse, H. H. Kelley, R. E. Nisbett, S. Valins, & B. Weiner (Eds.), *Attribution: Perceiving the causes of behavior.* Morristown, N.J.: General Learning Press, 1972.

Word, C. O., Zanna, M. P., & Cooper, J. The nonverbal mediation of self-fulfilling prophecies in interracial interaction. *Journal of Experimental Social Psychology,* 1974, *10,* 109–120.

Zadney, J., & Gerard, H. B. Attributed intentions and informational selectivity. *Journal of Experimental Social Psychology,* 1974, *10,* 34–52.

Zanna, M. P., & Pack, S. J. On the self-fulfilling nature of apparent sex differences in behavior. *Journal of Experimental Social Psychology,* 1975, *11,* 583–591.

III Research on Bias in Therapy

Chapter 6, the first chapter in Section III, presents a large-scale study that examined how a great number of variables might be related to sex bias in psychotherapy as conducted by psychologists, psychiatrists, and social workers. Murray and Abramson first discuss how socialization and other factors might lead to the occurrence of gender bias in psychotherapy. Next they review the methodological problems in the existing research literature in the area. They then describe a study designed to correct many of these methodological problems. The occurrence of sex bias—treating a male client differently from a female client solely because of his or her sex—in numerous dimensions of the psychotherapy process was investigated in this study through the use of a number of specific dependent measures, many of which would be expected to be related to sex roles. A number of moderator variables were also examined, including the patient's physical attractiveness and various characteristics of the therapist. Many possible interactions were considered.

In this comprehensive research, significant differences in therapists' judgments were found for both client and therapist variables. The client characteristics of gender and attractiveness had significant effects (both alone and in combination), some of which were related to sex roles. The therapist characteristics of gender, regional location in the United States, profession, orientation, and age all had significant effects on the therapists' judgments about the client and the client's prospective therapy. It seems clear that such influential factors need to be considered in future research in this area. Of particular interest was the finding that more complete care was recommended for attractive clients.

Davidson believes that the sex bias paradigm has "conceptual limitations" and makes a case for replacing it with a "more productive conceptual framework." She proposes in Chapter 7 that such a framework could be provided by the construct of countertransference, which would allow researchers to deal with therapists' dynamics.

She reviews the literature on sex bias and concludes that the evidence yields equivocal conclusions. This situation exists because the researchers were often politically motivated and therefore not objective. She then traces the development of the concept of countertransference, a concept that she feels could be used to resolve the stalemate in the area of sex bias in therapy. Whereas the sex bias construct is not capable of "moving beyond the surface structure of overt social attitudes," the countertransference concept would allow researchers to go further, into the therapist's personal history and interpersonal dynamics. How countertransference has been and could be operationalized in research on gender effects in psychotherapy is discussed.

Chapter 8, Stricker and Shafran's comprehensive review of research on gender bias in psychotherapy, encompasses three areas of empirical investigation—sex-role stereotyping, gender effects in psychotherapy, and patient attitudes and preferences. The authors make a distinction between biased attitudes and biased behavior, and effectively make the point that gender bias is not "monolithic" but must be considered in relation to variables besides client gender (e.g., therapist experience). They urge researchers to consider the patient's contribution to gender bias, arguing that because patients have differential expectations of male and female therapists, they may behave differently in therapy with different-sex therapists.

Definitive conclusions about the nature and extent of gender bias in psychotherapy are viewed as premature. Future research is required—research that examines the complex interactions between various patient and client characteristics.

In discussing race bias in psychotherapy, Abramowitz and Murray focus in Chapter 9 on the case of blacks because this particular group has been studied more than any other. They review research on three aspects of racial bias: (1) bias in diagnosis; (2) bias in treatment allocation and utilization; and (3) bias in process and outcome (effectiveness). These investigations have employed two paradigms, the archival records search (a naturalistic method) and the analogue (an experimental method).

Studies of diagnostic bias have produced inconsistent results, with the analogue studies not finding racial bias and the naturalistic studies finding some bias. As for allocation and utilization, whether racial bias exists is still open to question. The case for race bias in outcome is weak, but some differences in process have been found.

Overall, the authors feel that the empirical evidence has generally been negative, with findings of some subtle and circumscribed racial effects. But they caution us that these conclusions are based on research fraught with methodological problems. The analogue paradigm has several serious weaknesses, most noteworthy of which is a tendency to bias the research toward a finding of no race effect. Field research, too, has weaknesses that would lead to retaining the hypothesis of no race effects. Thus, many studies have been biased against finding any racial bias that does exist.

In Chapter 10, Schover reports an interesting investigation of bias in therapists' responses to sexual material from clients. An audiotape of a male or female client either describing a mild sexual dysfunction or being seductive toward the therapist was played for the male and female therapist/subjects. These psychiatrists, psychologists, and social workers were also shown a photograph and case history of the "client" on the tape. While listening to the tape, the subjects responded by saying what they would say to the client. Afterwards, they filled out rating scales and information about themselves.

Many differences emerged. Several important differences between male and female therapists were found; for example, women used more reflections and were less affected by the client's gender. Interestingly, male therapists rated a nonorgasmic female client as most disturbed, while female therapists rated her as least disturbed. Only male therapists reported any sexual arousal, and those who reported sexual arousal made more verbal approach responses. The seductive clients made the therapists more uncomfortable and anxious than the dysfunction cases did. Therapist profession was also a good predictor of verbal behavior, emotional reactions, and clinical judgments.

Therapists (mainly male ones) made two types of errors in responding to the client's sexual material—voyeuristic responses, and anxious responses encouraging the client to change the subject. There was also some evidence of homophobia, especially in male therapists.

Schover concludes that there is significant bias in therapists' current practices regarding sexuality and discusses implications for training.

Chapter 11 concerns erotic contact between patient and therapist—"perhaps the quintessence of sex-biased therapeutic practice." Evidence that other forms of sex bias actually occur in therapy may not be conclusive, but evidence of this particular form of sex bias is definitely so. Holroyd discusses erotic contact between patient and therapist at length, examining such issues as the frequency of such contact, the proper role for sex therapists, why some therapists have sex with their patients, how the patients are affected, what can be done to prevent the occurrence of such contact, and what remedies are available. She concludes that sex between patient and therapist occurs "when therapists who have mental and emotional problems also have sexist values."

Finally, in Chapter 12, Morin and Charles present a thought-provoking piece on a different type of bias—heterosexual bias, the belief that heterosexuality is somehow better than homosexuality. They discuss heterosexual bias in theory and practice, describe a cognitive-developmental approach to sex-role socialization in lesbians and gay men, and describe a bias-free approach to psychotherapy for these groups. In such a bias-free approach, the goals of the therapy must be the client's goals, not the therapist's; and the language of the therapist must be free of heterosexual bias, which can occur through connotation, inference, contiguity, and omission.

The authors conclude with some guidelines for mental health professionals working with lesbian and gay male clients.

6 An Investigation of the Effects of Client Gender and Attractiveness on Psychotherapists' Judgments

JOAN MURRAY AND
PAUL R. ABRAMSON

As psychotherapists, we know that we do not react to all clients in the same way. Even with our extensive training, we are still human beings and products of our culture. Because we are feeling human beings, we can be affected by a client's appearance, particularly by his or her physical attractiveness. It would be unfair to expect that a therapist meeting a client for the first time should have no reaction when he sees that the client is a beautiful, shapely 25-year-old woman, or she sees that the client is a handsome, well-built 25-year-old man.

Because we have grown up in and been socialized into a culture that views men and women differently, we are likely to have different expectations of men than we do of women. Given that most of us were raised with a traditional view of men and women, it would be unrealistic to expect that a therapist view men and women in just the same way. It would not be surprising if a therapist meeting a client for the first time, knowing little or nothing about that person, were to have traditional expectations about that client. For instance, a therapist might expect a male client to be more concerned about career problems than a female client would be, or a female client to be more concerned about social life or family problems than a male client would be.

129

There is nothing surprising or wrong in this. Traditionally, the husband in a family has been the breadwinner and has carried sole responsibility for earning money, while the wife has had the major responsibility for taking care of the home and raising the children. Even today, many families are still organized in this way.

WHAT'S THE PROBLEM?

However, when a client's physical appearance or gender influences the course of that client's therapy, then there is a problem. This is not to say that a man cannot or should not be concerned about his career or a woman about her children, but that a therapist should not *assume* that because a man *is* a man he therefore will be—or should be—concerned about his career and not his children, or because a woman *is* a woman she therefore will be— or should be—concerned about her children and not her career. Each client should be viewed as an individual, not simply as a member of the male or female gender.

Many writers have expressed concern that some therapists may be overly influenced by a client's gender, perceiving a client as having the characteristics traditional for his or her sex, and so may overlook other relevant information about the individual (Chesler, 1971; Howard & Howard, 1974; Kirsh, 1974; Pollock, 1972; Steiner, 1971). In addition, some have claimed that therapists apply different standards of mental health to males and females—standards paralleling traditional sex roles. The practical consequence of this concern is that if therapists define healthy males and females differently, then the selection of goals for individual clients may vary *solely* or largely on the basis of gender, with more relevant and individual considerations being ignored. For instance, a therapist might decide what areas to focus on in therapy according to expected role behavior, which in our culture emphasizes work for men and social relationships for women. Specifically, faced with a male client who presents with both career problems and social problems, the therapist might emphasize solving the career problems in his therapy; however, faced with a female client with both of these problems, the therapist might emphasize the social problems in her therapy. It is the possibility of such gender bias that is a major concern of the present investigation. For, if gender per se in any way determines the course of a client's therapy, such a process needs to be brought to light, examined, and, where necessary, modified.

There are numerous reasons why gender bias might enter into therapeutic judgments.[1] Primary are the strong, clear-cut, and widely shared role demands placed on women. A woman is expected to be first and foremost a wife and mother, with any activities outside the home being of only secondary significance (Keller, 1974; Russo, 1976). This female sex role is buttressed by religion, family, peers, teachers, the mass media, textbooks, and even elementary-school books—where working mothers are rarely found (Bem & Bem, 1970; Bernard, 1974; Women on Words and Images, 1972).

Many influential psychological theories—especially psychoanalytic theory (Freud, Rheingold, Horney, Deutsch, Erikson, Fine)—and the therapies derived from them have incorporated the traditional conception of women and have equated *normality* with conforming to the female sex role. From this perspective, motherhood is given central importance in the lives of women, and women who do want children are seen as deviant (Bernard, 1974). Furthermore, the psychoanalytic perspective encourages a double standard of mental health, since women are viewed as passive and as needing to be dominated by men.[2] Although these psychoanalytic notions lack an empirical basis and have been modified by some contemporary theorists, they have remained very influential in currently practiced psychotherapy. In addition, therapist training rarely includes any discussion of gender bias that might counteract the combined effects of society and theory.

Considering the strong and clear role demands placed on women, as well as the traditional view of women taken in psychological theories, one would expect individuals in our society—including psychotherapists—to have strong, definite, and traditional expectations about what women should be like. These traditional expectations are spelled out in the content of the stereotype of women, who are generally seen as socially skillful but lacking in the skills necessary to be competent in dealing with the environment, compared to men (who, conversely, are seen as active, rational, and competent) (Clifton, McGrath, & Wick, 1976; McKee & Sherriffs, 1959; Rosenkrantz, Vogel, Bee, Broverman, & Broverman, 1968). Such beliefs are widely held in our society (Broverman, Vogel, Broverman, Clarkson, & Rosenkrantz, 1972), and there is some direct evidence that therapists share the sex-role stereotypes (Drapkin & Ansel, Note 1). Moreover, therapists might remember stereotypic characteristics of a woman client more than other characteristics. Hamilton (Note 2) has shown that individuals recall traits that are consistent with their prior expectations more than other traits—especially if those traits confirm a stereotype.[3]

A more circumscribed area where gender bias may exist is in the judgment of whether a certain physical symptom is psychogenic or has an organic basis. One aspect of sex-role stereotypes is the expectation that women tend to have emotional illnesses, whereas men tend to have organic ones (Prather & Fidell, 1975). Two empirical analyses of drug advertisements in medical journals document the existence of such expectations. Mant and Darroch (1975) report a sex difference in the perceived legitimacy of the complaint (i.e., men's illnesses are shown as more legitimate than are women's illnesses). Similarly, Prather and Fidell (1975) find that men's problems are treated more seriously than women's problems are. Women tend to be portrayed as emotional, irrational, and complaining in the advertisements, while men are portrayed as nonemotional, rational, and stoic. In addition, Prather and Fidell quote a Department of Health, Education and Welfare report: "Physicians may be more likely to dismiss women's symptoms as neurotic or as 'normal' female problems" (p. 24). If physicians and/or therapists do dismiss women's symptoms because of sex-role expectations, the result could be severe consequences for those women who have organic problems that are continuously overlooked or made light of by the medical profession. Because of the importance of this issue, the present study includes an investigation of whether a physical symptom is viewed as organic versus psychogenic on the basis of gender.

The question of the existence of gender bias in psychotherapy has been directly addressed through a variety of research strategies. A number of investigators have reported evidence that therapists employ a double standard of mental health (i.e., one standard for males and another for females). Neulinger (1968), Broverman, Broverman, Clarkson, Rosenkrantz, and Vogel (1970), Cowan (Note 3), and Gomberg (1974) have provided such evidence for adults; Feinblatt and Gold (1976) have done the same for children. Moreover, therapists' standards of health tend to parallel sex-role stereotypes.

Some evidence that therapists actually treat men and women differently does exist. There is evidence that male therapists tend to show sexual curiosity toward women clients in various ways—from emphasizing sexual themes in testing to having sexual relationships with female clients (Asher, 1975; Holroyd & Brodsky, 1977; Kardener, Fuller, & Mensh, 1973; Masling & Harris, 1969; Perry, 1976). Specific verbal reactions to clients have also been found to vary with the client's gender (C. Hill, 1975).

However, two studies examining professional services received by clients (Hollingshead & Redlich, 1958; Sue, 1976); three studies assessing whether women are evaluated as less healthy than men (S. I. Abramowitz & C. V. Abramowitz, 1973; S. I. Abramowitz, Abramowitz, Jackson, & Gomes, 1973; S. I. Abramowitz, Abramowitz, Roback, Corney, & McKee, 1976; Zeldow, 1975); and a few studies investigating whether therapists foster traditional sex roles (C. V. Abramowitz, in press; C. V. Abramowitz, Abramowitz, Weitz, & Tittler, 1976; Billingsley, 1977; Gomes & Abramowitz, 1976) have not reported clear-cut differences as a function of gender. Yet this research is so fraught with methodological problems that no conclusions can be drawn from it at this time.[4]

METHODOLOGICAL PROBLEMS IN THE EXPERIMENTAL LITERATURE ON GENDER BIAS IN THERAPY

Investigations of differential treatment of men and women in therapy often employ procedures that are biased against finding an effect of gender. One continued limitation of the methodologies used in this research is that they are subject to social desirability effects. That is, the experimenter's concern with sex effects is so obvious (through, for example, inclusion of a traditionalism scale in the experimental materials) that the therapist/subject is aware of the purpose of the study and therefore likely to respond in a manner that obscures the very effects that are being investigated. Gender effects may also be hidden by designs in which client pathology is clearly defined in the case materials given to the subjects, and/or hints as to the appropriate responses to the dependent measures are given in the materials. In both cases, the therapists' responses are likely to be completely determined by the information given, and the subjects do not need to invoke sex and sex-role expectations to make the required judgments. Studies have also been subject to bias because of their use nonrepresentative samples, which may be skewed to the nontraditional. Samples have typically been small and/or regional and/or made up of inexperienced practitioners. In addition, investigations where subjects are led to consider extremes of behavior or where the design omits a crucial cell are similarly inconclusive.

A most serious, and very prevalent, methodological bias toward the finding of no gender effect is the use of broad, general dependent measures—for example, having therapists rate "social adjustment" or "emotional maturity." Studies employing such measures do not provide a fair test of whether gender bias exists in psychotherapeutic practice, because these dependent variables are not tied to sex-role expectations. If more specific measures that were related to sex roles were employed, a more fair test of whether sex effects exist would result. In fact, Coie, Pennington, and Buckley (1974) employed specific sex-role-related measures and found strong evidence of sex effects. They varied both types of stress (related to career or social life) and the type of reaction to that stress (aggressive behavior or somatic complaints) and were able to show that these interacted with client sex, and did so in a manner suggesting a strong influence of sex-role expectations on the judgments made. However, since the subjects were college students, the implications of this work for actual therapeutic practice are not known.

THE PRESENT RESEARCH

The present research investigates the effects of gender and attractiveness on therapists' judgments about a prospective client. In doing so, an attempt has been made to avoid the methodological problems enumerated above. First, the present research minimized social desirability effects, through veiling the true purpose of the study. Second, the experimental design presented the client's problems and had the subjects respond to them in ways that allowed the detection of the influence of sex-role expectations. At the same time, hints as to what responses were appropriate were now avoided. The sample was representative, including male and female therapists; psychiatrists, psychologists, and social workers; and subjects from various geographic regions of the United States. The factors of therapist gender, profession, and geographical location were crossed so that any interactions between them could be detected. Subjects were not led to consider extremes of behavior, and all relevant cells were included in the design.

Most important, the dependent measures used were both specific and related to sex-role expectations. At the same time, the questionnaire given to the clinician/subjects requested the kind of judgments that a therapist would be likely to make during an initial interview. It explored such questions as these: Do therapists evaluate mental health according to different standards for the two genders? Does gender affect specific aspects of the treatment—(1) type of treatment, frequency of sessions, length of treatment; (2) determination of whether a physical symptom is psychogenic or organic; (3) choice of what problem areas (role-related vs. non-role-related) to emphasize in the therapy; (4) a therapist's personal reaction to a client (perceived effectiveness, interest)? Even though such therapist variables as age and professional discipline have not been found to be related to gender effects, they were included here because the dependent measures in previous research may have been too insensitive to show such effects.

In addition, the present investigation examined the effects of physical attractiveness on therapists' judgments and the interactions of physical attractiveness with other factors, such as client's gender. Physical attractiveness has generally been neglected in research on gender bias in therapy. Yet it may be a mediator of gender effects, as well as an influence in itself. Physical attractiveness has been found to be a powerful determinant of impressions. There is plentiful evidence that physical attractiveness is associated with positive expectations and evaluations (Bar-Tal & Saxe, 1976) and with positive traits (Dion, Berscheid, & Walster, 1972; Miller, 1970). It seems that in many situations impressions are formed according to a principle of "what is beautiful is good" (Dion et al., 1972). Of great import is the finding that physical attractiveness may even influence decisions about an individual, specifically jury decisions. Leventhal and Kratt (1977) report that attractive defendants are assigned shorter sentences than are unattractive ones by college students. Similarly, the attractive plaintiff was favored by jurors over the unattractive one in a simulated personal damage suit (Stephan & Tully, 1977).

Some noteworthy findings further specify the influence of physical attractiveness. Bar-Tal and Saxe (1976) conclude that attractiveness is more important in the evaluation of females than in the evaluation of males, and speculate that for females—but not for males—physical attractiveness functions as an indicator of successful role fulfillment. M. Hill and Lando (1976) find that attractiveness is more salient for females than for males, both in trait ratings and in the prediction of performance. Miller (1970) reports that the less attractive a person is, the more that person's sex influences impressions of him or her. So it might be found that attractiveness enters into therapists' judgments of females more than into their judgments of males, and that sex-role appropriateness affect therapists' judgments only when clients are relatively physically unattractive.

A number of psychotherapy studies that have included the attractiveness variable have reported effects of attractiveness on therapists' judgments. Based on an investigation of a large and representative sample of practicing psychiatrists, psychologists, and social workers, Schofield (1964) concluded that clients were preferred if they presented the "YAVIS" syndrome—young, *attractive,* verbal, intelligent, and successful (italics are the present authors'). In a doctoral dissertation, Sandler (1976) reported effects of client attractiveness on therapists' judgments about the client's intellectual functioning, and, among subgroups of therapists, about a number of other client factors. Similarly, Barocas and Vance (1974) found that counselor ratings of attractiveness covaried in significant ways with clinical status ratings, especially for women clients. However, this study was inconclusive because it used therapists' judgments of their own clients. This procedure introduced a possible confound—attractive clients may have, in reality, differed from unattractive clients. A greater effect of attractiveness for females than for males was also discovered in a study by Hobfoll and Penner (1978). Clinical graduate students rated attractive women as having better self-concepts than unattractive women, attractive men, and unattractive men when they watched a videotape of the stimulus person. Also, Schwartz and Abramowitz (reported in C. V. Abramowitz & Dokecki, 1977) found that when male clinical and counseling graduate-student trainees observed a videotaped patient/actress, they regarded her as more likely to terminate therapy prematurely and made fewer relationship-building responses when she was made up to appear unattractive than when she was made up to appear attractive. The results of these studies suggest that therapists take a more positive view of attractive clients, especially in the case of women, and prefer to work with clients who are attractive. Such findings are consistent with the work on impression formation.

Method

Subjects

Questionnaires were mailed to 971 psychotherapists—322 psychiatrists, 325 psychologists, and 324 social workers—randomly selected from the directories of the American Psychiatric Association (1973), the American Psychological Association (1975), and the National Association of

Social Workers (1972). Only individuals who listed clinical practice as a main interest were selected. Subjects were sampled within each of the three professions and within each of the four major geographical regions of the United States—West, Midwest, South, and Northeast. Approximately one-fourth of the subjects in each profession resided in each of the four geographical areas.

A total of 397 therapists filled and returned usable questionnaires. Taking into account the number of questionnaires that were undeliverable ($n = 221$), the response rate was 52.9%, or $(397/971 - 221) \times 100$. Of the 397 respondents, 104 were psychiatrists (26.2%), 175 were psychologists (44.1%), 111 were social workers (28.0%), and 7 were in other professions (1.8%). So the response rates differed for the three main professions sampled, being 40.8% for psychiatrists, 62.7% for psychologists, and 51.2% for social workers. Of these 397, 276 were male (69.5%) and 121 were female (30.5%). The majority of the psychiatrists and psychologists were male; the majority of the social workers were female. In fact, over half of the women respondents were social workers. Respondents were fairly evenly distributed throughout the four geographic regions, there being 106 from the Northeast, 104 from the Midwest, 92 from the West, and 96 from the South.

Over 84% of the respondents were between the ages of 31 and 60; over 61% were between 41 and 60. They were quited experienced, with 96% having more than 5 years' experience conducting therapy and 78% having more than 10 years' experience. The most common theoretical orientation reported was eclectic (42%), with a strong representation of the analytically based therapies (36%).[5]

Procedure

Each therapist selected was mailed a packet of materials, which included a cover letter, instructions, materials purportedly belonging to a prospective client (Medical History Form and Presenting Problem Form), a questionnaire, and a stamped and addressed envelope for returning the questionnaire to the experimenter. Identical materials were sent to all subjects, with the exception that the sex and attractiveness of the prospective client were varied. All client materials had been constructed by the experimenter and did not represent an actual client.

Cover letter. In order to veil the purpose of the research, the cover letter presented the study as an investigation of the feasibility of developing computerized systems to perform the initial screening of clients at student mental health facilities of colleges and universities. Efforts were made to make this cover story believable, to assure confidentiality, and to encourage the subject to respond promptly. The cover letter and other materials appear in the Appendix.

Instructions. Consistent with the cover story, the instructions explained that the materials concerning the client were exactly those that a health service staff therapist received prior to first contact with the client, and asked the subject to read these and fill out the questionnaire.

Presenting Problem Form.   Adapted from a form used by the UCLA Student Mental Health Service, the Presenting Problem Form contained the prospective client's statement of his or her current problems, as well as the history of their occurrence. The same Presenting Problem Form was sent to all subjects. The client's problems had been constructed to include five possible distinguishable areas—uncertainty about career choice, lack of assertiveness, lack of a social life, past promiscuous sexual behavior, and a physical symptom (frequent diarrhea). These were chosen in order to investigate whether career and assertion problems, which are in areas more strongly representative of the male than of the female sex role, would be considered more serious problems for a male than for a female client; whether, conversely, lack of a social life and sexual promiscuity, which are more clearly departures from expected female than from expected male behavior, would be considered more serious problems for a female than for a male client; and whether the symptom of diarrhea, which could be seen as of organic or psychogenic origin, would be more often seen as psychogenic in the case of a female than of a male client.

Medical History Form.   The critical manipulations—of gender and attractiveness—were accomplished in the Medical History Form. An existing UCLA Student Health Service form was used. All nonessential identifying information was made to appear whited out. The student's sex was indicated on the second line from the top, where "M" or "F" was filled in. Near the lower left, there appeared a small black and white photograph—predetermined to be of high or low attractiveness.[6] The variation of gender and attractiveness produced four conditions: attractive male, attractive female, unattractive male, and unattractive female. But for the exceptions described below, all other information on the form was the same for each of these four clients, one of whom was presented to a subject. Each therapist was randomly assigned to one of the four conditions.

The rest of the information on the form had been completed in such a way as to be consistent with the Presenting Problem Form and the photograph (e.g., hair color, eye color), and to appear authentic. The average height and weight of the appropriate-age male or female was entered where required.

Questionnaire.   Divided into two parts, the questionnaire contained all the dependent measures of the therapists' responses to the hypothetical prospective client, as well as assessments of various therapist characteristics. It was constructed to be consistent with the cover story and thus to avoid raising suspicions about the true purpose of the research. Rationales for both sections were presented, explaining how each fit into the purported research strategy.

The first question explored the issue of whether women are seen as less mentally healthy than men, as did questions 3, 4, 5 and 11. The latter questions were also included to support the cover story. Whether sex-role expectations affect a therapist's judgment of what area(s) to focus on in therapy was investigated in questions 2, 6, and 7. Two areas considered critical for male role fulfillment (career and assertion) and two areas considered critical for female role fulfillment (social life and restriction of sexual behavior) were included in order to see whether therapists would emphasize problems in the former areas for males and in the latter areas for females. To explore possible gender bias further, therapists' reactions to a symptom (diarrhea) that could be considered either organic or psychogenic were assessed by questions 2, 4, 6, and 7. Literature already cited suggested that women's symptoms are more likely to be seen as psychogenic than men's. Question 2 investigated how much the symptom is related to judgments of mental health for men and women, while questions 6 and 7 examined whether the symptom would be seen as something to be worked on in therapy. If the symptom were seen as psychogenic for women but not for men, it would influence judgments of mental health and be seen as a topic for psychotherapy for women only. The most critical question on this issue is question 4: Would a woman's gender lead therapists to be so sure that her symptom is psychosomatic that they would not bother to recommend a medical checkup, which they would recommend for a man? Question 4 also supported the cover story, as a determination of what type of therapy is appropriate being of prime concern in the first contact. Similarly, question 8 asked about what type of therapist would be appropriate.

The therapist's personal, emotional reaction to the client was explored in questions 9 and 10. The subject's estimate of his or her effectiveness with the client (question 9) and his or her interest in working with the client might be related to the client's attractiveness. Judgments of mental health and expected length of therapy might be influenced by attractiveness as well.

The question asking subjects how confident they were in their judgments (question 12) was included in order to allow statistical analyses that investigated the relationship of confidence to other factors. The therapist variables of age, gender, profession, and so on were included so that it would be possible to examine whether any of these—or any combination of them—moderated therapists' judgments about the client.

Results and Discussion

Coding

The subjects' responses were numerically coded as the printed number circled on the questionnaire, except in the following cases. For questions 2 and 7, each of the five options received as a numerical code the rank assigned by the subject (e.g., first option received a 1); when a subject did not rank an option, it received a code of 6 to convey the idea that it had less importance than any item that was ranked (the lowest rank being fifth, or 5). On questions 4 and 19c, each option was again coded by the rank chosen, but here an unranked option was coded as a blank; the option "other" was not coded on question 4 and was coded only to indicate the presence or absence of any ranking on question 19c.

Statistical Analyses

Because of the large number of dependent measures, multivariate analyses of variance were performed first in order to guard against inflation of significance levels. After the multivariate analyses of variance had been performed, univariate analyses of variance were run in order to check on the validity of the dependent measures. When validity had been established, the main univariate analyses were carried out. A summary of all the significant main effects found is presented in Table 1, and a summary of the significant interactions is presented in Table 2.

Validity of the dependent measures. There are numerous indications that subjects took the questionnaire seriously and answered it carefully. First, certain trends were as would be expected, based on the therapists' theoretical orientations and professional affiliations. For instance, analytic and neoanalytic therapists favored more frequent sessions than other therapists did, recommending "individual therapy, twice per week or more" (question 4, option 2) more highly than therapists of any other orientation, $F = 2.37$, $p < .01$.[7] Analytic therapists also expected the client's therapy to last the longest, between 6 and 9 months, whereas eclectic therapists expected a length of between 3 and 6 months, $F = 9.39$, $p < .001$. In addition, psychiatrists recommended medication most strongly of all the professionals, $F = 4.16$, $p < .05$.

Second, intercorrelations between dependent variables suggest that therapists answered the questions consistently. Items indicating severity of illness correlated as expected: The better adjusted the client was perceived as being, the less he or she was believed to need therapy, questions 1 and 3; $r = .54$;[8] and if he or she was seen as needing therapy, the shorter the predicted duration of therapy was, questions 1 and 5; $r = -.39$. Also, lesser need for therapy was associated with prediction of shorter therapy, questions 3 and 5; $r = -.41$. Lastly, the three measures relating to the importance of each of the five problem areas were positively intercorrelated.

Third, the five problem areas were ranked in very similar orders on rank in influence on adjustment judgment (question 2), work on in therapy (question 6), and work on first in therapy (question 7).

Client Gender

Although the therapists did not rate the women clients as less well adjusted or more in need of therapy than the men clients, they were more like-

TABLE 1
Significance Levels of Main Effects

| | | | INDEPENDENT VARIABLES | | | | | |
DEPENDENT VARIABLES	CLIENT GENDER	ATTRAC-TIVENESS	THERAPIST GENDER	THERAPIST REGION	THERAPIST PROFESSION	THERAPIST ORIENTATION	THERAPIST AGE
Question 1. Judgment of client's adjustment					.05	.01	.001
Question 2. Problems influencing judgment of adjustment:							
Career							
Assertion							
Social life							.05
Sexual behavior				.05			
Diarrhea	.05		.05				
Question 3. Need for therapy							.01
Question 4. Therapy recommended:			.05				
Individual therapy, one time per week or less						.005	
Individual therapy, twice per week or more	.07					.01	
Group therapy, one time per week or less		.05			.05		

Group therapy, twice per week or more						
Medication			.01			
Hospitalization						
Board and care home						
Medical checkup			.01			
Question 5. Length of therapy		.05		.05	.001	.05
Question 6. Importance in therapy of:						
Career			.05			.05
Assertion		.005				
Social life		.05				.05
Sexual behavior		.05		.05		
Diarrhea				.05		
Question 7. Temporal priority in therapy:						
Career	.08					
Assertion			.05	.01		
Social life	.07					
Sexual behavior			.01			
Diarrhea				.01		
Question 9. Predicted effectiveness				.05	.05	
Question 10. Predicted interest	.005			.01	.01	
Question 12. Confidence in judgments				.005		.05

TABLE 2
Significance Levels of Interactions

DEPENDENT VARIABLES	INDEPENDENT VARIABLES							
	CLIENT GENDER BY CLIENT ATTRAC-TIVENESS	CLIENT GENDER BY THERAPIST RELIGION	CLIENT AT-TRACTIVE-NESS BY THERAPIST PROFESSION	CLIENT AT-TRACTIVE-NESS BY THERAPIST REGION	CLIENT AT-TRACTIVE-NESS BY THERAPIST RELIGION	THERAPIST GENDER BY CLIENT ATTRAC-TIVENESS	THERAPIST GENDER BY THERAPIST PROFESSION	THERAPIST GENDER BY THERAPIST RELIGION
Question 1. Judgment of client's adjustment							.05	
Question 2. Problems influencing judgment of adjustment:								
Career								
Assertion								
Social life			.05					
Sexual behavior								
Diarrhea							.05	
Question 3. Need for therapy								
Question 4. Therapy recommended								
Individual, once	.05							
Individual, twice								
Group, once	.001							
Group, twice								

Medication	.05							
Hospitalization								
Board and care home								
Medical checkup								
Question 5. Length of therapy								
Question 6. Importance in therapy of:								
Career								
Assertion			.05					
Social life						.05		
Sexual behavior								
Diarrhea		.005						.05
Question 7. Priority in therapy of:								
Career								
Assertion					.01			
Social life							.05	
Sexual behavior		.001		.005	.01		.05	
Diarrhea								
Question 9. Predicted effectiveness								
Question 10. Predicted interest								
Question 12. Confidence in judgments			.05					

ly to recommend "individual therapy, twice per week or more" for women than for men, $F = 3.42$, $p < .07$.[9] Perhaps participating in therapy was seen as more appropriate for a woman than for a man, since the majority of patients in therapy are women (in the present research, as well as reported by others— e.g., Chesler, 1972). The client's having a somatic complaint (frequent diarrhea) influenced the therapists' judgments of adjustment more for males than for females, $F = 5.81$, $p < .05$. This result may be related to sex-role appropriateness. Somatic complaints are perhaps more acceptable in women than in men, because they are in-role symptoms for females but out-of-role symptoms for males. Previous findings suggest that this may indeed be the case. Among college-student subjects, Coie et al. (1974) found that an individual with a somatic complaint was judged as sicker when that individual was presented as a male than when the individual was presented as a female. Similarly for child clients, Feinblatt and Gold (1976) concluded that a child who exhibited sex-role-inappropriate behavior was seen as more severely disturbed than a child who exhibited sex-role-appropriate behavior. In addition, the same behavior may be noticed more when it is out of role than when it is in role. Meyer and Sobieszek (1972) reported such a finding when raters viewed videotapes of very young children who were identified as boys for some observers, and as girls for others.

Sex-role expectations may also have been related to the present finding that therapists recommended working on the client's sexual behavior sooner in therapy when the client was a woman than when the client was a man, $F = 3.47$, $p < .07$. However, this was true only for Protestant and Jewish therapists, $F_i = 7.73$, $p < .001$, where $i =$ interaction. These respondents also saw working on sexual behavior as more important in the therapy of women than in the therapy of men $F_i = 5.34$, $p < .005$.

Contrary to sex-role expectations, working on assertion in therapy was given greater temporal priority for female than for male clients, $F = 3.28$, $p < .08$. However, this difference was due to the rankings of the unattractive clients only, the unattractive female being ranked higher and the unattractive male lower than the attractive male and female clients, $F_i = 4.15$, $p < .05$. Such a result is consistent with Miller's finding (1970) that gender is more influential at lower levels of attractiveness. Also, "group therapy, one time per week or less" and "individual therapy, one time per week or less" were recommended most strongly for the unattractive woman client, $F_i = 10.45$, $p < .001$; $F_i = 4.33$, $p < .05$. These findings may be related to the tendency of therapists to reserve "individual therapy, twice per week or more" for attractive clients, with the result that unattractive clients would be more likely to be assigned to less frequent individual therapy or to group therapy.

A trend emerged from inspection of the frequencies of the ranks assigned on the items dealing with the influence of the career problem on the therapists' judgments of adjustment and with the recommendation of inventory testing for career interest (question 4). In both cases, therapists most often failed to rank the item *at all* when the client was an attractive woman. This suggests that the career problem was seen as least important for the attractive woman client. Such a finding is consistent with the traditional view that a career is not important for a woman, with the difference that here a career is not important only for an *attractive* woman. Perhaps the attractive woman is seen as more likely to be able to fulfill the traditional female role (marry and stay at home) than the unattractive woman, because her appearance will make her more "socially" desirable (i.e., she is seen as more likely to find a husband).

Although client gender did have some effect on the therapists' judgments, it did not have the pervasive effects on the assessment of psychological health and the planning of therapy that some have claimed. The present data do provide some evidence that therapists encourage their clients to conform to traditional sex-role-appropriate behavior. And there was no evidence that a somatic complaint would be dismissed as psychogenic in a female client.

There are a number of possible reasons why client gender did not have wide-ranging effects in the present study. First, since therapists were told that their responses would be used as a data base for a computer screening system, they may have responded by giving "textbook" answers. That is, the respondents may have filled out the questionnaire according to what they believed to be the *consensus* of opinion among psychotherapists—not according to what each *personally* would do. Since effects of gender bias have been widely publicized as undesirable in recent years, such a mode of responding would certainly obscure the biases held by individual practitioners.

A second and related reason is the possible operation of *social desirability effects.* Once a therapist knows that he or she is taking part in a research project where his or her responses will be seen by others, that therapist is likely to censor any responses that would not appear socially desirable. That is a difficult problem to overcome. It is noteworthy that in more naturalistic studies —where the therapists generally are not aware that their written records will later be used for research purposes—more sex bias has been found than in analogue research. This dimension of *privacy* is probably of great importance in research on gender bias in psychotherapy.

Last, the present research did not involve a *real* situation. The therapists knew that they would never actually *see* the client. The anticipation of *personal contact*—and the contact itself—may be critical to the occurrence of gender bias.

It is interesting to note that in Schover's study (Chapter 10)—where it was clear that the therapist's own personal responses were desired; where the methodology did not allow the respondents much time to censor their responses; and where the situation was more realistic—considerably more sex bias was found.

Client Attractiveness

Evidence was found that the therapists sampled had a more positive reaction to the attractive clients than to the unattractive clients. They expressed greater interest in working with attractive clients, $F = 9.39$, $p < .005$ and recommended more frequent individual sessions for attractive than for unattractive clients, $F = 5.32$, $p < .05$—even though attractive clients were not seen as more poorly adjusted or more in need of therapy than unattractive clients were. The latter finding could also be interpreted in the context of providing better or more complete care to attractive clients. Such a tendency was also reflected in the findings that attractive clients were more likely to be referred for a medical checkup, $F = 7.74$, $p < .01$ and to be prescribed medication, $F = 8.38$, $p < .01$. Medication was most often recommended for the attractive woman, $F_i = 6.49$, $p < .05$.

Working on career choice in therapy was seen as more important for unattractive than for attractive clients, $F = 6.41$, $p < .05$; it was seen as most urgent for the unattractive female client and least urgent for the attractive female client, $F_i = 4.87$, $p < .05$. Perhaps, as noted earlier, the attractive woman is more likely to be expected to fulfill the traditional female sex role of marriage and family than is the unattractive woman, who must therefore support herself financially. Thus, career choice would be more important for the unattractive woman. Such an interpretation is consistent with Bar-Tal and Saxe's conclusion (1976) that attractiveness is more important in the evaluation of females than in the evaluation of males.

Therapist Gender

Women therapists stressed working on assertion in therapy more than did men therapists, $F = 8.47$, $p < .005$, but this difference was due to the ratings of the attractive clients only, $F = 4.85$, $p < .05$. The unattractive clients were rated similarly by male and female therapists. Female therapists also favored working on assertion sooner in the therapy than did male therapists, $F = 5.74$, $p < .05$. Perhaps the women respondents' greater emphasis on assertion was related to the fairly recent sensitization of women to the importance of assertiveness by the feminist movement.

Contrary to the results of previous research, the male therapists did not appear to be more interested in sexual problems—for male or for female clients—than female therapists appeared to be. In fact, it was not the male but the female therapists (excluding psychologists) who more strongly favored dealing with sexual behavior early in therapy, $F = 6.27$, $p < .01$; $F_i = 3.81$, $p < .05$, and who viewed sexual behavior as a more important area for therapeutic work, $F = 3.78$, $p < .05$.

Women practitioners viewed working on the physical symptom of diarrhea in therapy as more important than did men, $F=3.87$, $p<.05$. Also, the women ranked "diarrhea" as having a greater influence on their judgments of adjustment, $F=3.92$, $p<.05$; but this trend occurred mainly among psychiatrists, $F_i=3.13$, $p<.05$. Similarly, the responses of psychiatrists alone accounted for a significant difference in giving temporal priority to working on social life by female, as compared to male, therapists.

Male respondents recommended "individual therapy, one time per week or less" more highly than did female respondents, $F=5.24$, $p<.05$. This effect may be accounted for by the fact that more women than men in our sample were social workers, who more probably work in those settings where individual therapy is less available. Last, male therapists expected therapy to last a shorter time than did female therapists, $F=4.34$, $p<.05$.

Therapist Region

The effects of a therapist's regional location (Northeast, Midwest, West, or South) were difficult to group. No region had consistently extreme effects, except in the case of the Midwest on three variables. Midwestern therapists expected to be less effective with the client, $F=2.85$, $p<.05$; (possibly therefore) were least interested in conducting therapy with the client, $F=3.72$, $p<.01$; and (possibly also therefore) expected therapy to last the shortest time, $F=8.03$, $p<.01$. Conversely, the tendency of Northeastern therapists to foresee the longest duration of therapy may be related to there being a greater concentration, perhaps, of analytic therapists in that area. In the judgment of adjustment, sexual behavior was ranked as most influential by respondents in the Midwest and least influential by respondents in the West, $F=2.58$, $p<.05$.

Therapist Profession

A therapist's profession—psychiatrist, psychologist, or social worker—had numerous significant effects. In two cases, the effect of therapist profession was moderated by client attractiveness. Ratings of the influence of the problem with social life on the judgment of adjustment differed among professions when an attractive client was being rated (psychiatrists assigned the greatest weight to this problem, followed by psychologists and social workers), but not when an unattractive client was rated, $F_i=3.03$, $p<.05$. Social workers were most confident about their judgments, with psychologists next, and then psychiatrists, $F=5.64$, $p<.005$, but this finding was also moderated by client attractiveness, $F_i=3.43$, $p<.05$. Social workers expressed greater confidence than the other two groups only when judging an attractive client, and psychiatrists expressed lesser confidence only when judging an unattractive client.

Social workers and psychologists expected their therapy with the client to be more effective than did psychiatrists, $F = 3.67$, $p < .05$. Also, social workers anticipated that the client would be more interesting than did psychiatrists or psychologists, $F = 4.72$, $p < .01$. Perhaps, again, expecting lower effectiveness was related to lower interest in the case of the psychiatrists; however, such a relationship could not explain the lower interest of the psychologists. It is interesting to note that the social workers were highest (or, in one case, nearly tied for highest) in confidence judgments, anticipated effectiveness, and interest; and that psychiatrists were lowest (or, in one case, nearly tied for lowest) on these three variables.

In judging adjustment, psychiatrists tended to rate the client as less well adjusted than did psychologists or social workers, $F = 3.03$, $p < .05$. A profession $\times$ therapist gender interaction, $F = 3.04$, $p < .05$, showed that this trend was more pronounced for female than for male respondents.

Psychiatrists and psychologists were found to recommend "individual therapy, two times per week or more" more strongly than did social workers, $F = 3.86$, $p < .05$. This finding does not appear to be related to the therapists' orientations; for psychologists, not social workers, were the only professional group underrepresented in the sample among therapists with an analytic or neoanalytic orientation. Rather, the lesser tendency for social workers to recommend twice-weekly therapy may be related to the settings in which social workers are likely to practice, settings where perhaps such frequent therapeutic contact is not feasible. Similarly, orientation does not appear to account for the greater likelihood of psychiatrists, in contrast to the other professionals sampled, to expect therapy to last the longest time, $F = 3.01$, $p < .05$. If orientation were responsible, psychologists, many of whom use short-term techniques, should have expected the shortest therapy; but social workers expected therapy to last the shortest time. Again, setting may be a factor here, as well as in the tendency of social workers to prescribe medication more than psychologists. Availability and training are likely to account for the finding that the greatest tendency to prescribe medication occurred among psychiatrists, $F = 4.16$, $p < .05$. Seeing clients as needing medication is also consistent with their judging the clients as least well adjusted.

Therapist Orientation

A therapist's theoretical orientation had a significant effect on a number of variables. Analytic and neoanalytic therapists saw the client as least well adjusted, $F = 2.62$, $p < .01$. This finding may have to do with the tendency of therapists with these orientations to see a client's entire personality as pathological and in need of change, rather than certain behaviors. Behavioral therapists, who see the maladaptive behavior itself as what needs to be changed, saw the client as most well adjusted. Consistent with this line of reasoning and with their ideas about how long therapy takes, neoanalysts and analysts foresaw the longest duration of therapy, and behaviorists foresaw the shortest, $F=9.39$, $p<.001$. Also in line with their theory of therapy, neoanalytic and analytic therapists stressed twice-weekly sessions most, $F=2.87$, $p<.01$. "Individual therapy, one time per week or less" as ranked higher by analytic than by eclectic therapists, as would be expected, $F=3.03$, $p<.005$.

The importance of working on career choice was rated as much more important by the eclectic therapists than by the analytic and neoanalytic therapists, $F=2.38$, $p<.05$. This is as might be expected, since the latter two groups would be less likely than the eclectic group to see a client's concerns with career as falling within the province of therapy. Note that, conversely, the eclectic therapists saw working on sexual behavior as less important than the other two groups did, $F=2.07$, $p<.05$. This is not surprising, considering the stress that analytically based theory places on sexuality.

Therapist Age

Older therapists viewed the client as less well adjusted than did younger therapists, $F=6.18$, $p<.001$; consistently, the older practitioners judged the client as in greater need of therapy, $F=3.23$, $p<.01$. These findings suggest that therapists become less optimistic as they get older.

The older therapists saw the client's problem with social life as less important than did the younger therapists, in that they rated working on the social life problem in therapy as less urgent, $F=2.28$, $p<.05$, and were less influenced in their judgment of adjustment by it, $F=2.50$, $p<.05$. These results may be related to younger therapists' finding social life more important in their own lives than older therapists.

Therapist Orientation and Profession

The present data strongly suggest that a therapist's orientation is related to his or her professional affiliation. A cross-tabulation of therapist orientation × profession produced a significant chi-square statistic ($p<.001$). The percentages of psychiatrists, psychologists, and social workers ascribing to each orientation are presented in Table 3. Since psychiatrists made up 25.8% of the sample, psychologists 44.6%, and social workers 27.8%, tabled percentages considerably greater than these indicate an overrepresentation of the professional group in the orientation, and percentages considerably smaller indicate an underrepresentation. Psychiatrists were overrepresented among the analysts and were vastly underrepresented among all the newer therapeutic schools—Rogerian, Gestalt, transactional analysis, behavioral, and cognitive-behavioral. Psychologists were underrepresented among the

TABLE 3
Percent Relationship between Therapist Orientation and Therapist Profession

	PROFESSION				TOTAL	
	PSYCHIATRIST	PSYCHOLOGIST	SOCIAL WORKER	OTHER		
Percentage of sample	25.8	44.6	27.8	1.8	100.0	(387)
Orientation mainly:[c]						
Analytic	37.9[a]	24.2[b]	35.8[a]	2.1	100.0	(95)
Neoanalytic	26.1	50.0[a]	21.7[b]	2.2	100.0	(46)
Rogerian	0.0[b]	100.0[a]	0.0[b]	0.0	100.0	(6)
Gestalt	0.0[b]	83.3[a]	16.7[b]	0.0	100.0	(12)
Transactional analysis	11.1[b]	55.6[a]	33.3[a]	0.0	100.0	(9)
Behavioral	0.0[b]	55.6[a]	44.4[a]	0.0	100.0	(9)
Cognitive-behavioral	4.5[b]	81.8[a]	9.1[b]	4.5	99.9	(21)
Eclectic	26.9	44.3	26.9	1.8	99.9	(167)
Other	22.7	40.9	36.4[a]	0.0	100.0	(22)

[a]Overrepresented.
[b]Underrepresented.
[c]Percentages are percentages of each row.

analysts and overrepresented among the five newer schools of therapy. In fact, all the Rogerians were psychologists, and no psychiatrists were Gestalt or behavioral; few were cognitive-behavioral. These findings may be related to the fact that psychologists tend to have been trained more recently than psychiatrists have been. However, it is more likely that the newer therapeutic approaches have not yet been incorporated into the training of psychiatrists. Social workers were represented among the newer schools of therapy.

Overview

The respondents in the present study constituted a large, representative sample of therapists in the United States. Three professions—psychiatry, psychology, and social work—were represented; the subjects resided in four geographic regions—Northeast, Midwest, West, and South; and the response rate (53%) was adequate. Analyses of the data showed that individuals, from a variety of age groups, religions, and socioeconomic backgrounds were sampled, as expected. As a group, the respondents were experienced, practicing therapists who worked with adult clients and dealt with a wide range of emotional problems.

The method employed in assessing the therapists' reactions succeeded in veiling the true purpose of the research and thus prevented social desirability effects. In addition to simulating real clinical decisions made in intake situations, the procedure also controlled for variation in clients, so that any effects found could be attributed to factors that were either controlled or measured by the experimenter—client gender, client attractiveness, therapist gender, therapist location, therapist profession, therapist orientation, or therapist age. The dependent measures also proved to be valid.

Although client gender, alone and in combination with client attractiveness, did influence therapists' judgments in some cases, the present data do not support prior claims of broad gender bias. It has been noted that the necessary conditions for detecting sex bias effects may include the absence of social desirability effects, which may involve respondents' not having time to censor their responses, as well as privacy; and a realistic situation, where the therapist anticipates or has personal contact with the client. Further investigation into the area of sex bias in therapy is definitely required, and the topic of sex bias should be discussed in therapist training.

On the other hand, client attractiveness did seem to have a consistent effect on the decisions of the therapist/respondents, with high attractiveness engendering more positive responses than low attractiveness. The tendency that was found for attractive clients to be given more thorough care requires further investigation.

Interestingly, the effects of the client characteristics (gender and attractiveness) were not as numerous as the effects of the therapist characteristics examined (gender, region, profession, orientation, and age). The measures employed in the present study were evidently sensitive enough to show up effects of variables not previously found to be significant. The finding of so many and varied effects of therapists factors should encourage those who conduct future research in the area of psychotherapy to be aware of these in the planning of their research and in the analysis of their data.

For the prospective client, the present data pinpoint differences among therapists, including the following: Women therapists stress working on assertion and sexual behavior more than men therapists do; psychiatrists are more likely to favor including medication in the therapeutic regime than are the other types of professionals sampled; analytic and neoanalytic therapists view clients as least well adjusted and foresee the longest duration of therapy, while behavioral therapists see the client as most well adjusted and foresee the shortest course of therapy; eclectic therapists see working on career concerns in therapy as much more important than do analytic and neoanalytic therapists; older therapists view the client as more poorly adjusted and place less emphasis on problems with social life than do younger therapists.

Implications for the Consciousness Raising of Practicing Therapists and the Training of New Therapists

For practicing therapists, the present findings point up biases of which they should be aware. This is especially true of the finding that attractive clients receive more complete care than unattractive clients do. Therapists need to be made cognizant of their reactions to unattractive clients so that they can make an effort to ensure that these patients receive the best possible care. Such awareness could be promoted by means of dissemination of the present results and discussion of their implications, through such channels as continuing education courses, professional journals, and professional meetings.

In order to reach new therapists, these findings should be incorporated into textbooks on psychotherapy and into training programs for psychotherapists, whether in graduate schools, medical schools, institutes, or elsewhere. Discussion of the problem of unconscious biases on the part of therapists should be encouraged, and the likely directions of such biases should be communicated.

Methodological Comments

In a recent article, Maher (1978) has offered a number of cautions to those who would conduct research on psychotherapy. First, he has pointed out that generalizations can be made from the subjects to the population only if the subjects are representative of that population, and that experimenters' conclusions must be confined to the range of values covered by the experimental stimuli. In the present study, it has been shown that the respondents were indeed quite representative of the population of therapists who are psychiatrists, psychologists, or social workers. As for the stimuli, the case materials employed here presented only nonpsychotic, college-age patients with one specific set of problems. So it is strictly true that the conclusions cannot—without further experimentation—be generalized to patients with other problems and of other ages. However, the inclusion of a range of stimuli covering patients with all possible problems and of all possible ages, as well as all combinations of these, would have required a sample larger than the total population of therapists available. And such variation of stimuli with a sample of the size employed would have introduced the problem of having so many possible explanations for (factors accounting for) any effect found that *no* conclusions at all could have been drawn. Last, Maher's concern that case materials constructed by the experimenter be realistic (i.e., naturally occurring) is not a problem here. For concerns with career, assertion, social life, sexual behavior, and physical symptoms—alone and in combination—are commonly found among college students seeking treatment at a student mental health facility.

Moreover, the procedure employed in the present study demonstrates one method for increasing the external validity of experimental research—namely, combining the experimental manipulations with the use of survey research techniques of subject selection and data collection. External validity (Campbell & Stanley, 1963) deals with the question of the generalizability of research to real populations and real settings. The findings of many psychology experiments are of severely limited generalizability because of the reliance on college students as subjects. By combining experimental and survey techniques, it is possible to attenuate the disadvantages of each method while maintaining their unique advantages. The ability to isolate experimental variables (the major advantage of the experimental method[10]) is retained, while the generalizability of the findings is increased (the advantage of survey methodology).

APPENDIX

Computer Screening Project

INSTRUCTIONS

The following materials are exactly those which a therapist on the Student Mental Health Service staff would receive prior to seeing the client. Before this initial contact, the client has completed a description of the presenting problem(s), which is given to the therapist along with the client's medical history (Form 101 A). You are receiving copies of both of these forms, taken from existing files (nonessential identifying data have been deleted). Please read these forms and respond to the accompanying questionnaire, indicating what you would recommend for this student.

Date 10·3·77

Name _____ _____ _____ Age: 20
   Last,   First   Middle

Briefly state the nature and history of your problems:

I'm starting my junior year in college + I need to decide what career I want. The trouble is I don't have any idea.

Another problem is that I let people push me around. I may not want to do something, but I do it anyway if somebody wants me to.

Also, I've been pretty lonely lately since I haven't been dating at all. History—well this wasn't a problem before—I used to date, slept with a lot of people, but not now.

I've had diarrhea pretty often lately.

This form dated 5-24-77/jz

UNIVERSITY OF CALIFORNIA   **STUDENT HEALTH SERVICE**   LOS ANGELES

PLEASE PRINT IN INK OR TYPE – MUST BE COMPLETED IN FULL.

Full Legal
Student's Name ___ _ _ ___ _ ___ First _ ___ Middle · _ SHS No. ___ (to be filled in by SHS)

Date of Birth 7/12/57 Sex f Social Security No. ___

Local address ___ Number, Street ___ City, Zip Code ___ Phone ___

Next of kin:
Name ___ Relationship ___
Address ___ Number, Street ___ City, State, Zip Code ___ Phone ___

Person to be notified in emergency (if not next of kin):
Name ___ Relationship ___
Address ___ Number, Street ___ City, State, Zip Code ___ Phone ___

CONFIDENTIAL MEDICAL HISTORY

Marital status: single [X] married [ ] divorced [ ] widowed [ ] maiden name ___
Birthplace Los Angeles Religion (optional) ___
Class in UCLA freshman Major Still deciding Vocational goal Still deciding
Current Place of Employment student
Medical Insurance Company Kaiser Policy No. ___
    name
Personal physician ___ Address LA CA
    name   city state zip
Personal dentist ___ Address LA CA
    name   city state zip

Family history – must be filled in:

Did your mother take female sex hormones during pregnancy? No

Relation	Age	State of Health	Age at Death	Cause of Death
Father	57	fine		
Mother	54	fine		
Brothers and Sisters	22	''		
	16	''		
Children	none			

Which blood relative has had:
Allergy sister
Cancer ___
Diabetes ___
Heart disease ___
High blood pressure ___
Kidney disease ___
Tuberculosis ___
Familial or hereditary disease ___
    specify

Additional Identifying Information:
Height: 5'4"
Weight: 126
Hair Color: brown
Eye Color: brown
Identifying Marks: ___

Picture

Mother's Family Name: ___
When did you first attend UCLA:? Fall 1975
    (quarter, year)

PREVENTIVE IMMUNIZATION INFORMATION. Answer "yes" or "no." Give dates if known. Must be filled in.

DIPHTHERIA SERIES COMPLETED yes BOOSTER ___ MEASLES no
POLIOMYELITIS SERIES COMPLETED yes BOOSTER ___ MUMPS no
    ORAL SABIN yes BOOSTER ___ SMALLPOX yes
    INJECTED SALK yes BOOSTER ___ OTHER (SPECIFY) ___
TETANUS SERIES COMPLETED yes BOOSTER 1973
    (OVER)

Form 101A 10 May 1973

HAVE YOU EVER HAD OR DO YOU NOW HAVE ANY OF THE FOLLOWING:

Please amplify, by number, in this space, the course and outcome of ALL situations identified in the "yes" column. Use as many lines as necessary.

#		YES	NO	AGE	
1.	Drug sensitivity or drug allergy		X		
2.	Non-medical drug use		X		
3.	Skin disease, including acne		X		
4.	Frequent or severe headaches		X		
5.	Severe head injury		X		
6.	Corrective lenses (glasses or contacts)		X		Circle one
7.	Eye disease		X		
8.	Ear, nose, or throat trouble		X		
9.	Hearing difficulty		X		
10.	Ruptured or perforated ear drum		X		
11.	Hay fever or other non-drug allergy		X		
12.	Severe tooth or gum trouble	X		17	wisdom tooth
13.	Thyroid disorder		X		
14.	Close contact with tuberculosis		X		
15.	Tuberculin skin test (positive or negative)		X		Circle one
16.	Abnormal chest X-ray		X		
17.	Asthma		X		
18.	Shortness of breath		X		
19.	Chest pain or pressure		X		
20.	Chronic cough		X		
21.	Heart pounding		X		
22.	Heart murmur		X		
23.	High or low blood pressure		X		
24.	Severe or recurrent abdominal pain		X		
25.	Stomach or duodenal ulcer		X		
26.	Chronic or recurrent diarrhea		X		
27.	Gall bladder disease		X		
28.	Venereal disease (specify type)		X		
29.	Hernia (rupture)		X		
30.	Hemorrhoids (piles)		X		
31.	Urinary problem		X		
32.	Blood, sugar, albumin in urine		X		
33.	Bone or joint disability or deformity		X		
34.	Loss of an extremity or portion thereof		X		
35.	"Trick" joint		X		
36.	Varicose veins		X		
37.	Foot trouble		X		
38.	Frequent or severe back trouble		X		
39.	Paralysis (including polio)		X		
40.	Dizzy or fainting spells		X		
41.	Convulsions or epilepsy		X		
42.	Psychiatric disorder		X		
43.	Diabetes		X		
44.	Rheumatic fever		X		
45.	Hepatitis (specify type)		X		
46.	Infectious mononucleosis		X		
47.	San Joaquin-Valley fever		X		
48.	Mumps	X		?	
49.	Whooping cough		X		
50.	Chicken pox		X		
51.	Rubella (German measles or "3 day")	X		?	
52.	Rubeola ("red" measles or "2 week")		X		
53.	Scarlet fever		X		
54.	Malaria		X		
55.	Menstrual abnormality		X		
56.	Pregnancy		X		
57.			X		

Name any illness, injury, disability, surgery not mentioned and state year and outcome. Include tonsillectomy and appendectomy.

broken wrist, tonsillectomy

Specify any medical and/or psychiatric therapy you are receiving. List ALL medications, including vitamins, birth control pills, etc.

vitamins

I consider my health ☒ excellent ☐ good ☐ fair ☐ poor. The foregoing information is accurate to the best of my knowledge. I am aware that inaccuracies or omissions may jeopardize my health.

SIGNATURE _____ Date 6/30/75

(Do not fill in) Impressions: _normal_　　FOR STUDENT HEALTH SERVICE USE ONLY　　Recommendations: _none_　(Do not fill in)

SHS Reviewer _____, M.D. _____ Date 8-12-75

Computer Screening Project Questionnaire

We understand that we are supplying you with only limited information. Please try to answer *all* questions, as this is all the information that is available to us to feed into the computer. The following questions require one of two types of responses. For some questions, check over the number next to the appropriate response; for others, rank order the choices by writing in the appropriate numbers.

1. How well adjusted does the prospective client appear to be? (check one)

    (1) Seriously maladjusted

    (2) Somewhat maladjusted

    (3) Slightly maladjusted

    (4) Adequately adjusted

    (5) Well adjusted

    (6) Extremely well adjusted

2. Which of the client's problems most influenced your judgment of adjustment? (Please rank-order all of the areas that contributed by writing 1 for the most important influence, 2 for the next most important, etc., up to the number necessary to indicate all the areas that influenced your evaluation.)

    _____ No idea what career to choose

    _____ Lack of assertiveness

    _____ Loneliness/No social life

    _____ Sexual behavior

    _____ Diarrhea

3. How much does this person need therapy at the present time? (check one)

    (1) Urgent need for therapy

    (2) Serious need for therapy

    (3) Moderate need for therapy

    (4) Slight need for therapy

    (5) Does not need therapy

4. If therapy were to be initiated with this person, what type(s) of therapy would you recommend? (Please rank all that apply, with 1 indicating the most important, 2 the next most important, etc., up to the number that you would include.)

    _____ Individual therapy, one time per week or less

    _____ Individual therapy, twice per week or more

_____ Group therapy, one time per week or less

_____ Group therapy, twice per week or more

_____ Medication

_____ Hospitalization

_____ Board and care home

_____ Career interest inventory testing

_____ Referral for medical checkup to investigate the cause of the diarrhea

_____ Other, please specify _____

5. How long would you expect this client's therapy to last? (Do not consider what is practical at the Student Mental Health Service. Referrals can be made where necessary.) (check one)

   (1) 6 weeks or less

   (2) 7 weeks to less than 3 months

   (3) 3 months to less than 6 months

   (4) 6 months to less than 9 months

   (5) 9 months to less than 1 year

   (6) 1 year or more

6. How important would it be to work on _each_ of the following areas in this person's therapy? (check one for _each_ of the 5 areas listed below)

	very important	moderately important	somewhat important	slightly important	not at all important
1. Career choice	(1)	(2)	(3)	(4)	(5)
2. Assertion	(1)	(2)	(3)	(4)	(5)
3. Social life	(1)	(2)	(3)	(4)	(5)
4. Sexual behavior . .	(1)	(2)	(3)	(4)	(5)
5. Diarrhea	(1)	(2)	(3)	(4)	(5)

7. Which area would you work on first, second, etc., in therapy? (Please indicate all those that you would work on by writing 1st, 2nd, 3rd, etc., up to the number of areas you would try to include in the therapy.)

   _____ Career choice

   _____ Assertion

   _____ Social life

   _____ Sexual behavior

   _____ Diarrhea

8. What type of therapist would be most appropriate for this client?

   a. Sex (check one)

      _____ Male

      _____ Female

      _____ Either

   b. Age (check one)

      _____ 21–30

      _____ 31–40

      _____ 41–50

      _____ 51–60

      _____ Over 60

      _____ Any age

9. How effective do you think that *you* could be with this client? (check one)

   (1) Very effective

   (2) Moderately effective

   (3) Somewhat effective

   (4) Slightly effective

   (5) Not at all effective

10. As a therapist, how interesting do you think working with this client would be for you? (check one)

   (1) Very interesting

   (2) Moderately interesting

   (3) Somewhat interesting

   (4) Slightly interesting

   (5) Not at all interesting

11. If the Student Health Service were not able to see this person, what referral would be most appropriate? (check one)

   (1) Minister, priest, or rabbi

   (2) Analytic therapist

   (3) Rogerian therapist

   (4) Gestalt therapist

   (5) Behavioral therapist

   (6) Transactional therapist

(7) Cognitive-behavioral therapist

(8) Eclectic therapist

(9) Other type of therapist, please specify _____

(10) Referral to a psychiatric hospital

(11) Other referral, please specify _____

(12) None, referral not necessary

12. In answering the above questions, how confident were you about your judgments? (check one)

(1) Very confident

(2) Moderately confident

(3) Somewhat confident

(4) Slightly confident

(5) Not at all confident

In order to determine similarities and dissimilarities between you and the Student Health Service staff members, we need some demographic information about you. Please give the following information about *yourself* by checking the appropriate response:

13. Age

(1) Under 30

(2) 31–40

(3) 41–50

(4) 51–60

(5) 61–70

(6) Over 70

14. Sex

(1) Male

(2) Female

15. Marital Status

(1) Married

(2) Divorced

(3) Separated

(4) Widowed

(5) Single

16. Profession

(1) Psychiatrist

(2) Psychologist

(3) Social Worker

(4) Other, please specify _____

17. Therapeutic Orientation

(1) Mainly Analytic

(2) Mainly Neoanalytic

(3) Mainly Rogerian

(4) Mainly Gestalt

(5) Mainly Transactional Analysis

(6) Mainly Behavioral

(7) Mainly Cognitive Behavioral

(8) Eclectic

(9) Other, please specify _____

18. Number of years you have been a practicing therapist (total number of years, not necessarily continuous)

    (1) Less than 2 years

    (2) 2 years to less than 5 years

    (3) 5 years to less than 10 years

    (4) 10 years to less than 15 years

    (5) 15 years to less than 20 years

    (6) Over 20 years

19. Are you currently conducting therapy?

    (1) Yes. If yes, answer 19a through 19e.

    (2) No. If no, go on to question 20.

19a. How many hours per week are you involved in conducting therapy?

    (1) 5 hours or less

    (2) 6 to 15 hours

    (3) 16 to 25 hours

    (4) 26 to 35 hours

    (5) More than 35 hours

19b. In what setting do you conduct therapy? (check the setting where you do the majority of your therapeutic work)

    (1) Student health or counseling service at a college or university

    (2) Other college or university position, please specify _____

    (3) Elementary or secondary school

    (4) Public clinic or institute

    (5) Private clinic or institute

    (6) Public hospital

    (7) Private hospital

    (8) Private practice

    (9) Other, please specify _____

19c. What types of problems do you generally deal with? (Place a 1 beside the category you treat most often, a 2 beside the category you treat next most often, etc., up to the number necessary to indicate all the kinds of problems that you treat.)

    _____ Psychoses

    _____ Character disorders

_____ Drug or alcohol dependency

_____ Neuroses

_____ Problems in living

_____ Crisis situations

_____ Specific behavioral problems (e.g., phobias, weight reduction)

_____ Other, please specify _____

19d. Of your clients, what percentage are

Male?	Female?
(1) Between 0% and 10%	(1) Between 0% and 10%
(2) Between 11% and 40%	(2) Between 11% and 40%
(3) Between 41% and 60%	(3) Between 41% and 60%
(4) Between 61% and 90%	(4) Between 61% and 90%
(5) Between 91% and 100%	(5) Between 91% and 100%

19e. Of your clients, what percentages are in the following age groups?

	0–10%	11–40%	41–60%	61–90%	91–100%
Under 10 years old	(1)	(2)	(3)	(4)	(5)
11 to 20 years old	(1)	(2)	(3)	(4)	(5)
21 to 30 years old	(1)	(2)	(3)	(4)	(5)
31 to 45 years old	(1)	(2)	(3)	(4)	(5)
46 to 60 years old	(1)	(2)	(3)	(4)	(5)
Over 60 years old	(1)	(2)	(3)	(4)	(5)

20. Place a check where

	West	Midwest	South	Northeast
a. You grew up (i.e., spent most of the years before age 18)	(1)	(2)	(3)	(4)
b. The school that granted your highest degree was located	(1)	(2)	(3)	(4)
c. You have practiced therapy the majority of your professional career	(1)	(2)	(3)	(4)

21. What religion were you raised in?

(1) Protestant

(2) Catholic

(3) Jewish

(4) Other, please specify _____

22. To what ethnic group do you belong?

    (1) Caucasian

    (2) Black

    (3) Chicano, Puerto Rican, or other Spanish-speaking group

    (4) Oriental

    (5) Other, please specify _____

23. When you were growing up, was your family

    (1) Upper-class

    (2) Upper-middle-class

    (3) Middle-class

    (4) Lower-middle-class

    (5) Working-class

    (6) Other, please specify _____

24. Is there anything you would like to add? (Please use the space below.)

_____

PLEASE MAIL BACK THE QUESTIONNAIRE IN THE ENCLOSED STAMPED RETURN ENVELOPE.

                                        THANK YOU.

NOTES

[1]In discussing these, the focus is on the case of women; a complementary case could be developed for men.

[2]See Chapter 2 for a more complete discussion of women in psychological theory.

[3]See Chapter 5 for more details.

[4]See Chapter 8 for a detailed review of the literature.

[5]More detailed information about the sample's characteristics is available from the authors on request.

[6]The attractiveness of the photographs had been determined in a prior study.

[7]Relevant tables of means and standard deviations, as well as analysis-of-variance tables, are available from the authors on request.

[8]The signs of the correlations must be interpreted in conjunction with looking at the ordering of the alternatives on the questions.

[9]Statistical results are from the analysis of variance unless otherwise stated.

[10]This discussion of the advantages and limitations of the experimental method draws on Babbie (1973).

REFERENCE NOTES

1. Drapkin, R., & Anzel, A. *Sex-role bias in clinical judgments.* Manuscript in progress, 1977.

3. Hamilton, D. *Contextual factors in stereotyping.* Paper presented at University of California, Los Angeles, October 1977.

3. Cowan, G. *Therapists' judgments of sex-role problems of clients.* Paper presented at the meeting of the Western Psychological Association, San Francisco, April 1975.

REFERENCES

Abramowitz, C. V. Blaming the mother: An experimental investigation of sex-role bias in countertransference. *Psychology of Women Quarterly,* in press.

Abramowitz, C. V., Abramowitz, S. I., Weitz, L. J., & Tittler, B. Sex-related effects on clinicians' attributions of parental involvement in child psychopathology. *Journal of Abnormal Child Psychology,* 1976, 4, 129–133.

Abramowitz, C. V., & Dokecki, P. R. The politics of clinical judgment: Early empirical returns. *Psychological Bulletin,* 1977, 84, 460–476.

Abramowitz, S. I., & Abramowitz, C. V. Should prospective women clients seek out women practitioners? Intimations of a "dingbat" effect in clinical evaluation. *Proceedings of the 81st Annual Convention of the American Psychological Association,* 1973, 8, 503–504. (Summary)

Abramowitz, S. I., Abramowitz, C. V., Jackson, C., & Gomes, B. The politics of clinical judgment: What nonliberal examiners infer about women who do not stifle themselves. *Journal of Consulting and Clinical Psychology,* 1973, 41, 385–391.

Abramowitz, S. I., Abramowitz, C. V., Roback, H., Corney, R., & McKee, E. Sex-role-related countertransference in psychotherapy. *Archives of General Psychiatry,* 1976, 33, 71–73.

American Psychiatric Association. *Biographical directory of the fellows and members of the American Psychiatric Association.* New York: Jaques Cattell Press, 1973.

American Psychological Association. *Biographical directory of the American Psychological Association.* Washington, D.C.: Author, 1975.

Asher, J. Sex bias found in therapy. *APA Monitor,* April 1975, pp. 1, 4.

Babbie, E. R. *Survey research methods.* Belmont, Calif.: Wadsworth, 1973.

Barocas, R., & Vance, F. Physical appearance and personal adjustment counseling. *Journal of Counseling Psychology,* 1974, *21,* 96–100.

Bar-Tal, D., & Saxe, L. Physical attractiveness and its relationship to sex-role stereotyping. *Sex Roles,* 1976, *2,* 123–133.

Bem, S. L., & Bem, D. J. Case study of a nonconscious ideology: Training the woman to know her place. In D. J. Bem (Ed.), *Beliefs, attitudes, and human affairs.* Belmont, Calif.: Brooks/Cole, 1970.

Bernard, J. *The future of motherhood.* New York: Dial Press, 1974.

Billingsley, D. Sex bias in psychotherapy: An examination of the effects of client sex, client pathology, and therapist sex on treatment planning. *Journal of Consulting and Clinical Psychology,* 1977, *45,* 250–256.

Broverman, I., Broverman, D., Clarkson, P., Rosenkrantz, P., & Vogel, S. Sex-role stereotypes and clinical judgments of mental health. *Journal of Consulting and Clinical Psychology,* 1970, *34,* 1–7.

Broverman, I., Vogel, S., Broverman, D., Clarkson, F., & Rosenkrantz, S. Sex-role stereotypes: A current appraisal. *Journal of Social Issues,* 1972, *28,* 59–78.

Campbell, D. T., & Stanley, J. C. *Experimental and quasi-experimental designs for research.* Chicago: Rand McNally, 1963.

Chesler, P. Men drive women crazy. *Psychology Today,* July 1971, pp. 18, 22, 26–27, 97–98.

Chesler, P. *Women and madness.* New York: Doubleday, 1972.

Clifton, A. K., McGrath, D., & Wick, B. Stereotypes of women: A single category? *Sex Roles,* 1976, *2,* 135–148.

Coie, J. D., Pennington, B. F., & Buckley, H. H. Effects of situational stress and sex roles on the attribution of psychological disorder. *Journal of Consulting and Clinical Psychology,* 1974, *42,* 559–568.

Dion, K., Berscheid, E., & Walster, E. What is beautiful is good. *Journal of Personality and Social Psychology,* 1972, *24,* 285–290.

Feinblatt, J. A., & Gold, A. E. Sex roles and the psychiatric referral process. *Sex Roles,* 1976, *2,* 109–121.

Gomberg, E. Women and alcoholism. In V. Franks & V. Burtle (Eds.), *Women in therapy.* New York: Brunner/Mazel, 1974.

Gomes, B., & Abramowitz, S. Sex-related patient and therapist effects on clinical judgment. *Sex Roles,* 1976, *2,* 1–13.

Hill, C. Sex of client and sex and experience level of counselor. *Journal of Counseling Psychology,* 1975, *22,* 6–11.

Hill, M., & Lando, H. Physical attractiveness and sex-role stereotypes in impression formation. *Perceptual and Motor Skills,* 1976, *43,* 1251–1255.

Hobfoll, S., & Penner, L. Effect of physical attractiveness on therapists' initial judgments of a person's self-concept. *Journal of Consulting and Clinical Psychology,* 1978, *46,* 200–201.

Hollingshead, A., & Redlich, F. *Social class and mental illness: A community study.* New York: Wiley, 1958.

Holroyd, J., & Brodsky, A. Psychologists' attitudes and practices regarding erotic and nonerotic physical contact with patients. *American Psychologist,* 1977, *32,* 843–849.

Howard, E., & Howard, J. Women in institutions: Treatment in prisons and mental hospitals. In V. Franks & V. Burtle (Eds.), *Women in therapy.* New York: Brunner/Mazel, 1974.

Kardener, S., Fuller, M., & Mensh, I. A survey of physician's attitudes and practices regarding erotic and nonerotic contact with patients. *American Journal of Psychiatry*, 1973, 10, 1077–1081.

Keller, S. The female role: Constants and change. In V. Franks & V. Burtle (Eds.), *Women in therapy*. New York: Brunner/Mazel, 1974.

Kirsh, B. Consciousness-raising groups as therapy for women. In V. Franks & V. Burtle (Eds.), *Women in therapy*. New York: Brunner/Mazel, 1974.

Leventhal, G., & Kratt, R. Physical attractiveness and severity of sentencing. *Psychological Reports*, 1977, *40*, 315–318.

Maher, B. A. Stimulus sampling in clinical research: Representative design reviewed. *Journal of Consulting and Clinical Psychology*, 1978, *46*, 643–647.

Mant, A., & Darroch, D. B. Media images and medical images. *Social Science and Medicine*, 1975, *9*, 613–618.

Masling, J., & Harris, S. Sexual aspects of TAT administration. *Journal of Consulting and Clinical Psychology*, 1969, *33*, 166–169.

McKee, J., & Sherriffs, A. Men's and women's beliefs, ideals, and self-concepts. *American Journal of Sociology*, 1959, *64*, 356–363.

Meyer, J. W., & Sobieszek, B. J. The effect of a child's sex on adult interpretations of its behavior. *Developmental Psychology*, 1972, *6*, 42–48.

Miller, A. G. Role of physical attractiveness in impression formation. *Psychonomic Science*, 1970, *19*, 241–243.

National Association of Social Workers. *Directory of professional social workers*. Washington, D.C.: Author, 1972.

Neulinger, J. Perceptions of the optimally integrated person: A redefinition of mental health. *Proceedings of the 76th Annual Convention of the American Psychological Association*, 1968, *3*, 553–554. (Summary)

Perry, J. Physicians' erotic and nonerotic physical involvement with patients. *American Journal of Psychiatry*, 1976, *33*, 838–840.

Pollock, M. J. Changing the role of women. In H. Wortis & C. Rabinowitz (Eds.), *The women's movement: Social and psychological perspectives*. New York: Wiley, 1972.

Prather, J., & Fidell, L. S. Sex differences in the content and style of medical advertisements. *Social Science and Medicine*, 1975, *9*, 23–26.

Rosenkrantz, P., Vogel, S., Bee, H., Broverman, I., & Broverman, D. Sex-role stereotypes and self-concepts in college students. *Journal of Consulting and Clinical Psychology*, 1968, *32*, 287–295.

Russo, N. F. The motherhood mandate. *Journal of Social Issues*, 1976, *32*, 143–153.

Sandler, A. The effects of patients' physical attractiveness on therapists' clinical judgment. *Dissertation Abstracts International*, 1976, *36*, 3624B.

Schofield, W. *Psychotherapy: The purchase of friendship*. Englewood Cliffs, N.J.: Prentice-Hall, 1964.

Steiner, C. Radical psychiatry: Principles. In J. Agel (Ed.), *The radical therapist*. New York: Ballantine, 1971.

Stephan, C., & Tulley, J. The influence of physical attractiveness of a plaintiff on the decisions of simulated jurors. *Journal of Social Psychology*, 1977, *101*, 149–150.

Sue, S. Clients' demographic characteristics and therapeutic treatment: Differences that make a difference. *Journal of Consulting and Clinical Psychology*, 1976, *44*, 864.

Women on Words and Images. *Dick and Jane as victims: Stereotyping in children's readers*. Princeton, N.J.: Authors, 1972.

Zeldow, P. B. Search for sex differences in clinical judgment. *Psychological Reports*, 1975, *37*, 1135–1142.

7 Making the Conceptual Leap from Sex Bias to Countertransference: A Closer Look at the Patient-Therapist Dyad

CHRISTINE V. DAVIDSON

A retrospective examination of the literature on sex bias in clinical practice inevitably reveals that much of the formative research in this area was driven by a rather clear political agenda to expose the pernicious effects of "sex-biased" attitudes and behavior in the mental health professions. Since a good part of these research activities were stimulated by the radical psychiatry and feminist movements, one can also note the political and social "relevance" (to recall a phrase from the 1960s) of the topics themselves, the language of "oppressors and victims," and the clamor for an immediate redress of grievances. To be sure, in many instances the barbs were well aimed and deserved, a significant case in point being the public and professional discussion of the once unrecognized, even taboo, subject of unethical sexual behavior by therapists with their patients. By and large, however, sex bias researchers directed their attention to such questions as these: Do clinicians have sex-role-stereotypic conceptions of the mentally healthy man and woman? Are there differential (read "sex-biased") diagnostic criteria for men and women? Are women whose behavior departs from traditional sex-role norms viewed as less adjusted than their more conventional counterparts? And do "conser-

The contributions of Ronald H. Davidson to this chapter are gratefully acknowledged.

vative" therapists make more evaluative discriminations according to patient sex or sex-role attributes than do their "liberal" colleagues? Clearly, then, the sex bias literature has had a major consciousness-raising function in simply bringing the variables of patient and therapist sex and sex role to the attention of clinical researchers and the general public, though the paradoxical result of these efforts may have been to lead researchers further afield from the true heart of the psychotherapeutic interaction. Indeed, it does not seem unfair to remark that sex bias researchers often seemed to proceed as if there was nothing more to sex than bias.

Without detracting from the genuine contributions that the sex bias literature made in its time, this author would argue that there are compelling methodological and conceptual reasons why researchers interested in the study of sex and sex-role effects in psychotherapy ought to begin to reassess the value of the sex bias paradigm as an appropriate and productive line of investigation. Following a discussion of the problematic nature of the sex bias approach, this chapter offers some reasons for shifting our attention to the psychoanalytically derived notion of *countertransference* as an alternative research strategy. In defense of the sex bias position, it might well be argued that the concept was never meant to deal with the sort of phenomena that are subsumed under the heading of "countertransference," nor have the sex bias researchers shown much inclination to embark upon that path. However, insofar as the sex bias concept is fundamentally inadequate to the task of capturing the full complexity of the therapist's behavior, it also does not seem unfair to raise this as a prima facie reason to seek an alternative mode of inquiry. Whether or not countertransference may prove itself adequate to the task is equally problematic, though, and researchers interested in adopting this approach should note the emphasis given in the discussion below to the empirical difficulties that examining such a concept entails.

Finally, a separate objection to much of the sex bias literature is raised that goes beyond the consideration of the relative merits of a territorial dispute between two competing paradigms. With respect to both the political roots of the sex bias research and the seeming disinclination of most of its contributors to concern themselves with anything beyond a simplistic, attitudinal view of psychotherapeutic interaction, this chapter suggests that the very process of scientific investigation in this area represents a form of countertransference distortion in itself. Put another way, from the perspective of the philosophy of science, it is argued here that the purported data (i.e., "sex bias effects in psychotherapy") are epiphenomenal to the subjective investments and distortions of the observers. That *all* behavioral and social science methodology is inherently riddled with such subjective patterns of disturbance or sources of error is the operational premise of a countertransference position in general, and specifically so with regard to the implementation of realistic research on patient-therapist interaction.

THE SEX BIAS LITERATURE

The intense interest in sex bias in clinical practice is evidenced by the numerous literature reviews (C. V. Abramowitz & Dokecki, 1977; American Psychological Association, 1975; Davidson & Abramowitz, 1980; Kirshner, 1978; Maffeo, 1979; Sherman, 1980; Smith, 1980; Stricker, 1977; Whitley, 1979; Zeldow, 1978) that have appeared within a relatively brief period, let alone the published studies and unpublished doctoral dissertations examined in these reviews. By way of developing the case for the redirection of attention from sex bias to countertransference, it is important to turn first to an examination of the basic approaches that have been utilized in the studies of sex bias. Representative studies are therefore discussed here for their heuristic value, focusing on the question of the profitability of each particular approach for revealing the operation of sex and sex-role effects in the patient-therapist dyad. It is not the intent of this chapter, however, to serve as yet another detailed literature review, so readers interested in summaries of specific findings should turn instead to the reviews cited above.

Studies of Sex-Role-Stereotyped Mental Health Standards

The frequently cited study by Broverman, Broverman, Clarkson, Rosenkrantz, and Vogel (1970) on sex-role-related standards of mental health has had a major influence in shaping inquiry into sex bias in clinical practice. Not only did a rash of essentially similar investigations follow closely on its heels, but the study itself has been cited almost religiously in most of the subsequent papers on bias. In the study, clinicians were given a bipolar adjective list, all items of which were presumed to have a masculine and a feminine pole, with the masculine pole of some and the feminine pole of others being socially desirable. They were asked to use this list to describe a "mature, healthy, socially competent adult man," "woman," or "person" (Broverman et al., 1970, p. 2). One key data analysis examined consensus as to the characteristics of the healthy man and those of the healthy woman; another compared the similarity of each of these descriptions to that of the sex-unspecified "person," which was presumed to be a neutral standard of mental health. A host of methodological criticisms have been leveled at the study by previous reviewers (Stricker, 1977; Whitley, 1979), including the questionable evidence of item bipolarity and the scale's potential for generating artifactual findings linking masculinity to mental health. Furthermore, the investigators have come under deserved attack for editorializing about specific trait differences in clinicians' conceptions of the healthy man and woman in the absence of appropriate statistical tests of such differences.

Our primary concern here, however, is with the conceptual limitations of this type of approach. Even if it were established that clinicians have sex-role-biased stereotypes of mental health, this would still not be sufficient to demonstrate that these stereotypes influence their judgments of mental illness (Smith, 1980) or that these biases are activated in treatment (Smith, 1980; Stricker, 1977), although such conclusions have been widely drawn. These hypothetical linkages become even less clear when one considers that the studies in the tradition of Broverman et al. have typically provided no information about the patient other than sex, whereas, in reality, clinicians are faced with a complex array of patient information on which to base diagnostic and treatment decisions. Stearns, Penner, and Kimmel (1980) have thus commented that "it is difficult to conceive of a therapist who considers only the sex of a client before making a treatment recommendation" (p. 548). Indeed, they found that clinicians responded primarily to the patient's case history and symptomatology—not to his or her sex—in formulating treatment plans, as well as in describing the patient's current personal characteristics and those that they would expect the patient to have after a successful course of treatment. Patient psychopathology likewise proved more important than patient sex in a similar study by Billingsley (1977), who interpreted her data as suggesting that therapists work to promote androgynous rather than sex-role-stereotypic characteristics in their patients. Nevertheless, these data, like the Broverman et al. (1970) findings, remain within the realm of attitudinal or intellectual responses to paper and pencil tests; their generalizability to the affect-laden encounter between patient and therapist in the real world is as yet undetermined (Stricker, 1977).

Studies in the tradition of the Broverman et al. (1970) research—and, in fact, in the sex bias literature as a whole—have not attempted to examine the contributions of clinician attributes beyond sex and sex-role attitudes. The discussion returns to this point later, as such restriction poses a major limitation on what has been learned. It should be clear, however, at this point that while the studies of sex-role stereotyping have seemingly made much ado about sexism in clinical practice, their failure to extend beyond the attitudinal surface has sharply limited the usefulness of this conceptual paradigm.

Analogue Studies of Patient and Clinician Sex and Sex-Role Effects on Clinical Judgment

Most of the extant data on sex bias in clinical practice are from analogue studies of patient and clinician sex and sex-role effects on clinical judgment that, in their heyday, incorporated many of the methodological refinements of the well-controlled experiment. However, like the studies on sex-role stereotyping of mental health standards, they generally fell short of revealing much about real clinical phenomena, although their approximation to these phenomena was much better. For example, in one study (Gomes & Abramowitz, 1976) done at the peak of this research, patient sex and sex-role attributes were factorially varied in a fairly lengthy written case description, with all other information about the patient held constant. While such written protocols were the mode in analogue studies, a few investigators (e.g., Johnson, 1978; Schwartz & Abramowitz, 1978) made use of videotaped presentations of bogus patients in order to increase external validity. Each clinician/subject in the Gomes and Abramowitz study was given one of the four case reports and asked to rate, along Likert-type continua, the patient's emotional maturity, social adjustment, mental disorder and prognosis; their feelings of empathy and liking for the patient; and the normativeness of the patient's traits. This latter served as an empirical check on the efficacy of the experimental manipulation of patient sex-role attributes. Subjects also completed a sex-role attitude scale and were subsequently blocked for the data analyses into subsamples, according to their scores on this scale and their sex. With regard to the results of analogue research, interactions between patient and clinician characteristics were of particular interest, since they could most clearly demonstrate the intrusion of clinician factors in the evaluation of patients.

Both the patient material and the typical dependent variables—diagnosis, prognosis, and treatment recommendations—in these studies are considerably more similar to clinical reality than are the patient material and the dependent variables in the Broverman-type studies. Moreover, many analogues examined the question of whether patient sex-role attributes affect clinicians' evaluations of psychosocial dysfunction, a linkage to everyday clinical practice that was lacking in the research on sex-role stereotypes of mental health. Despite these improvements, however, this approach is vulnerable to the same basic criticism as the work in the Broverman tradition; by and large it, too, taps only clinicians' attitudes, and thus its findings may not validly mirror clinicians' behavior when faced with real patients. In fact, doubts have frequently been raised about the generalizability of findings of no bias, on the grounds that those findings might have been an artifact of social desirability. The generalizability of positive findings is also suspect, because the patient stimulus material in the typical analogue study is limited to a few "patients" (e.g., a male and a female version of the same protocol) and thus does not represent the range of individual differences among the patients of each sex that the practicing therapist routinely encounters (Smith, 1980).

As Zeldow (1978) has already noted, these studies are characterized by "an absence of a theoretical framework coupled with a 'shotgun' empirical approach involving numerous dependent variables of unknown reliability" (p. 92), both of which make interpretation of the data ambiguous, if not extremely risky. In a previous paper (Davidson & Abramowitz, 1980), this author suggested that the time has come to move beyond analogue research to more in-depth examination of the patient-therapist dyad, a comment that was limited in that paper to the methodological constraints and clinical impoverishment of the analogue. Such a step, however, requires a theoretical framework for understanding whatever sex or sex-role phenomena that are to be found in clinical data, least we replicate the conceptual barrenness of the analogue research.

Naturalistic Research Pertinent to Bias

Most reviewers of the sex bias literature have called for more data from actual clinical practice. Thus, Stricker (1977) has argued that "if one wished to discover how females are treated in psychotherapy, the methodology of choice would be to observe the therapy, describe it in a systematic way, and then draw conclusions. The problems in sampling patients, therapists, and therapies would be enormous, but if they were solved, one could reach a definitive conclusion" (p. 14). To be sure, various attempts have been made to bring naturalistic data to bear on the issue of sex bias, but these approaches have all had important limitations. For example, epidemiological statistics indicating that women have higher rates of mental illness and psychiatric treatment than men do have often been construed as evidence of clinician bias. Such an interpretation is extremely simplistic and hazardous, at best, because it overlooks the contributions to these rates of other factors such as strains in sex and marital roles (Gove, 1980).

Another, more direct approach has been to tap archival clinic records for comparative data on the diagnosis and treatment of men and women. The designs of many archival studies include clinician variables, so that the combined effects of patient and clinician attributes can be examined. However, since no active data collection is done in these studies, the clinician variables are necessarily confined to broad demographic and professional indexes such as sex and mental health discipline, which in many ways are even more tangential than clinician sex-role attitudes to the concerns that clinicians' personal attributes color their professional work with their patients. The value of some archival investigations is also limited by their dependent variables. Thus, findings of differences in the initial diagnosis or treatment assignment of male and female patients, while based on data from real patient-clinician dyads, do not automatically shed light on what transpires in the course of treatment. Archival data concerning treatment length that move us a small step closer to an examination of the latter phenomena have been reported in a handful of studies (e.g., S. I. Abramowitz, Davidson, Greene, & Edwards, 1980; Del Gaudio, Carpenter, & Morrow, 1978). However, in the absence of any information about session-to-session transactions, we are left to guess about the sex-related dynamics in the patient-clinician dyad that may have contributed to even the most intriguing differentials in treatment duration. In this spirit, the operation of "sex-role-related countertransference in psychotherapy" (p. 71) was inferred in one study (S. I. Abramowitz, Abramowitz, Roback, Corney, & McKee, 1976) from archival data on caseload composition and number of therapy sessions according to patient and therapist sex, although there was, in fact, neither the information about clinician personal history nor the information about patient-clinician interaction that is central to the concept of countertransference. The fit here between data and concept, then, was more suggested than established. Analysis of the methodological limitations of archival studies is available elsewhere (e.g., Davidson & Abramowitz, 1980; Werner & Block, 1975). The conclusion to be drawn from the present discussion, however, is that even these data from clinical records are unlikely to be able to yield much in the way of increasing our understanding of sex and sex-role effects in clinical practice.

Summary and Suggestions for a Redirection

The direction of the empirical findings on sex bias, as noted in the previous literature reviews, has been equivocal at best—a state of affairs that has unfortunately invited interpretation of the data "both as strong and weak evidence for sexism in the mental health field, depending on the view of the interpreter" (Zeldow, 1978, p. 93). Holding this empirical stalemate aside, however, a more pressing and cogent objection to the sex bias research can and should be made on conceptual grounds: that a legitimate, but politically fueled, concern engendered an inadequate and poorly conceptualized investigatory paradigm, which, by definition, limited its persuasive power as a unit of scientific achievement. In other words, this research could ultimately tell us little of value about either sex, bias, or psychotherapy. To recapitulate, the work has displayed a self-limiting tendency to remain at the attitudinal perimeter of psychotherapy, as demonstrated in particular by the heavy reliance on an analogue methodology that was designed to gauge clinicians' opinions about bogus patients, but that inevitably could not establish the fidelity of those opinions to clinicians' "real-life" behavior. Moreover, the wide dissemination of the results of the earlier sex bias analogues within the mental health professions may have in itself spoiled whatever potential this method had for eliciting anything other than socially desirable responses in subsequent studies, thereby limiting even the potential of this approach to reveal much about attitudes per se. Second, in the research to date, the key clinician variables have been limited to sex and sex-role attitudes. What has been sorely missing is information about clinicians' personal history that would better elucidate their contribution to sex or sex-role dynamics in therapy. This topic is more fully discussed later, as it is central to the primary argument that is to be developed in the next part of this chapter. Third, what we have come to know as the sex bias literature has been advanced, willy-nilly, from an essentially atheoretical position—a difficult enough task under ordinary circumstances of investigation, but a treacherous one for the investigator attempting to orient himself or herself in a domain of experience in which the findings are so prey to misappropriation in the service of politics.

Finally, the sex bias literature, because of its inherent limitations and inadequacies, simply begs the question of what actually transpires in the special relationship between therapist and patient. In keeping with the general recognition among clinical researchers of the complexity of questions about psychotherapy (i.e., Kiesler, 1971), it would therefore now seem appropriate to find ways to shift our activities in the direction of a potentially more fruitful, in-depth examination of that relationship. The epistemological lesson we may derive from the failure of the sex bias paradigm to give a clearer account of itself may also suggest a more productive line of approach in a domain of knowledge where the conditions for analysis and synthesis of experience exhibit an elusive, less accessible character than does the simplistic notion of bias—conditions that require an investigatory and explanatory paradigm equal to the task. For this reason, what is being suggested here as a point of departure is a reconsideration of the psychoanalytic concept of *countertransference*, a concept that claims as its phenomenological domain the complex interplay of clinician and patient personal histories and characteristics—particularly their expression, distortion, and perception—as a major component of psychotherapeutic process and an important contributor to treatment outcome.

THE CONCEPT OF COUNTERTRANSFERENCE

Historical Development of the Concept

Since Freud's initial introduction and rather specific definition of the term *countertransference* (1910/1957), considerable discussion, elaboration, and redefinition has occurred in the clinical literature, so that some understanding of the historical permutation of this concept is necessary both to avoid confusion and to appreciate the complexity of the process it was meant to signify. Freud clearly viewed the existence of countertransference feelings in the therapist as detrimental to the course and outcome of treatment, and he commented on the necessity for the therapist to "recognize this counter-transference in himself and overcome it . . . [since] no psychoanalyst goes further than his own complexes and internal resistances permit" (p. 145). This view would hold that the therapist must remain a neutral screen onto which the patient may project those conflict-ridden (presumably early parental) relationships that form the core of his or her neurotic difficulties. In the normal course of treatment, this therapeutic neutrality would allow the patient opportunity for a constructive reevaluation of his or her own hindered past and present functioning; hence Freud's suggestion that the therapist should reveal "nothing but what is shown to him" (1912/1957, p. 118).

When this central task of eliciting and facilitating the working through of the patient's transference reactions gives rise to analogous distorted perceptions of the patient by the therapist, then a "classical" countertransference reaction may be said to exist. For example, in psychotherapy supervision, a third-year medical student reported difficulty in attending carefully to his patient's productions. When asked by his supervisor to attempt to trace this blocking of his normally intuitive and empathic skills, the student eventually arrived at an understanding that his patient (a male homosexual whose transference behavior was of a clinging and otherwise passively demanding style) had aroused in him anxiety over his own unresolved feelings of dependency and passivity, which the student identified himself as being "perhaps a fear of seeing myself as soft or feminine." Further investigation of these feelings by the medical student revealed that both he and his patient shared considerable amounts of unresolved hostility toward their fathers, a reconstruction that allowed the student to understand more fully what was occurring in the treatment hour and to take appropriate steps to modify his behavior toward the patient (R. Davidson, Note 1).

Sandler, Dare, and Holder (1973) have summarized the classical view of countertransference:

> . . . for Freud, the fact that the psychoanalyst has feelings towards his patients, or conflicts aroused by his patients, did not in itself constitute countertransference. . . . Countertransference was seen as a sort of "resistance" in the psychoanalyst towards his patient, a resistance due to the arousal of unconscious conflicts by what the patient says, does or represents to the analyst. . . . In Freud's view, the conflicts were not in themselves countertransference, but could give rise to it. . . . [Additionally,] the "counter" in countertransference may . . . indicate a reaction in the analyst which implies a parallel to the patient's transference (as in "counterpart") as well as being a reaction to them (as in "counteract"). (pp. 62–64)

Subsequent contributors to the psychoanalytic literature who have held more or less to the classicial position on countertransference include Fenichel (1941), Fleiss (1953), Gitelson (1952), Glover (1955), Reich (1951, 1960), and Stern (1924). While there are some technical variations among those who maintain this classical stance, their work is generally marked by an adherence to the view of countertransference as a deleterious by-product that ought to be eradicated inasmuch as possible from the therapeutic encounter.

A number of other writers (e.g., Fromm-Reichmann, 1950; Heimann, 1950, 1960; Weigert, 1952; Winnicott, 1960) moved in the direction of extending the concept to cover the full range of the therapist's feelings and reactions toward the patient, not merely those that are provoked by the transference situation. Moreover, embedded in this view was the seemingly more heretical notion that, rather than a process to be avoided, certain types of countertransference phenomena could serve an instructive function for the therapist—that is, as an extension of the specifically honed cognitive processes learned and employed as part of the therapist's technical armamentarium. Kernberg (1975) has referred to this latter approach as the "totalistic" stance, in the sense that its advocates choose to subsume under its rubric the fullest possible range of clinical phenomena. While Kernberg encourages a broad conceptualization of countertransference and its place in therapy, he nevertheless criticizes much of the extant totalistic literature for its ambiguous and poorly defined set of operating boundaries, inadequacies that he suggests "[make] the term countertransference lose all specific meaning" (p. 50). In advancing his argument for a broad view, Kernberg lists several main objections that adherents of the totalistic orientation have directed toward the classical approach. First, the narrow classical definition implies that something is "wrong" if the therapist experiences an emotional reaction to a patient, thereby encouraging a "phobic" attitude toward his or her own reactions that restricts the therapist's understanding of the patient. Second, attempts to eliminate the therapist's emotional reactions negate a potentially vital source of information about the nonverbal communication between patient and therapist, whereas a reemphasis on the *controlled* assessment of these reactions allows for their utilization in the service of the therapeutic task. Third, certain patients (primarily those with borderline character disorders) are notorious for their ability to provoke extreme countertransference reactions in their therapists, so that a willingness and a trained ability to analyze one's own countertransference reactions may provide the therapist with "the most meaningful understanding of what is central in the patient's chaotic expression" (p. 51).

The reader may recognize an apparent contradiction in the example of the medical-student therapist described above. Although the student's countertransference reaction was stimulated by the transference situation (which is consistent with the classical formulation), the introspection that occurred during supervision about the reaction clearly demonstrates the utilitarian manner in which totalists would employ countertransference as a data source to inform the therapist about an important process in the psychotherapy. So as to avoid any misunderstanding, it should be stressed that few if any workers in this area, including this writer, approve of the extremely "radical" position taken by Little (1951) that the patient may benefit from the therapist actually sharing (in the form of a *countertransference interpretation*) his or her own distortions with the patient. Conversely, the example would fully support the classical position had the student's pathological reaction resulted in an uncontrolled negative response to the patient (i.e., fostering deterioration or premature termination). In effect, then, the movement away from the classical position allows us a more reasonable compromise focus on countertransference as an invaluable diagnostic and therapeutic tool. It is from this advantageous viewpoint that we may begin to consider how the concept of countertransference may come to fill a central role in the investigation of sex and sex-role effects in the therapeutic relationship.

Countertransference as a Conceptual Advancement beyond Bias

In a general sense, both the sex bias researchers and those involved in the study of countertransference share a mutual concern over the detrimental, irrational factors (whether one calls them "unstated" or "unconscious") that the clinician may bring to the treatment situation. This concern has been further encouraged by the extraordinary receptivity of social and behavioral scientists to the application of philosophy of science premises (e.g., Kuhn, 1970) in examining the professional infrastructure of their respective scientific communities. In attempting to assess the relative merits of a countertransference position over the arguments of sex bias researchers, it would behoove us to keep in mind Kuhn's advice that

> paradigm debates are *not really* [italics added] about relative problem-solving ability, though for good reasons they are usually couched in those terms. Instead, the issue is which paradigm should in the future guide research on problems many of which neither competitor can yet claim to resolve completely. A decision between alternative ways of practicing science is called for, and in the circumstances that decision must be based less on past achievement than on future promise. (1970, pp. 157–158)

It has already been suggested above that, while sex bias research has made some sound contributions in its time, it nevertheless has come to a stalemate due largely to its limited scope and atheoretical nature. More importantly, however, for those interested in further development of our understanding of sex and sex-role effects, one might legitimately raise the issue of whether the political roots and motivations of much of the bias research may have paradoxically resulted in the establishment of an "investigator countertransference effect," whereby well-intentioned but overdriven, even crusading, zeal was substituted for dispassionate investigation. The notion of "heartpotheses" in the face of disconfirmatory findings regarding sex bias has been discussed elsewhere (Davidson & Abramowitz, 1980). Whereas *hypotheses* accommodate themselves to data, *heartpotheses* allow the investigator to circumvent or continue to resist the evidence by appealing to the "common-sense" logic and personal beliefs of one's cohorts. To cite some examples, "all research is colored by the biases of the investigator and as long as a certain segment of the profession believes that sex bias does not exist, we will have to demonstrate what we, with feminist-biased eyes and ears, know to be true" (Brodsky, 1980, p. 334). Another writer (Sherman, 1980), apparently frustrated over the "ambivalent" findings regarding sex bias, seriously proposed that "if one wished to gain more information . . . knowledge of the prevalence of bias against women and sex-role stereotyping in psychotherapy might be obtained from surveys of women's groups" (p. 62). Such an investigatory ethos, a rather clear vestige of the political origins of this field, tends to undermine whatever reserves of credibility that scholars may normally expect to draw upon and, more importantly, even to alienate many of those clinicians and investigators whom the sex bias researchers had allegedly sought most to influence.

Where the development of a scientific undertaking eventuates in a "them and us mind set" (Davidson, 1980, p. 903), and particularly where normal discourse gives way to a shrill, polemical tone, one may speculate whether or not rational theory building has given way to an irrational element—that is, to a reliance on a narcissistically invested paradigm that serves something of a mystical function for the group. Rothstein (1980) has commented on the difficulties for science where such narcissistically invested theories are "perceived (consciously and/or unconsciously) to be perfect" (p. 387) or felt to be the ultimate arbiter of reality for their adherents. In attempting to understand the world "the scientist subliminally perceives his helplessness. Intelligence is invested as the vehicle to actively undo that helplessness. One seeks to defend against accepting one's intellectual limitations by adopting the narcissistically invested theory that holds out the possibility of having all the answers" (p. 388). Such prior commitments have both metaphysical and methodological implications, dictating to scientists the nature of the entities the universe does and does not contain, what ultimate laws and explanations must be like, and even what research problems are permissible (Kuhn, 1970).

Ultimately, however, the case for making a transition from sex bias to countertransference as an organizing conceptual matrix involves more than a mere shift in terminology. The work on sex bias has failed to provide meaningful, enduring insight into sex and sex-role effects in psychotherapy, because the construct itself is fundamentally incapable of moving beyond the surface structure of overt social attitudes to the less accessible level of covert deep structures inherent in the reciprocal exchange between patient and therapist, a realm whose charting offers the most fruitful possibilities for informing our inquiry into this special relationship. The data base for the study of countertransference, on the other hand, necessarily brings into view specific information about the therapist's personal history and interpersonal dynamics, with particular attention being paid to the operation of those dynamics in the therapist's cognitive process and behavior in the treatment situation. No such intricate scrutiny of the therapist's history and functioning is mandated in the sex bias formulation, where investigators are content to rest with knowing the therapist's sex and sex-role attitudes or supposed political beliefs. Since countertransference is, by definition, a process that occurs *in* therapy (and that is presumably linked to outcome), a decision to adopt this concept as a research stratagem would overcome a major objection to the sex bias research: that the most cogent dependent variables are those that come to grips with actual therapy rather than those that are limited to attitudes *about* therapy.

From a related perspective, Kaplan (Kaplan, 1979; Kaplan & Yasinski, Note 2) has already attempted to show that our understanding of the relational aspects of the therapeutic process can be enhanced by reference to the therapist's development as a gendered and socialized person. Thus, given the presumably differential early experience of male and female therapists in being mothered by women, including such salient factors as sex-related differences in the phase of separation-individuation from the mother (Chodorow, 1978), Kaplan and Yasinski (Note 2) have proposed the study of three particular relational components of therapy: (1) *level of intimacy* (related in part to "the daughter's early development of a sense of self within the context of a relationship with another female"); (2) *empathic understanding* (e.g., "is empathic understanding between two women in therapy influenced by the mother's projection of her own needs into the daughter . . . ?"); and (3) *ability to be aware of and use emotional responses* (i.e., "do the empathic, intimate dimensions of the pre-Oedipal relationship influence women's ability to be aware of and use their own emotional states in therapy, as either patient or therapist?") In another vein, Wolfe (Note 3), noting the lack of attention to cognitive meanings of sex and sex role in psychotherapy research, has commented that "to give the gender variable its due . . . a conceptualization of the role of gender in psychotherapy is required which reflects the *meanings* that therapists and patients attach to their own gender-related behavior, as well as to the gender behavior of the other therapy participant" (p. 2).

The discussion returns below to an elaboration of the various ways in which this type of innovative research question could be implemented. One final comment is needed here, however, with respect to the attempts of many sex bias researchers to squeeze overtime performance from their operational paradigm as both a research puzzle and a call to arms. While this effort has clearly condemned itself to failure, it should not pass unnoticed that the rehabilitation of such a clinically derived notion as countertransference offers applied advantages beyond our general research focus—a situation that may paradoxically facilitate the kind of sensitization to the operation of sex and sex-role effects in psychotherapy that has proven so elusive a goal to date. In contradistinction to the simplistic dichotomy of sexist versus nonsexist therapists, the countertransference approach redefines the issue of sex- and sex-role-related transactions by allowing that clinicians are products of their socialization as *men or women*, thereby inviting them to partake in a potentially more productive self-examination of interpersonal distortions that may arise from the question of gender. It may be hoped that this self-examination would serve to foster both a therapeutic utilization of countertransference phenomena (as previously illustrated in the example of the medical-student therapist) and the eradication of countertherapeutic (i.e., neurotic) emotional conflicts in the therapist that would impair his or her work. Although one would not want to fault the desirability or usefulness of the reeducative and consciousness-raising efforts that have been proposed as elixirs in the sex bias literature, it should be clear by now that the operation of sex and sex-role influences in human relationships is of such subtlety and complexity as to demand a remedial strategy that is more equal to the task.

Attempts to Operationalize the Concept of Countertransference

To recapitulate the argument so far, it has been suggested that the conceptual barrenness of the sex bias paradigm, coupled with the narcissistic investment of many politically motivated researchers in that field, has led to a state of affairs where the very process of research itself has been contaminated by the latent potential for unrecognized and uncontrolled countertransference distortion—an epistemological predicament that has, in effect, brought this entire investigatory enterprise to the edge of bankruptcy. Acknowledging this impasse as a form of "countertransference resistance masquerading as methodology" (Devereux, 1967, p. xvi) is a first step toward coming to grips with the inherent anxiety that the observer of clinical data must confront. For those who are willing to follow the direction of this argument a bit further, it must also be recognized that there is no prefabricated solution at hand, since extant research on countertransference as a general clinical phenomenon has been fraught with conceptual and methodological difficulties of its own. Without a doubt, the expansion of the concept of countertransference, as outlined previously, from the original classical intent (i.e., linkage to the transference situation) to the more recent all-incorporative defusion characterized by the totalistic position (i.e., that *all* feelings toward the patient represent countertransference) has enormously confounded the problems of operationalization.

Taking this issue as a point of departure, Luborsky and his colleagues (Luborsky & Spence, 1971, 1978; Singer & Luborsky, 1978), in a series of literature reviews, have identified a host of difficulties in the operationalization of the concept; they note especially that the subtleties and complexities implicit in the theoretical qualitative studies have eluded quantitative translation. The bulk of the quantitative research cited in their most extensive review paper on countertransference (Singer & Luborsky, 1978) employed conceptual and operational definitions that illustrate Kernberg's comment (1975) that the plasticity of definitional criteria of the totalistic view runs the risk of rendering the notion of countertransference all but meaningless. In discussing the range of studies that purport to deal with countertransference, Singer and Luborsky tend to echo Kernberg's sentiments, remarking that the types of questions addressed further obscure the subject matter. Moreover,

> the difficulties involved in controlling variables in such a complex field as psychotherapy research have been so enormous that investigators have not been able to work very well with the more subtle, yet substantial, aspects of countertransference. Rather, these studies have been limited to more simplified and superficial problems, and restricted in terms of what could be measured (p. 448).

Nevertheless, they are able to point to a handful of studies that attempted to assess the therapist's own conflicts and to explore how those conflicts were manifested in his or her interactions with patients.

In one study, Bandura, Lipsher, and Miller (1960) obtained information about therapists' (in this case, clinical psychology graduate students') emotional conflicts by having clinical psychology staff members who knew them well rate them on several dimensions of hostility, anxiety, and dependency behavior. Tapes of sessions involving these therapists were reviewed for instances of expression of hostility by the patient; the object (e.g., spouse, self, therapist) toward which the hostility was directed was recorded; the therapists' reactions to this hostility were scored as either approach or avoidance responses; and the occurrences of further expression of hostility subsequent to the therapists' responses were counted. The findings of this study were consistent with theoretical predictions regarding the operation of countertransference. Therapists who tended to express anger directly and who had a low need for approval were more likely than their peers were to permit and encourage patients' expressions of hostility; such approach reactions by the therapist were found, in turn, to be more likely to stimulate further (presumably constructive) expression of hostility by the patient. Additionally, therapists were more likely to avoid patient hostility when it was directed at them rather than at others.

Cutler (1958), on the other hand, sought to define areas of therapists' conflicts in interpersonal functioning by reference to the magnitude of the discrepancy between self-reports and judges' ratings on a variety of dimensions, such as "dominating," "rejecting," "respectful," and "agreeable." Therapy sessions conducted by these clinicians and the therapists' dictated accounts of those sessions were both scored for instances of these same interpersonal issues. Again, consistent with countertransference formulations, there proved to be significant discrepancies between the data from the session and the data recalled (i.e., overreported or underreported) by the therapist when the interpersonal issue at hand was an area of conflict for the therapist. Additionally, a relationship obtained between the type of material the patient presented and the adequacy of the therapist's response to it, with conflictual topics eliciting ego-defensive as opposed to task-oriented behaviors (i.e., responses geared toward stimulating the flow of therapeutically relevant material) from the therapists.

Therapists' general level of anxiety was found to affect their behavior in two other studies (although one must question whether, in fact, this particular phenomenon is relevant to countertransference in the ways that the investigators suggested). Graduate-student therapists, who had been judged to have high or low anxiety on the basis of content of extemporaneous speech samples, were asked by Yulis and Kiesler (1968) to listen to taped interviews in which the content of the patient's verbalization was either sexual, aggressive, or neutral. Pauses had been built into the tapes, during which the subjects had to choose which of two comments they would make to the patient; one alternative reflected recognition that the therapist was the object of the patient's feelings, and the other alternative (defined in this study as indicative of greater countertransference) was marked by avoidance or denial of such recognition. The more anxious therapists selected the defensive remarks more often than the less anxious therapists did. In a study by Milliken and Kirchner (1971), counseling students who had obtained higher scores on an anxiety scale recalled less of what had occurred in a simulated interview with an actor (recall being measured by an objective true-false test) than did their less anxious peers.

While none of these investigations are directly germane to the area of sex- and sex-role-related transactions in psychotherapy, they nevertheless serve to illustrate some ways in which we might begin to retrench and retool for a new approach. The most salient features of these studies for our purposes, therefore, are that some attempt was made, most notably by Bandura et al. (1960) and Cutler (1958), to gauge conflictual areas in a therapist's own emotional functioning (although this was by no means the type of exhaustive and genetic treatment of the therapist's personal contributions that a full appreciation of the question of countertransference would require); to relate those areas to the therapist's responses to the patient; and, in the Bandura et al. and Cutler studies, to link the therapist's responses to the patient's subsequent productions.

RESEARCH DIRECTIONS FOR THE STUDY OF SEX- AND SEX-ROLE-RELATED COUNTERTRANSFERENCE

Having critically reviewed the inherent difficulties of the sex bias research as well as the usefulness of a countertransference paradigm, and also having suggested the potential windfall gains that such a redirection might yield, we are now left with the task of indicating just how one might go about implementing such a revised strategy for the examination of sex and sex-role effects in psychotherapy. To begin with, it is imperative that researchers identify those sex and sex-role issues that might be manifested in the form of countertransference reactions in therapy. While it is beyond the scope of this chapter to offer an encyclopedic list of pertinent variables, even a cursory glance at the literature on sex-role socialization, including the recent work on patterns of mothering and fathering (Biller, 1974; Chodorow, 1978), and sex differences in personality and behavior (Block, 1978) suggest ample opportunities for integrating into psychotherapy research major organizing variables that have proven their value in developmental, personality, and social psychology. Similarly, the smaller body of work on therapist life history might provide an additional source of variables. For example, with respect to the differential socialization of males and females to assume positions of authority and power, a key question related to the process and outcome of psychotherapy might be pursued in examining therapists' responses to what Neill (1979) has termed "the difficult patient"—that is, an individual who is "perceived to be significantly more demanding . . . , dangerous, difficult to empathize with, manipulative, and likely to polarize the staff" (p. 209). In this instance, one might consider a study in which therapists' reactions to such resistant, uncooperative, and rejecting patients would be examined in light of their own history of rehearsal for authority. Given the well-known chaotic transference-countertransference struggles for control that these patients typically provoke, what might we be able to learn about sex- or sex-role-related patterns of "managing" such patients, as well as therapists' ways of coping with their own anxiety? Among the hypothetical countertransference issues that might be raised here are the resultant sex-role-conditioned moves toward either attempting to reassert control over the patient or evading the power aspects of the conflict—behaviors that might tell us a great deal about male and female therapists' differential styles of empathy and identification with the patient. A related topic for study in such an area would obviously center around the handling of anger toward the patient, along with the narcissistic threat to therapists' clinical self-esteem and interpersonal skills. Given the overemphasis in the sex bias literature on the difficulties of male therapists with female patients, it seems only equitable that a few writers have begun to suggest sex-role-related areas of countertransference difficulties experienced by female therapists toward their patients (e.g., confusion regarding attraction to or fear of male patients; issues surrounding pregnancy or homosexuality of female patients) ("Countertransference—and Female Trainees," 1979). Interestingly, Lothstein (1977) has identified some patterns of acute countertransference anxieties experienced by male and female therapists confronted by gender-dysphoric patients, noting differential responses according to sex of the therapist and gender orientation of the patient (i.e., female therapist with male-to-female gender-dysphoric patient, male therapist with male-to-female gender-dysphoric patient, etc.).

The nature of this type of research places the added burden upon the investigator of separating those more surface attitudinal constructs that have been the focus of so much attention in the sex bias literature from the more authentic enduring patterns of countertransference phenomena that are the sequelae of developmental experiences and emotional conflicts within the therapist. The gathering of the latter information represents an investigatory challenge in its own right. If we accept the premise that certain events (e.g., object loss of one's father, mother, or sibling due to divorce or death) during one's childhood tend, on the average, to have predictable and observable effects on one's personality and behavior as an adult, then we might be able to make limited use of simple demographic data as a source of information about likely conflictual areas for therapist/subjects. A more substantial data pool could be obtained from in-depth, retrospective clinical interviews concerning early childhood memories, experiences, and so forth. Although these kinds of approaches would yield a considerably more informed basis on which to judge whether or not particular clinicians are likely to be prone to specific forms of countertransference (i.e., forms centered around the sex- and sex-role-related issues under investigation in a study), they are admittedly only capable of scratching the surface in this regard. A more potent, though correspondingly more inaccessible, source of information would be third parties who are uniquely privy to the relevant personal and interpersonal data: In increasing order of their informational value for our purposes, those supplying ratings could include professional peers or colleagues, therapy supervisors, training analysts, or even the therapists' own therapists. Obviously, the procedural and ethical issues here would be enormously complex, but the price would inevitably be worth the wager in that we would be able to develop a three-generational schema of psychotherapy. In other words, such an approach would allow us to look at the historical permutation of an emotional conflict in the therapist as experienced by patient, therapist, and observer (C. V. Davidson, Note 4; Gediman & Wolkenfeld, 1980). It should also be noted that this sort of methodology is applicable to research efforts that take either a single-case perspective (choosing to trade off broader generalizability for the ability to make a more sensitive microanalysis of the operation of countertransference) or a more standard large-sample approach. Regarding the potential applications for single-case studies, one should not overlook the possibilities for a rich historical review of extant published cases or other clinical sources (e.g., Blacker & Abraham, in press; Elms, 1980).

At the same time, key situations in the interaction between patient and therapist that have the potential for eliciting countertransference responses (of whatever kind that are being examined in a particular study) from the therapist need to be isolated. If one is employing transcripts of actual therapy sessions, this can readily be done by independent raters. Analogue methodology, keeping in mind its limitations as noted earlier in this chapter, may still have some residual utility here as an alternative to studying real therapy sessions, since the analogue does allow a sharp, deliberate portrayal of specific events that might stimulate countertransference. To illustrate, in a study of counselor sex differences in reactivity to clients, Johnson (1978) showed a videotape of either an angry male, an angry female, a depressed male, or a depressed female to each of her subjects, who were asked to report their immediate subjective feelings about the client and to indicate what they would say to him or her during built-in pauses in the tape. These verbal responses were then scored for sympathy for the client, identification with the client, defensiveness toward the client, and anger toward the client; the subjects themselves rated their liking for, comfort with, and empathy for the client, as well as client attractiveness for counseling. The point to be emphasized here is that this study, both in terms of the type of pull created in the videotapes and the technique of free verbal response with which some of the clinicians' reactions were captured, came remarkably close to fulfilling the necessary criteria for an authentic study of countertransference. Its major oversight in this regard was that the requisite personal data on the therapists were lacking—a shortcoming that could certainly be easily remedied in future studies.

Assuming that critical countertransference-prone incidents could be reliably identified in transcripts, audiotapes, or videotapes of psychotherapy sessions, we might be in a better position to assess the theoretical and clinical assumptions regarding inappropriate countertransference interference or acting out (depending on the type and intensity of the particular behavior). For example, certain effects on the patient might occur immediately and be more readily observable, such as the hypothetical formulation whereby the patient reacts in anger and disappointment when the therapist falls into a seductive transference trap by not recognizing that the real motivation stems from the patient's need to "test" the therapist as well as reality (Sampson & Wallerstein, 1972; Silberschatz, 1978). This same situation may likewise result in such longer-term consequences as inappropriate prolongation of treatment, premature termination, or poor outcome, including deterioration. We should also keep in mind the distinction made by Reich (1951) between "acute" and "chronic" patterns of countertransference in the therapist. The term *chronic* here is meant to describe those instances in which a therapist has established a personal tradition of countertransference reactions to *all* patients, regardless of their characteristics (e.g., a therapist who consistently elicits and rewards dependency behavior in his or her patients in order to satisfy unresolved needs for control and power), while the term *acute* refers to idiosyncratic, case-by-case therapist reactions to particular stimuli in the interaction with the patient (e.g., the instance of the medical student referred to in the discussion above).

It must also be remarked that researchers interested in developing this line of inquiry ought to make their first order of business the opening up and expansion of those naturalistic laboratories in which the in-depth study of countertransference may best flourish. This would entail, among other things, a concerted effort on the part of researchers to establish formal associations with psychoanalytic institutes (and for those so inclined, perhaps even seeking training as analysts themselves); the initiation of collaborative research within psychiatric residency and clinical psychology internship programs; and the implementation of workshops and seminars on methods of intensive psychotherapy supervision (i.e., geared toward the conjoint examination of and sensitization to therapists' personal functioning, in addition to their mastery of treatment techniques) as part of regular clinical training.

CONCLUSIONS

This chapter has touched upon a number of theoretical, clinical, and empirical issues by way of developing the case for adopting a more productive conceptual framework than sex bias for the study of sex and sex-role effects in psychotherapy. Undoubtedly, some readers may protest the choice of countertransference as an alternative organizing concept, whether out of scientific or political objections to psychoanalytic theory in general. It has not been the intent here to make a case for psychoanalysis as well, nor to suggest that countertransference is the only useful vantage point from which to view patient-therapist dynamics. Certainly, other workers may wish to bring to bear additional constructs from the related areas of personality and social psychology, while still others may yet see some remaining value in retaining the concept of sex bias.

At the same time, given the predilections of polemically driven writers to misunderstand or misrepresent psychoanalytically oriented work—that is, selectively citing badly dated early psychoanalytic paradigms, overlooking what is lasting, failing to acknowledge the systematic updating and critical reexamination that has always been a central characteristic of the analytic tradition—it would nevertheless seem prudent to reemphasize what (to most readers) is no doubt patently obvious about the nature of countertransference as a clinical phenomenon and a research position. Since the area of concern in this chapter is directly related to such anxiety-arousing topics as sexuality, sex-linked personality development, and the psychology of women, the accountability of clinicians and researchers needs to be phrased accordingly: Advancing from a countertransference position in these types of research activities does not imply a concomitant disregard for misinformed or poor clinical practice with women patients. On the contrary, where iatrogenic effects in psychotherapy are shown to be a function of therapist personality or behavior, the moral and ethical imperative implicit in the countertransference position requires, as a prerequisite to further patient contact, that the noxious components of characterology by demonstrably resolved, not merely denied or covered over in the form of socially desirable attitude change. Parenthetically, with respect to the separate instance of sexual contact between therapist and patient, the countertransference concept is perhaps of little more value than that of sex bias, since most responsible clinicians of whatever theoretical persuasion maintain that such behavior is nothing short of a special category of rape. The psychoanalytic position is particularly unequivocal in this regard, insisting not only that such contact is never allowable under *any* circumstances, but that where such ethical violations do occur there is clear evidence of irreparable harm to the patient and to the course of treatment (e.g., often resulting in a situation in which the patient is rendered unanalyzable or untreatable in any subsequent therapy, because the frightening erotic component of the Oedipal transference has been inappropriately gratified by the therapist) (Blum, 1973; Marmor, 1972).

One might say, paradoxically, that the clinically derived notion of countertransference, with its locus of concern rooted in the continual struggle for maintaining therapeutically and ethically appropriate boundaries between therapist and patient, draws a "harder line" in many respects than the polemically inspired hunt for sex bias. That this is so is related, in large part, to the basic psychoanalytic assumptions concerning the reciprocal nature of disturbances in the field between the observer and the observed—between clinician and patient—in a situation where "the subject most capable of manifesting scientifically exploitable behavior is the observer himself" (Devereux, 1967, p. xix). For our purposes as observers and chroniclers of the unique patterns of communication and human interaction found in psychotherapy, the data provided by the study of sex- and sex-role-related countertransference may serve to inform us equally as much about our own pseudomethodological distortions as researchers. That such data may ultimately force us to come to grips with both extremes of our professional ego defenses—whether in the form of anxiety-ridden denial or counterphobic, polemical posturing—is reason enough to warrant our attention to the countertransference paradigm.

REFERENCE NOTES

1. Davidson, R. Personal communication, December 1980.
2. Kaplan, A. G., & Yasinski, L. Research issues on women and therapy: Can a theoretical perspective inform investigations of process? Paper presented at Women and Psychotherapy: An Assessment of the State of the Art of Research on Psychotherapy with Women, Washington, D.C., March 1979.
3. Wolfe, B. E. *The Imperatives of gender differentiation: Implications for psychotherapy research.* Paper presented at the meeting of the Society for Psychotherapy Research, Asilomar, California, June 1980.
4. Davidson, C. V. *Gender influences in the patient-therapist dyad.* Paper presented at the meeting of the Society for Psychotherapy Research, Asilomar, California, June 1980.

REFERENCES

Abramowitz, C. V., & Dokecki, P. R. The politics of clinical judgment: Early empirical returns. *Psychological Bulletin*, 1977, *84*, 460–476.

Abramowitz, S. I., Abramowitz, C. V., Roback, H. B., Corney, R. T., & McKee, E. Sex-role-related countertransference in psychotherapy. *Archives of General Psychiatry*, 1976, *33*, 71–73.

Abramowitz, S. I., Davidson, C. V., Greene, L. R., & Edwards, D. W. Sex-role-related countertransference revisited: A partial extension. *Journal of Nervous and Mental Disease*, 1980, *168*, 309–311.

American Psychological Association. Report of the Task Force on Sex Bias and Sex-Role Stereotyping in Psychotherapeutic Practice. *American Psychologist*, 1975, *30*, 1169–1175.

Bandura, A., Lipsher, D. H., & Miller, P. E. Psychotherapists' approach-avoidance reactions to patients' expressions of hostility. *Journal of Consulting Psychology*, 1960, *24*, 1–8.

Biller, H. B. *Paternal deprivation: Family, school, sexuality, and society.* Lexington, Mass.: Heath, 1974.

Billingsley, D. Sex bias in psychotherapy: An examination of the effects of client sex, client psychopathology, and therapist sex on treatment planning. *Journal of Consulting and Clinical Psychology*, 1977, *45*, 250–256.

Blacker, K. H., & Abraham, R. The Rat Man revisited: A look at the maternal conflict. *International Journal of Psychoanalytic Psychotherapy*, in press.

Block, J. H. Another look at sex differentiation in the socialization behaviors of mothers and fathers. In J. A. Sherman & F. L. Denmark (Eds.), *The psychology of women: Future directions in research.* New York: Psychological Dimensions, 1978.

Blum, H. P. The concept of erotized transference. *Journal of the American Psychoanalytic Association*, 1973, *21*, 61–76.

Brodsky, A. M. A decade of feminist influence on psychotherapy. *Psychology of Women Quarterly*, 1980, *4*, 331–344.

Broverman, I. K., Broverman, D. M., Clarkson, F. E., Rosenkrantz, P. S., & Vogel, S. R. Sex-role stereotypes and clinical judgments of mental health. *Journal of Consulting and Clinical Psychology*, 1970, *34*, 1–7.

Chodorow, N. *The reproduction of mothering: Psychoanalysis and the sociology of gender.* Berkeley: University of California Press, 1978.

Countertransference—and female trainees. *Psychiatric News*, August 3, 1979.

Cutler, R. L. Countertransference effects in psychotherapy. *Journal of Consulting Psychology*, 1958, *22*, 349–356.

Davidson, C. V. From politics to method in the psychology of women. (Review of *The psycholo-*

gy of women: Future directions in research, ed. by J. A. Sherman & F. L. Denmark.) *Contemporary Psychology,* 1980, *25,* 902–903.

Davidson, C. V., & Abramowitz, S. I. Sex bias in clinical judgment: Later empirical returns. *Psychology of Women Quarterly,* 1980, *4,* 377–395.

Del Gaudio, A., Carpenter, J. R., & Morrow, G. Male and female treatment differences: Can they be generalized? *Journal of Consulting and Clinical Psychology,* 1978, *46,* 1577–1578.

Devereux, G. *From anxiety to method in the behavioral sciences.* The Hague: Mouton, 1967.

Elms, A. C. Freud, Irma, Martha: Sex and marriage in the "dream of Irma's injection." *Psychoanalytic Review,* 1980, *67,* 83–109.

Fenichel, O. Problems of psychoanalytic technique. *Psychoanalytic Quarterly,* 1941, *27,* 71–75.

Fleiss, R. Countertransference and counteridentification. *Journal of the American Psychoanalytic Association,* 1953, *1,* 268–284.

Freud, S. The future prospects of psycho-analytic therapy. In J. Strachey (Ed.), *Standard Edition* (Vol. 11). London: Hogarth, 1957. (Originally published, 1910.)

Freud, S. Recommendations to physicians practicing psycho-analysis. In J. Strachey (Ed.), *Standard Edition* (Vol. 12). London: Hogarth, 1957. (Originally published, 1912.)

Fromm-Reichmann, F. *Principles of intensive psychotherapy.* Chicago: University of Chicago Press, 1950.

Gediman, H. K., & Wolkenfeld, F. The parallelism phenomenon in psychoanalysis and supervision: Its reconsideration as a triadic system. *Psychoanalytic Quarterly,* 1980, *49,* 234–255.

Gitelson, M. The emotional position of the analyst in the psychoanalytic situation. *International Journal of Psycho-Analysis,* 1952, *33,* 1–10.

Glover, E. *The technique of psycho-analysis.* New York: International Universities Press, 1955.

Gomes, B., & Abramowitz, S. I. Sex-related patient and therapist effects on clinical judgment. *Sex Roles: A Journal of Research,* 1976, *2,* 1–13.

Gove, W. R. Mental illness and psychiatric treatment among women. *Psychology of Women Quarterly,* 1980, *4,* 345–362.

Heimann, P. On counter-transference. *International Journal of Psycho-Analysis,* 1950, *31,* 81–84.

Heimann, P. Countertransference. *British Journal of Medical Psychology,* 1960, *33,* 9–15.

Johnson, M. Influence of counselor gender on reactivity to clients. *Journal of Counseling Psychology,* 1978, *25,* 359–365.

Kaplan, A. G. Toward an analysis of sex-role-related issues in the therapeutic relationship. *Psychiatry,* 1979, *42,* 112–120.

Kernberg, O. F. *Borderline conditions and pathological narcissism.* New York: Jason Aronson, 1975.

Kiesler, D. J. Experimental designs in psychotherapy research. In A. E. Bergin & S. L. Garfield (Eds.), *Handbook of psychotherapy and behavior change: An empirical analysis.* New York: Wiley, 1971.

Kirshner, L. A. Effects of gender on psychotherapy. *Comprehensive Psychiatry,* 1978, *19,* 79–82.

Kuhn, T. S. *The structure of scientific revolutions* (2nd ed.). Chicago: University of Chicago Press, 1970.

Little, M. Counter-transference and the patient's response to it. *International Journal of Psycho-Analysis,* 1951, *32,* 32–40.

Lothstein, L. M. Countertransference reactions to gender dysphoric patients: Implications for psychotherapy. *Psychotherapy: Theory, Research, and Practice,* 1977, *14,* 21–31.

Luborsky, L., & Spence, D. P. Quantitative research on psychoanalytic therapy. In A. E. Bergin & S. L. Garfield (Eds.), *Handbook of psychotherapy and behavior change: An empirical analysis.* New York: Wiley, 1971.

Luborsky, L., & Spence, D. P. Qualitative research on psychoanalytic therapy. In S. L. Garfield

& A. E. Bergin (Eds.), *Handbook of psychotherapy and behavior change: An empirical analysis* (2nd ed.). New York: Wiley, 1978.

Maffeo, P. A. Thoughts on Stricker's "Implications of research for psychotherapeutic treatment of women." *American Psychologist*, 1979, *34*, 690–695.

Marmor, J. Sexual acting out in psychotherapy. *American Journal of Psychoanalysis*, 1972, *32*, 3–8.

Milliken, R. L., & Kirchner, R. Counselor's understanding of student's communication as a function of the counselor's perceptual defense. *Journal of Counseling Psychology*, 1971, *18*, 14–18.

Neill, J. R. The difficult patient: Identification and response. *Journal of Clinical Psychiatry*, 1979, *40*, 209–212.

Reich, A. On counter-transference. *International Journal of Psycho-Analysis*, 1951, *32*, 25–31.

Reich, A. Further remarks on counter-transference. *International Journal of Psycho-Analysis*, 1960, *41*, 389–395.

Rothstein, A. Psychoanalytic paradigms and their narcissistic investment. *Journal of the American Psychoanalytic Association*, 1980, *28*, 385–395.

Sampson, H., & Wallerstein, R. S. New research directions: Comment from a psychoanalytic perspective. In H. Strupp & A. E. Bergin (Eds.), *Changing frontiers in the science of psychotherapy*. Chicago: Aldine-Atherton, 1972.

Sandler, J., Dare, C., & Holder, A. *The patient and the analyst: The basis of the psychoanalytic process*. New York: International Universities Press, 1973.

Schwartz, J. M., & Abramowitz, S. I. Effects of female client physical attractiveness on clinical judgment. *Psychotherapy: Theory, Research, and Practice*, 1978, *15*, 251–257.

Sherman, J. A. Therapists' attitudes and sex-role stereotyping of women. In A. M. Brodsky & R. Hare-Mustin (Eds.), *Women and psychotherapy*. New York: Guilford Press, 1980.

Silberschatz, G. Effects of the analyst's neutrality on the patient's feelings and behavior in the psychoanalytic situation (Doctoral dissertation, New York University, 1978). *Dissertation Abstracts International*, 1978, *39*, 3007B. (University Microfilms No. 7824277)

Singer, B. A., & Luborsky, L. Countertransference: The status of clinical versus quantitative research. In A. Gurman & A. Razin (Eds.), *Effective psychotherapy: A handbook of research*. New York: Pergamon Press, 1978.

Smith, M. L. Sex bias in counseling and psychotherapy. *Psychological Bulletin*, 1980, *87*, 392–407.

Stearns, B. C., Penner, L. A., & Kimmel, E. Sexism among psychotherapists: A case not yet proven. *Journal of Consulting and Clinical Psychology*, 1980, *48*, 548–550.

Stern, A. On the counter-transference in psychoanalysis. *Psychoanalytic Review*, 1924, *11*, 166–174.

Stricker, G. Implications of research for psychotherapeutic treatment of women. *American Psychologist*, 1977, *32*, 14–22.

Weigert, E. Contribution to the problem of terminating psychoanalyses. *Psychoanalytic Quarterly*, 1952, *21*, 465–480.

Werner, P. D., & Block, J. Sex differences in the eyes of expert personality assessors: Unwarranted conclusions. *Journal of Personality Assessment*, 1975, *39*, 110–113.

Whitley, B. E., Jr. Sex roles and psychotherapy: A current appraisal. *Psychological Bulletin*, 1979, *86*, 1309–1321.

Winnicott, D. W. Countertransference. *British Journal of Medical Psychology*, 1960, *33*, 17–21.

Yulis, S., & Kiesler, D. J. Countertransference response as a function of therapist anxiety and content of patient talk. *Journal of Consulting and Clinical Psychology*, 1968, *32*, 413–419.

Zeldow, P. B. Sex differences in psychiatric evaluation and treatment: An empirical review. *Archives of General Psychiatry*, 1978, *35*, 89–93.

8 Gender and Psychotherapy: A Review of the Emprical Literature

GEORGE STRICKER AND
ROBIN SHAFRAN

The possible occurrence of sex bias and sex-role stereotyping in psychotherapy has been an area of major concern in recent years. The potential impact of therapist attitudes toward women has been frequently discussed, and accusations that stereotypic attitudes serve to hinder, rather than facilitate, the growth of female clients are often heard among both professionals and nonprofessionals. Despite the importance of the topic and the amount of attention it is given, definitive data are still sorely lacking. For example, in their examination of gender and psychotherapy outcome, Orlinsky and Howard (1980) reviewed the research and commented on how little data were available. Maracek and Johnson (1980), writing in the same volume, reached a similar conclusion in regard to research on gender and the process of therapy. This chapter again scans the research literature, in an attempt to compile findings on different aspects of the relationship between gender and psychotherapy.

Findings based on analogue designs are not reviewed in this chapter. Although analogues vary in the degree to which they approach ecologically sound designs, their limitations are such that their external validity may be questionable. In their review article, Maracek and Johnson (1980) considered both naturalistic and analogue studies, and commented that "evidence on the validity of the analogue methodology is not reassuring" (p. 70). They pointed out that two out of three times, when an analogue is repeated in a natural setting, agreement is disappointing. This lack of correspondence between analogue and naturalistic data has been demonstrated directly by Kushner, Bordin, and Ryan (1979). In a review of therapy research, Cartwright (1968) also expressed skepticism about analogue designs, stating that, in some cases, an analogue can so distort a situation as to be irrelevant. Accordingly, this chapter is restricted to studies of actual psychotherapists and patients. For a review of analogue studies in this area, interested readers are referred to Sherman (1980).

Sex-role stereotypes—clearly identifiable behavioral characteristics that are attributable to either men or women (Broverman, Vogel, Broverman, Clarkson, & Rosenkrantz, 1972; Kravetz, 1976)—influence the manner in which men as well as women are viewed in our society. However, largely because stereotypically "male" traits are more likely to be seen as socially desirable than stereotypically "female" traits are, the consequences of stereotyping are more often discussed in regard to women. Consistent with this trend, psychotherapy research addressing this question generally examines therapists' attitudes toward women, with the goal of determining if, and how, sex-role stereotyping is operative in the treatment of female patients.

The major focus of interest concerning sex-role stereotyping in psychotherapy lies in the manner in which therapists stereotype. There is less attention paid to the importance of patient attitudes regarding sex-role stereotypic characteristics and their influence on the psychotherapy experience. This is an important omission, since there is substantial literature regarding the importance of patient expectations and attitudes in psychotherapy (Goldstein, 1962; Gurman, 1977; Wilkins, 1973; Ziemelis, 1974), as well as data suggesting that patients working with a therapist with preferred characteristics will have more successful psychotherapy experiences (Gurman, 1977; Ziemelis, 1974). Accordingly, following a review of the research on therapist attitudes, the literature on patient attitudes and preferences is examined. Finally, some summary conclusions are drawn about the empirical findings concerning gender and psychotherapy. Since this topic has been the subject of a series of major review articles, the chapter relies heavily on these summaries, and only cites specific studies that have not been included in prior reviews.

SEX-ROLE STEREOTYPING

The continued interest in the impact of sex-role stereotyping in psychotherapy is reflected by the research literature, both in the number of investigations directed toward examining the incidence and nature of such stereotyping, and in several recent review articles that have attempted to organize the often disparate and contradictory findings by individual researchers. Clinical anecdotes that support stereotypes abound, and analogue studies, from which bias in the treatment situation is generalized, make up a large proportion of the published literature. In this section, the direct empirical evidence regarding sex-role and psychotherapy is examined in some detail, so that we may learn more about the nature and extent of the influence of gender in psychotherapy. There have been a half dozen comprehensive reviews of the literature, and these provide the basis of the discussion.

Despite the fact that it was published over a decade ago, a study by Broverman, Broverman, Clarkson, Rosenkrantz, and Vogel (1970) continues to be regarded as the most striking and influential demonstration of the hazards of sex-role stereotyping in psychotherapy. As such, it is still widely cited in the professional literature. Using the Sex-Role Stereotype Questionnaire (Rosenkrantz, Vogel, Bee, Broverman, & Broverman, 1968), Broverman and her associates asked male and female clinicians to rate either a "healthy male," a "healthy female," or a "healthy adult." They found that "clinicians strongly agree on the behavior and attributes which characterize a healthy man, a healthy woman, and a healthy adult" (Broverman et al., 1970, p. 3). Further, they found that ratings of a healthy man and a healthy adult did not differ, but that significant differences did exist between ratings of a healthy adult and a healthy woman, with the latter characterized as possessing significantly fewer socially desirable attributes. "These results, then, confirm the hypothesis that a double standard of health exists for men and women, that is, the general standard of health is actually applied only to men, while healthy women are perceived as significantly less healthy by adult standards" (p. 6).

The Broverman et al. study was considered at length by Stricker (1977) in his review of the literature concerning the treatment of women in psychotherapy. He criticized the published presentation for its lack of raw data, for the absence of individual item analyses, and for the assumption of significant differences without statistical evidence. Stricker saw the conclusions reached by Broverman and her colleagues as unsubstantiated and overly dramatic, suggesting that more parsimonious, though less striking, explanations of the results may have been appropriate. Whitley (1979) pointed out that Broverman et al. did not investigate the extent to which attitudinal bias leads to discriminatory behavior, commenting that subsequent research has "generally found no such discrimination and casts doubt on the generality of the bias" (p. 1309). Despite these criticisms, the conclusions drawn by Broverman et al. have been accepted and cited by many who challenge the validity of psychotherapy as a viable option for women in our society.

On the basis of his examination of the research literature, Stricker concluded that sex of therapist is of little consequence with regard to sexist practice, an assertion consistent with Broverman et al.'s finding of high agreement between experienced female and male therapists concerning mental health and stereotypes of men and women. Stricker goes on to say that the widely cited conclusion concerning a double standard of mental health and negative evaluations of women are premature in light of the data.

Zeldow (1978) reviewed the research regarding sex bias in psychotherapy, including Broverman et al.'s work, and concluded that, in general, practicing mental health professionals share the values and norms of their society. However, he attempted to soften what might be heard as an indictment by stating that "differential judgment does not automatically prove differential treatment, nor do double standards of optimal mental health necessarily imply differential assessments of mental illness" (p. 89). He also commented that it seems likely that "sex differences in psychiatric assessment are rare or embedded in complex contexts" (p. 90). He highlighted the need to study treatment and disposition variables in order to find support for the assumption of sex bias in psychotherapy. After examining the literature and finding that female therapists may be more empathic, while male therapists are more authoritarian, he commented that such differences in the therapeutic style of men and women have not been connected to gender-related differences in therapy outcome.

After considering approximately 25 studies, Zeldow reached many of the conclusions arrived at by Stricker, noting that, by itself, patient gender is rarely a factor in determining diagnosis, prognosis, degree of psychopathology assessed, or treatment goals. He concluded that a large, but possibly diminishing, minority of clinicians hold separate standards of mental health for men and women, but cautioned that the ways in which such stereotypes affect therapy are not known. Further, Zeldow pointed out that it is still not known whether responses to questionnaires reflect actual behavior. The external validity of such ratings must be determined.

Zeldow saw the available data as sufficiently diverse and ambiguous to be perceived according to the predisposition of the reader, and agreed with Stricker that the most compelling evidence is anecdotal. Biases are probably more limited in scope and more complex than had been previously thought. According to Zeldow, "the most strident claims of sex discrimination in this field cannot be supported by current research evidence" (p. 93).

Whitley (1979) also reviewed the research on sex roles and psychotherapy, again taking Broverman et al. (1970) as a starting point. Whitley addressed three questions, asking (1) whether there are different, sex-role-related, standards of mental health for men and women; (2) whether violations of sex-role-related norms lead to negative mental health judgments; and (3) whether therapists set sex-role-related goals for their patients.

Although Whitley found support for the existence of differential standards of mental health in the 12 studies reviewed, he cautioned that many of them contained flaws limiting their validity. One such flaw is the use of subjects who are not professional clinicians, such as college students and therapist trainees.

There also were difficulties in the measurement of sex-role stereotyping, which seeks to determine the set of beliefs held about a particular group. Whitley defined two problems currently faced by researchers in this regard.

He first addressed the question of whether stereotyping should be assessed in a forced-choice or a free-response format. He saw the more commonly used forced-choice method as maximizing stereotypic responses (perhaps artificially), in that subjects are permitted to respond only with what is provided, whether or not it is what they would actually choose to say.

The second question Whitley raised is whether it is more important to tap stereotypic beliefs about specific behaviors or about more generalized personality traits. In his view, stereotyping is more easily elicited with questions about specific behaviors. Thus, the use of trait scales might reduce measured stereotypes. This, of course, raises the possibility of artificially controlling results by varying the nature of the dependent variable, a problem considered primary by Zeldow (1978).

Whitley believed that the overreliance on the Sex-Role Stereotype Questionnaire (Rosenkrantz et al., 1968) was another major limitation of research in this area. In discussing that questionnaire, he pointed out that the incidence of stereotyping is increased by its forced-choice format, but decreased by its use of traits. Whitley's main concern, however, was that it was used in 10 of the 12 reviewed studies concerning differential standards of mental health. He commented that the Sex-Role Stereotype Questionnaire "hardly represents a consensual definition of sex roles" (p. 1312); he also noted that Bem (1974) and Spence, Helmreich, and Stapp (1974) both developed viable measures of sex-role identity.

Another methodological concern to Whitley was the dichotomous scoring of many stereotyping measures. Here he concurred with Stricker (1977), warning that dichotomous scoring does not permit an assessment of the degree to which a trait is thought to be characteristic of either a man or a woman. Rather, scoring in this manner tends to inflate the extremity of scores by eliminating the option of giving a qualified or a neutral rating. This was one basis of Stricker's assertion that the Broverman et al. conclusions were somewhat dramatic for the data.

In reference to his third question, whether therapy goals are sex-role-related, Whitley found effects of violations of sex roles on judgments of mental health among nonprofessionals, but not when professional therapists were queried. This conclusion was based predominantly on analogue evidence. Finally, he did not find support for the contention that treatment goals are often sex-role-related.

Smith (1980) addressed the literature on sex bias in psychotherapy in a somewhat different fashion. After reviewing the research on counselor attitudes, stereotypes, and behavior, much of which was analogue in nature, she did a "meta-analysis" of sex bias studies. This method converts the results of all studies to a common metric, the "effect of sex bias" (ESB). Smith presented this as a more satisfactory method of assessing the results of many studies than simply totaling those that reported either positive or negative findings.

Reviewing her own calculations, she called the results "clear" and stated: "There is no evidence for the existence of counselor sex bias when the research results are taken as a whole" (p. 404). Looking at each individual category (i.e., attitudes, judgments, and behavior), Smith was equally clear about her results. Again, sex bias was not demonstrated in the meta-analyses she performed. Smith concluded that the empirical support for sexism in psychotherapy is weak, and that the evidence leaning toward bias is balanced by the evidence against it. "Stripped of the selectivity, motivation, and rhetoric, the body of evidence looks both different and more clear: Counselor sex bias has not been demonstrated despite a dozen years of attempts to do so" (p. 407).

In her review of therapists' attitudes toward women and sex-role stereotyping, Sherman (1980) reached different conclusions. She judged the data as providing evidence that sex-role values of therapists are operative during counseling; that there is sex-role stereotyping in mental health standards; and that behavior that crosses sex-role norms is judged more negatively. While Sherman agreed that there is some evidence that stereotyping is decreasing, her conclusions contrast sharply with the four reviews previously discussed, and thus warrant some consideration.

In assessing attitudes toward women among therapists and counselors, Sherman reviewed 10 studies, of which half found male therapists to hold more conservative views than female therapists did. One such study, reported by Rabkin (1977), was based on psychiatrists' responses to a questionnaire. Rabkin reported that 73% of the respondents believed that psychiatrists have stereotypes of "normal healthy females" and "normal healthy males," and that 66% believed that psychiatrists attempt to influence patients to adjust to these stereotypes. Rather than concurring with Sherman that these results indicate that psychiatrists hold stereotypes about their patients, it seems that they can more accurately be indicative of stereotypes psychiatrists hold of psychiatrists. Further, this is a clear example of how notions about stereotyping continue to persist, even to flourish, whether or not there is data to support their existence.

Sherman noted four studies in which therapists were found to hold more liberal attitudes toward women than therapist trainees were—results that argue against the existence of bias among professional practitioners. However, she minimized these results, cautioning that, for a number of reasons, it is unwise to assume that these liberal attitudes are truly typical of the population of therapists and counselors as a whole. The therapists sampled were not nationally representative and, in some cases, were probably biased in a liberal direction. Additionally, Sherman commented that if a respondent were not planning to answer truthfully, he or she would be more likely to misrepresent in a liberal direction.

Sherman discussed her own research (Sherman, Koufacos, & Kenworthy, 1978), in which a questionnaire was sent to mental health practitioners in order to survey their attitudes about women and their knowledge of the psychology of women. Despite the fact that she felt that this sample, too, was biased in a liberal direction, she found that their fund of information about the psychology of women was not up to date. Over half the therapists sampled missed 38% of the items. "The fact, however, that their information about the psychology of women did not reflect equally up-to-date views underscores the fact that response to attitude scales basically reflects what people want to tell you" (p. 44). Sherman suggested that a more useful research strategy would be to measure information about, rather than attitudes toward, women.

Although Sherman concluded that the results of the 10 studies of therapists' attitudes supported the existence of sex bias in therapy, this was not as clear to the present authors in their reading of her tabular presentation of the results. This is an example of an area where, as Zeldow warns, the data are sufficiently ambiguous to be interpreted in more than one direction. Sherman also called for more cogent conceptualizations in future research, including reasonable hypotheses that are fairly tested. In this regard, she is in accord with the other reviewers discussed thus far.

The final review article to be discussed is somewhat broader in scope, covering studies on the influence of gender in general on the process of psychotherapy. Maracek and Johnson (1980) looked at three areas: the influence of both the therapist's and the client's gender, influence of the therapist's sex-role stereotypes on therapist behavior, and the incidence of sexist statements and actions in the therapy situation. They pointed out that an understanding of the influence of gender on therapy will improve our understanding of how therapy works, and will thereby make it more successful. In addition, they believed that such understanding will improve our knowledge of the effects of various gender pairings on the treatment process.

Maracek and Johnson looked first at therapist behavior, studying client selection, preference for either male or female clients, judgments about client need for therapy, and duration of treatment, finding inconsistent data from which few conclusions could be drawn. In looking at the literature on client behavior and preferences, they concluded that the modal client does not have a preference. Among those who state preferences, better-educated, younger, and women clients are more likely to prefer female therapists. Again, Maracek and Johnson were cautious in generalizing from any of the evidence, commenting instead on the striking absence of clear data, especially in the form of process studies.

The literature reviews seem to agree on a number of points. The data are generally insufficient to draw any definitive conclusions. Assertions of demonstrated effects are more likely to be anecdotal or political than they are to be based on sound research. It is important to realize that the crucial findings will not concern attitudinal characteristics of therapists, but the effect of those attitudes on treatment intervention and outcomes. It is most likely that this effect will be a complex one, and gender will have to be considered in interaction with a number of moderator variables if we are to have a clear picture of its impact.

GENDER EFFECTS

A small number of studies have looked at the effect of therapist gender on psychotherapy. The studies do not focus on any single topic, but explore a variety of gender-related issues.

Shullman and Betz (1979) were interested in the factors influencing assignment of a client to counseling, and looked at the relationship between presenting problem and sex of client in the assignment of a client to a male or female counselor, using as their sample the files of terminated cases at a university counseling center. Male and female counselors at the center from which their data were obtained rotated in doing intakes, and had the option of continuing with the client seen or making a referral to another staff member. Shullman and Betz found that 73% of the clients who were referred were matched with a counselor of the same sex. Female counselors were as likely to make a referral to a same-sex counselor for both male and female clients, while male counselors were more likely to do so for males than for females. The type of presenting problem (educational, personal/social, or both) was not significantly related to the sex of the assigned counselor.

Kirschner, Genack, and Hauser (1978) studied the effects of gender on short-term psychotherapy. After reviewing the relevant literature, they delineated four trends and addressed themselves to those issues. Kirschner et al. first highlighted the tendency for female patients to be more responsive than male patients to psychotherapy, and the tendency for patients to be more satisfied with female than with male therapists. They pointed out that variables such as age, experience, and marital status may interact significantly with the influence of gender on treatment outcome. Finally, they concurred with others in the field (e.g., Maracek & Johnson, 1980; Orlinsky & Howard, 1980) that systematic differences as a consequence of the gender of either therapist or patient have not yet been demonstrated in the empirical literature.

Kirschner et al. mailed 395 questionnaires to past patients at a university clinic, of which 189 were returned. The questionnaire asked for the sex of the therapist seen, whether a request had been made to see a therapist of a specific sex, and for ratings of improvement and satisfaction with the therapy. Therapists (17 male and 5 female) were also asked to rate their satisfaction with the treatment. Most of the male therapists were less experienced, "junior" therapists (residents or postdoctoral fellows), while the female therapists were more "senior."

Female patients reported higher self-improvement scores than did male patients. Both female and male patients reported greater improvement and satisfaction, and more congruence with the ratings of their therapists, when they were seen by female therapists. Junior therapists reported more satisfaction with female than with male patients, while, for senior therapists, gender of patient did not make a difference. Male therapists reported more satisfaction with female than with male undergraduates, with no differences found for graduate students.

In concluding, Kirschner and his associates emphasized that their study investigated gender, rather than gender attitudes. They reported that women do better in therapy and that, controlling for experience level, women make better therapists. In most cases, same-sex patient and therapist pairs do not do better than cross-sex pairs. They believed that their results added empirical support to a gender effect in psychotherapy, saying that "women appear to be both more responsive and effective in psychotherapy than men" (p. 167).

In an attempt to replicate an analogue study in a natural setting, Helms (1978) studied counselor attitudes toward female clients. Designing her study along the lines of the analogue investigation by Hill, Tanney, Leonard, and Reiss (1977), Helms looked at the relationship between client age and the importance of educational, vocational, or personal problems, as judged by male or female counselors. She was also interested in the number of contacts that either younger or older clients had with male and female counselors.

Helms found that personal and interpersonal problems were considered most important for all clients. Vocational problems were considered more important for younger than for older clients. Helms suggested, however, that younger clients may have presented with more vocational problems than their older counterparts may have. For the female counselors, there was a significant correlation between the number of sessions and the number of problems. This was not so for the male counselors.

Discussing her results, Helms commented on their surprising similarity to the results of Hill et al. (1977). She pointed out that, in Hill et al.'s analogue, counselors estimated that their pseudoclients would required 6 to 10 sessions, a figure close to the average 5 to 6 sessions of clients with female counselors in the natural setting. Male counselors, in contrast, used half that number. Helms suggested that the estimate provided by Hill's therapist/subjects may be an ideal that the male counselors in her own study did not reach; in general, she saw these results as support for the use of analogue designs in psychotherapy research. It should be noted that the similar findings in the two studies involved a specific outcome criterion (number of sessions), rather than a treatment behavior or attitude.

Most studies assessing sex bias in psychotherapy use outpatient facilities, often university counseling centers, as sources for subject samples. Doherty (1976) and Doherty and Liang (Note 1) considered gender-related issues in hospitalized populations. Doherty (1976), in a study of length of hospitalization, found that both female and male patients who demonstrated stereotypically feminine behavior were discharged earlier. These were patients who accepted the rules of the therapeutic community, conforming to situational expectations.

Examining a different aspect of the hospital situation, Doherty and Liang (Note 1) investigated whether women staff members are less helpful to female patients than to male patients, a belief often commented upon in the literature. These researchers looked at staff members' perceptions of whom they had helped, in order to see whether female staff helped female patients less, and whether this was so for both professional and nonprofessional staff. Female staffers reported that they helped more patients than did male staffers, and that they helped more female than male patients. Female staff helped more female patients than did male staff, and professional women helped more women than men. The contention that women staff members discriminate against women patients was clearly not supported.

The studies in this section are so scant and disparate that an overall conclusion would be difficult to sustain. One point that does appear clearly, however, is that the effect of gender is not monolithic, and must be considered in a variety of complex interactions.

PATIENT PREFERENCES

The psychotherapy literature thus far reviewed has focused on therapist gender effects, particularly on therapist sex-role stereotyping and attitudes toward women, attempting to assess the impact of such beliefs and attitudes on the treatment process. There is also a growing literature emphasizing the importance of patient reactions to therapist variables in successful therapy. Carter (1978) emphasized the importance of patient preferences in psychotherapy, citing counseling literature suggesting that the degree to which a client is attracted to his or her therapist is related to the success of psychotherapy. Since therapist bias appears to be complex and multidetermined, it is instructive to view the patient contribution to any possible gender effects.

The role of sex of the therapist was discussed by Turkel (1976), who believed it is a factor too frequently ignored in the psychoanalytic literature. Turkel commented that "the whole area of therapist sex variables has been ignored almost in the proportion to that in which patient sex variables have been discussed" (p. 119). In her view, female and male therapists bring different attitudes to their work and are perceived differently by their patients. Further, she suggested that societally based, stereotypic conceptions of men and women enter into the choice of a therapist of a particular sex. In discussing the influence of sex-role stereotyping on the part of the patient, she has commented:

> Sexual stereotyping carried over into the masculine view of the woman analyst. She has been portrayed as a quiet, patient, nurturant, practical person endowed with natural warmth, empathy, intuition, sensitivity, and understanding—a virtual earth mother. Of course, few of the qualities have been scientifically validated as more characteristic of females. Nevertheless, this stereotype of the healing mother persists. (p. 120)

This review now turns to the research dealing with patient stereotypes and preferences, with the assumption that understanding the gender-related transference of the patient will illuminate the gender-related countertransference of the therapist.

There is a small literature focused on patient preferences for male or female psychotherapists, from which two tentative conclusions have emerged. Prior to treatment, those patients who express a preference for a therapist of a particular sex prefer to work with a male therapist (e.g., Davidson, 1976) and, once in treatment, women working with female therapists report greater satisfaction than do women working with male therapists (e.g., Orlinsky & Howard, 1976).

Howard, Orlinsky, and Hill (1970) are among the few who have studied the impact of patient-therapist gender pairings from the point of view of the patient. As part of a study of patient satisfaction in psychotherapy, these investigators explored the extent to which personal characteristics of patients and therapists influenced the satisfaction reported by patients following a series of psychotherapy sessions. Their sample of 188 female patients was classified according to age, marital, and parental status. The therapist group was classified by the same variables and by sex. The authors acknowledged that the results were confounded by a potentially biased assignment of patients and by the small sample size, such that only 29 of the 55 possible patient-therapist combinations occurred at all, and many of these only infrequently.

No consistent trend was discernible from the data collected, but different patient classifications did report differential satisfaction with the various groups of therapists. The authors saw their findings as suggesting that the personal characteristics of therapists "definitely and differentially" influence the experienced satisfaction of patients. With such a small sample, however, it is unclear whether the differences obtained reflect the specified variable, other characteristics of the patients or therapists, or some combination.

Orlinsky and Howard (1976) reported a reanalysis of the data obtained from 118 patients previously sampled. This time the authors were interested in assessing the impact of sex of therapist on content of therapy interviews, reactions of patients (again all female) to their therapists (male and female), and on patient perceptions of their therapists' attitudes toward them. The data, which had been collected via questionnaires filled out after each session in ongoing therapies, were factor-analyzed, and 46 dimensions were obtained. Differences between patients being seen by male and female therapists were found on 15 of the 46 dimensions. This seemingly dramatic result is, again, considerably weakened by the small sample size relative to the type of data analysis employed, but it still warrants discussion.

Analyses determined that certain groups of patients, particularly young single women, are most sensitive to therapist gender. "Independent" women (defined by the authors as over 29, single, and working) are virtually indifferent to the sex of their therapists. The two groups of patients most sensitive to sex of therapist, "younger single" (aged 18–22) and "young single" (aged 23–28) women, both reported more favorable experiences with female therapists. In discussing their findings, Orlinsky and Howard minimized the possibility that the male therapists studied were less able or sensitive than the female therapists. They stated:

> Rather, it seems to us that our results direct attention to the patients' more than to the therapists' attributes. Whether the therapist is able and sensitive may be less important than what a male or female therapist means to a patient. It may also be the case that male and female therapists behave differently or react differently to female patients and/or patients in specific life situations. (p. 87)

More recently, Orlinsky and Howard (Note 2) discussed predictors of therapy outcome for women, basing their comments on the data collected previously. They reported a statistically nonsignificant trend for women patients to be more successful when in treatment with women therapists. Young women clearly and significantly benefited from assignment to a female therapist, as did women with diagnoses of anxiety reaction and schizophrenia.

On the basis of average outcome ratings of their patient population, Orlinsky and Howard commented that "some male therapists were as good with women as their female colleagues, but that the women therapists were much more consistent in their effects on women patients" (p. 10). In further examining their outcome data, they found that highly experienced male therapists were as good as female therapists were, doing as well as their female counterparts with anxious and schizophrenic women. Experience level did not differentiate female therapists; moderately experienced women were as successful as were their more experienced colleagues. There were no inexperienced therapists in the subject pool.

Hill (1975) also studied patient satisfaction with male and female therapists, but sampled male as well as female patients. An additional variable in this study was counselor experience level (counselor/subjects were either therapists with 2 years of experience or students). In addition to asking 12 counselors and two of each counselor's patients (one female and one male) to assess satisfaction, tape recordings of the sessions were rated for therapist activity level, empathy, and self-exploration. Hill found that inexperienced counselors, both male and female, were most empathic and active, and elicited the most feeling, with same-sex clients. The more experienced counselors were more focused on feelings and more empathic with clients of their own sex, and more active and directive with opposite-sex clients.

Of special interest is Hill's finding that clients of female counselors reported more satisfaction than did clients with male counselors. The investigator suggested that female counselors may have been perceived as more empathic and understanding, although female and male counselors did not differ behaviorally on these dimensions. In discussing these results, Hill referred to previous findings that clients more frequently prefer male counselors—a preference usually attributed to expectations of authority and prestige that accompany the stereotypic male role. "However, during counseling, those paired with males may have discovered they were not as potent as expected, whereas those paired with female counselors may have been surprised that they were more competent than expected" (p. 10).

Persons, Persons, and Newmark (1974) studied patients' perceptions of characteristics important in paraprofessional therapists, and found that the attributes clients ascribed to their undergraduate therapists were markedly similar to characteristics of professionals. Not primarily interested in looking at gender issues, Persons et al. remarked: "It was not our original intention to study sex of the therapist and the client as a variable, but in analyzing the data it became clear that sex was an important factor" (p. 63).

The Persons et al. results indicated that male and female clients queried following their final therapy session were responsive to different characteristics in their therapists. The men sampled cited honest feedback more frequently, while the women indicated greater responsiveness to encouragement of risk taking, perception, insightfulness, and supportiveness. When asked what they had gained from treatment, women gave four times as many responses as men, and women working with women therapists gave twice as many responses as did those working with male therapists.

Davidson (1976) emphasized the importance of the sex of both patient and therapist in the therapeutic relationship in her investigation of attitudes held by prospective patients regarding sex of therapist, and of preferences for either male or female therapists. She was interested in how frequently preferences were stated, and on what expectations such preferences were based. Male and female applicants for psychotherapy at a university-affiliated clinic were first asked whether they preferred a male or female therapist; 50% indicated no preference, 35% indicated they would prefer a male therapist, and 15% preferred a female therapist. Few differences were found in patterns of preference for the different demographic variables checked, including patient sex.

Subjects who expressed a preference were asked to note, on a checklist of six qualities, those that were relevant to their choice. Subjects most frequently expressed the belief that they would feel more comfortable, and would be able to talk more freely, with a therapist of their preferred sex. When these reasons were related to the sex of the subject, it was found that "talking freely" was checked less frequently by women preferring male therapists than by women preferring female therapists. Davidson interpreted this finding as an indication that patients, particularly women, prefer male and female therapists for different reasons. She further suggested that female therapists are perceived as possessing different personality characteristics from those of male therapists, at least by those individuals who seek out female therapists.

In her conclusions, Davidson implied that patient preferences may be related to sex-role-based assumptions of personality characteristics inherent in men and women. She commented that "the relationship of sex and sex-role behavior of both patients and therapists has yet to be carefully investigated with regard to process and outcome of psychotherapy" (p. 167).

Delk and Ryan (1975) are among the few who have addressed this issue from the point of view of psychotherapy patients, looking at patient sex-role stereotypes and preference for male and female therapists. In their study, Delk and Ryan investigated A-B status and sex-role stereotyping. Subjects were also asked to rank-order their preferences for either male, female, or male or female therapist. For those subjects who chose the "male or female" (no preference) option first, their second choices were used in the data analysis. In this study, then, there was no comparison of patients with preferences and patients without preferences.

Using an adaptation of the Sex-Role Stereotype Questionnaire, Delk and Ryan had their subjects rate male therapists, female therapists, and themselves on each item. Difference scores were calculated and used as a dependent variable. Significant and "sizable" differences in ratings of male and female therapists are seen by the authors as an indication that patients, when evaluating the personality traits of male and female therapists, "endorse culturally loaded male and female stereotypes which tend to denigrate the female therapist" (p. 5). Male patients were found to stereotype more than female patients were, and A-status patients of either sex stereotyped more than B-status patients did. A-status patients of either sex tended to prefer male therapists, while B-status patients tended to prefer female therapists. Of particular interest to Delk and Ryan was their finding that, with the exception of female patients who expressed a preference for male therapists, all patients perceived themselves as more similar (in sex-role identity) to the preferred than to the nonpreferred therapist. They concluded that most people seek therapists whom they see as similar to themselves.

Shafran (1978) investigated differential sex-role-related expectations patients have of male and female therapists and preferences for male or female therapists. The relationship between stereotypic characteristics associated with an "ideal" (sex-unspecified) therapist and preference was also studied, in order to determine the degree to which therapists of the preferred sex are expected to possess more of the characteristics considered important.

In this study, new clinic psychotherapy patients were given a questionnaire assessing expected differences between male and female therapists on sex-role-stereotypic characteristics, and were asked to rate the importance of each of the same characteristics for an "ideal" therapist. A modified version of the Personal Attributes Questionnaire (Spence et al., 1974) was used for this purpose. Subjects were also asked to indicate the strength of their preferences for a male or female therapist. Unlike the Delk and Ryan (1975) study, "no preference" was a category used in the data analyses.

Similar to the Delk and Ryan findings, a greater percentage of men than women endorsed the stereotypic expectations of differences between male and female therapists. On those characteristics for which both male and female subjects expected differences, these differences fell in the same, stereotypic direction. Subjects of both sexes concurred in their ratings of characteristics important to an "ideal" therapist, and the majority of characteristics seen as most important were female-valued traits.

Although the male patients sampled were more likely to expect differences between male and female therapists, they were less likely than were their female counterparts to express preferences. Male patients with preferences were divided between preferring a male or female therapist. Women, who were more egalitarian in their expectations of differences, were more likely to express a preference, and more often preferred to see a woman therapist.

An increasing number of studies indicate patient preferences for female therapists, and for stereotypically feminine characteristics in their therapists, regardless of sex. The way in which preferences affect the behavior of a patient who gets a therapist who is (or is not) compatible with that preference, and the way in which that behavior in turn influences subsequent therapist behavior, remain unknown. Here, too, it appears that the role of patient preference in regard to gender must be considered in combination with a variety of other characteristics, and a simplistic summary will not fit the data.

DISCUSSION AND CONCLUSIONS

Bias can occur when patients are systematically offered treatment that is inappropriate for them but would be appropriate for other patients, or when some patients are systematically denied appropriate treatment that is offered to other patients. If the treatment is inappropriate for all groups it is not bias, but simply poor treatment; and if the problem is not systematic, it is likely to represent an idiosyncratic countertransference issue. There has been no suggestion that women are not given the opportunity to receive treatment; if anything, there is a suggestion of overutilization. Rather, concern is about the nature of treatment. The Procrustean bias—the treatment of women as though they were men, without regard to any special needs they may have—is one potential problem that has been noted. The chauvinist bias—the treatment of women differently from men, reflecting the imposition of cultural stereotypes—has also been a major source of concern.

In evaluating the literature dealing with the role played by gender in psychotherapy, it becomes clear that this is an area charged with emotion. There is a group of people who have unshakable convictions that women in psychotherapy are subject to sexist regimentation of roles; there is also another, perhaps less vocal, group of people who do not believe that the present documentation for such assertions is sufficient, even if they should ultimately prove to be accurate. The key lies with data interpretation, which is often colored by the side of the argument that is being supported. Explanations are offered to accommodate the chosen side (whichever that may be), and merciless attention is given to methodological laxity on the part of one's opponents. Some of the issues involved in this still heated debate are now discussed.

Three different, but related, areas of research have been covered in this review. The literature on sex-role stereotyping has been examined, as has the more general "gender effect" in psychotherapy. Patient preferences for male and female therapists have been discussed as well, particularly as these preferences relate to sex-role attitudes of psychotherapy patients regarding therapists. The tone of debate is most heated for the first of these three issues, and becomes less controversial as the questions of gender effect and patient preferences are discussed. Heat, however, does not always generate light, and definitive conclusions remain elusive.

The question of whether psychotherapists adhere to sex-role-stereotypic conceptions of their patients that serve to limit their patients' options, particularly those of female patients, has been addressed extensively in the literature in the past decade. Five out of the six major reviews discussed in this chapter have concluded that clear-cut stereotyping in psychotherapy has not been empirically documented, despite numerous attempts to do so. The sixth reviewer has disagreed, concluding that sex-role stereotyping continues to be a problem for the mental health field, and that it is evidenced in the research literature.

In looking at one aspect of this issue—the charge of a "double standard of mental health" initiated by the Broverman group (Broverman et al., 1970)—questions arise concerning whether such stereotyping exists, and what the impact of therapists' sex-role-based assumptions is on the psychotherapy experiences of their women patients. In response to the first part of the question, those who believe that psychotherapists do stereotype their patients and accept the conclusions reached by Broverman et al. cite their results and those of similar studies (see Sherman, 1980) in support of their contention that psychotherapy, in its present form, is a sexist institution. Those who are not so quick to agree with such a dramatic condemnation of the profession have either discredited the findings on methodological grounds, sought to minimize their impact, or attempted to explain them away.

An alternative explanation for the Broverman group's striking results, in addition to the methodological criticisms directed toward both the Broverman et al. study and research in this area in general, lies in the lack of identifying data provided about the healthy male, female, and adult that therapist/subjects were asked to rate. In the absence of such information, and without anything else upon which to rely, subjects fell back on what is "known" about men and women. In that situation it is not surprising that culturally maintained stereotypes appeared, since, by definition, stereotypes are required when characteristics of a general group must be used to describe an individual member of that group. In regard to the similarity of stereotypes of "adult" and "male," in contrast to "female," it has been suggested that "male" or "man" is the generic term for person in our language (Stricker, 1977).

Several points must be raised in evaluating this argument. Detrimental stereotypes have no place in the descriptions of healthy individuals regardless of the situation, but subjects were required to respond, and the questionnaire was designed to elicit stereotyping. Stearns, Penner, and Kimmel (1980) have noted that sexism cannot be concluded if a therapist uses sex-role stereotypes when given no information other than sex. It appears to the present authors that such studies do little more than investigate the familiarity of therapists with cultural stereotypes. The more crucial question, which was not addressed, is whether such stereotyping occurs in the face of a live patient, complete with personal history, a particular style of relatedness, and so forth. The argument asserting a double standard of mental health would be more convincing in such a case.

Another common response to claims that sex-role-stereotypic attitudes of therapists are detrimental to their women patients is the rejoinder that documenting sexist attitudes is not the same as demonstrating sexist behavior. Here the opposing sides claim either that attitudes and behavior are not necessarily related, or, alternatively, that they are intimately linked.

The social-psychological literature can be somewhat helpful in this regard. Borgida, Locksley, and Brekke (1980) discuss the persistence of stereotypic modes of thought, despite the prominence of evidence proving them invalid. They cite Snyder's reasons (1980) for this occurrence and delineate some of the potential effects of adherence to stereotypic characterization, both for the holder of the stereotype and for the individual so characterized. According to Snyder, stereotypes can guide interactions with members of the stereotyped group, such that the group member is induced to behave in a manner consistent with the stereotype. Stereotyping, then, can "create" its own apparent behavioral confirmation. If this can be demonstrated in psychotherapy, it presents a very real danger to female patients. Again, since the pivotal field studies have not yet been done, definitive conclusions are premature. The literature points to some adherence to traditional attitudes toward women, particularly among nonprofessionals, older professionals, and men; however, the extent of such attitudes and their impact remain controversial. Similarly, the evidence suggesting the conclusion that therapists penalize women for behaviors that violate sex-role norms is not clearly convincing.

Although the pervasiveness of occurrence is not clear, there is little dispute that any patient who is asked to conform to a therapist's stereotype of appropriate behavior, rather than being allowed and enabled to develop in a unique and satisfying manner, is being poorly served. It should be noted that the effect is not unidirectional, and the danger is from the imposition of a stereotype, not the specific nature of the stereotype. A woman who is discouraged from exploring her wish to seek a career despite the objections of her husband and children is receiving patently poor and destructive treatment, as is the woman who is made to feel guilty about her satisfaction with the role of a homemaker.

The methodological flaws that beset this whole area of research have been mentioned in regard to specific studies as they have become apparent. The extent of difficulties in designing valid, reliable, and replicable research on the nature of sex-role stereotyping in psychotherapy is such, however, as to warrant additional elaboration.

The subjects from whom data is collected constitute a major source of variability. "Therapist" samples can include students and trainees, as well as junior and senior colleagues. Experience level has been found to make a difference (Kirschner et al., 1978), yet it is not routinely controlled. Concern that samples are not random and may be biased have also been raised (Sherman, 1980). Stearns et al. (1980) have discussed this with particular reference to the survey done by the American Psychological Association's Task Force on Sex Bias and Sex-Role Stereotyping in Psychotherapeutic Practice (American Psychological Association, 1975). They have pointed out that the return rate for that survey was low (16%) and not likely to have been random, in that interested persons were more likely to respond. They have also noted that, while anecdotes regarding sexist incidents were solicited, no information was collected regarding whether the same sex-role-stereotypic therapists were equally incompetent with men.

The choice of dependent measures is another area where investigations of sex-role stereotyping have had problems. Whitley raised this issue in regard to what he believed to be an overreliance on the Sex-Role Stereotype Questionnaire. The need to assess the external validity of a dependent variable was highlighted by Zeldow. This is a particularly important point, since it leads to the possibility that investigators are not really clear about what is being measured. Converging results obtained by separate, individually validated scales would add considerable strength to claims made on the basis of findings from those scales. Finally, Whitley's discussion of measures that yield higher or lower incidences of stereotyping raises the possibility that results can be artificially influenced by the choice of a dependent variable.

Sherman (1980) raised an interesting point when she suggested that measuring therapist attitudes may be less useful than measuring therapist knowledge may be. Regardless of intention, if one possesses outdated or insufficient information about the psychology of women, the particular difficulties faced by women in contemporary society, and so on, psychotherapy will not be maximally effective. Of course, in assessing therapist knowledge, investigators must first determine what is crucial to the conduct of successful psychotherapy. It may be, for example, that a therapist would need to know the effects of hormonal changes during the menstrual cycle, but need not know the signs of sexual harassment on the job; or the reverse might be true; or neither might be necessary; or both might be necessary. It seems likely that a therapist should be educated about matters crucial to the patient, but the specific parameters are undetermined.

Turning to the more general question of the influence of gender in psychotherapy, the literature becomes less clouded by rhetoric, accusations, and denial. It appears that sex of therapist, in isolation, may be less an issue than the interrelationship of therapist sex with other factors. Here, the importance of moderator variables such as experience level must be considered.

Therapist experience level appears to be a factor of greater importance with male than with female therapists. Data suggest that less experienced male therapists are less successful, on a number of variables, than their more experienced male colleagues are and than both lesser and more experienced female therapists are. It might be that the maturational process proceeds differently for male and female therapists, but this supposition requires empirical verification. It is also unclear as to whether inexperienced male therapists are equally hampered in their work with male patients.

Brodsky (Note 3) discusses the need to investigate more complex, higher-order interactions in order to learn more about the manner in which gender influences psychotherapy—an opinion shared by Zeldow. These factors may be therapist or patient characteristics, as illustrated by Orlinsky and Howard's finding (1976) that among female patients, those of different ages worked with differential satisfaction with male and female therapists.

Working with a male or female therapist may be differentially meaningful to some patients, regardless of the actual characteristics possessed by the therapist in question. In some situations, sex-role-related biases of patients may result in their seeking a therapist of a particular sex, or in their responding more favorably to a male or female therapist.

In the area of patient preferences, common lore has held that patients traditionally prefer male therapists (Bent, Putnam, Kiesler, & Nowicki, 1975; Chesler, 1971; Davidson, 1976). This phenomenon has been changing in recent years. Women have begun to question whether a male therapist is necessarily "better," and there has been an increase in the number of women seeking female therapists. Tanney and Birk (1976) reviewed the literature regarding women's preferences for male or female therapists, described it as "sparse," and concluded: "Women clients' perceptions and preferences for sex of counselor need to be monitored carefully; rising social consciousness may create among women clients a greater demand for women counselors and therapists" (p. 31).

Interestingly, certain trends in the data indicate that some women may be correct in their beliefs that they are better off with female therapists; several recent studies have suggested that women are more successful as therapists and have more satisfied patients. What began as a political call to seek out feminist or, at least, female therapists may evolve into a thoughtful examination of exactly what it is that is important about a therapist, and what makes the process work. While data are not complete, it appears likely that this thoughtful examination will lead some women to the recognition that they would be best served by a woman, others to a choice of a male, and many to direct their attention to factors other than gender.

As a result of this review, a number of points seem to be clear. First, we do not have the information to make any definitive statement about the nature, pervasiveness, extent, or parameters of bias in psychotherapy with women. It does, however, appear unlikely that any conclusions ultimately drawn will be simple and unilateral. The complexity of the phenomenon is becoming increasingly clear, and gender is but one of many variables that must be considered. Just as gender was ignored, inappropriately, in prior years, it may now be overemphasized, with a resultant neglect of variables such as experience, orientation, and personal characteristics.

There is increasing recognition that the patient must be taken into account in any situation. Patient biases and preferences, which form the basis of initial alliances and resistances, may be critical in determining therapist assignment. Here it must be noted that these patient attitudes may be irrational and must be examined within the treatment. The preference for a male because he is an omnipotent authority, or for a female because she is a nurturant earth mother, cannot be taken at face value and allowed to remain unexplored. On the other hand, the potential value of a competent, successful woman therapist as a role model for a younger woman, or the similar value of a male therapist for an adolescent boy, should not be ignored.

It is recognized that the question as to whether therapy works is too oversimplified. Rather, investigators are asked to determine what type of therapy produces what type of effect with what type of patient when offered by what type of therapist. Similarly, the question as to the effect of gender must also be expanded. We cannot make a definitive statement about gender, but we can note that the ultimate answer to the questions "what type of therapist" and "what type of patient" will have to include gender along with a variety of other parameters.

The issue of therapist gender received little systematic attention prior to 1970. The Broverman et al. (1970) study, regardless of the methodological problems, represents a watershed that accomplished a great service in the way of consciousness raising. Since that date there has been a plethora of theoretical, clinical, review, political, and anecdotal papers; an increasing number of analogue studies; and a paucity of field studies. It may be that we have finally reached the point where the importance of the issue is clearly recognized, and we can now move on to performing the research that will allow for definitive conclusions.

REFERENCE NOTES

1. Doherty, E. G., & Liang, J. *Do women staff discriminate against women psychiatric patients?: Chesler reexamined.* Paper presented at the meeting of the American Psychological Association, New York, 1979.
2. Orlinsky, D. E., & Howard, K. I. *Predictors of psychotherapeutic outcome for women.* Paper presented at the meeting of the American Psychological Association, New York, 1979.
3. Brodsky, A. *A decade of feminist influence on psychotherapy.* Paper presented at the meeting of the American Psychological Association, Toronto, 1978.

REFERENCES

American Psychological Association. Report of the Task Force on Sex Bias and Sex-Role Stereotyping in Psychotherapeutic Practice. *American Psychologist,* 1975, *30,* 1169–1175.
Bem, S. L. The measurement of psychological androgyny. *Journal of Consulting and Clinical Psychology,* 1974, *42,* 155–162.
Bent, R. J., Putnam, D. G., Kiesler, D. J., & Nowicki, S., Jr. Expectancies and characteristics of outpatient clients applying for services at a community mental health facility. *Journal of Consulting and Clinical Psychology,* 1975, *43,* 280.
Borgida, E., Locksley, A., and Brekke, N. Social stereotypes and social judgment. In N. Cantor and J. Kihlstrom (Eds.), *Cognition, social interaction, and personality.* Hillsdale, N.J.: Erlbaum, 1980.
Broverman, I. K., Broverman, D. M., Clarkson, F. E., Rosenkrantz, P. S., & Vogel, S. R. Sex-role stereotypes and clinical judgments of mental health. *Journal of Consulting and Clinical Psychology,* 1970, *34,* 1–7.
Broverman, I. K., Vogel, S. R., Broverman, D. M., Clarkson, F. E., & Rosenkrantz, P. S. Sex-role stereotypes: A current appraisal. *Journal of Social Issues,* 1972, *28,* 59–78.
Carter, J. A. Impressions of counselors as a function of counselor physical attractiveness. *Journal of Counseling Psychology,* 1978, *25,* 28–34.

Cartwright, R. D. Psychotherapeutic processes. *Annual Review of Psychology*, 1968, *19*, 387–416.

Chesler, P. Women psychiatric and psychotherapeutic patients. *Journal of Marriage and the Family*, 1971, *33*, 746–759.

Davidson, V. Patient attitudes toward sex of therapist: Implications for psychotherapy. In J. L. Claghorn (Ed.), *Successful psychotherapy*. New York: Brunner/Mazel, 1976.

Delk, J. L., & Ryan, T. T. Sex-role stereotyping and A-B therapist status: Who is more chauvinistic. *Journal of Consulting and Clinical Psychology*, 1975, *43*, 589.

Doherty, E. G. Length of hospitalization on a short-term therapeutic community: A multivariate study by sex across time. *Archives of General Psychiatry*, 1976, *33*, 87–92.

Goldstein, A. P. *Therapist-patient expectancies in psychotherapy*. New York: Pergamon Press, 1962.

Gurman, A. S. Therapist and patient factors influencing the patient's perception of facilitative therapeutic conditions. *Psychiatry*, 1977, *40*, 218–231.

Helms, J. E. Counselor reactions to female clients: Generalizing from analogue research to a counseling setting. *Journal of Counseling Psychology*, 1978, *25*, 193–199.

Hill, C. E. Sex of client and sex and experience level of counselor. *Journal of Counseling Psychology*, 1975, *22*, 6–11.

Hill, C. E., Tanney, M. F., Leonard, M. M., & Reiss, J. Counselor reactions of female clients: Type of problem, age of client, and sex of counselor. *Journal of Counseling Psychology*, 1977, *24*, 60–65.

Howard, K. I., Orlinsky, D. E., & Hill, J. A. Patient's satisfaction in psychotherapy as a function of patient-therapist pairings. *Psychotherapy: Theory, Research, and Practice*, 1970, *7*, 130–134.

Kirshner, L. A., Genack, A., & Hauser, S. T. Effects of gender on short-term psychotherapy. *Psychotherapy: Theory, Research, and Practice*, 1978, *15*, 158–167.

Kravetz, D. F. Sex-role concepts of women. *Journal of Consulting and Clinical Psychology*, 1976, *44*, 437–443.

Kushner, K., Bordin, E. S., & Ryan, E. Comparison of Strupp's and Jenkins' audiovisual psychotherapy analogues and real psychotherapy interviews. *Journal of Consulting and Clinical Psychology*, 1979, *47*, 765–767.

Maracek, J., & Johnson, M. Gender and the process of therapy. In A. M. Brodsky and R. Hare-Mustin (Eds.), *Women and psychotherapy: An assessment of research and practice*. New York: Guilford Press, 1980.

Orlinsky, D. E., & Howard, K. I. The effects of sex of therapist on the therapeutic experience of women. *Psychotherapy: Theory, Research, and Practice*, 1976, *13*, 82–88.

Orlinsky, D. E., & Howard, K. I. Gender and psychotherapeutic outcome. In A. M. Brodsky & R. Hare-Mustin (Eds.), *Women and psychotherapy: An assessment of research and practice*. New York: Guilford Press, 1980.

Persons, R. W., Persons, M. K., & Newmark, I. Perceived helpful therapists' characteristics, client improvement, and sex of therapist and client. *Psychotherapy: Theory, Research, and Practice*, 1974, *11*, 63–65.

Rabkin, J. G. Therapists' attitudes toward mental illness and health. In A. S. Gurman & A. M. Razin (Eds.), *Effective psychotherapy: A handbook of research*. New York: Pergamon Press, 1977.

Rosenkrantz, P., Vogel, S., Bee, H., Broverman, I., & Broverman, D. Sex-role stereotypes and self-concepts in college students. *Journal of Consulting and Clinical Psychology*, 1968, *32*, 287–295.

Shafran, R. B. *Patient sex-role stereotypic expectations of therapists and preferred sex of therapist*. Unpublished doctoral dissertation, Adelphi University, 1978.

Sherman, J. Therapist attitudes and sex-role stereotyping. In A. Brodsky and R. Hare-Mustin (Eds.), *Women and psychotherapy: An assessment of research and practice.* New York: Guilford Press, 1980.

Sherman, J., Koufacos, C., & Kenworthy, J. A. Therapists: Their attitudes and information about women. *Psychology of Women Quarterly,* 1978, *2,* 299-313.

Shullman, S. L., & Betz, N. E. An investigation of the effects of client sex and presenting problem in referral from intake. *Journal of Counseling Psychology,* 1979, *26,* 140-145.

Smith, M. L. Sex bias in counseling and psychotherapy. *Psychological Bulletin,* 1980, *87,* 392-407.

Snyder, M. On the self-perpetuating nature of social stereotypes. In D. L. Hamilton (Ed.), *Cognitive processes in stereotyping and intergroup behavior.* Hillsdale, N.J.: Erlbaum, 1980.

Spence, J. T., Helmreich, R., & Stapp, J. The Personal Attributes Questionnaire: A measure of sex-role stereotyping and masculinity-femininity. JSAS *Catalog of Selected Documents in Psychology,* 1974, *4,* 43-44. (Ms. No. 617)

Stearns, B. C., Penner, L. A., & Kimmel, E. Sexism among psychotherapists: A case not yet proven. *Journal of Consulting and Clinical Psychology,* 1980, *48,* 548-550.

Stricker, G. Implications of research for the psychotherapeutic treatment of women. *American Psychologist,* 1977, *32,* 14-22.

Tanney, M. F., & Birk, J. M. Women counselors for women clients? A review of the research. *The Counseling Psychologist,* 1976, *6,* 28-32.

Turkel, A. R. The impact of feminism on the practice of a woman analyst. *American Journal of Psychoanalysis,* 1976, *36,* 119-126.

Whitley, B. E. Sex roles and psychotherapy: A current appraisal. *Psychological Bulletin,* 1979, *86,* 1309-1321.

Wilkins, W. Expectancy of therapeutic gain: An empirical and conceptual critique. *Journal of Consulting and Clinical Psychology,* 1973, *40,* 69-77.

Zeldow, P. Sex differences in psychiatric evaluation and treatment: An empirical review. *Archives of General Psychiatry,* 1978, *35,* 89-93.

Ziemelis, A. Effects of client preference and expectancy upon the initial interview. *Journal of Counseling Psychology,* 1974, *21,* 23-30.

9 Race Effects in Psychotherapy

STEPHEN I. ABRAMOWITZ
AND JOAN MURRAY

Research on the effects of social class and race in psychotherapy is a rather recent phenomenon. Such research did not really occur until Thomas Szasz published a series of penetrating analyses portraying the mental health establishment as a bastion of middle-class interests (1961, 1965, 1970). His and other widely read essays (Braginsky & Braginsky, 1974; Goffman, 1961, 1963; Halleck, 1971) provided a scholarly perspective from which to consider the disturbing question of whether the imposing array of psychotherapeutic remedies was merely an ingenious invention for stigmatizing minority and counternormative subcultures and preserving the status quo. These authors were viewing psychotherapy from a new perspective—a politicoeconomic perspective that focused on an individual's location in the politicoeconomic system as defined by his or her social class, race, and sex.

Oddly enough, much of the ground-breaking work on the politics of psychotherapy was done not by psychologists and psychiatrists, but by sociologists. Why was this the case? The different philosophies of science underlying these disciplines may be part of the explanation. Another part may be territorial defensiveness in those who were closer to—or actually involved in —the phenomenon under study. In addition, psychology's heritage in physical science directed researchers to examine the curative effects of psychotherapy, not its sociopolitical implications. Also, the experimental methodology of psychology could not as easily be applied to research on the hidden political agenda of psychotherapy as could the archival and survey strategies of sociology. Moreover, at the time that such research began, clinical psychology was still young and could not be expected to spearhead what might turn out to be an assault on its own professional beachhead. As for the psychiatric establishment, the silence with which it greeted Szasz's fusillade and the chill that many within it still accord his views testify to the relevance of politico-economic perspectives to the development of a science.

Research addressing the issue of psychotherapy as social control (Hurvitz, 1973; Sarbin & Mancuso, 1970) has run the gamut of the treatment spectrum, addressing issues ranging from the cultural relativism of symptomatology and "abnormal" behavior at intake to the rationale for termination or discharge. To date, studies have spoken to three principal issues raised in the polemic literature: *diagnostic bias* (Are lower-class patients diagnosed more harshly than middle-class patients with the same presenting problems are?); *treatment utilization and allocation* (Do blacks receive their fair share of individual and other "elite" forms of therapy?); and *effectiveness* (Do female patients fare better with a female therapist?). Such questions, as noted, have been investigated in the context of three primary demographic indicators of an individual's location in the politicoeconomic system: social class, race, and sex.

Several factors led to an early emphasis on social status. Perhaps foremost among these were the federal government's war on poverty and subsequent community mental health initiatives, which aimed to ameliorate the suffering of the poor. The landmark epidemiological studies of Hollingshead and Redlich (1958) and Srole's mid-Manhattan group (Srole, Langner, Michael, Opler, & Rennie, 1962) had just linked mental illness to social class. Although not directly related to the politics of therapy, these influential findings focused attention on the unequal distribution of culturally defined mental disorder in our society and thus heightened concern about the diagnostic and treatment implications of lower-class status (Scheff, 1966).

The civil rights movement ushered in a second wave of investigations, now centered on racial bias in diagnostic labeling and treatment brokering. This period is memorable for exposure of patterns of covert discrimination perpetrated under the banner of mental health care (L. H. Gardner, 1971; Thomas, 1962; Thomas & Sillen, 1972). However, an integrative review by Sattler (1970) revealed that there was a paucity of empirical data relevant to the questions at hand—a gap partly filled in recent years with respect to black Americans, if not to those of Hispanic, Asian, or Indian descent (C. V. Abramowitz & Dokecki, 1977; Sattler, 1977).

Next the emergence of the women's movement stimulated social scientists to examine the contention that *sex bias* pervades psychotherapy (Chesler, 1972[1]; Levine, Kamin, & Levine, 1974). In a relatively short time, researchers of sex bias in psychotherapy have laid a base of empirical data that eclipses by some measure its social class and race counterparts (Davidson & Abramowitz, 1980). Why research on the racial politics of therapy has tended to lag behind that for social class and sex is not immediately clear, although the few minority investigators and the greater delicacy of ferreting out racial prejudice among professional colleagues are likely possibilities.

RESEARCH METHODOLOGY

C. V. Abramowitz and Dokecki (1977) have offered a brief overview of the competing paradigms employed in studying the politics of psychotherapy—the archival records search, and the clinical (actually, experimental-clinical) analogue. The former strategy involves the retrieval of case records to examine associations between patient variables, on the one hand, and therapist or treatment variables, on the other, either or both of which are suspected to have political implications. The archival search has been popular among sociologists and a handful of applied social psychologists, whose scholarly mandate places a premium on ecological and external validities. deHoyos and deHoyos (1965), for example, found that practitioners (regardless of discipline) recorded fewer psychiatric symptoms in the hospital charts of black patients than in those of white patients.

Despite persuasive exhortation from within their own discipline to adopt archival and other "unobtrusive" strategies (Webb, Campbell, Schwartz, & Sechrest, 1966), psychologists have for the most part remained true to their experimental approach. This orientation leads to a discounting of archival research on the grounds of threats to internal validity. Foremost among these are the correlational constraint, the disproportionate weighting of therapists with large caseloads, and the notorious unreliability of institutional records (Davidson & Abramowitz, 1980). The *correlational* nature of archival research means that some uncontrolled third variable, such as level of psychopathology, may explain any relationship found between a patient variable and a treatment variable. Thus, it would be difficult to conclude that any relationship found was politically motivated. For instance, although deHoyos and deHoyos (1965) attributed the underrecording of symptoms in black patients' charts to the social distance between white professionals and black patients, another possible explanation would be the existence of a differential level or configuration of maladjustment in the two races (C. V. Abramowitz & Dokecki, 1977; Schermerhorn, 1956). The disproportionate weighting given to more active therapists results from the convention of using the patient as the case rather than the clinician in analyzing data. In instances where a relatively small number of therapists carry a disproportionate number of patients, results seemingly based on heterogeneous patient and therapist samples may be actually attributable to a handful of clinicians. In addition, consideration of each patient's data as independent, when in fact the same therapist has worked with a number of patients, has statistical consequences that have routinely been overlooked (Werner & Block, 1975). Last, one can hardly dispute the contention that agency files are rife with error variance and that unreliable data precipitate an interpretive dilemma in the event of null results. However, confirmatory findings, despite an appreciable number of misclassifications, are all the more impressive.

Experimentally inclined psychologists have placed greater credence in the results of clinical analogues (C. V. Abramowitz & Dokecki, 1977; Heller, 1971; Kazdin, 1978; Munley, 1974). This paradigm, in many respects the logical complement to archival and field methods, puts considerations of internal validity above considerations of external validity. Adapting the laboratory procedure used by social psychologists to study impression formation (Asch, 1946), many clinical researchers have experimentally manipulated stimulus patients' politically relevant characteristics within a bogus written case report, videotaped session, or role-played interview. Practitioners, presumably blind to the study's true concern, are asked to respond to one of the randomly distributed versions of the stimulus materials. Since expressly clinical input is held constant across all conditions and only race, class, or sex is varied, the idea is that any difference found can be attributed to the factor varied. In this way, the problem of differential psychopathology that plagues the archival search is neatly circumvented. To illustrate, Levy and Kahn (1970) determined that clinicians made more severe evaluations when fabricated Rorschach responses were designated as belonging to a lower-class than to a middle-class patient.

The analogue motif compromises many principles of external validity. Clinician/subjects may discern the true objectives of the study and adjust their responses so as to put themselves and their profession in a favorable light. Or such features of the research as the clinical situation or rating scale employed may be unrepresentative of those encountered in real-life settings. Moreover, critics of analogue methods maintain that a contrived transaction cannot be expected to evoke the intensity of emotion and thus the degree of evaluative distortion aroused in a face-to-face encounter. Practitioners in particular regard the analogue as an impoverished replica of clinical reality (Stricker, 1977). Nevertheless, most of these factors would bias the research toward finding no effect of class, race, or sex. It is not possible to discern whether the effects of employing unrepresentative research situations would increase or decrease the chance of finding political biases.

Surely, the methodological squabbles among psychotherapy researchers of the politics of therapy have made it easier for many professionals to indulge their temptation simply to discount this research altogether (Bergin & Strupp, 1972). The potential of this research for making an impact on clinical practice has been further eroded by a confusing pattern of findings suggesting that the direction of the evidence varies appreciably with the methodology employed (C. V. Abramowitz & Dokecki, 1977; Davidson & Abramowitz, 1980). Archival inquiries have turned up a substantial amount of data supportive of political bias formulations. However, while a cluster of early analogues yielded data consistent with the notion of social class bias (C. V. Abramowitz & Dokecki, 1977), such efforts have, overall, led to mixed results in the case of race (Griffith & Jones, 1979; Sattler, 1977).

Investigator Effects

Empirical discrepancies of the sort just described in a value-laden and ego-involving context invite cognitive distortion and interpretive gerry-mandering (Campbell, Note 1). Observers who champion consumer interests have tended to highlight and even to dramatize the generally confirmatory archival and anecdotal findings, to the virtual exclusion of the disconfirma-tory analogue data (American Psychological Association, 1975). Cor-respondingly, those whose allegiances appear to lie with the professional es-tablishment have been inclined to do just the reverse (Stricker, 1977). To be sure, practitioners have lamented that they are in a no-win situation. Taking another look at the finding that mental health professionals recorded fewer symptoms in the hospital charts of black than of white patients, we may be tempted (as deHoyos and deHoyos were) to infer a process of social distanc-ing. However, had more rather than less symptoms been been imputed to black patients, we might well be inclined to charge the staff with labeling bias derived from negative racial stereotypes. ("Heads we win, tails they lose.")

The methodological and substantive ego involvements and sometimes flagrant violations of usual scientific precautions so evident in this literature have inspired the characterization as "heartpotheses" of many of the socially sensitive questions raised (S. I. Abramowitz, 1978; Bloch, Abramowitz, & Weitz, 1980). Heartpotheses, such as the theory that minority patients are in-evitably shortchanged by majority therapists, masquerade as hypotheses but are actually political beliefs based on personal experience. By casting heart-potheses as hypotheses, those with a large personal stake in the outcome of their research gain a scientific credibility for and a chance to promote their political ideology.[2] Note that the notion of a heartpothesis does not imply the direction of the underlying political opinion; the conviction in some profes-sional circles that black patients are most assuredly not given short shrift by white therapists qualifies as well.

Another often-neglected investigator effect involves the choice of method (Barber, 1973; Carlson, 1972). Since archival searches are more likely to yield findings of political bias than are analogues, the investigator can choose the method that is more likely to produce the results desired.

Introduction to the Literature on Race Effects in Psychotherapy

Of the three political factors mentioned, social class and sex have been widely researched to detect any bias that they might engender in ther-apy. In contrast, research on the racial politics of treatment has been distin-guished by a "benign neglect." For reasons that probably lie in the politics of research and are not difficult to fathom, the research on the racial politics of clinical practice has not enjoyed the attention given the class and sex research. The chapter now turns to a review of the research that has been done. This review begins with an overview of previous reviews, and then examines the individual studies, divided according to whether they attempted to relate race to diagnosis, to treatment allocation, or to outcome.[3]

Before the review begins, some qualifications are in order. First, many studies touch on more than one patient parameter, so that classification within a section is somewhat arbitrary. The chapter places a study in what seems to be the most suitable context and returns to it in a subsequent section whenever appropriate. Second, the great majority of investigations have involved one-to-one treatment. Thus, modality is noted only when it is other than individual therapy. The absence of compelling evidence that persons from certain mental health professions or with certain orientations or levels of experience are more effective than others (Meltzoff & Kornreich, 1970) has led to the inclusion here of investigations of psychiatrists, psychologists, and social workers with varying approaches and seniority.

A final caveat: Prominent among the value judgments embedded in the enterprise of social science are those of reviewers (Barber, 1973; F. G. Singer, 1971; M. B. Smith, 1961). In the end, the reader must judge the weight of empirical evidence and attempt to reconcile the interpretive stalemate.

Issues in Interpretation

Although the political implications of data on race and diagnosis, treatment utilization, and outcome are for the most part straightforward, the implications of certain issues broached by the research are less obvious than are others. For example, the meaning of differential utilization of mental health services by blacks is far from self-evident. Until very recently, a large segment and perhaps even a majority of the black community regarded psychotherapy as a racist pacification program whose goal was social amnesia (Statman, 1971). From this vantage point, underutilization might be seen as an expression of informed avoidance and thus hardly a cause for concern. However, many black observers have now come to reject the premise that intensive psychotherapy is merely a middle-class opiate, and they insist that any withholding of such treatment from blacks by white institutions deprives blacks of the potential for personal growth that therapy affords (Griffith & Jones, 1979). As soon becomes clear, various observers apparently arguing from markedly different value assumptions have disagreed sharply over the implications of research on cross-racial treatment (i.e., treatment involving black patients and white therapists). If the search for empirical verities teaches one lesson, it is that the road from data to interpretation in this socially sensitive area is particularly treacherous.

The Present Strategy

Space constraints have dictated that this chapter concentrate on one particular ethnic group or settle for a cursory examination of the empirical work relevant to many. A focus on blacks and psychotherapy has been chosen because of the sheer number of black consumers of mental health services, an abundant and provocative scholarly heritage on race and psychiatry, and a substantial empirical beachhead. Moreover, many of the issues confronted in that literature have corresponding implications for other minorities, although experience reminds us that each group has its unique questions to ask of the field and thus deserves attention in its own right (M. L. Smith, 1974).

A Review of Previous Reviews

Dreger and Miller (1960, 1968) were among the first to attempt to synthesize the burgeoning research on the comparative psychologies of blacks and whites. While only small sections of both far-ranging reviews were devoted to clinical diagnosis and psychotherapy, the tentative inferences drawn from these very limited data are of historical interest. Based on a handful of studies conducted in the 1940s and early 1950s, Dreger and Miller (1960) inferred that "treatment of psychiatric disturbance is more difficult with Negroes than with whites" (p. 394). However, citing Schermerhorn's sociological caveats (1956), they acknowledged that "investigators have frequently been in error in assuming that the Negro and white populations are alike except for the variable in question and that the experimental meaning of these variables is culturally equivalent in both groups" (p. 394). In their subsequent paper, Dreger and Miller (1968) observed that "questions continue to be asked about the perceptions of the middle-class psychiatrist as he examines Negro patients . . . [but that] it continues to be impossible to draw meaningful conclusions regarding the relation between race and the incidence of mental disorder" (pp. 41–42). Significantly, the reviewers also noted the "irrelevancy and inappropriateness of many conclusions drawn from the not-too-distant past" (p. 42). The paucity of research on racial differences in treatment responsiveness was specifically lamented.

Siegel (1974) considered the research evidence relating to race as a factor in psychological testing, counseling, and psychotherapy. Although his review was not exhaustive, his conclusions are noteworthy for their compatibility with those of subsequent commentators.

> In psychological testing with blacks, the factor of the race of the examiner is probably no more salient than any other aspect of the testor. Despite much clinical speculation about the possibile inability of white clinicians to help black pa-

tients, there is little evidence to suggest that this is the case. In fact there is no research on therapeutic outcome comparing black and white therapists with black
patients. (p. 561)

As part of a larger review of the politics of clinical judgment, C. V.
Abramowitz and Dokecki (1977) examined several analogue and field in-
vestigations of the impact of patient and therapist race on clinical assessment.
They concluded:

Caucasian clinicians have for the most part shown immunity from negative racial expectancies and have on occasion manifested seemingly problack sentiment. [While] some observers may regard these outcomes as sufficiently counterintuitive to call into serious question the internal validity of patient racial
analogues . . . correlational data themselves offer only marginal support for the
notion of a negative racial halo. (p. 473)

But the mandate carried out by Dreger and Miller in the 1960s was passed
for the ensuing decade to Sattler (1970, 1977). His earlier paper dealt primarily with experimenter and interviewer race effects, only touching on the
therapeutic transaction. He observed that "research on racial therapist-client
variables is meager . . . [and] controlled investigation of interracial psychotherapy dyads is only in its beginning phase" (p. 155). Sattler's more recent
contribution spanned a period of accelerated research activity in the area of
race and mental health care. Focusing exclusively on the therapist-client interaction, it represents by far the most thorough and well-executed attempt to
organize this literature around the fundamental questions of diagnosis, utilization, and outcome. Sattler's handling of the empirical evidence was systematic and comprehensive, and his overall conclusion was clear and un-
hedged: "White therapists have been effective helping agents with a variety of
Black clients" (p. 278).

We have seen that some recent reviewers of the empirical literature on race
and psychotherapy—Siegel (1974), C. V. Abramowitz and Dokecki (1977),
and Sattler (1977)—have tended to reject allegations of pervasive discrimination in the name of mental health. A similar conclusion was recently reached
by a team of researchers at the National Institute of Mental Health (Parloff,
Waskow, & Wolfe, 1978). In a major generic review of the impact of therapist
outcome, Parloff et al. (1978) noted that "there are almost no findings with
regard to [race and] outcome. . . . Whether white therapists are as helpful as
or more helpful than black therapists cannot . . . be inferred" (p. 258). The
cumulative evidence thus appears to argue for tentative retention of the hypothesis of no racial differences.

But since most observers would agree that "one-to-one therapeutic relationships provide the same racial interaction patterns found in other forms of

interpersonal contacts [in our culture]" (Sattler, 1970, p. 153), this hypothesis is quite contradictory to the racist experiences of black Americans and an affront to liberal sensibilities. Is the clinical domain as well insulated from the racial undercurrents of the cultural environment as the previous white reviewers have suggested? Even Sattler (1977), after concluding that the "therapist's race is for the most part not a significant variable" (p. 271) in affecting the behavior of black clients in initial interview analogues, regarded his own verdict as "surprising in view of the clear documentation (Sattler, 1970) of *experimenter* race effects in subjects' performance in many other (test) situations" (p. 290).

Certainly, the divergent conclusions reached by black observers only confuse the situation. On the basis of less extensive reviews of the pertinent research, Griffith (1977) asserted that "racial differences have a somewhat negative effect upon psychotherapy" (p. 33), and Griffith and Jones (1979) concluded that "the mental health system does not serve the needs of blacks as well as it does those of whites" (p. 229). Focusing on vocationally oriented counseling, one black reviewer struck a more cautious note: "There is some evidence that the facilitative functioning of counselors is affected by race of the client, but the studies are few and the findings mixed and inconclusive" (Harrison, 1975, p. 131). Borrowing Sattler's heuristic tripart schema (1977) (diagnosis, utilization, and outcome), this chapter now scrutinizes the major findings on race and therapy that produced the white reviewers' negative verdict and the generally positive verdict of their black counterparts. Certain perspectives offered by the social psychology of research are invoked toward resolving this interpretive standoff.

REVIEW OF THE LITERATURE
ON RACE EFFECTS
IN PSYCHOTHERAPY

Diagnosis

Race effects in psychiatric diagnosis is an important area of concern because a patient's diagnosis can have a significant effect on the treatment he or she receives and on his or her later readjustment to the community. For instance, a verdict of schizophrenia might relegate an individual to inpatient status or to a pharmacotherapeutic regimen, and at a later time might become an obstacle to employment. Szasz (1971) has argued that white therapists impute greater maladjustment to minority patients, thereby shortchanging and stigmatizing them. Empirical examination of this proposition has involved two different methodological approaches. Clinical analogue studies have typically presented white (and sometimes black) professionals with identical hypothetical case descriptions, which are designated as belonging to either black or white patients. Archival investigations, by contrast, have consisted of retrospective searches of actual clinical records. While such naturalistic research obviously does not provide the same degree of control over patient characteristics as does the analogue research, it offers a more ecologically valid glimpse of real-life clinical transactions.

Analogue Research

C. V. Abramowitz and Dokecki (1977) and Sattler (1977) independently conducted partly overlapping reviews of some 10 analogue studies of racial bias. Significantly, both interpreted the data as largely vindicating white practitioners of evaluative discrimination: "Analogue research has not substantiated the contention that clinical verdicts rendered by Caucasian clinicians inevitably penalize racial minorities" (C. V. Abramowitz & Dokecki, 1977, p. 466). Illustrative of the method used in the analogues, Schwartz and Abramowitz (1975) mailed a racially labeled case description depicting a nonpsychotic patient referred for inpatient treatment to 102 participating psychiatrists randomly selected from the national register. The main outcome was "the inability to detect consistent psychiatric bias against [black-identified] patients" (p. 1528). M. L. Smith (1974) likewise failed to elicit counseling judgment bias with Chicano-designated materials.

Paradoxically, Schwartz and Abramowitz and others reported scattered indications of what C. V. Abramowitz and Dokecki (1977) tentatively identified as "seemingly problack effects" (p. 466). Moreover, data from additional analogues suggest that negative racial expectancies are not only the white therapist's burden (Celnak, 1970). Thus, Benefee, Abramowitz, Weitz, and Armstrong (1976) found that the direction of a black clinician's bias depends not only on the client's racial designation, but also on the therapist's own social values. While relatively untraditional black practitioners were partisan toward the client designated as black, the reverse was true for their more traditional colleagues.

Recent findings only reinforce these earlier trends. Umbenhauer and De-Witte (1978) persuasively reproduced Schwartz and Abramowitz's null results (1975). Employing an unusually credible sample of over 400 psychiatrists and psychologists, they obtained abundant evidence of social class effects on clinical judgment, but no evidence of racial attribution effects, and no race × class interactions. Warner (1979) also inferred minimal racial bias from the diagnoses given by 173 black and white mental health professionals shown same- or opposite-race patient protocols. In addition, 10 unpublished doctoral dissertations that employed racial bias analogues also reported results not supportive of race effects.

In a related arena, 217 school psychologists randomly selected from the national directory were presented with a bogus psychoeducational report of a 10-year-old pupil labeled black or white (Amira, Abramowitz, & Gomes-Schwartz, 1977). Based on the pattern of these psychologists' diagnostic impressions, the investigators concluded that "the school psychologists . . . acquitted themselves rather well overall" (p. 438); "in addition to being weak, socially charged expectancy effects do not necessarily penalize the socially disenfranchised" (p. 439). That is, expectancy effects may be *problack*. In another independent confirmation of problack effects, 86 graduate students from six counseling programs rated cases significantly more positively when they thought the patients were black than when they thought the patients were white (Merluzzi & Merluzzi, 1978). Warner (1979) noted occasional tendencies for professionals of both races to make judgments favoring the cross-racial patient, failing to support the Benefee et al. (1976) finding of anti-white stereotyping among some black clinicians. No other new analogue evidence directly relevant to this question has appeared. However, using the same patient materials employed by Benefee et al. (1976), Bloch et al. (1980) were unable to detect evidence of racial attribution effects in white practitioners.

There are a number of possible explanations for the finding of problack bias. C. V. Abramowitz and Dokecki (1977) noted that the clinician/subjects might be aware of the hidden agenda of the racial bias analogue and that they might give socially desirable responses because of professional defensiveness. Others have invoked the idea of overcompensation motivated by white guilt in attempting to account for the unexpected problack patterns in their own data (Amira et al., 1977; Fischer & Miller, 1973; Merluzzi & Merluzzi, 1978; Schwartz & Abramowitz, 1975). A related interpretation hinges on the notion of white paternalism. According to this view, black patients are regarded more favorably because they are not expected to meet as high standards as their white counterparts are (Mercer, 1973).

Altogether, the analogue data stack up as follows: (1) Charges that white therapists frequently discriminate according to race in making psychiatric diagnoses have generally not been confirmed; (2) scattered problack effects have been found; and (3) the issue of racial stereotyping on the part of black clinicians remains open. The chapter returns to the nagging question of how to reconcile such counterintuitive empirical data with street wisdom in a later discussion of analogue methodology and the politics of research.

Field Research

Some 20 naturalistic investigations have examined various aspects of diagnosis as a function of the patient's race. Griffith and Jones (1979) reported that blacks indeed seem to "receive more severe diagnoses" (p. 228), but they reached this conclusion on the basis of what appears to have been a limited review of the epidemiological research. On the basis of overlapping subsets of about half of the studies then available, two independent reviewers reached a tentative null conclusion. Sattler (1977) concluded from five relevant studies that "White mental health professionals do not, for the most part, appear to be differentially biased in the diagnostic decisions they make for Black and White patients" (p. 259). C. V. Abramowitz and Dokecki (1977) characterized the corresponding data from six studies as slightly less negative: "The relevant findings are inconclusive and thus . . . repudiate the claim of pervasive antiminority/sentiment" (p. 466).

Thus, the weight of the early archival data failed to support the claim of diagnostic bias against blacks. However, on consideration of an enlarged pool of earlier findings, along with more recent data, one would tend to refrain from granting a blanket pardon to white practitioners quite yet. Such a stance seems justified, even though several investigations bypassed by Sattler (1977) actually support the inference of no antiblack diagnostic bias. For one, B. D. Singer (1967) found fewer rather than more symptoms recorded for black than for white patients. Similarly, data reported by Derogatis, Covi, Lipman, Davis, and Rickels (1971) suggest that race per se does not have as strong an effect on symptomatology as does social class. Such a conclusion in fact appears to be entirely consistent with the results of several major epidemiological surveys of mental disorder among blacks and whites (Ilfeld, 1978; Langner, Gersten, Greene, Eisenberg, Herson, & McCarthy, 1974; Srole et al., 1962; Tischler, 1977).

Despite all of these findings, a reappraisal of the data now available suggests that the weight of cumulative evidence no longer clearly rests on the side of the defense. Even in his generally meticulous review, Sattler (1977) overlooked numerous pertinent field studies whose findings were consistent with racial bias formulations. Liss, Weiner, Robins, and Richardson (1973) and Vitols, Waters, and Keeler (1963), for example, determined—contrary to de-Hoyos and deHoyos (1965) and to B. D. Singer (1967)—that more symptoms were ascribed to black than to white patients. While archival records' searches do not control for such potential confounds as race-differential maladjustment patterns, the foregoing kind of divergence nonetheless advises against rigid retention of the hypothesis of no racial difference. Rather, in light of the pattern of positive findings of varying direction, a more tenable hypothesis would be one postulating the operation of patient or therapist mediator variables, such as the former's social class or the latter's social values.

There is also other evidence in favor of retaining the hypothesis of racial bias in mental health services. First, even though Sattler (1977) did note Lane's finding (1968) of a higher proportion of black than white patients among process (i.e., poor-prognosis) than reactive schizophrenics, he neglected to cite Allon's virtual replication of this finding (1971). In addition, he was apparently unaware of several reports indicating that black patients receive more severe diagnostic labels than do white patients in the same program or system (Gross, Herbert, Knatterud, & Donner, 1969; Locke & Duval, 1965; Malzberg, 1965; Pollack, Redick, Norman, Wurster & Gorwitz, 1964; Simon, Fleiss, Gurland, Stiller, & Sharpe, 1973). Gross et al. (1969) concluded from their results that "as the sociocultural distance between the clinician and his patient increases, diagnoses become less accurate and dispositions more nonspecific" (p. 638). In that regard, Gynther and his associates (Gynther, 1972; Gynther, Lachar, & Dahlstrom, 1978) have secured evidence that use of the Minnesota Multiphasic Personality Inventory (MMPI), the most popular psychiatric screening instrument in the United States, leads to more inaccuracies in diagnosing black than white individuals.

Besides the previously overlooked evidence, recent archival research is virtually unanimous in indicating that black patients receive more than their proportional share of schizophrenic and paranoid diagnoses (Balch & Balch, 1975; Cole & Pilisuk, 1976; Davis & Jones, 1974). Although psychosocial variables as well as prejudicial evaluation can explain such overrepresentation, it is significant that the relationship between minority status and diagnostic stringency has been found to hold across educational level in at least one investigation (Watkins, Cowan, & Davis, 1976).

Data retrieved from the program evaluation archives of a constellation of urban community mental health centers have likewise revealed that a large sample of white therapists of varying disciplines and theoretical orientations rendered slightly more severe diagnostic impressions of black than of white child and adolescent outpatients (Davidson, Edwards, Greene, & Abramowitz, Note 2). This investigation, one of the handful to incorporate a subsample of black professionals, disclosed a corresponding trend toward same-race favoritism among them. If valid, these findings raise the disturbing specter of mental health professionals of both races "favoring their own kind." Moreover, since the direction of differential severity varied by clinician race, and since assignment of patients to therapists was presumably independent of race, actual race-differential levels of childhood maladjustment cannot be invoked as a rival explanation.

Conclusion

There can be no blanket acceptance of Sattler's conclusion (1977) that 'The trends resulting from clinical judgment studies and from the archival and field diagnostic studies are similar. The diagnostic judgments of [white] clinicians are not systematically biased in favor of or against Black clients" (p. 260). However, the present reanalysis advises that this conclusion be accepted only to the degree that it is limited to the analogue findings, and then with the qualification that the scattered problack patterns demand careful methodological scrutiny. Many apparently overlooked earlier data and

newer archival findings are incompatible with the predominantly disconfirmatory evidence from naturalistic studies reviewed by Sattler (1977) and
C. V. Abramowitz and Dokecki (1977). Although the cumulative data present
a mixed and contradictory picture, the newer evidence has been disconcerting-
ly amenable to racial bias formulations. Once unwarranted and premature,
Griffith and Jones's (1979) assertion of race-differential severity of psychiatric judgment may yet turn out to be the correct diagnosis.

The inconsistency between the overwhelmingly negative analogue data
and the partially supportive field results should be kept in mind. As is argued
later, certain weaknesses of the analogue approach to studying political bias
seem likely to tilt the odds in favor of obtaining null results. To be sure, this is
not to minimize the interpretive pitfalls inherent in attempting to distinguish
between the plausibility of the bias formulation and that of such rival accounts
of the apparent archival confirmations as race-patterned manifestations of
psychopathology. To permit the disconfirmation of such alternative
explanations, archival studies are needed in which potential patient confounds are controlled via covariance or matching procedures.

Allocation and Utilization of Mental Health Resources

The political consequences of treatment allocation and utilization
are of major import. If any therapeutic effect is granted to the cornucopia of
psychiatric remedies, then it seems clear that underutilization by any group
in acute need only prolongs their psychosocial maladies—and, ultimately,
maintains their social disadvantage. The community mental health movement and affirmative action programs have attempted to make psychiatric
services more attractive, relevant, and available to minority populations.
Still, so long as the professional establishment continues to claim that some
methods and programs are more suitable than others for certain designated
problems, then appropriate treatment assignment is inseparable from effi-
cient relief. Also, different treatments carry differential social stigmata.

In this regard, an especially heated race-related question concerns the appropriateness of insight-oriented psychotherapy for minority patients. Once
regarded as an opiate that duped blacks into blaming themselves rather than
their circumstances for their plight (L. H. Gardner, 1971; Halleck, 1971;
Thomas & Sillen, 1972), traditional psychodynamic therapy is enjoying something of a renaissance in minority circles. Whereas giving insight-oriented
treatment was once considered part of the latent racist pacification program
(Grier & Cobbs, 1968; Statman, 1971), withholding it in favor of a more direct problem-solving approach is increasingly being equated with denying
black people legitimate access to personal exploration (Griffith & Jones,
1979; A. Jones & Seagull, 1977).

Analogue Research

The issue of *utilization* has been operationalized in the research analogue largely through expression of differential preference for a same- or opposite-race therapist presented in a clinical sketch or on videotape. *Disposition* (allocation) has been cast in terms of suitability for a generic treatment, a specific modality or orientation, and length.

Sattler (1977) reviewed over 20 analogue and interview studies that compared a broad spectrum of black and white consumers' preferences for race of therapist. In about half of the investigations, blacks clearly disclosed a preference for black therapists. "However, a competent White professional is preferred to a less competent Black professional and the therapist's style and technique are more important in affecting Black clients' choices than the therapist's race. . . . a simple unequivocal answer cannot be given to the question, "Do Black people prefer Black therapists or counselors?" (p. 267). From a more selective review, Griffith (1977) likewise inferred that "black clients have not revealed a clear preference for black therapists over white therapists" (p. 36). However, a review of vocationally oriented studies produced a dissenting opinion. According to Harrison (1975), counselees do indeed "prefer counselors of the same race, particularly if they are black counselees" (p. 131). The therapist's race appears to be of minimal importance to white people, Sattler suggests, perhaps because they perceive the likelihood of encountering a minority therapist to be small.

Recent data have in the main supported Sattler's and Griffith's observations. Minority counselees have tended to prefer same- over opposite-race counselors (Atkinson, Maruyama, & Matsui, 1978; Harrison, 1977), although opposite-race counselors with certain qualities have been perceived as helpful (Peoples & Dell, 1975) or likable (Harrison, 1977). One recent study found that Caucasian female delinquents actually preferred a black counselor (Gamboa, Tosi, & Riccio, 1976), while a dissertation disclosed that white counselees rarely chose a black counselor (Briley, 1977).

Since several of the analogue studies reviewed in the preceding section also elicited treatment recommendations, the picture here might be expected to be starkly negative as well. In fact, while the evidence tends in that direction, the case is not nearly so open-and-shut. To be sure, most of the data reviewed by Sattler (1977) fail to indicate that blacks are perceived as less appropriate psychotherapy candidates than whites are. Fischer and Miller (1973) even found that a severely disturbed lower-class client identified as white was seen as particularly ill suited for psychotherapy, while a mildly disturbed upper-class black client was seen as especially well suited. Of course, the failure to control for the class difference could explain this apparently counterintuitive finding due to race.

The picture with respect to particular modalities and orientations seems less clear, however. The results reviewed by Sattler (1977) are mixed. Some imply that patient racial attribution does not affect assignment to supportive therapy or treatment having a social emphasis. However, others suggest that a teenager is more likely to be assigned to individual than family treatment only when he or she is identified as black, and that in 1966 only about a third of a sample of group therapists would admit a black businessman into an ongoing group of Southern whites. Moreover, the national sample of psychiatrists solicited by Schwartz and Abramowitz (1975) rated black-designated patients as less suitable than white-designated patients for inpatient treatment, and black-designated men as especially inappropriate for insight-oriented treatment.

Paradoxically enough, data collected from a national convention sample of black clinicians are comparatively straightforward (Benefee et al., 1976):

> Despite the relatively unfavorable assessment of the white-identified patient's level of functioning, the untraditional [black] clinicians recommended slightly shorter-term therapy for him than for the black-identified patient. The white patient was also disproportionately likely to be singled out for behavior therapy by the traditional [black] clinicians. [Untraditional black practitioners] may cope with anxieties aroused by the prospect of an ongoing personal relationship with a white patient simply by foreclosing that possibility. Their conventional and presumably more protocol-minded coworkers may resort to more discreet forms of distancing, including deployment of a professionally sanctioned approach that legitimizes some impersonalization in the therapeutic hour. (p. 272)

The newer data likewise offer just enough support for the hypothesis of antiblack effects on treatment brokerage to argue against our abandoning it at this early juncture. The weight of evidence is still disconfirmatory. Bloch et al. (1980) failed to find differential recommendations for either therapy length or modality according to the stimulus patient's racial designation. Nor did Umbenhauer and DeWitte's impressive sample of professionals (1978) relegate the black-identified patient to treatments previously rated by expert judges as having second-class status. However, Amira et al. (1977) obtained evidence that a national sample of school psychologists advised placement in a custodial program at a separate facility more strongly when the pupil was believed to be black and middle-class than they did when the pupil was believed to be either black and lower-class or white and of any social standing. And Crossley, Weitz, and Abramowitz (1977) reported that Southern white abortion counselors were more likely to encourage an adolescent to have her child rather than to abort when her case materials were black-identified. Regardless of whether these perplexing findings are construed as antiblack or problack, their import seems clear enough. Although the analogue data are again largely negative, they do not allow the possibility of some circumscribed or subtle racial effects on treatment recommendations to be ruled out.

Field Research

Paralleling the relationship between the overwhelmingly negative analogue data on diagnostic bias and the more equivocal field data, the naturalistic results for treatment utilization and disposition are more consistently supportive of political bias formulations than are the analogue data. In fact, Sattler (1977) noted more evidence of racial effects in this particular realm than in any other in his review: "Black clients usually are underrepresented in mental health facilities; when offered treatment, they usually, but not always, after the initial interview have higher dropout rates than White clients; they are assigned less often to individual therapy than are White clients; once in therapy they are likely to have higher dropout rates than White clients, and when hospitalized usually are discharged more quickly than White patients" (p. 267). These conclusions are consistent with those reached by Griffith and Jones (1979), who noted that blacks "utilize psychiatric services at a rate far lower than the proportion of blacks in the surrounding community, are afforded different treatment . . . and remain in treatment for far briefer periods of time than whites" (pp. 228–229).

A closer look at the five studies on which Sattler's inference regarding race-differential utilization patterns is based reveals that only one of them unequivocally indicated an underrepresentation of black patients in mental health clinics (Kadushin, 1969). Although it was an extensive cross-agency investigation, this study alone probably should not outweigh the other, less decisive data. Such data include the results of two investigations overlooked by Sattler (1977). In one, Rosenblatt and Mayer (1972) found that black persons underutilized marital and family services; in the other, Gullatee (1972) found that middle-aged nonwhite males were overrepresented in public mental hospitals. Since public mental hospital admission may be involuntary, any pattern of underutilization of outpatient programs concomitant with overutilization of inpatient programs among blacks might reflect their lesser willingness to seek out traditional mental health services voluntarily. E. E. Jones (1978) reached a consistent but somewhat different conclusion: "Black men, for as yet undetermined reasons, do not seek [outpatient] psychotherapy nearly as frequently as do black females, or to the same extent as do their white counterparts" (p. 228).

The newer evidence germane to the question of race-differential utilization of psychiatric services is meager and ungeneralizable. B. L. Weiss and Kupfer (1974) reported a relative absence of blacks on psychiatric research wards, and Kirstein (1978) found an overrepresentation of black enlisted officers among military psychiatric inpatients. Thus, while "sometimes" might be substituted for Sattler's (1977) "usually," the weight of the evidence suggests that black males in particular are underrepresented in other than inpatient mental health facilities.

Almost two-thirds of the numerous relevant studies examined by Sattler (1977) indicated a difference in length of treatment according to patient race, and in each case the direction was toward earlier termination among blacks. More recent data, however, have not confirmed any tendency for black patients to be shortchanged in regard to length of therapy with whites. In a direct reversal of earlier findings, Davidson et al. (Note 2) found that black children were actually seen for more sessions than white children were by white as well as black practitioners. Both they and Craig and Huffine (1976) failed to find that therapeutic matching according to race affected continuation in treatment. E. E. Jones (1978) reported no tendency for black women to terminate earlier from therapy conducted by a white than by a black professional. And Vail (1978) obtained no correlation between black patients' attitudes toward whites and their persistence in treatment with a white therapist. Thus, Sattler's impression (1977) that black patients tend not to remain in cross-racial treatment must be tempered in light of recent findings— among the first to suggest that the decade-long moderation of racial tensions in the broader culture may be facilitating the establishment of a working alliance in cross-racial therapy. Garfield (1978) sounds a caveat from another vantage point: "While there appears to be a tendency for a more frequent early termination from psychotherapy by black clients than by whites, this is by no means a consistent pattern. This problem is also compounded by social class factors that generally have not been partialled out" (p. 200).

Regarding race-differential patterns in hospitalization discharge rates, the two more methodologically sound of the three investigations covered by Sattler disclosed that black patients indeed have a shorter length of stay (Mayo, 1974; B. D. Singer, 1967). However, these findings cannot be clearly adduced as evidence for or against a patient-based explanation of racial differences in length of treatment, because discharge from a hospital is not determined solely by the patient's preference. The professional staff often has a part in the discharge decision. So, it does not reflect simply the patient's desire to leave treatment.

Sattler (1977) cited four investigations that were unanimous in demonstrating that black patients were less likely to be offered individual psychotherapy than other treatment modalities. Similarly, Cole and Pilisuk (1976) recently reported that black men in a crisis clinic were less likely than white men were to be referred for psychotherapy. To the contrary, Lowinger and Dobie (1968) found no greater tendency to assign black than white patients to psychotherapy.

The tendency for black patients to be referred more often for treatment other than individual therapy is not the only suggestion that they receive less desirable forms of treatment than their white counterparts do. Sue, McKinney, Allen, and Hall (1974), for example, reported that blacks were more likely to be seen by paraprofessionals, and B. D. Singer (1967) found that they were given less intensive kinds of care. Gross et al. (1969) noted that black females were more likely to be treated in the emergency room, whereas white females were more often referred for outpatient treatment. Lubin, Hornstein, Lewis, and Bechtel (1973) found a relationship between race and referral to inpatient treatment, and Greene, Abramowitz, Davidson, and Edwards (1980) recently related race to referral to group therapy. However, notwithstanding this impressive but somewhat selective array of positive findings, the empirical case for race-differential assignment to drug, inpatient, and group treatment is decidedly mixed.

Scattered indications that blacks sometimes are underrepresented among those referred for individual and other intensive forms of therapy, treated for a shorter period of time, and more likely to be seen by a nonprofessional would appear to be cause for concern. Sattler (1977) largely dismissed the import of the latter finding on the grounds of the lack of evidence that professionals are any more effective with black clients than nonprofessionals are (Cowen, 1973). The presumption that one-to-one treatment is necessarily more powerful than alternative modalities are can likewise be challenged (Meltzoff & Kornreich, 1970). From the standpoint of cultural preference and social desirability, however, most people would prefer to be treated for their psychological problems in individual therapy conducted by a professional (Griffith & Jones, 1979; Sanua, 1966).

Explanation

To the extent that one is inclined to accept on a tentative basis the implication of the naturalistic data that the allocation of certain mental health resources is differential by race, one is left to grapple with how best to understand this phenomenon. Explanations have varied considerably, according to whether they focus on the patient's personality, racial attitudes, and other transferential encumbrances, or whether they focus on the therapist's own excess baggage. Hence, the trend toward shorter, less intensive care of black patients has been linked to their collusion in making fewer demands on themselves (B. D. Singer, 1967) and to interference from hourly work schedules (Krebs, 1971). In attempting to account for the overrepresentation of blacks among his voluntary inpatients, Cripps (1973) proposed that they may actually have sought hospital treatment. Obviously, any negative opinions a black patient holds about the benefits he or she can derive from intimate interaction with a middle-class white would also be expected to contribute to shorter, less intensive care. As Griffith (1977) observed, ''The black man's sense of distrust in encounters with whites is well documented for its survival function. . . . this tendency of black clients represents a healthy cultural paranoia . . . that white therapists must learn to distinguish from pathological states" (pp. 31–32).

Unlike the patient-based model, which involves white clinicians only indirectly in black patients' treatment fate, therapist-based models directly implicate the clinicians' social values. B. D. Singer's notion (1967) of "sociological realism" suggests that these values operate in the interest of effective cue utilization—clinical staff members "recognize" that the problems of blacks are more social than psychiatric, and therefore appreciate the irrelevance of intensive intrapsychic therapy. Other conceptualizations cast therapists in a less benign mold. White clinicians have been accused of fatalistic attitudes toward the pathogenic conditions of lower-class black culture (B. D. Singer, 1967), subtle discrimination in treatment referral (Sue et al., 1974), and outright rejection of black patients (Krebs, 1971). How covert discrimination might operate in the clinic was neatly demonstrated by Yamamoto, James, Bloombaum, and Hattem (1967), whose white therapists completed several indirect measures of racial stereotyping. Although degree of stereotyping was unrelated to therapy length for white patients, black patients seen by more prejudiced therapists received shorter treatment than did those seen by less prejudiced therapists. The clear implication is that the negative racial expectancies of some white clinicians are communicated to the patient and culminate in early termination.

Conclusion

Altogether, the field data provide some support for the position that patients' treatment careers are partly determined by their and their therapists' ethnicity. Although the findings are for the most part only suggestive and highly circumscribed by program, patient, and therapist characteristics, they nonetheless constitute the most persuasive empirical case yet for racial effects in the clinic. Nevertheless, as a precaution against overinterpretation in the service of ideological fervor, it should be emphasized that the positive naturalistic data are amenable to multiple interpretations, and that these have been largely conjectural, post hoc, and value-laden. It is important to remember that patients as well as therapists contribute to decisions about which treatment to enter and when to terminate. Notwithstanding the notable exception by Yamamoto and his associates (1967), few investigators have described the staff members involved or have assessed therapists' social beliefs sufficiently well to pinpoint the problem of race-differential treatment patterns *within the racial attitudes of white therapists*. That having been said, the cumulative evidence would seem to warrant accelerated empirical attention, professional sensitization, and administrative vigilance. It would also appear to legitimate the movement toward local control of mental health services by minority communities (Nassi, 1978).

Process and Outcome

Even if blacks were shown to receive a fair shake from white diagnosticians and referring clinicians, this would all be for naught unless they
were in fact also shown to benefit from undergoing conventional forms of
mental health care. The paramount question concerning the cross-racial therapy process involves black patients' ability to trust and willingness to disclose
to white therapists, and the latter's ability to transcend negative stereotypes
about blacks and willingness to facilitate their personal growth. Skepticism
that a favorable working alliance could be forged between majority therapists and minority patients provided the momentum for affirmative action
programs in mental health training (Padilla, Boxley, & Wagner, 1973).

The issue of outcome is straightforward: Do minorities in fact prosper in
therapy with whites? One particular corollary of this question is, however,
considerably more subtle: To what extent is any enhanced "psychosocial adjustment" deriving from blacks' enrollment in the traditional intrapsychic
therapies offered by whites merely majority highbrow for what actually
amounts to political co-optation? Statmen (1971) is one among many who
have underscored that the therapeutic assumption of personal responsibility
is incompatible with the conviction of patterned institutional discrimination
that lies at the core of the minority community's political awareness. However, since even when the objectives of the research clearly call for doing so,
measures of political beliefs have rarely been included in patients' outcome
batteries (Nassi & Abramowitz, 1978), there is not as yet an empirical answer
to this pressing question.

This is not to imply by contrast that studies bearing on the expressly psychological outcomes of conventional verbal psychotherapy are especially
abundant. Moreover, the methodological pitfalls common to all psychotherapy outcome research are only magnified when placed in a socially sensitive
context, and therefore dictate more than the usual caution in interpretation.
For example, in the therapy and counseling analogues, the typical methodologies employed are exemplified by this comment: "Therapists were most often not professionals, 'patients' were usually college students recruited as research subjects, and 'therapy' consisted of a single interview" (Griffith &
Jones, 1979, p. 229). The seemingly more preferable naturalistic investigations "have not employed extensive outcome measures . . . [or] control
groups" (Sattler, 1977, p. 274) and suffer from insufficient demographic and
social attitude information about the white interviewers, the small pools of
black professionals and longer-term black male patients from which to draw,
and brief treatment duration. Such weaknesses no doubt contribute to the
ambiguity of the evidence and the various interpretations of it. The picture is
further clouded by the frequent failure of researchers to demonstrate beneficial effects of psychotherapy involving white clients and white therapists.[4]

For if the effectiveness of therapy in relation to a control group cannot be easily demonstrated, how can one expect to demonstrate differences between blacks and whites in improvement in therapy?

Analogue Research

Sattler (1977) reviewed 10 pertinent analogue studies, all with black and white clinicians and all but three with clients of both races as well. He concluded that the results of those studies "suggest that the therapist's race is for the most part not a significant variable in affecting the client's performance and reactions. . . . The position that Blacks prefer to be counseled only by Blacks or that White therapists cannot be effective in working with Black clients does not receive support" (pp. 271, 273). The counterintuitiveness of this conclusion seems to have troubled Sattler himself, who noted in a revealing aside (1977, pp. 289–290) that such a conclusion is curiously at odds with earlier findings of experimenter race effects in psychological testing (Sattler, 1970).

A rereading of the research covered by Sattler in fact suggests that he somewhat overstated the case against race effects. Four analogue studies appear to exonerate the white counselor (Cimbolic, 1972; Ewing, 1974; Tanney, 1973; Young, 1973). Of the remaining six, however, three look equivocal (Bryson & Cody, 1973; Grantham, 1973; Mullozzi, 1972). And both Banks (1972) and Carkhuff and Pierce (1967) determined depth of self-exploration to be higher in same- than in opposite-race dyads. In addition, all black subjects in Banks, Berenson, and Carkhuff (1967) wanted to return to see the black counselor, but only one-third would return to see white counselors. The black counselor, though less experienced, was judged to be more facilitative than the white counselors were. While Sattler is technically correct in noting that the generalizability of these provocative data is constrained by the small number of counselors (one black, three white) and by the confound of race with experience level and orientation, he nonetheless understated its message.

It is instructive to learn what black observers have to say about the therapy analogue data. E. E. Jones (1978) cited several of the studies reclassified here from Sattler as mixed or troublesome, and another investigation in which therapist race and experience were both found to be of primary importance (W. Gardner, 1972). Three of the four negative findings noted by Sattler were not mentioned. Presumably on the basis of the evidence cited, Jones inferred that "The preponderance of the studies indicates that blacks respond more favorably to black counselors than to white counselors" (p. 277). More recently, Griffith and Jones (1979) observed in the context of a broad overview of cross-racial therapy issues that "the results of analogue studies concerning black-white interactions in interviews simulating counseling situations support the conclusion that white therapist–black patient interactions are frequently ineffective" (p. 229).

In the interest of possibly resolving the foregoing dispute, a literature search covering the period 1975–1979 has been conducted. Unfortunately, only five new studies could be located and these were of negligible import. The setting was always educational rather than clinical per se; the "counselors" were in fact trainees; and the findings are inconsistent. Furthermore, since all five analogues are unpublished doctoral theses summarized in *Dissertation Abstracts International*, important descriptive information is often lacking.

In considering the evidence germane to the question of utilization, the present authors have happily observed that previous reviewers of the research concurred, in the main, about certain race-differential patterns. In the discussion of the data on race and diagnosis, it has been suggested that some overlooked and some recent investigations probably account for the discrepancy between previous white reviewers' treatment of the data as largely negative, their black colleagues' strongly positive characterization, and the present authors' mixed reaction.

Although the direction of the discrepancy among reviewers is the same for the process and outcome analogue research, and the breadth of coverage is likewise not identical, the ultimate resolution appears to lie elsewhere—in the reviewer's race. The split is now clearly along racial lines. Sattler (1977), a white reviewer, saw little evidence that blacks get short shrift in therapy with whites; while Griffith and Jones (1979), black reviewers, found ample evidence that this is in fact so. In their brief but discerning review of this literature, Parloff et al. (1978) attribute this discrepancy in conclusions to Sattler's more extensive coverage of null and counterintuitive data and to the differential significance that the black reviewers apparently placed on measures of self-exploration. While this explanation probably accounts for some portion of the variance and has the virtue of diplomacy, it does not go far enough. Notwithstanding Parloff et al.'s observation about the somewhat different empirical domains, black and white reviewers alike examined many of the same studies, and no new persuasive evidence has appeared in the interim. Moreover, rather than sweeping the issue of nonoverlapping coverage under the rug, it behooves socially concerned investigators to ask what psychological processes help explain the phenomenon of different-race reviewers' differentially *locating as well as interpreting* data in a way that is consistent with their probable overt and covert political beliefs and professional stakes. It has continued to appear that, despite the thoroughness and undeniable scholarship of his review, Sattler (1977) succumbed to overstating the negative case. For their part, although Griffith and Jones (1979) were sensitive to the problem of overgeneralizing from the often methodologically weak positive investigations, they largely overlooked the negative evidence compiled by Sattler.

In all likelihood, the empirical "truth" lies somewhere in between the polarized positions. As Parloff et al. (1978) noted, "Although there may be some benefits to communication and to feelings of satisfaction in same-race pairs in single-interview situations" (p. 258), few findings bear on actual outcome. The counseling analogue data indeed seem as inconclusive as they are suggestive with regard to the presence of racial effects. The need for research with more credible professional and client samples and measures of outcome is acute. Furthermore, one might well choose to elevate to the status of a hypothesis the suggestion that the black and white reviewers' differing social experiences and conscious and unconscious racial attitudes help to explain the discrepancy between their readings of the empirical evidence. Accelerated construction of a racial politics of research as a branch of the social psychology of knowledge and a special case of investigator bias is long overdue (Sherwood & Nataupsky, 1968).

Field Research

Sattler (1977) reviewed 10 *in vivo* studies of the impact of race on therapeutic outcome. Half included white as well as black clients; the other half included black clients only (two of the latter included black and white therapists). Sattler regarded all but one of these investigations as pointing to a single inexorable conclusion: "Black clients report that they have benefited from treatment received from White therapists, who have used, so far as can be determined, traditional forms of therapy" (p. 276).

Again, the present reviewers are less sanguine than Sattler that these earlier returns are unequivocally negative. In the first place, certain methodological constraints idiosyncratic to this sensitive area of research increase the likelihood of overestimating the benefits that the typical black patient derives from therapy with a white professional. For example, white practitioners who agree to cooperate in the research are probably more liberal than are their colleagues who do not, and thus less reactive to race-related issues (Parloff et al., 1978). Similarly, black people willing to seek out traditional mental health services and to be seen by white practitioners are probably less alienated and more trusting of white institutions than are those who prefer to seek assistance from predominantly black institutions. In addition, we already know that black patients are more likely to terminate therapy prematurely than are white patients (E. E. Jones, 1978); those black clients who remain to complete the outcome measures are thus less representative of the original subsample than are the whites who remain. Finally, the question is not whether minority patients benefit at all from treatment with a white professional, but whether they benefit as much as they would have with a same-race therapist. As only a handful of studies have yet systematically varied both therapist race and patient race to address this question directly, it remains largely unanswered (Parloff et al., 1978).

Turning to the specific investigations covered in Sattler's review, it appears that the balance of the evidence is indeed negative—but less so than Sattler believed. To be sure, three of the studies are definitely negative (Aronow, 1967; Lerner, 1972; Silverman, 1971). Lerner (1972) paid more than the usual attention to such important factors as therapist values and experience, and employed sophisticated outcome measures. The inability to find that 15 severely disturbed white patients achieved greater success with white therapists than their 15 black counterparts did is therefore particularly noteworthy. A counterintuitive finding by Goldberg (1973) also belongs in the null camp. Urban lower-class black women reported fewer problems after than before treatment (three or more sessions) with a white therapist, whereas the whites in the study reported no such improvement.

On the other side of the ledger, two of the inquiries noted by Sattler yielded mixed findings regarding race-differential outcome, and a third produced positive results. Williams (1974) found that white male professional counselors and black peer counselors were equally successful in eliciting trust and self-disclosure from black college students after five interviews. The question here—whether the white professionals should have been more facilitative than the black peers—cannot be answered due to the confound of training with race. Warren, Jackson, Nugaris, and Farley (1973) studied matched samples of 20 white and 20 black parents who had at least three sessions with white therapists at an urban child guidance clinic. The two groups held similar opinions about the helpfulness of therapy and the therapist's attitude toward treating them. Still, on some dimensions, black parents seemed ambivalent about the white therapists, regarding them as supportive yet not involved with the struggles of black people. Moreover, black parents thought that the race issue had been neglected in therapy. Warren et al. concluded that although the black parents had perhaps not experienced as many problems with the white therapists as expected, they nonetheless experienced noteworthy disappointments. The authors also considered the possibility that the unavailability of alternative clinics staffed by blacks contributed to an underreporting of criticisms, thereby throwing another monkey wrench into the delicate interpretive apparatus. While the findings yielded by the foregoing two studies were mixed, Phillips (1960) was unequivocally positive. Black counselors at a predominantly black urban high school regarded themselves as effective with their adolescent counselees (whom they found to be relaxed and responsive), whereas white counselors regarded themselves as ineffective.

The remaining three studies included in Sattler's section on effectiveness should not have been characterized as outcome studies per se, because no relevant conclusions can be drawn from them. S. L. Weiss and Dlugokinski (1974) used the criterion of treatment length, a crude index of outcome that Sattler discussed separately in his section on utilization. Likewise, Overall and Aronson (1963) studied rate of return, not outcome itself. Walker (1973) employed a more convincing measure of treatment success, but the study compared the effectiveness of two forms of counseling within the white therapist–black client dyad and included neither black therapist nor white client controls.

The picture becomes even more clouded when one considers that Sattler overlooked one counterintuitive study and did not return to three important studies in his section on outcome. With regard to the former, Rosenblatt and Mayer (1972) found that while the black community underutilized marital and family services, those blacks who did use them expressed greater satisfaction than their white counterparts did. Each of the latter three studies was mentioned in Sattler's review, but not in the context of outcome. Although Hughes (1972) reported equivalent levels of success for white and nonwhite clients seen by white therapists, he also secured several findings suggestive of racial effects on outcome. These included the therapists' belief that they understood their white clients better and felt more comfortable with them; the tendency for clinicians using personal therapy to produce better results with their nonwhite patients; and the less positive effectiveness ratings given the therapists by the nonwhite than by the white clients. But, as if more contradictory data were needed, Rosenthal and Frank (1958) failed to uncover a relationship between race and outcome as part of their classic investigation of the implications of patients' social class for psychotherapy. Furthermore, Winston, Pardes, and Papernick (1972) determined that black inpatients were treated as successfully with individual and milieu therapy as white inpatients were, and that the black inpatients actually had a somewhat *higher* rate of improvement. As E. E. Jones (1978) has pointed out, however, the confound produced by combining individual therapy (conducted by white psychiatrists) with milieu therapy (coordinated by a predominantly black nursing staff) imposes a serious constraint on internal validity.

Sattler felt that nine of the 10 then-extant naturalistic findings pertinent to the question of racial effects on outcome were null. After deleting three tangential studies and adding four others, the revised scorecard reads seven null or problack studies (including Lerner's persuasive 1972 report), three mixed-positive studies, and one decidedly positive study. Obviously, such a configuration does not warrant rejection of the hypothesis of no difference in outcome between black and white patients seen by white therapists in individual psychotherapy. But neither would it appear to present as closed a case for the defense as Sattler intimated. This characterization applies as well to the corresponding data on group therapy that he reviewed.

If the present authors discern more shades of grey than Sattler, then black reviewers must have been looking through a wholly different lens. Griffith (1977) concluded from a selective review of analogue and field studies that racial differences have a "somewhat negative effect upon psychotherapy" (p. 33). He cited an investigation by Wolken, Moriwaki, and Williams (1973) that does not appear in Sattler's outcome section. Although black female college students were not found to hold less favorable global attitudes toward psychotherapy, they reported greater dissatisfaction with their personal experiences in therapy than did their white counterparts. Both E. E. Jones (1978) and Griffith and Jones (1979) characterized the naturalistic research as having produced somewhat less evidence of racial effects on outcome than the analogue data, but they maintained that the direction was still positive. While Sattler's verdict from an exhaustive review appears overly negative, these latter assertions from a narrower data base appear overly positive.

The newer naturalistic evidence does not promise an easy resolution. Rather, it suggests that the ways in which race influences the course of treatment are more subtle and complex than many had previously thought. Ten studies were discovered—one unpublished report, four published reports, and five dissertation abstracts. E. E. Jones (1978) examined the effects of racial matching on the process and outcome of short-term intensive psychotherapy. Patients were seven black and seven white middle-class neurotic women. The two black and three white therapists averaged about 3½ years of professional experience and espoused a traditional psychodynamic orientation. Racial matching had no impact on either therapists' or patients' satisfaction with the progress of therapy. However, differences according to race were found on four of seven process ratings made by an experienced pair of black and white clinical judges. The black therapist–black patient dyads scored higher than the white therapist–white patient dyads on race salience and depth efficacy, as well as lower on rapport and liking. Moreover, the black pairing evoked greater erotic transference than did either racially unmatched pairing. Jones also found important process shifts between the first and subsequent sessions and cautioned against overgeneralizing from single-session analogues of cross-racial psychotherapy.

Another study similarly implicates the influence of racial matching on therapeutic process. Wright (1975) randomly assigned black and white college students at different levels of trust to several counseling sessions with a black or white counselor. Students initially held preconceived notions of the opposite-race counselors, but perceived them as increasingly empathic over the counseling period. If valid, this finding has several important implications. Perhaps foremost, it may help to explain the more positive nature of the brief-treatment analogue outcome data with respect to racial effects—the working alliance in the cross-racial dyad is weakest at the outset. Moreover, evidence of *increasing rapport over the course of treatment* militates against the contention that studies of truly long-term psychotherapy would turn up more pervasive racial countertransference than the available data thus far suggest. Significantly, Griffith and Jones (1979) have observed that the "race difference appears to have its greatest impact early in treatment, particularly at the first encounter. If the white therapist can establish effective rapport at initial contact and build a therapeutic alliance in relatively rapid fashion, successful outcome can be achieved" (p. 230). Another recent finding suggests that cross-racial therapy can plunge therapists into countertransferential depths (Armstrong & Turner, in press). White therapists indicated higher levels of distress over clients' negative attitudes, not being able to help or confront opposite-race clients, and being oversolicitous with them than did black therapists.

Notwithstanding the foregoing evidence of racial effects on therapy process (though not on outcome), the bulk of the previously overlooked and recent research must still be counted as negative. In their large-scale study of children undergoing treatment at an urban community mental health center, Davidson et al. (Note 2) failed to find that outcome (as assessed by the therapist following treatment) varied as a function of racial match. Other data reported by Genthner (1973) and Redfering (1971, 1975) could actually be interpreted as problack in the context of race and outcome.

Overview

To retrace our steps, Sattler's impressions (1977) of the early 1970s data on race and *outcome* were overwhelmingly negative. Noting certain methodological considerations and reclassifying some of the studies Sattler reviewed, the present reviewers have shown that he again seems to have overstated the negative case. On the other hand, the claims of Griffith and Jones that this earlier evidence is largely positive would appear to be an exaggeration. In fact, the earlier data do not, in the main, support the assertion that black patients fare poorly in therapy with whites, although the empirical case should hardly be considered closed. More recent naturalistic studies of racial effects on outcome are, however, for the most part null.

What these newer outcome data do suggest is that the *process* in cross-racial treatment may differ from the process in treatment involving two persons of the same race. Thus, white reviewers Parloff et al. (1978) acknowledged "some short-term process differences in actual therapy . . . but almost no findings with respect to outcome" (p. 258). Harrison (1975), a black reviewer, seems to have agreed: "There is some evidence that the facilitative functioning of the counselor is affected by race of the client, but the studies are few and the findings mixed and inconclusive. Limited evidence exists that prejudice is related to counseling effectiveness" (p. 131).

The presence of racial differences in therapeutic process in the context of no outcome differences is paradoxical. Presumably, distinctive ingredients should produce distinctive results. Either investigators do not yet have a handle on the critical parameters of therapeutic process, or present measures of process and treatment effectiveness are insufficiently sensitive. The failure of numerous studies of white clients in therapy with white therapists to demonstrate any improvement suggests that this is indeed the case. Solving the problems of identifying the essence of therapeutic process and measuring change in therapy are two of the most pressing charges to future researchers in this area.

SUMMARY AND CONCLUSIONS

In the foregoing sections, the present authors have set out to answer the question of whether blacks and other minorities who seek out traditional mental health services are victims of covert discrimination. Are blacks more likely to receive the kind of pejorative psychiatric diagnoses that can label them for life, or to be shunted off to second-class or briefer treatments? Are they unresponsive to conventional therapy conducted by white professionals?

Unfortunately, there is no simple answer. The conclusions reached by reviewers of research in the area run the gamut from negative (i.e., no evidence of discrimination) through inconclusive (Harrison, 1975; Parloff et al., 1978) to positive (i.e., definite evidence of discrimination). And the direction of the conclusion appears to be related to the race of the reviewer. Siegel (1974), C. V. Abramowitz and Dokecki (1977), and Sattler (1977), all white, believe that the empirical data are largely negative. Jones and Griffith (Griffith, 1977; Griffith & Jones, 1979; E. E. Jones, 1978), both black, have waged a positive campaign from a relative handful of the available studies.

On the basis of empirical returns to date, it seems that racial bias does not appear to be rife in the clinical setting. However, in some contrast to most of the previous reviews, race has been found to be a salient enough parameter in the clinical marketplace. While the case for confirmation seems weakest with respect to outcome and diagnosis (where some seemingly problack trends have even been detected), the case with respect to treatment utilization, allocation, and process remains very much open. Black patients are more likely to drop out of therapy; are less frequently referred to individual treatment; are sometimes discharged more quickly from psychiatric hospitalization; and are somewhat reluctant early in treatment to express themselves openly to white therapists.

With the benefits of the previous reviewers' efforts, hindsight, and recent evidence, a *judiciously negative stance that acknowledges subtle and circumscribed racial effects* seems generally warranted and represents a closer approximation to present empirical reality. Significantly, black as well as white investigators have contributed to the data failing to confirm allegations of racial bias of one sort or another. Moreover, since the complications of cross-racial therapy appear to have been rather mild even during periods of racial strife, it seems unlikely that they would become more pronounced as racial attitudes in the broader culture continue to moderate. And despite a dearth of information about intensive cross-racial therapy over the longer term, what process data there are suggest that the therapeutic interaction itself can dissolve some initially unfavorable stereotypes.

Those who would continue to press the charge of pervasive racial bias must explain why racial bias eludes detection when social class bias has been found (C. V. Abramowitz & Dokecki, 1977; Parloff et al., 1978). Since blacks and other minorities are overrepresented among the lower classes, and undoubtedly suffer various subtle and not so subtle psychosocial stresses that are spared underprivileged whites, the failure of empirical research to demonstrate that race has at least as great a clinical impact as social class does is surprising and paradoxical. If the available data are to be taken at face value, then blacks are victimized mostly to the extent that they share certain lower-class characteristics with other similarly disadvantaged nonwhites and whites; blacks who transcend the class barrier are, empirically speaking, only marginally more vulnerable than likewise privileged nonblacks. Thus, Umbenhauer and DeWitte (1978) turned up ample evidence of patient *social class* effects on clinical judgment but neither *race* effects nor class × race interactions among a compelling interdisciplinary sample of diagnosticians. While possible differential professional sensitivity to and thus transparency of the race manipulation raises a question about the internal validity of such racial bias analogues, most of the methodological features of the extant research seen above as militating against confirmation of racial bias formulations should logically have been operative as well against the hypothesis of social class bias.

Research Limitations

The most meticulous review by far, Sattler's contribution (1977), has two fundamental flaws. First, although the precision and quality of the research descriptions are excellent, Sattler's summations characteristically overstated the negative findings at the expense of the positive. Second, while Sattler offered an exhaustive recapitulation of methodological limitations and cautioned appropriately against premature interpretation, he failed to point out that the great majority of those limitations had the systematic effect of decreasing the likelihood of confirming the alternate hypothesis (i.e., that racial bias exists), and thereby the effect of increasing the likelihood of retaining the null hypothesis (i.e., that no racial bias exists). Moreover, once consideration is given to the fact that the research analogue is more vulnerable to such systematic effects than is the naturalistic study, the disproportionate number of negative findings yielded by the racial bias analogue relative to the naturalistic study appears in a different light.

The analogue paradigm has several serious weaknesses, most of which bias the research toward retention of the null hypothesis of no race effects. During the 1970s, most white mental health professionals could discern the hidden agenda in a mailed request to evaluate the psychosocial well-being of a black patient described in enclosed materials. As a result, it seems safe to assume that the more conservative and race-reactive clinicians would be less likely to take part in the research, with the result that therapists with such attitudes are underrepresented among participants in research on race effects. As Parloff et al. (1978) have astutely pointed out, "It is probable that research that depends on the participation of self-selected therapists may inadvertently underrepresent the prevalence of racial biases that may continue to exist among the population of therapists" (p. 258).

Following the same line of reasoning, an appreciable number of those who did cooperate in such research undoubtedly saw through the experimental facade and so tempered their ratings in the socially desirable direction (i.e., not race-biased). Yet another possibility has to do with subjects' perception of racial identity per se, which was usually designated in a demographic list in one corner of one page of the clinical notes. Attempting to cooperate in the midst of a busy professional schedule, many respondents may simply have never noticed the racial cue. In addition, "subtle effects of biases may be difficult for the researcher to identify. Such research may require more precise and sophisticated measures of process and outcome than are generally used" (Parloff et al., 1978, p. 258).

Even in field research, there are methodological features that militate against turning up evidence that blacks fare poorly in therapy with whites. For example, the data pool for such research includes only the blacks who seek out traditional mental health services, and especially those who remain in treatment long enough to complete the questionnaires. The more alienated segments of the black community are certainly underrepresented in such a sample, and so that sample is biased. And research with such biased samples probably overestimates the therapeutic responsiveness of the typical black. Another possible contributor to spuriously inflated therapeutic results from cross-racial treatment would be any tendency by blacks to respond benignly to questionnaire items from fear of antagonizing the white authority structure (Warren et al., 1973). Then too, although abundant evidence suggests that many black patients improve during the course of therapy with white practitioners, the frequent absence of black patient–black therapist dyads and attention-placebo controls leaves open the possibility that change is less positive than it might be with racially matched pairs or is reflective of spontaneous remission rather than of treatment effects. Also, the prospective naturalistic method (though not the retrospective archival study) is no less susceptible then its analogue counterpart to biased recruitment of white professionals and the latter's defensive behavior (Parloff et al., 1978). Even some records searches are compromised by value-biased recruitment to the extent that facilities generating a high level of minority utilization and interest in investigating racial bias phenomena are probably staffed disproportionately by liberal clinicians. Importantly, though, most of the studies that have yielded treatment distribution and have used data compatible with racial bias formulations have been archival and thus relatively free of value-biased sampling and attempts by clinicians to present themselves and their profession in a favorable light.

The foregoing methodological loopholes systematically tilt the odds against discovering any racial bias that does exist and so warrant far more recognition than they have heretofore received. They impose a severe constraint on the interpretability of the extant data base on race and psychotherapy. As foreshadowed earlier in this review, a call for the development of a racial politics of psychotherapy research at the intersection of the burgeoning personology of research (Carlson, 1971; F. G. Singer, 1971; M. B. Smith, 1961) and the venerable sociopolitics of knowledge (Buss, 1975; X, 1975) seems more than justified. Articulation of the political implications of various methodological anomalies would be one starting point for such an enterprise. More penetrating analysis of the racial "heartpotheses" of observers is also in order (S. I. Abramowitz, 1978). Racial bias formulations have persisted in the face of substantial empirical disconfirmation largely because the heartpotheses sustaining them are steeped in personal experience. When all is said and done, how many among us readily exchange our personal convictions and cherished family ideals for hard data? Was Sattler inclined to slay certain findings suggestive of racial bias with the methodological (1977, p. 274) and the conceptual (1977, p. 270) sword because his social expectancies unwittingly commanded that racial bias could not be a factor? Was it street wisdom that led Griffith and Jones to attend selectively to the positive findings and to reach a verdict compatible with a legacy of generations? Is the present reviews' closer alignment with previous white than with previous black reviewers tantamount to a white psychotherapy research establishment, and is the litany of methodological lacunae an expression of white guilt over this inclination? Such questions are the proper province of the racial politics of research.

Research Recommendations

Turning now to more conventional matters, several recommendations for future research seem appropriate. The first is for designs that embrace the treatment cycle in its entirety—from initial intake and diagnosis through the referral process and on to therapeutic results. Studies to date have, in the main, provided cross-sectional snapshots of single junctures in patients' treatment careers, leaving no clear sense of a process of interrelated decisions with consequences for patients' psychosocial and political well-being. As noted earlier, investigators need to reconcile some intriguing process data, which have sometimes implicated racial effects, with the outcome data, which typically have not. Even when an investigator has attempted to examine both process and outcome, the tendency has been to examine each separately in relation to race, rather than to study their interrelationship in different racial contexts. Moreover, in formulating the study itself and in discussing the results in the context of previous work, greater attention must be paid to such culturally relevant variables as the past and present state of race relations nationally, in the local community, in the clinic, and in the patient and therapist samples. Certainly, the neglect of patients' and therapists' sociopolitical attitudes represents an avoidance of core propositions of the racial bias viewpoint—a once-compelling etiquette that the growing tide of racial moderation may be hoped to have made obsolete.

From a methodological perspective, the present thinking is that the analogue study's systematic biases against the racial bias hypothesis are such as to render that approach well-nigh irredeemable. A moratorium on its continued wholesale adoption thus seems entirely justified. As has been indicated, field methods are not wholly without such vices, but they appear to have offsetting virtues. The present reviewers would stress the need in naturalistic research to control statistically for any difference in initial impairment between black and white consumers of mental health services. And finally, readers and reviewers should beware the premature inference about therapeutic success with blacks from archival data that reflect those remaining in therapy only. Since research has shown that a higher proportion of white than black patients who undertake treatment will complete it, one must take pains to insure that a spurious comparison is not being made between white continuers, who comprise the bulk of those who enter, and black continuers, who do not and may well represent an elite group. But by far the most valuable counsel one can offer colleagues in this area is to be alert to the subtle ways in which our own racial heartpotheses can influence our choice of method, interpretation of data, and attempts to reconcile conclusions with those of others.

A Final Note

Although the present review draws a somewhat negative conclusion concerning the existence of racial effects in therapy from the existing data, it must be emphasized that these existing data may not present a very accurate picture of the reality of the therapeutic situation. Recall that much of the negative data comes from analogue research—which is plagued with methodological problems. Note that as the research setting more closely approaches reality, fewer negative and more positive findings emerge. Also, the methodologies that are more similar to the real therapy situation are subject to fewer methodological problems. Taking all of this together, it seems apparent that no definite conclusions can be drawn at this point. That is, no one really knows how prevalent race effects are in therapy as it is practiced today. There still remains the possibility that race effects are quite common, but investigators have yet to detect them.

NOTES

[1]See Chapter 2 for a presentation of Chesler's views.

[2]The topic of investigator effects and other expectancy effects is discussed at length in Chapter 4.

[3]Although race and social class are certainly related, social class has its own literature. Data pertaining to social class and psychotherapy have been intensively examined by C. V. Abramowitz and Dokecki (1977), Garfield (1971, 1978), Goldstein (1971, 1973), Hollingshead and Redlich (1958), E. E. Jones (1974), Lorion (1973, 1974, 1978), Meltzoff and Kornreich (1970), and Parloff, Waskow, and Wolfe (1978).

[4]See Bergin, 1971; Eysenck, 1952, 1961, 1964, 1966a, 1966b; Malan, 1973; and Strupp, 1963 for overviews of outcome research. For discussions of problems with outcome measures, see Bergin, 1971; Howard and Orlinsky, 1972; Kellner, 1966; Kiesler, 1966; Meltzoff and Kornreich, 1970; and Strupp and Bergin, 1969.

REFERENCE NOTES

1. Campbell, D. T. Systematic errors to be expected of the social scientist on the basis of a general psychology of cognitive bias. In R. Rosenthal (Chair), *The problem of experimenter bias.* Symposium presented at the 66th Annual Convention of the American Psychological Association, Cincinnati, 1959.

2. Davidson, C. V., Edwards, D. W., Greene, L. R., & Abramowitz, S. I. *Patient and clinician race effects on child psychotherapy.* Paper presented at the 87th Annual Convention of the American Psychological Association, Montreal, 1980.

REFERENCES

Abramowitz, C. V., & Dokecki, P. R. The politics of clinical judgment: Early empirical returns. *Psychological Bulletin, 1977, 84,* 460–476.

Abramowitz, S. I. Splitting data from theory on the black patient–white therapist relationship. *American Psychologist, 1978, 33,* 957–958.

Allon, R. Sex, race, socioeconomic status, social mobility, and process-reactive ratings of schizophrenics. *Journal of Nervous and Mental Disease, 1971, 153,* 343–348.

American Psychological Association. Report of the Task Force on Sex Bias and Sex-Role Stereotyping in Psychotherapeutic Practice. *American Psychologist*, 1975, *4*, 1169–1175.

Amira, S., Abramowitz, S. I., & Gomes-Schwartz, B. Socially charged pupil and psychologist effects on psychoeducational decisions. *Journal of Special Education*, 1977, *11*, 433–440.

Armstrong, S. H., & Turner, S. Cross-racial psychotherapy: What the therapists say. *Psychotherapy: Theory, Research, and Practice*, in press.

Aronow, A. *The Negro client's use of casework treatment.* Unpublished master's thesis, Smith College School for Social Work, 1967.

Asch, S. E. Forming impressions of personality. *Journal of Abnormal and Social Psychology*, 1946, *41*, 258–290.

Atkinson, D. R., Maruyama, M., & Matsui, S. Effects of counselor race and counseling approach on Asian Americans' perceptions of counselor credibility and utility. *Journal of Counseling Psychology*, 1978, *25*, 76–85.

Balch, P., & Balch, K. A racial comparison of admissions, diagnoses, and releases in a state mental hospital system: A five-year review. JSAS *Catalog of Selected Documents in Psychology*, 1975, *5*, 197. (Ms. No. 868)

Banks, G., Berenson, B. G., & Carkhuff, R. R. The effects of counselor race and training upon counseling process with Negro clients in initial interactions. *Journal of Clinical Psychology*, 1967, *23*, 70–72.

Banks, W. M. The differential effects of race and social class in helping. *Journal of Clinical Psychology*, 1972, *28*, 90–92.

Barber, T. X. Pitfalls in research: Nine investigator and experimenter effects. In R. M. W. Travers (Ed.), *Second handbook of research on teaching.* Chicago: Rand McNally, 1973.

Benefee, L. M., Abramowitz, S. I., Weitz, L. J., & Armstrong, S. H. Effects of patient racial attribution on black clinicians' inferences. *American Journal of Community Psychology*, 1976, *4*, 263–273.

Bergin, A. E. The evaluation of therapeutic outcomes. In A. E. Bergin & S. L. Garfield (Eds.), *Handbook of psychotherapy and behavior change.* New York: Wiley, 1971.

Bergin, A. E., & Strupp, H. H. *Changing frontiers in the science of psychotherapy.* Chicago: Aldine, 1972.

Bloch, P. M., Abramowitz, S. I., & Weitz, L. J. Racial attribution effects on clinical judgment: A failure to replicate among white clinicians. *American Journal of Community Psychology*, 1980, *8*, 485–493.

Braginsky, B. M., & Braginsky, D. D. *Mainstream psychology: A critique.* New York: Holt, Rinehart & Winston, 1974.

Briley, C. E. The relationship between race, sex, type of problem, and interpersonal trust in determining ethnic-racial preference for counselor (Doctoral dissertation, East Texas State University, 1977). *Dissertation Abstracts International*, 1977, *38*, 3282A–3283A. (University Microfilms No. 77-27, 539)

Bryson, S. L., & Cody, J. Relationship of race and level of understanding between counselor and client. *Journal of Counseling Psychology*, 1973, *20*, 495–498.

Buss, A. R. The emerging field of the sociology of psychological knowledge. *American Psychologist*, 1975, *30*, 988–1003.

Carkhuff, R. R., & Pierce, R. Differential effects of therapist race and social class upon patient depth of self-exploration in the initial clinical interview. *Journal of Consulting Psychology*, 1967, *31*, 632–634.

Carlson, R. Where is the person in personality research? *Psychological Bulletin*, 1971, *75*, 203–219.

Carlson, R. Understanding women: Implications for personality theory and research. *Journal of Social Issues*, 1972, *28*, 17–32.

Celnak, M. Racial factors in the countertransference: The black therapist and the black client. *American Journal of Orthopsychiatry*, 1970, *40*, 39–46.

Chesler, P. *Women and madness.* New York: Doubleday, 1972.

Cimbolic, P. Counselor race and experience effects on black clients. *Journal of Consulting and Clinical Psychology,* 1972, *39,* 328–332.

Cole, J., & Pilisuk, M. Differences in the provision of mental health services by race. *American Journal of Orthopsychiatry,* 1976, *46,* 510–525.

Cowen, E. L. Social and community interventions. *Annual Review of Psychology,* 1973, *24,* 423–472.

Craig, T. J., & Huffine, C. L. Correlates of patient attendance in an inner-city mental health clinic. *American Journal of Psychiatry,* 1976, *133,* 161–165.

Cripps, T. H. Sex, ethnicity, and admission status as determinants of patient movement in mental health treatment. *American Journal of Community Psychology,* 1973, *1,* 248–257.

Crossley, B., Abramowitz, S. I., & Weitz, L. J. Race and abortion: Disconfirmation of the genocide hypothesis in a clinical analogue. *International Journal of Psychiatry in Medicine,* 1977, *8,* 35–42.

Davidson, C. V., & Abramowitz, S. I. Sex bias in clinical judgment: Later empirical returns. *Psychology of Women Quarterly,* 1980, *4,* 377–395.

Davis, W. E., & Jones, M. H. Negro versus Caucasian psychological test performance revisited. *Journal of Consulting and Clinical Psychology,* 1974, *42,* 675–679.

deHoyos, A., & deHoyos, G. Symptomatology differentials between Negro and white schizophrenics. *International Journal of Social Psychiatry,* 1965, *11,* 245–255.

Derogatis, L. R., Covi, L., Lipman, R. S., Davis, D. M., & Rickels, K. Social class and race as mediator variables in neurotic symptomatology. *Archives of General Psychiatry,* 1971, *25,* 31–40.

Dreger, R. M., & Miller, K. S. Comparative psychological studies of Negroes and whites in the United States. *Psychological Bulletin,* 1960, *57,* 361–402.

Dreger, R. M., & Miller, K. S. Comparative psychological studies of Negroes and whites in the United States: 1959–1965. *Psychological Bulletin,* 1968, *70*(3, Pt. 2), 1–58.

Ewing, T. N. Racial similarity of client and counselor and client satisfaction with counseling. *Journal of Counseling Psychology,* 1974, *21,* 446–449.

Eysenck, H. J. The effects of psychotherapy: An evaluation. *Journal of Consulting Psychology,* 1952, *16,* 319–324.

Eysenck, H. J. The effects of psychotherapy. In H. J. Eysenck (Ed.), *Handbook of abnormal psychology.* New York: Basic Books, 1961.

Eysenck, H. J. The outcome problem in psychotherapy: A reply. *Psychotherapy: Theory, Research, and Practice,* 1964, *1,* 97–100.

Eysenck, H. J. (Ed.) *The effects of psychotherapy.* New York: International Science Press, 1966.(a)

Eysenck, H. J. Reply. In H. J. Eysenck (Ed.), *The effects of psychotherapy.* New York: International Science Press, 1966.(b)

Fischer, J., & Miller, H. The effect of client race and social class on clinical judgments. *Clinical Social Work Journal,* 1973, *1,* 100–109.

Gamboa, A. M., Tosi, D. J., & Riccio, A. C. Race and counselor climate in the counselor preference of delinquent girls. *Journal of Counseling Psychology,* 1976, *23,* 160–162.

Gardner, L. H. The therapeutic relationship under varying conditions of race. *Psychotherapy: Therapy, Research, and Practice,* 1971, *8,* 78–87.

Gardner, W. The differential effects of race, education, and experience on helping. *Journal of Clinical Psychology,* 1972, *28,* 87–89.

Garfield, S. L. Research on client variables in psychotherapy. In A. E. Bergin & S. L. Garfield (Eds.), *Handbook of psychotherapy and behavior change: An empirical analysis.* New York: Wiley, 1971.

Garfield, S. L. Research on client variables in psychotherapy. In S. L. Garfield & A. E. Bergin

(Eds.), *Handbook of psychotherapy and behavior change: An empirical analysis* (2nd ed.). New York: Wiley, 1978.

Genthner, R. W. Differences between Black and white patients in the effects of short-term hospitalization (Doctoral dissertation, Kent State University, 1973). *Dissertation Abstracts International,* 1973, *34,* 2303B. (University Microfilms No. 73-27, 250)

Goffman, E. *Asylums.* New York: Doubleday, 1961.

Goffman, E. *Stigma: Notes on the management of spoiled identity.* Englewood Cliffs, N.J.: Prentice-Hall, 1963.

Goldberg, M. The black female client, the white psychotherapist: An evaluation of therapy through clients' retrospective reports (Doctoral dissertation, California School of Professional Psychology, San Francisco, 1972). *Dissertation Abstracts International,* 1973, *33,* 3302B. (University Microfilms No. 72-33, 287)

Goldstein, A. P. *Psychotherapeutic attraction.* New York: Pergamon Press, 1971.

Goldstein, A. P. *Structured learning therapy.* New York: Academic Press, 1973.

Grantham, R. J. Effects of counselor sex, race, and language style on black students in initial interviews. *Journal of Counseling Psychology,* 1973, *20,* 553-559.

Greene, L. R., Abramowitz, S. I., Davidson, C. V., & Edwards, D. W. Gender, race, and referral to group psychotherapy: Further empirical evidence of countertransference. *International Journal of Group Psychotherapy,* 1980, *30,* 357-364.

Grier, W. H., & Cobbs, P. M. *Black rage.* New York: Bantam, 1968.

Griffith, M. S. The influence of race on the psychotherapeutic relationship. *Psychiatry,* 1977, *40,* 27-40.

Griffith, M. S., & Jones, E. E. Race and psychotherapy: Changing perspectives. In J. H. Masserman (Ed.), *Current psychiatric therapies* (Vol. 8). New York: Grune & Stratton, 1979.

Gross, H. S., Herbert, M. R., Knatterud, G. L., & Donner, L. The effect of race and sex on the variation of diagnosis and disposition in a psychiatric emergency room. *Journal of Nervous and Mental Disease,* 1969, *148,* 638-642.

Gullatee, A. C. Mental health planning and evaluation for the black and the poor. *Journal of the National Medical Association,* 1972, *64,* 134-138.

Gynther, M. D. White norms and black MMPIs: A prescription for discrimination? *Psychological Bulletin,* 1972, *78,* 386-402.

Gynther, M. D., Lachar, D., & Dahlstrom, W. G. Are special norms for minorities needed? Development of an MMPI F scale for blacks. *Journal of Consulting and Clinical Psychology,* 1978, *46,* 1403-1408.

Halleck, S. L. *The politics of therapy.* New York: Science House, 1971.

Harrison, D. K. Race as a counselor-client variable in counseling and psychotherapy: A review of the research. *The Counseling Psychologist,* 1975, *5,* 124-133.

Harrison, D. K. The attitudes of Black counselees toward White counselors. *Journal of Non-White Concerns in Personnel and Guidance,* 1977, *5,* 52-59.

Heller, K. Laboratory interview research as analogue to treatment. In A. E. Bergin & S. L. Garfield (Eds.), *Handbook of psychotherapy and behavior change: An empirical analysis.* New York: Wiley, 1971.

Hollingshead, A. B., & Redlich, F. C. *Social class and mental illness.* New York: Wiley, 1958.

Howard, K. I., and Orlinsky, D. E. Psychotherapeutic processes. *Annual Review of Psychology,* 1972, *23,* 615-668.

Hughes, R. A. *The effects of sex, age, race, and social history of therapist and client on psychotherapy outcome.* Unpublished doctoral dissertation, University of California, Berkeley, 1972.

Hurvitz, N. Psychotherapy as a means of social control. *Journal of Consulting and Clinical Psychology,* 1973, *40,* 232-239.

Ilfeld, F. W., Jr. Psychologic status of community residents along major demographic dimensions. *Archives of General Psychiatry*, 1978, *35*, 716–724.

Jones, A., & Seagull, A. A. Dimensions of the relationship between the black client and the white therapist: A theoretical overview. *American Psychologist*, 1977, *32*, 850–855.

Jones, E. E. Social class and psychotherapy: A critical review of the research. *Psychiatry*, 1974, *37*, 307–320.

Jones, E. E. Effects of race on psychotherapy process and outcome: An exploratory investigation. *Psychotherapy: Theory, Research, and Practice*, 1978, *15*, 226–236.

Kadushin, A. *Why people go to psychiatrists*. New York: Atherton, 1969.

Kazdin, A. E. Evaluating the generality of findings in analogue therapy research. *Journal of Consulting and Clinical Psychology*, 1978, *46*, 673–686.

Kellner, K. Discussion. In H. J. Eysenck (Ed.), *The effects of psychotherapy*. New York: International Science Press, 1966.

Kiesler, D. J. Some myths of psychotherapy research and the search for a paradigm. *Psychological Bulletin*, 1966, *65*, 110–136.

Kirstein, L. Sociodemographic factors and military psychiatric hospitalization. *Journal of Nervous and Mental Disease*, 1978, *166*, 299–303.

Krebs, R. L. Some effects of a white institution on black psychiatric outpatients. *American Journal of Orthopsychiatry*, 1971, *41*, 589–596.

Lane, E. A. The influence of sex and race on process-reactive ratings of schizophrenia. *Journal of Psychology*, 1968, *68*, 15–20.

Langner, T. S., Gersten, J. C., Greene, E. L., Eisenberg, J. G., Herson, J. H., & McCarthy, E. D. Treatment of psychological disorders among urban children. *Journal of Consulting and Clinical Psychology*, 1974, *42*, 170–179.

Lerner, B. *Therapy in the ghetto: Political impotence and personal disinteraction*. Baltimore: Johns Hopkins University Press, 1972.

Levine, S. V., Kamin, L. E., & Levine, E. L. Sexism and psychiatry. *American Journal of Orthopsychiatry*, 1974, *44*, 327–336.

Levy, M., & Kahn, M. Interpreter bias on the Rorschach test as a function of patients' socioeconomic status. *Journal of Projective Techniques and Personality Assessment*, 1970, *34*, 106–112.

Liss, J. L., Weiner, A., Robins, E., & Richardson, M. Psychiatric symptoms in white and black inpatients: I. Record study. *Comprehensive Psychiatry*, 1973, *14*, 475–481.

Locke, B. Z., & Duval, H. J. Patterns of schizophrenic admissions to Ohio public mental hospitals. *Quarterly Journal of Studies on Alcohol*, 1965, *49*, 220–229.

Lorion, R. P. Socioeconomic status and traditional treatment reconsidered. *Psychological Bulletin*, 1973, *79*, 263–270.

Lorion, R. P. Patient and therapist variables in the treatment of low-income patients. *Psychological Bulletin*, 1974, *81*, 344–354.

Lorion, R. P. Research on psychotherapy and behavior change with the disadvantaged: Past, present and future directions. In S. L. Garfield & A. E. Bergin (Eds.), *Handbook of psychotherapy and behavior change: An empirical analysis* (2nd ed.). New York: Wiley, 1978.

Lowinger, P., & Dobie, S. The attitudes of the psychiatrist about his patient. *Comprehensive Psychiatry*, 1968, *9*, 627–632.

Lubin, B., Hornstein, R. K., Lewis, R. V., & Bechtel, B. S. Correlates of initial treatment assignment in a community mental health center. *Archives of General Psychiatry*, 1973, *29*, 497–504.

Malan, D. H. The outcome problem in psychotherapy research: A historical review. *Archives of General Psychiatry*, 1973, *29*, 719–729.

Malzberg, B. Mental disease among Negroes: An analysis of first admissions in New York State, 1949–51. *Mental Hygiene*, 1959, *43*, 422–459.

Mayo, J. A. Utilization of a community mental health center by blacks: Admission to inpatient status. *Journal of Nervous and Mental Disease,* 1974, *158,* 202–207.

Meltzoff, J., & Kornreich, M. *Research in psychotherapy.* New York: Atherton, 1970.

Mercer, J. R. *Labeling the mentally retarded.* Berkeley: University of California Press, 1973.

Merluzzi, B. H., & Merluzzi, T. V. Influence of client race on counselors' assessment of case materials. *Journal of Counseling Psychology,* 1978, *25,* 399–404.

Mullozzi, A. D., Jr. Interracial counseling: Clients' ratings and counselors' ratings in a first session (Doctoral dissertation, Southern Illinois University, 1972). *Dissertation Abstracts International,* 1972, *33,* 2175A–2176A. (University Microfilms No. 72-28, 546)

Munley, P. H. A review of counseling analogue research. *Journal of Counseling Psychology,* 1974, *21,* 320–330.

Nassi, A. J. Community control or control of the community?: The case of the community mental health center. *Journal of Community Psychology,* 1978, *6,* 3–15.

Nassi, A. J., & Abramowitz, S. I. Raising consciousness about women's groups: Process and outcome research. *Psychology of Women Quarterly,* 1978, *3,* 139–156.

Overall, B., & Aronson, H. Expectations of psychotherapy in patients of lower socioeconomic class. *American Journal of Orthopsychiatry,* 1963, *33,* 421–430.

Padilla, E. R., Boxley, R., & Wagner, N. N. The desegregation of clinical psychology training. *Professional Psychology,* 1973, *4,* 259–264.

Parloff, M. B., Waskow, I. E., & Wolfe, B. E. Research on therapist variables in relation to process and outcome. In S. L. Garfield & A. E. Bergin (Eds.), *Handbook of psychotherapy and behavior change: An empirical analysis* (2nd ed.). New York: Wiley, 1978.

Peoples, V. Y., & Dell, D. M. Black and White student preferences for counselor roles. *Journal of Counseling Psychology,* 1975, *22,* 529–534.

Phillips, W. B. Counseling Negro pupils: An educational dilemma. *Journal of Negro Education,* 1960, *29,* 504–507.

Pollack, E. S., Redick, R. W., Norman, V. B., Wurster, C. R., & Gorwitz, K. Socioeconomic and family characteristics of patients admitted to psychiatric services. *American Journal of Public Health,* 1964, *54,* 506–518.

Redfering, D. L. Differential effects of group counseling with Negro and white delinquent females. *Corrective Psychiatry and Social Therapy,* 1971, *17,* 29–34.

Redfering, D. L. Differential effects of group counseling with Black and White female delinquents: One year later. *Journal of Negro Education,* 1975, *44,* 530–537.

Robins, L. N., Murphy, G., Woodruff, R., & King, L. Adult psychiatric status of black school boys. *Archives of General Psychiatry,* 1971, *24,* 338–345.

Rosenblatt, A., & Mayer, J. E. Help seeking for family problems: A survey of utilization and satisfaction. *American Journal of Psychiatry,* 1972, *128,* 1136–1140.

Rosenthal, D., & Frank, J. D. The fate of psychiatric outpatients assigned to psychotherapy. *Journal of Nervous and Mental Disease,* 1958, *127,* 330–343.

Sanua, V. D. Sociocultural aspects of psychotherapy and treatment: A review of the literature. In L. E. Abt & B. F. Reiss (Eds.), *Progress in clinical psychology.* New York: Grune & Stratton, 1966.

Sarbin, T. R., & Mancuso, J. C. Failure of a moral enterprise: Attitudes of the public toward mental illness. *Journal of Consulting and Clinical Psychology,* 1970, *35,* 159–173.

Sattler, J. M. Racial "experimenter effects" in experimentation, testing, interviewing, and psychotherapy. *Psychological Bulletin,* 1970, *73,* 137–160.

Sattler, J. M. The effects of therapist-client racial similarity. In A. S. Gurman & A. M. Razin (Eds.), *Effective psychotherapy: A handbook of research.* New York: Pergamon Press, 1977.

Scheff, T. *Being mentally ill: A sociological theory.* Chicago: Aldine, 1966.

Schermerhorn, R. A. Psychiatric disorders among Negroes: A sociological note. *American*

Journal of Psychiatry, 1956, *112*, 878–882.

Schwartz, J. M., & Abramowitz, S. I. Value-related effects on psychiatric judgment. *Archives of General Psychiatry*, 1975, *32*, 1525–1529.

Sherwood, J. J., & Nataupsky, M. Predicting the consequences of Negro-white intelligence research from biographic characteristics of the investigator. *Journal of Personality and Social Psychology*, 1968, *8*, 53–58.

Siegel, J. M. A brief review of the effects of race in clinical service interactions. *American Journal of Orthopsychiatry*, 1974, *44*, 555–562.

Silverman, P. R. The influences of race on the Negro patient dropping out of psychiatric treatment. *Psychiatric Opinion*, 1971, *8*, 29–36.

Simon, R. J., Fleiss, J. L., Gurland, B. J., Stiller, P. R., & Sharpe, L. Depression and schizophenia in hospitalized black and white mental patients. *Archives of General Psychiatry*, 1973, *28*, 509–512.

Singer, B. D. Some implications of differential psychiatric treatment of Negro and white patients. *Social Science and Medicine*, 1967, *1*, 77–83.

Singer, F. G. Toward a psychology of science. *American Psychologist*, 1971, *26*, 1010–1015.

Smith, M. B. Mental health reconsidered: A special case of the problem of values in psychology. *American Psychologist*, 1961, *6*, 299–306.

Smith, M. L. Influence of client sex and ethnic group on counselor judgments. *Journal of Counseling Psychology*, 1974, *21*, 516–521.

Srole, L., Langner, T. S., Michael, S. T., Opler, M. K., & Rennie, T. A. C. *Mental health in the metropolis: The midtown Manhattan study.* New York: McGraw-Hill, 1962.

Statman, J. Community mental health as a pacification program. In J. Agel (Ed.), *The radical therapist.* New York: Ballantine, 1971.

Stricker, G. Implications of research for psychotherapeutic treatment of women. *American Psychologist*, 1977, *32*, 14–22.

Strupp, H. H. The outcome problem in psychotherapy revisited. *Psychotherapy: Theory, Research, and Practice*, 1963, *1*, 1–13.

Strupp, H. H., & Bergin, A. E. Some empirical and conceptual bases for coordinated research in psychotherapy: A critical review of issues, trends, and evidence. *International Journal of Psychiatry*, 1969, *7*, 18–90.

Sue, S., McKinney, H., Allen, D., & Hall, J. Delivery of community mental health services to black and white patients. *Journal of Consulting and Clinical Psychology*, 1974, *42*, 794–801.

Szasz, T. S. *The myth of mental illness: Foundations of a theory of human conduct.* New York: Hoeber-Harper, 1961.

Szasz, T. S. *Psychiatric justice.* New York: Macmillan, 1965.

Szasz, T. S. *The manufacture of madness: A comparative study of the inquisition and the mental health movement.* New York: Harper & Row, 1970.

Szasz, T. S. The sane slave: An historical note on the use of medical diagnosis as justificatory rhetoric. *American Journal of Psychotherapy*, 1971, *25*, 225–259.

Tanney, M. F. The initial impact of racial differences on clients: An analogue study (Doctoral dissertation, Ohio State University, 1972). *Dissertation Abstracts International*, 1973, *33*, 5527B. (University Microfilms No. 73-11, 588)

Thomas, A. P. Pseudo-transference reactions due to cultural stereotyping. *American Journal of Orthopsychiatry*, 1962, *52*, 894–900.

Thomas, A. P., & Sillen, S. *Racism and psychiatry.* New York: Brunner/Mazel, 1972.

Tischler, G. L. Ethnicity and the delivery of mental health services. In G. Serban & B. Astrachan (Eds.), *New trends of psychiatry in the community.* Cambridge, Mass.: Ballinger, 1977.

Umbenhauer, S. L., & DeWitte, L. L. Patient race and social class: Attitudes and decisions among three groups of mental health professionals. *Comprehensive Psychiatry*, 1978, *19*, 509–515.

Vail, A. Factors influencing lower-class Black patients remaining in treatment. *Journal of Consulting and Clinical Psychology*, 1978, *46*, 341.

Vitols, M. M., Waters, H. G., & Keeler, M. H. Hallucinations and delusions in white and Negro schizophrenics. *American Journal of Psychiatry*, 1963, *120*, 472–475.

Walker, P. L. The effect of two counseling strategies with black disadvantaged clients (Doctoral dissertation, Georgia State University, 1972). *Dissertation Abstracts International*, 1973, *33*, 4106A–4107A. (University Microfilms No. 73–4345)

Warner, R. Racial and sexual bias in psychiatric diagnosis: Psychiatrists and other mental health professionals compared by race, sex, and discipline. *Journal of Nervous and Mental Disease*, 1979, *167*, 303–310.

Warren, R. C., Jackson, A. M., Nugaris, J., & Farley, G. K. Differential attitudes of black and white patients toward treatment in a child guidance clinic. *American Journal of Orthopsychiatry*, 1973, *43*, 384–393.

Watkins, B. A., Cowan, M. A., & Davis, W. E. Differential diagnosis imbalance as a race-related phenomenon. *Journal of Clinical Psychology*, 1975, *31*, 267–268.

Webb, E. J., Campbell, D. T., Schwartz, R. D., & Sechrest, L. *Unobtrusive measures: Nonreactive research in the social sciences.* Chicago: Rand McNally, 1966.

Weiss, B. L., & Kupfer, D. J. The black patient and research in a community mental health center: Where have all the subjects gone? *American Journal of Psychiatry*, 1974, *131*, 415–418.

Weiss, S. L., & Dlugokinski, E. L. Parental expectations of psychotherapy. *Journal of Psychology*, 1974, *86*, 71–80.

Werner, P. D., & Block, J. Sex differences in the eyes of expert personality assessors: Unwarranted conclusions. *Journal of Personality Assessment*, 1975, *39*, 110–113.

Williams, B. M. Trust and self-disclosure among black college students. *Journal of Counseling Psychology*, 1974, *21*, 522–525.

Winston, A., Pardes, H., & Papernick, D. S. Inpatient treatment of blacks and whites. *Archives of General Psychiatry*, 1972, *26*, 405–409.

Wolken, G. H., Moriwaki, S., & Williams, K. J. Race and social class as factors in the orientation toward psychotherapy. *Journal of Counseling Psychology*, 1973, *20*, 312–316.

Wright, W. Relationships of trust and racial perception toward therapist-client conditions during counseling. *Journal of Negro Education*, 1975, *44*, 161–169.

X (Clark), C. The role of the white researcher in black society: A futuristic look. *Journal of Social Issues*, 1975, *29*, 109–118.

Yamamoto, J., James, Q. C., Bloombaum, M., & Hattem, J. Racial factors in patient selection. *American Journal of Psychiatry*, 1967, *124*, 630–636.

Young, A. H. Race of psychotherapist and client and perception of variables relevant to therapy outcome (Doctoral dissertation, University of Illinois at Urbana-Champaign, 1972). *Dissertation Abstracts International*, 1973, *33*, 5506A. (University Microfilms No. 73–10, 093)

10 Psychotherapists' Responses to Client Sexuality: A Source of Bias in Treatment?

LESLIE R. SCHOVER

A young, bearded psychiatrist listens to his attractive blonde patient talk about a date with a new lover. The doctor leans forward intently in his chair as she recounts the details of the evening. "We went back to my place," she says softly, her voice beginning to tremble, "and everything was fine until after we made love. Even then, he held me for a while, and I was really relaxed, but just when I was about to fall asleep, he got out of bed and said he had to go home." She is crying in earnest now. "I know I'm being irrational, but why did he have to do that? And I remembered, one of the times that my father split, seeing my mother cry and feeling that same horrible, empty, feeling—"

"Wait a minute." The doctor shifts in his chair impatiently. "What about the sex? You haven't talked about the sex at all."

The psychologist is a woman in her late 40s, wearing an expensive, blue

The author's research described in this chapter was supported by a Woodrow Wilson Research Grant in Women's Studies. The grant is endowed by the Helena Rubinstein Foundation. The author would also like to thank Joseph Sheehan, Ph.D., Professor of Psychology at the University of California at Los Angeles, for his invaluable aid during the research process; and Donald Guthrie, Ph.D., Adjunct Professor of Psychiatry and Biostatistics at the University of California at Los Angeles, for his statistical consultation.

256

wool dress. Her patient, a heavy-set truck driver, has been out of the hospital on medication for 3 weeks subsequent to an acute paranoid schizophrenic episode. "There's something I've been meaning to ask you," he says, 10 minutes before the end of the session. He looks at the floor. "It's about my sex life." The psychologist looks at her watch, but the patient does not appear to notice the gesture. "Ever since I came home from the hospital, whenever my wife and I—you know, want to have sex, I—I can't. I mean, I'm—I guess I'm—it just won't get hard! I've never had this problem before! Is this part of my sickness, or what? What's wrong with me?"

The psychologist gazes obliquely at her desk calendar. "I'm afraid it's one of the effects of your medication," she says. "You'll just have to bear with it. Now I'm going to have to move your appointment up an hour next week, to 11:00. Is that O.K.?"

The social worker has had many homosexual patients in his 10 years at the free clinic. He considers himself a liberal man, a believer in gay rights who would never try to talk someone into heterosexuality. Nevertheless, this particular young man, with his carefully pleated pants, silk shirt, and gold earring, evokes an inner chuckle when he walks (or "minces," thinks the social worker) into the office. They have spent many sessions working on the patient's lack of assertiveness in his job. Today he greets his therapist with unusual jauntiness, "Hey, man, it worked! I asked for a raise, just like we rehearsed it, and I got it!"

The social worker congratulates him, but the patient's enthusiasm does not abate. "I don't know how to thank you for all the help you've given me," he says. "You didn't judge me like my other therapists. You've made me feel like I'm really somebody, not just a pretty boy." He reaches over to shake his therapist's hand. Startled, the social worker pulls away from the contact. His revulsion is evident, for a moment, on his face. The patient stares in shocked silence.

Are these vignettes unwarranted stereotypes of professional psychotherapists, or do they depict behavior that is all too common? This chapter examines the hypothesis that therapists' responses to client sexuality are a significant source of bias in psychotherapy.

There are a number of important questions: Are clients often encouraged to reveal sexual material merely to satisfy a therapist's voyeurism? Do some therapists ignore clients' sexual issues because of their own discomfort? Which therapists, with which clients, are most effective in dealing with sexual problems? Which therapists are likely to be especially unskilled in this area? Is a seductive client more difficult to treat than is a client who has sexual concerns that do not involve the therapist? What are the effects of gender of therapist and client on the therapist's reaction to sexual material?

WHAT IS AN UNBIASED RESPONSE?

Many attempts have been made to define the proper response of a psychotherapist confronted with a client's sexual issues. The concern of early psychoanalysts with countertransference led to a particular concern with the situation in which a client expresses attraction to his or her therapist. How can the therapist respond without succumbing to temptation or being too harshly rejecting?

As one would expect, there is an encyclical from Freud on the subject. In an essay entitled "Observations on Transference Love" (Freud, 1915/1949), he cautioned the analyst not to ascribe his analysande's sexual desires for him to "the charms of his person" (p. 379). Rather, a seductive female client was reacting to transference feelings and exhibiting a type of resistance. The conscious love or lust masked an unconscious wish to destroy the analyst's authority and undermine treatment. Freud admonished the analyst to overcome the pleasure principle and renounce his erotic feelings for the patient, demonstrating his parental resistance to temptation. The analysande should be allowed to acknowledge her sexual feelings, yet should be told to save her libido for real life rather than wasting it on the analyst. Freud warned that acting out sexually with the patient, or even claiming to return her passion but saying it was taboo to act on it, would stop the therapeutic work.

Freud directed his essay only to the male therapist, particularly the young and unmarried analyst. His recognition that it was useless to exhort the patient to cool her infantile ardor may have come from his attitudes about female frailty as much as from analytic theory. The male analyst, however, was forbidden to nurture even an ember of desire.

The problem with the Freudian tenet that any intense feeling about a patient is countertransferential (and detrimental to treatment; see Berman, 1949) is that it ignores human nature. It calls for a monastic discipline on the part of the therapist that few can, or even want to, attain. Consider Freud's disciples who married former analysandes (Marmor, 1970). Are they comparable to early Christians who decided it was better to marry than to burn? While their conduct has been seen as misguided, they were not labeled as heretics—unlike Ferenczi, with his doctrine of parental affection; Reich, with his quest for the orgone (Marmor, 1970); or McCartney (1966), who published an account of his active sexual liberation of 10% of his female patients' libidos (which works out to 82 women over 40 years who "needed" to express their transference love in a sexual manner).

In any event, this rigid code did not endure. Psychoanalytic theorists soon recognized that it was not possible to rid oneself of feelings toward a client, and that countertransference was a useful tool in exploring the client's issues (Cohen, 1952; Flescher, 1953). While some analysts, such as Annie Reich (1951), maintained that sexual feelings for a client represented a therapist's failure to sublimate voyeurism, others were beginning to acknowledge their own erotic responses to clients. There also was more permission to discuss emotional reactions to client sexual material that was not strictly seductive in nature.

Searles (1959) revealed that he experienced romantic and sexual feelings for clients during every successful analysis. He suspected that other therapists also had such reactions. Just as the parent, that often neglected term of the Oedipal equation, must overcome incestuous desires for the child, Searles felt that the analyst must relinquish the patient as a love object by the end of treatment. He proposed that it is harmful for therapists to ignore erotic feelings for clients. Such denial may give the clients the message that they are worthless, or conversely that they are so powerful that their therapists would be overwhelmed if the sexual attraction was brought to light. The healthy alternative is for therapists to be fully aware of their sexual arousal and sometimes even to tell clients about it, if a disclosure is appropriate. Searles noted that such sharing can boost clients' low self-esteem, satisfy their demand for affection, and keep therapists interested in difficult work. Searles did not, however, advocate sexual contact between therapists and clients, any more than he would advocate incest. He agreed with earlier theorists than an erotic response to a client could be due to a therapist's unresolved conflicts, or to the narcissism of a Pygmalion contemplating his Galatea, but he also suggested that it can be a response to the client's new, healthy maturity.

Searles's assertion that sexual feelings between therapist and client are an integral part of the therapeutic interaction was supported by Scheflen's work (1965). Taking an ethological perspective, Scheflen studied what he called "quasi-courtship" behavior during therapy sessions. He found that therapist and client regularly give each other nonverbal, sexual courtship signals, such as muscular tensing, preening, inviting postures, eye contact, and exposure of a vulnerable wrist or thigh. At the same time, the pair remind each other with "decourting" cues, such as a glance at the diploma on the wall, or a breaking of eye contact, that they are not in a sexual situation. Thus it is only a quasi-courtship. Scheflen believed that these communications maintain mutual interest in the task of therapy and in the therapeutic relationship. As long as the courting-decourting pattern retains its intricate balance, it is a positive force in therapy. If therapists or clients cannot distinguish quasi-courtship from real courtship, however, they may retreat from the relationship in dismay or attempt to violate the sexual limits.

Thus more recent psychodynamic theory admits that even well-adjusted therapists are going to have some sexual feelings about clients. Whether these should be squelched, analyzed away, or used as therapeutic tools remains controversial.

Psychotherapists of other orientations have addressed this issue less systematically. Humanistic practitioners vary widely in their definitions of what is ethical sexual conduct between encounter group leaders and group members (Cinnamon & Morris, 1976). The humanistic movement's emphasis on therapist self-disclosure, genuineness, being in the moment, and doing one's own thing seems to promise a more relaxed attitude toward accepting and communicating erotic feelings between therapist and client, if not toward acting out such attractions. There are also fewer value judgments made about sexual behavior than there are in psychoanalytic theory. Little has been directly written on these issues by humanistic therapists, however.

The other major orientation that has devoted a great deal of thought to sexuality in the therapy context is behavioral sex therapy. Sex therapists have, by and large, been careful to dissociate themselves from those who engage in sexual activities with clients (LoPiccolo, 1978; Masters & Johnson, 1976), but the public has been confused by the use of surrogate partners and by such practices as the "sexological exam," in which the therapist actually stimulates the client's genitals (Hartman & Fithian, 1972). While training for behavioral sex therapists often includes films and discussions aimed at liberalizing sexual attitudes, or role-playing exercises designed to make clinicians less anxious in talking about sex, little has been written on ways for a therapist to cope with sexual feelings evoked during a session. In fact, it is only quite recently that sex therapists have described the operation of transference (Levay, Kagle, & Weissberg, 1979) and countertransference (Dickes & Strauss, 1979) in their work. Kaplan (1977) has commented:

> If one of our trainees reports more than once a year an erotic response on the part of the patient, we assume that he is doing something seductive, something countertransferential that is outside of his awareness. This is a terribly important area of training. (p. 186)

Kaplan does not explain, however, how a novice sex therapist attains the conflict-free attitude toward sex that she advocates, nor what the therapist must do if made aware of seductive behavior on his or her own part. Other behavioral sex therapists have pointed out the difficulties caused by feelings of attraction or sexual competition occurring between male and female cotherapists in sex therapy teams (Dunn & Dickes, 1977; Golden & Golden, 1976; Zentner & Pouyat, 1978). These therapists call for direct communication about sexual feelings within the cotherapy team, but again this is a difficult task, and few concrete suggestions are made for easing the way.

The reader may have noticed Kaplan's use of "he" in the above description of the seductive trainee. This was not sexism, but reflects Kaplan's belief (and that of others) that male and female therapists react differently to attractive clients:

> Discussions with our psychiatric residents at Cornell, about one-third of whom are now women, indicate that the male residents often have feelings of sexual desire for female patients, whereas female residents rarely have such feelings. I think the discrepancy is real and significant. (Masters, Johnson, & Kolodny, 1977, pp. 170–171)

Research on sexual contact between therapist and client, which is discussed by Jean Holroyd in Chapter 11 of this volume, also consistently shows that it is the older male therapist who has sex with an attractive female client (Belote, 1974; Butler & Zelen, 1977; Dahlberg, 1970; Holroyd & Brodsky, 1977; Kardener, Fuller, & Mensh, 1973; Perry, 1976). Explanations for this gender difference range from Marmor's speculation (1976) that female therapists are bound by the mother-son incest taboo, which is stronger than the Oedipal version, to Davidson's suggestion (1977) that female therapists identify with victimized female clients or wives of philandering therapists, rather than with the male role of seducer.

Perhaps female therapists are not as likely as males are to be exposed to the temptation of a seductive client. Lief (1978) reported that 72% of psychiatrists responding to a questionnaire published in *Medical Aspects of Human Sexuality* had had seductive clients. The sample, however, was almost entirely male. Anecdotal reports (Benedek, 1973; Brodsky, 1977; Miller, 1976; Saretsky, 1977), however, suggest that female therapists often must contend with the sexual advances of male clients. We do not know, as yet, whether the differences in the percentage of men versus women who have sex with clients is due to a gender difference in therapist style, or whether female therapists simply have less opportunity to act out with clients because they see fewer opposite-sex cases than men do.

Byrne (1977) has pointed out that research on sex has become respectable in the field of psychology by stages. First psychologists studied animal sex; then "native sex" in other cultures; then "crazy sex" in those labeled abnormal in our society; and finally, ordinary, everyday sex. In Byrne's scheme, we are still studying "crazy sex" in psychotherapy by concentrating on the therapists who violate accepted ethical standards of professional conduct. Such research is important. We need to know how many therapists engage in sexual relationships with clients, and why they do so, but it is also useful to look at less extreme situations to see whether the majority of clinicians are comfortable with client sexuality.

EVIDENCE FOR AN EROTIC BIAS

Some empirical evidence has now been gathered on therapists' erotic responses to clients. It suggests that many therapists are not comfortable dealing with sexual issues, and that there are differences in the typical styles of male versus female therapists in this regard.

Most researchers have begun with the hypothesis that due to traditional sex roles, male therapists are more likely to respond to female clients' sexuality in a voyeuristic, encouraging way, while female therapists would feel guilty about any erotic response to a patient and therefore avoid dealing with male clients' sexual issues. Abramowitz, Abramowitz, Roback, Corney, and McKee

(1976) analyzed records from 316 cases seen in an outpatient clinic. They looked at gender of therapist and client, as well as the number of total sessions in the treatment. The patterns they found suggested that female therapists avoided seeing male clients. This was most likely to be true if the therapist was unmarried, or if the man was younger and better educated (i.e., more apt to be sexually attractive). Male therapists, on the other hand, did not seem to avoid taking on opposite-sex clients, and indeed treated their female clients for more sessions than they did their male clients. The records of female therapists' cases did not reveal such a bias. Safer (1975) confirmed this gender difference in length of treatment in another setting. Other researchers, however, have not discovered such therapist effects in their clinics (Helms, 1978; Kirshner, Genack, & Hauser, 1978).

Surprisingly, when therapists' emotional reactions to female clients were studied (Howard, Orlinsky, & Hill, 1969), male therapists were the ones who had negative feelings during sessions. Most of the difference between male and female therapists was due to the men's discomfort with sexual attraction occurring between therapist and client. Unfortunately, the project did not include male clients, so there was really no direct comparison of reactions in opposite-sex pairings of therapist and client.

Another relevant group of studies explored the projective testing situation. Some researchers found that male therapists modified their testing procedures for female clients, giving them more Thematic Apperception Test (TAT) cards with sexual or romantic themes (Masling & Harris, 1969; Siskind, 1973), or eliciting more Rorschach responses than they did with male clients (Harris & Masling, 1970). Female therapists' behavior did not differ according to the gender of the testee. Other researchers, however, have tried unsuccessfully to reproduce these results (Hersen, 1971; Milner & Moses, 1974).

Thus the literature purporting to demonstrate a voyeuristic bias in male therapists or excessive inhibition in female therapists remains controversial. In addition, none of the research cited thus far has studied verbal interaction during therapy sessions, or has related therapist and client gender to treatment outcome. In order to claim that such biases exist, one should really have evidence that the genders of therapist and client affect therapists' verbal and nonverbal behaviors during the process of treatment. Also, such biases are only important if they can be shown to affect treatment outcome adversely.

AN ANALOGUE STUDY OF THERAPISTS' RESPONSES TO CLIENT SEXUAL MATERIAL

The study that the present author undertook at the University of California at Los Angeles does not meet all these criteria either, but it is a first direct attempt to assess the effect of client gender and sexual content on therapists' verbal responses, as well as on emotional reactions and clinical judgments.

The present research used psychotherapy analogue methodology, which means that the psychotherapists who participated were presented with a male or a female client photograph and case history, and then asked to respond to seven audiotaped excerpts of sexual material from the client's sessions. A therapist heard either a tape of a client describing a mild sexual dysfunction, or a tape of a client being sexually seductive toward the therapist. In actuality, the description and excerpts were written for the study, and the clients were actors.

The major hypothesis was that the different dyads formed by crossing therapist and client gender are typically vulnerable to different therapeutic errors when sexual problems are a focus of treatment. Specifically, male therapists with female clients are likely to respond voyeuristically to sexual material, paying too much attention to it. Female therapists with male clients, however, may avoid dealing with sexual problems, since traditionally women in our society are taught to inhibit both sexual arousal and talking about sex to males. For same-gender pairings, the therapists in male dyads are less comfortable than the female therapist with a female client is. This is due to the lack of a traditional male model for discussing sexual problems (Zilbergeld, 1978), and to the stronger male reaction to any implication of homosexuality (Mosher & Abramson, 1977). All therapists are more comfortable discussing a client's sexual problems than dealing with sexual attraction directed at themselves.

Generalizability

Why go to all this trouble to gather data in an artificial context? Why not observe *real* sessions in which the client brings up sexual material? First of all, consider the number of hours of therapy tapes necessary to provide several excerpts of client sexual material for each of a large sample of therapists. Then take into account the difficulty of obtaining informed consent for such research from clients and permission to tape from therapists, not to mention the reactive effects of being taped on the therapeutic session, particularly if the therapist knows the purpose of the study. Finally, what about uncontrolled client characteristics that would certainly affect the therapists' responses, such as client age, education, socioeconomic status, psychopathology, and physical attractiveness? The effects of such variables could be strong enough to overwhelm evidence of any bias due to therapist and client gender, or to the type of material.

While a study in naturalistic settings is necessary before firm conclusions can be drawn, the results of an analogue study can be used to design a more economical naturalistic study by narrowing the target population. For example, as later becomes evident, this analogue study suggests that male therapists with female clients have the most extreme emotional and verbal responses to sexual material. It would thus be interesting to look intensively at factors affecting the behavior of male therapists with female clients, and thus to try to confirm the analogue results, rather than to begin with the gargantuan task of getting an adequate sample of all four therapist-client gender combinations.

Maher (1978) feels that analogue designs depending on a script and actor as stimuli are useless. He notes that an implausible script can produce atypical responses in therapists, so that the results would not generalize to real sessions. He also points out that extraneous variables—for example, an actor's regional accent or clothing—might interact with the factors being studied (i.e., client gender and type of sexual material), so that significant results might not really be due to the variables of interest.

This analogue has tried to answer Maher's criticisms in several ways. The scripts for the audiotapes were developed from role-plays of five men and five women, each of whom pretended to be a client with either a mild problem with premature ejaculation (male dysfunction condition), an inability to reach orgasm during intercourse (female dysfunction condition)[1], or a sexual attraction to the therapist (both male and female attraction conditions). The scripts were rated by a group of psychotherapy trainees in the UCLA Human Sexuality Program and by graduate students in a seminar on sex research. Ratings were conducted to insure plausibility in the four therapist-client gender combinations, and to make sure that the dysfunction client was not seductive while the attraction client was. Even though the male and female seduction scripts were identical in wording, and the dysfunction scripts were the same except for a few changes to make the sexual problem male versus female, they were rated as equally plausible for each therapist-client gender combination. Raters had a slightly harder time imagining a client talking about being attracted to the therapist as opposed to revealing a sexual problem. This difference may be due to the fact that seductiveness in a client is more unusual than a sexual problem, rather than to script implausibility.

In order to minimize extraneous variables, the male and female client descriptions were identical except for pronoun changes. The history was rather brief and vague. Its purpose was to let the therapist know that the client was a 31-year-old art director in an advertising agency, had not had previous therapy, and was referred to a private practitioner by his or her physician due to mild anxiety and depression subsequent to a divorce. The taped excerpts were said to be taken from several different sessions during the sixth month of therapy. This later period was chosen to make the seductive vignette seem less pathological and more plausible than such material might seem if revealed earlier in treatment. It was hoped that taking excerpts from several sessions would minimize the problem for the therapist of responding to the client, and then not getting an answer in the next excerpt. The client photographs were equated by graduate-student raters for a high degree of physical attractiveness. The male and female pictures were taken against an identical, neutral background. Both the man and woman were dark-haired and wore casual but attractive sweaters.

Procedure

The whole procedure was designed to take about 45 minutes. A total of 72 therapists participated. They were recruited through staff meetings at several Los Angeles mental health facilities, or through phone contacts from lists of private practitioners. There were 12 men and 12 women from each of the categories of postresidency psychiatrists, Ph.D.-level clinical psychologists, and M.S.W.-level social workers. There was a surprisingly high proportion of clinicians who agreed to give an hour of their time to the study (subjective estimate, 70% of those asked). The informed consent form detailed the procedure, but did not say that the content of the tapes would be sexual. That information was left out to avoid biasing the sample by forewarning therapists less comfortable with sexual issues, who might then decline to participate.

Six experimenters, three men and three women, went to the therapists' offices and took them through the procedure. Half of the subjects were run by a same-sex experimenter, and half by an opposite-sex experimenter, in order to control for reactive effects of experimenter gender on the therapists' responses to the client tapes (Abramson, Goldberg, Mosher, Abramson, & Gottesdiener, 1975; Abramson & Handschumacher, 1978).

The design is explained in Table 1. As can be seen, half of the therapists

TABLE 1
Experimental Design

	DYSFUNCTION VIGNETTE		ATTRACTION VIGNETTE	
	MALE CLIENT	FEMALE CLIENT	MALE CLIENT	FEMALE CLIENT
Male Therapists	3 M.D.s 3 Ph.D.s 3 M.S.W.s	3 M.D.s 3 Ph.D.s 3 M.S.W.s	3 M.D.s 3 Ph.D.s 3 M.S.W.s	3 M.D.s 3 Ph.D.s 3 M.S.W.s
Female Therapists	3 M.D.s 3 Ph.D.s 3 M.S.W.s	3 M.D.s 3 Ph.D.s 3 M.S.W.s	3 M.D.s 3 Ph.D.s 3 M.S.W.s	3 M.D.s 3 Ph.D.s 3 M.S.W.s

were presented with a same-sex client, and half with an opposite-sex client. Within each of the four resulting groups, half of the therapists heard an attraction tape, and half heard a dysfunction tape. The profession of the therapist was also evenly distributed across groups so that it could be examined as a factor.

After seeing the client description and photograph, therapists were left alone in their offices with the client tape. The tape consisted of seven 45-second excerpts, each followed by a 60-second pause. During the pause the therapists were asked to record on another tape exactly what they would say next to the client, as if in a real session.

After the tape, the experimenter came back and gave the therapists a set of 7-point scales on which to rate their anxiety and sexual arousal during the tape, the client's physical attractiveness and degree of disturbance, the importance of the issue discussed on the tape, the ease of establishing a good therapy relationship with the client, the therapists' estimated need for a consultation on the case, and how much they would enjoy treating the client.

After completing that form, therapists filled out demographic information about themselves, including age; relationship status (five categories from "married" through "not dating at all"); years of experience as a therapist; primary orientation as a therapist; settings of current clinical work; age, gender, socioeconomic status, and psychopathology of their typical client; and whether or not they had specific training in human sexuality and/or in behavioral sex therapy. Therapists also completed an abbreviated version of the Mosher Sex Guilt Scale (Mosher, 1966, 1968); the attitudes subscale of the Sex Knowledge and Attitudes Test (SKAT) (Lief & Reed, 1972), which breaks down into attitudes about abortion, heterosexual relations, masturbation, and sexual myths; and the UCLA Loneliness Scale (Russell, Peplau, & Ferguson, 1978). At the end of the procedure, they completed a debriefing form that assessed their reactions to participating and their guesses about the hypotheses of the research.

Results and Discussion

Therapists' verbal responses to the tapes were transcribed and then coded in two ways. By the first method, the author and two undergraduates (who did not know the therapist's gender or profession) rated a therapist's response to each of the seven excerpts as either "approaching" the client's material (i.e., encouraging the client to say more about the topic), or "avoiding" it (i.e., discouraging the client from pursuing the subject). A rating scale for this purpose was designed by Bandura, Lipsher, and Miller (1960), and has been used to assess therapist's responses to their clients' hostility (Bandura, Lipsher, & Miller, 1960; Varble, 1968) and dependency (Caracena, 1965;

Schuldt, 1966; Winder, Ahmad, Bandura, & Rau, 1962). Approach responses would include statements approving or supporting the client; exploring the
topic further; labeling the client's feelings, attitudes or actions; making a reflection or interpretation of the material; answering a question; or normaliz-
ing the client's actions or reactions. Avoidances might be remarks expressing
disapproval, mislabeling the client's feelings, changing the subject, ignoring
the client's statement, or harshly setting limits on the therapy relationship.

Some examples give a feeling for the client material and the therapists'
responses to it. Here is excerpt 7 from the dysfunction tape. The words that
differ in the male and female scripts are italicized, with the female version in
parentheses.

> I guess a few *women (men)* have tried to, uh, to help me with this—this prob-
> lem, and, uh, the ones that really get to me are the ones that sort of do a martyr
> trip, like, you know, "Don't worry about getting me off. You just concentrate
> on yourself." That just makes it all worse. I mean, then I can hardly even feel
> turned on. Uh—the more helpful they are, the more frantic I get, and, uh, some-
> times I feel like—why bother with sex at all? Or maybe I'd be better off just mas-
> turbating.

One therapist responded,

> Yeah, I can really see that you have a lot of frustration and concern about all
> this. And maybe you would be better off masturbating, but somehow the way
> we keep talking about it, I'm not sure that's true. I also wonder if maybe you
> don't have some real concerns about intimacy and closeness in these relation-
> ships.

This is clearly an approach response. It is supportive and does not change the
subject.

Another therapist said,

> Well, you're probably right. You would be much better off doing that. Sounds
> like you're only comfortable with sex when you're the martyr.

This kind of confrontive sarcasm was coded as an avoidance. It would not encourage the client to reveal more of such feelings.

Excerpt 2 from the seductive tapes was identical for both male and female
clients:

> All this time—since the divorce—you're really the person I've been closest to,
> and, uh, sometimes I really miss that—that physical closeness. You know, like
> sleeping in the same bed with someone, or just touching someone, and I—I re-
> member, the first time I came here, you, uh, you shook my hand—and you

never did that again. And, uh, I really need that kind of contact with people. And, uh, you know I can still almost feel that nice touch of your hand, and, uh, I wish you would touch me again.

One therapist's approach response was as follows:

I imagine that you are in touch right now with feelings that are very difficult for you, very painful, perhaps reminders of times when you have felt untouched or unconnected with people. And there's a longing to experience that here. You're very aware of the many areas of your life where this has been missing. We have a close relationship, and it's natural for you to be frustrated.

The contrast with the avoidance response below should be obvious:

Michael, you're still talking in that stylized way. Why don't you try telling me the same thing, this time as though you were talking to a friend? This time as though you really mean it, if you do.

The second coding system was a response modes scale (Whalen & Flowers, 1977), which classified each segment of a therapist's response in one of 19 categories, including types of reflections, interpretations, advisement, process statements, self-disclosures, questions, and confrontations. This system was included to provide more specific response categories that might reveal differences due to the type of sexual material, or to the gender of therapist and client. Two trained undergraduates also did these ratings. Both coding systems turned out to be quite useful.

Since there were so many different measures included in the study, the most coherent way to present the results is in an integrated fashion.

There were several important differences between male and female therapists. Female therapists made more verbal approach responses to the clients than male therapists did. The response modes scale showed that the women used reflections more often than the men did, and were less apt to make disapproving, confrontive responses or to comment on the psychotherapy process. Female therapists also felt that it would be easier to establish a good therapy relationship with these clients than men felt it would be.

The male therapists did report mild sexual arousal in response to tapes of a female client. Female therapists, however, indicated they felt little arousal in any condition. When male therapists were sexually excited by a tape, they made more verbal approach responses and rated the client as more physically attractive.

It was expected that both male and female therapists would react more positively to female clients. The only clear evidence that this occurred was that therapists rated female clients as more enjoyable to treat. All therapists were more likely to make directive requests that the client do or say something during the session to female clients, which may be due to a greater feeling of authority or comfort with women.

Seductive clients did make therapists more uncomfortable than the dysfunction cases did. All therapists made more verbal avoidance responses to the seductive clients than to the clients complaining of sexual problems. Therapists discouraged clients from continuing to be seductive by omitting information-seeking questions and reflections. Instead, they made disapproving comments or statements about the process going on in the session. Therapists also reported feeling more anxious in response to attraction tapes than they did with the dysfunction tapes. Therapists felt that it would be harder to establish a good relationship with seductive clients, and that such cases would be less enjoyable to treat.

Therapists' age, years of experience, relationship status, psychotherapy orientation, training in sexuality or sex therapy, and work setting were not good predictors of their verbal behavior, emotional reactions, or clinical judgments. What was important, surprisingly, was a therapist's profession. Psychiatrists seemed the most authoritative of the therapists. They felt less need for a consultation and gave the client more advice and interpretations. They also showed more evidence of believing that women should have orgasms during intercourse, of indicating discomfort with homosexually seductive clients, and of enjoying heterosexual seductiveness from clients. Male psychiatrists were particularly extreme on these dimensions. Social workers seemed to have some discomfort with sexuality. They reported the most sexual arousal of any of the professionals, but had more conservative sexual attitudes than the others and were the group least likely to have had training in behavioral sex therapy. Psychologists did not stand out in any way as a group.

The three personality and attitude scales were also useful predictors. Lonelier therapists were simply more anxious with all clients. This may represent discomfort with client sexuality rather than with interpersonal situations in general, since lonelier therapists also had more conservative sexual attitudes. Therapists who were higher in sex guilt felt more need for a consultation on the cases and thought their verbal responses did not closely resemble what they would say in a real session. Thus sex guilt seemed to result in a feeling of tentativeness. Sexual attitudes were good predictors of male therapists' responses to female clients. Male therapists who had liberal beliefs about abortion and about sexual relations outside of marriage were sexually aroused by the seductive female client tape. They got mildly anxious, and gave a fair number of verbal approach responses. Men who had conservative attitudes on these dimensions were turned on by the woman who talked about her problem in reaching orgasm. This group, however, got quite anxious and made verbal responses that would discourage the client from talking about sex. Men who agreed with present-day cultural myths about sex were less anxious with the seductive female tape than were those who rejected these misconceptions, and also gave the client more verbal encouragement to continue with the topic.

Therapist Errors in Dealing with Sexually Attractive Clients

One of the most important issues that this study hoped to address was whether therapists deal adequately with attractive opposite-sex clients, particularly when the topic of a session is sex. There were two possible therapist errors in responding to client sexual material The first was the voyeuristic response to the client's sexuality, with therapists using the interaction to further their own erotic pleasure. This kind of process in the session might be associated with sexual acting out between therapist and client. The second therapist error was to get overly anxious in response to client sexual material and to shut off the expression of sexual feelings by giving disapproving responses or by changing the subject. This could prevent the client from resolving sexual conflicts or receiving treatment for sexual dysfunctions. Voyeurism had been predicted to be more likely in male therapists, while the phobic response was seen as more probable for female therapists.

There was a good deal of evidence that male therapists had erotic responses to female clients. The male therapist–female client dyads, particularly in the attraction condition, stood apart on a number of measures. This was the combination in which the client was judged as most physically attractive and sexually arousing, and in which the most therapist self-disclosures occurred. In fact, the men found these tapes so disturbing that they reported more loneliness, more conservativism about premarital or extramarital sex, and less sex guilt after hearing them. When male therapists were sexually aroused, they gave more verbal encouragement to the client to keep talking about sex, even though men as a group made more avoidance responses than women.

What kinds of things did the men say? Self-disclosures to the seductive female client fell into several categories. A number of therapists revealed sexual feelings for the client, but always added that there were limits on sexual behavior in the therapy relationship. For example, in one segment, the client says:

> I'd really like to know, like, what you think of me. I mean, not just do you like me, or do you think I'm an O.K. person, because, uh, I think you care about me as a—a patient, but, you know, if you think I'm attractive, or, you know, nice-looking. Like if you notice the way I dress, or if you think I have a good body. I've even wondered if you ever get a little, you know, turned on to me, like even

right now. I don't know—probably even if you were, you wouldn't tell me about it. It's probably against the 10 commandments of Freud or something. But that doesn't stop me from wondering.

A male social worker replied:

> Well, I am turned on to you. I find you very attractive. I like the way you dress. I think you have a good body. You're bright, talented, etc., etc. And again I feel a lot of pressure in this respect; that you want something from me, and, uh, I find it difficult because it seems as if I keep wanting to set limits, and you're keeping wanting to go beyond the limits. Uh, is that true that you do want more?

One could imagine this interaction escalating into a seduction if the therapist had poor impulse control.

Other therapists spoke of their own anxiety and anger at the seductive client. One male psychologist told her:

> You're having a lot of feelings about me. I find myself getting very anxious and nervous.

Later in the sequence of excerpts he became quite disapproving:

> Again, I find myself feeling quite annoyed. I'm wondering what in the world you're trying to get at. And I just don't find myself being very sexually attracted.

This kind of response might stop the seductiveness, but at the cost of alienating the client.

It is interesting that female therapists paired with the male seductive client did not feel a need to share their feeling reactions. They were much less likely to answer client questions about their feelings. Instead, they said they understood how the client felt, but turned the inquiry back to the client's emotional experience. By using this sort of passive limit setting, they were less likely to get drawn into a confrontation about the issue of therapist-client sex.

A number of indicators make up a tentative profile of a therapist who might act out with a seductive female client. He is generally a psychiatrist whose typical client is a young, upper-middle-class woman with little psychopathology. He believes that premarital and extramarital sex, as well as abortion, are permissible, but he agrees with sexual myths and stereotypes common in our culture. This profile fits reasonably well with sexually acting-out therapists interviewed by Butler and Zelen (1977) or described by ex-clients in Belote's (1974) project.

The group of men who had conservative attitudes about abortion and sex outside of marriage seemed to be making the second therapist error of shutting off the client's sexual material. These men were aroused by the woman who recounted details of her sexual life, but not by the seductive client. They were highly anxious and verbally avoided the topic of sex.

There was little evidence that female therapists were either overly voyeuristic or rejecting of sex. Like the female testers in the Masling and Harris (1969) study, women were less affected by client gender in their responses than men were. There were very few interaction effects here involving female therapists. There were no particularly positive or negative reactions to attractive male analogue clients, whether they were seductive or merely discussing their sex lives.

Women therapists reported very little sexual arousal in any context. It is possible that women in our culture do not become aroused with an attractive male client immediately, but might have an erotic response later in treatment. Recent studies of women's sexual arousal to erotic tapes and films, however (Abramson et al., 1975; Heiman, 1977; Mosher & Abramson, 1977), show that college-age women report arousal as high as men's. Sex between therapist and client usually does not occur until well into the therapy (Belote, 1974), but there is still a therapist gender difference in its frequency. Thus, there is little evidence to suggest that women are at risk for making therapeutic errors in response to client sexual material, but a good deal of evidence that men are apt to overreact in either direction.

It may be that some errors made by women were not assessed in this design, however. Female therapists may need help in setting assertive limits with seductive clients and in focusing on hostile or resistive aspects of such interactions. Women may avoid confronting male clients, particularly on issues such as seductiveness or anger, out of a fear of bodily harm. Female therapists also may be more practiced and skillful in ignoring seductiveness. In our society, it is usually the woman who thinks of an innocuous way to refuse a sexual invitation.

Women could also be more likely to worry that they have elicited client sexual material by their own seductiveness. Women graduate students in psychology who had seductive professors and clinical supervisors were slightly more likely than men to feel they had also been seductive (Levenson, Note 1).

As a result of these inhibitions, female therapists may have overly severe controls on their erotic responses to clients. As Scheflen (1965) has pointed out, a certain amount of "courting" is necessary between therapist and client to maintain interest in the therapy relationship. Sexual arousal can also be a useful indicator of something unusual in the process of the therapy session.

Does Talking about Sex Elicit Sexism?

There were a few specific findings suggesting sexist attitudes in this group of therapists. Female therapists had more liberal attitudes on abortion than males did, which may reflect some conservatism about feminism on the men's part. The place where men's clinical judgments differed from women's was in response to the female client who could not have orgasms during intercourse. Men gave her the highest ratings of disturbance of any client, and women the lowest. Within the group of psychiatrists, men felt that it would be the most difficult to have a good therapy relationship with this particular client, while women felt that it would be the easiest. Male therapists, then, and especially male psychiatrists, do not seem affected by recent research suggesting that lack of orgasm during intercourse is within the normal range of female sexuality (Morokoff, 1978).

All therapists rated the female seductive client's problem as more important in the context of the whole treatment than that of the male seductive client. Because women in our culture are not expected to initiate sex directly, those who are seductive may be seen as more in need of treatment than "macho" men are.

And a Little Homophobia?

Therapists did seem to have a negative response to the homosexually seductive clients. The same photograph and voice was rated as less physically attractive when it belonged to a same-sex seductive client compared to a same-sex client complaining about a sexual problem. Seductiveness did *not* decrease the perceived attractiveness of opposite-sex clients.

Male therapists were especially harsh in their judgment of the attractiveness of the homosexually seductive male client. Thus we do see the stronger male reaction to homosexuality predicted in the hypotheses.

Again, psychiatrists had a stronger bias against the homosexually seductive client than did other professionals. M.D.s indicated that they would enjoy treating such a client less than psychologists or social workers would, and they made fewer verbal approaches to same-sex than opposite-sex seductive clients.

Thus homosexual seductiveness was, in some respects, even more difficult and upsetting for the therapists than heterosexual seductiveness was. Therapists may need special training to learn to cope with this kind of sexual material.

Therapist Preferences
for Client Gender

The therapists in this sample felt it would be easier to establish a good therapy relationship with a same-sex client. Their actual caseloads reflect this preference to some extent. Both men and women were most likely to have practices equally divided between male and female clients, and then next most likely to see mainly same-sex clients (42% of female therapists and 31% of male therapists). Only 17% of male therapists and 11% of women had mostly opposite-sex caseloads. Female therapists were a little more likely to restrict their practices to same-sex clients than males were, but it was unclear whether this was due to institutional pressures or because of the therapists' own preferences. Female clients were only slightly "preferred" (i.e., 50% of the sample saw both genders equally often, 29% saw mainly women, and 21% saw mostly men). These proportions are similar to those in an extensive therapist sample interviewed by Schofield (1964).

Those therapists who usually did see women clients were more anxious during the tapes than other clinicians were. It may be that therapists who prefer female clients are more conventional and conforming. This was true of college students in a recent study (Wilder, Hoyt, Zettle, & Hauck, 1978) who preferred same-sex therapists. Such a personality difference might well lead to anxiety when a client brings up sexual material.

Implications for Behavioral Sex Therapy

In this sample, 75% of therapists had specific training in human sexuality, and 61% had been trained in behavioral sex therapy. The quantity and quality of this training, however, is unknown. Psychologists were most likely to be trained in sex therapy, followed by psychiatrists and then by social workers. Eclectically oriented therapists were more likely than were psychodynamic or psychoanalytic practitioners to have had such training.

The fact that training in sexuality or sex therapy was not predictive of therapist verbal behavior or therapist affect, or even of felt need for a consultation, is disappointing. Recent California laws (Assembly Bills 4178 and 4179) require training in sexuality for licensure or license renewal for physicians, psychologists, social workers, and marriage and family counselors. Some workshops designed to help professionals satisfy the requirement, however, may be inadequate to their task.

This study does show that therapists' knowledge of the treatments available for sexual dysfunctions is not always evident. A number of therapists took the classic psychoanalytic position that sexual dysfunctions are a sign of serious psychological disturbance. One male psychiatrist said, in response to the female who complained of lack of orgasm during intercourse,

> If you have pent-up energy, that is a problem. The only channel that you are sure in, that you can manage it, or mismanage it, is in the bed, or the couch, or whatever. Again, it is my firm opinion that the so-called sex problem is only a manifestation of deeper problems.

Another clinician said this to the male client who described a mild problem with premature ejaculation:

> Yes, maybe deep inside you are afraid to satisfy a woman, or maybe you don't want to satisfy a woman. Maybe you feel that there would be something dangerous for you. You may be guilty and you are afraid to. So as soon as you feel the excitement, you have an orgasm to stop her from enjoying it or for you to avoid something which is probably sinful or bad.

Another implication of this study is that therapists may feel more comfortable, and hence may be more successful, in treating same-gender clients with sexual dysfunctions, rather than opposite-gender clients. The data supports Dickes and Strauss's contention (1979) that focusing on client sexual material may exacerbate countertransference feelings, particularly in male therapist–female client dyads, disrupting the process of sex therapy.

Generalizability Revisited

Is there evidence that these clinicians were responding as they would to an actual client? Out of 72 therapists, only one guessed that the purpose of the study was to compare male and female therapists or clients. The others mainly saw it as an attempt to correlate the personality and attitudes of the therapist with reactions to client sexual material. Their behavior, therefore, was not biased by knowledge of the major hypotheses.

Therapists were asked to rate the resemblance of their verbal responses to the tape to their comments in a real session. The mean rating was 5.1 out of a possible 7 (a rating of 7 would mean that their responses were identical). Mean ratings did not differ between groups of therapists who were male versus female, heard male versus female tapes, or were in the dysfunction versus attraction conditions. Response resemblance did correlate significantly with other variables, suggesting that it has concurrent validity as a measure (i.e., therapists who rated their responses as closely resembling those in a real session were also less anxious, had a shorter verbal response reaction time, used more words per response, were less guilty about sex, and had more liberal attitudes about masturbation).

Therapists also rated their emotional involvement in listening to the tape. The mean was a respectable 4.5 out of 7. Therapists who were more involved judged the client to be more physically attractive, saw the material as more important, and felt more need for a consultation on the case.

Finally, evidence for generalizability of these results can be seen in the consistency of verbal responses, emotional reactions, and clinical judgments.

The differing reactions of male versus female therapists to male versus female clients, and to the two types of sexual material, are consistent with each other and with common-sense expectations. It is difficult to see how extraneous variables or atypical scripts could account for this body of data.

IMPLICATIONS FOR TRAINING

These findings suggest that psychotherapists need a new type of training. Workshops on sexuality emphasizing behavioral techniques and physiological information are not enough. One may be able to recite the ana-tomical changes of the sexual response cycle backwards and forwards, but may still be tongue-tied when a client wants to know what to do about sex play between her son and daughter. Therapists must be exposed to conscious-ness raising about the wide range of "normality" in the human sexual reper-toire. They need to be made aware of their own sexual attitudes, especially the ways in which their beliefs about sex can color their reactions to clients.

The stereotype of the nonjudgmental therapist is an unfortunate fiction. Few are inscrutable enough to conceal shock, disgust, or sexual excitement from clients, and most of us experience such powerful emotions many times during our careers. The cool "Mm-hmm" can only partially disguise the inner squawk of "You did *what*?" Perhaps our attempts to seem unshakable serve more to protect ourselves than our clients. It might seem prudish to admit that we have never taken (or perhaps even had) the opportunity to have sex with two partners, as a proud but confused client may have done. It might seem narrow-minded to reveal that we do not see why one should learn to like anal intercourse, or that we do not understand what is pleasurable about be-ing urinated on by a partner. Yet it might be a better experience for the clients if we said something about our feeling reactions, as long as we make it clear that we do not think less of the clients as people or seek to impose our judg-ments on them. Not only can such self-disclosures validate the clients' percep-tions of us, but it would more likely resemble the reaction they could expect from other significant others. The goal is to allow sexuality to be explored as a topic of importance to personal growth.

Therapists make mistakes when they try to ignore their sexual responses to attractive clients. The first step is for therapists to be aware of their own arousal. Then the anxiety or seductiveness that sometimes go along with arousal can be interrupted. Therapists may be more accepting of their own erotic responses to a client if the reaction is labeled as a normal human feeling rather than as countertransference.

What does it mean to be attracted to a client? It may be due to the client's good looks or appealing personality. The client may remind the therapist of a past lover or of a parent. The therapist may be lacking a good sexual relationship in his or her current life and hence may be more vulnerable. None of these reasons is "unhealthy" in itself. Problems arise if the attraction gets in the way of the therapeutic work. If the therapist is often distracted by sexual fantasies or finds that he or she is being overly ingratiating or avoiding needed confrontations, some extra attention must be paid to such feelings.

It is probably most useful to have an objective consultation with a trusted colleague. Direct observation of the therapeutic interaction, or at least the use of videotapes or audiotapes, is the easiest way to spot problems in the therapy process. If the therapist has not consistently taken an authoritarian and aloof role, discussion of sexual feelings with a client should not be any more disruptive to therapy than discussing anger or empathy should be. The therapist can clearly state that the purpose of talking about feelings of attraction is to explore their meaning rather than to act them out. Important issues to assess include the client's perception of the therapist's feelings; the client's positive and negative reactions to the attraction; the client's fears or hopes about its effect on the therapy; similar patterns in the client's current or past experience with parents or authority figures; and the client's beliefs about sex and nurturance. If the therapist can discuss these issues in a calm and matter-of-fact way, not only will they be defused, but valuable insights may result for both clinician and client. The criterion for revealing a therapist's attraction to the client must of course be the probable benefits to the therapy. If the feeling is clearly evoked by the therapist's unresolved issues rather than by the client's behavior, or if the therapeutic alliance is unusually fragile, such a revelation may not be in the best interests of the client. Occasionally, both therapist and client may feel that an attraction between them is so disruptive that a referral to another therapist, perhaps of a different gender or age, is in order.

Obviously most therapists do not reach the point of being comfortable with sexual material in the absence of good training. Few programs discuss sexual issues in any systematic way. Experiential workshops on sexual attitudes can play a useful role. These could include films and discussions about such charged issues as homosexuality, incest, therapist-client sex, and other unconventional sexual practices. It is especially important to present relevant cases, and if possible to do live interviews of clients who have had such experiences. Clinicians need to role-play situations so that they know what "pushes their buttons" and how they can regain their equanimity. Individual supervisors also should monitor and discuss their students' tendencies either to dwell on or to avoid sexual content. A student should be assigned both male and female supervisors and clients (Brodsky, 1977), so that sex-role and sexual issues can be fully explored during the important beginning years.

Not only do present training programs ignore these issues, but they often provide just the kind of models that are not needed. Two colleagues and the present author (Pope, Levenson, & Schover, 1979) recently sent surveys to 500 male and 500 female psychologists in the American Psychological Association's Psychotherapy Division (29). The psychologists were asked about their experiences as graduate students with seductiveness from educators, including academic psychology teachers, clinical supervisors, and departmental administrators. They were asked about types of seductive behaviors; whether they felt they had also been seductive in the situation; and their feelings about the incidents, then and now. They were also asked whether, as graduate students, they had had sexual contact (defined as intercourse or genital stimulation) with any of the three types of psychology educators. Another question covered their current sexual behavior with students or clients in their professional roles of psychology teacher, clinical supervisor, administrator, or psychotherapist. Finally, the psychologists were asked whether they felt that sexual contact between educator and graduate student could be mutually beneficial.

There was a 48% return rate, with equal proportions of men and women replying. Only 14% of the men, but 60% of the women, had experienced seductive behavior, such as flirting, joking about sex, excessive attention, or touching from an educator (Levenson, Note 1). At the time, about a third of all respondents felt positively about the interaction. From their current perspectives, however, while a similar percentage of men still remembered the incidents with fondness, only 17% of women had positive memories. This may represent a raising of consciousness for women in the interim, or it may reflect more negative consequences of such flirting for women than for men. About half of the men and women who reported having seductive educators also felt that they had acted seductively in the situation. The figure for women (55%) was somewhat, but not significantly, higher than that for men (46%).

When it came to actual sexual contact (Pope et al., 1979), the older, higher-status man with the younger woman was clearly the predominant pattern. As graduate students, 16.5% of women, but only 3% of men, had had sex with an educator. The more recent the Ph.D., the more likely such affairs became. Of women who received their degrees within the past 6 years, 25% had had sexual contact with a psychology professor, supervisor, or administrator. As professionals, 20% of the men and 6% of the women had had sex with a student or client.

One important question raised by these data is whether the educator's seductiveness represented sexual harassment, or whether the relationships that resulted were merely pleasurable encounters of mutually consenting adults. The women respondents were more likely to give personal accounts on the backs of their questionnaires that were examples of harassment. This story told by a recent female Ph.D. was typical (Schover, Note 2):

> It was a nightmare in graduate school. My chairman kept after me and I was forced into a position of utter stupidity—I never "noticed" his attentions. He

finally came out with a direct proposal and I had to act that too. "Oh, Dr. So-and-So, you are like a father to me. Such a great thinker and seer. I respect you as a mentor, etc., etc." Anything not to deflate his ego. My career depended on that pose. It was loathsome and caused me a great deal of anxiety."

The few men who recounted their seductions did not show the same anxiety and disgust about the experience:

The basic (nonverbal) message throughout, from two female professors in clinical psychology, to me and certain other male graduate students, was something like—"John (Tom/Dick/Harry), I sure wish you'd get your damned degree *done,* so I could go to bed with you!" Eventually we *did,* so the "prompt"/S^D/ cue was apparently *helpful*—as well as, in *my* book, ethical.

The most popular sexual partner was the academic psychology teacher. Some 12% of female graduate students and 1% of men had had sex with a teacher, and of the professionals who indicated they were teachers ($n = 247$), 18% of men and 4% of women had had sex with a student. Clinical supervisors were also frequent participants; 8% of women and 2% of men as graduate students had sex with a supervisor. Of the 263 supervisors included in our sample, 6% of men and 2% of women had had affairs with students. Administrators were cited more rarely, but psychotherapists came in for their share. Of 305 psychotherapists in the sample, 12% of men and 3% of women had had sex with a client. This compares closely to the numbers of psychologists in Holroyd and Brodsky's survey (1977) who reported having had erotic contact with clients.

One important finding (Pope et al., 1979) was that of women who had had sexual affairs as students, 23% also had had sex with their own students or clients as professionals. Only 6% of other women had sexual contacts as professionals. The number of men having affairs as students was too small ($n = 7$) to allow a similar comparison. If one looks at the correlation between having seductive educators as a student and having actual sexual contact with students or clients as a professional, there is a specific and significant relationship between having had a seductive supervisor and being a seductive supervisor. Similarly, those respondents who gave affirmative answers to questions about observing or directly hearing about other graduate students' experiences with seductive psychology teachers or who knew of others' affairs with teachers were more likely to indulge in such relationships when they attained positions of authority.

There are two alternative explanations for these results: Either people who are sexually active are active with the ones they are with; or professors, supervisors, and administrators are teaching young psychologists that sexual relationships with students and clients are not only permissible, but fun. The uselessness of the maxim, "Do what I say, not what I do," was legendary even before Bandura. Its ubiquity is seen in the statistic that 43% of respondents who had had sex with a student or client felt such relationships were *not* beneficial to both parties. A mere 2% of all respondents said that sex between psychology educators and graduate students could be mutually beneficial.

These problems are certainly not exclusive to psychology training. A paper by Benedek, Barton, and Bieniek (1977) mentions seductive supervisors and sexual harassment by mentors as significant problems for the female psychiatry resident. Outside of the mental health professions, Quinn (1977) studied sexual relationships between workers in white-collar organizational settings and found that affairs were quite common. The men in 74% of the couples had higher-level jobs than the women. The women were also twice as likely to be fired due to the affairs as the men were. Sexual harassment of women on the job is currently a "hot" issue in the news media. Educators in mental health fields, however, have an ethical responsibility beyond that of business people or even academics in other disciplines to refrain from such behavior. Graduate students in psychology or social work, and residents in psychiatry, are dependent on their educators—not only in terms of finances and evaluations that can affect the courses of their careers, but for learning the professional standards that will guide them with their own clients.

It is this author's guess that professionals who are comfortable with themselves as sexual beings are less likely to have affairs with their students or clients. Someone who is secure about his or her sexual attractiveness and worth as a person, may not need to choose a subordinate as a sexual partner. As one of the respondents (Pope et al., 1979) wrote,

> My impression is that there are lonely, dissatisfied, searching people among graduate students and department faculty. This is not meant to excuse the behavior on the part of either since, ultimately, the behavior is not likely to be constructive and growthful for either. I would, however, suggest that the motivation for the acting out of sexual behavior on the part of faculty or graduate students is, in my perception, less likely to be prurient or lascivious and more likely to be a misguided attempt at putting an end to one's doubts about one's self.

Of course, as Quinn (1977) and some of the other respondents in the Pope et al. study noted, sometimes one meets a person in the workplace who is simply very attractive, and who is interested in a long-term relationship. Such couples may have a difficult time, however. As anyone living in this era of social change is aware (let alone anyone practicing as a psychotherapist), happy, nonsexist relationships are difficult enough to build, without beginning with the handicap of a status differential.

CONCLUSIONS

A good training program should not only encourage, but demand, that the future professional examine his or her sexual attitudes and ethics. From the present author's point of view, a psychotherapist who does not believe in the equality of women; who will not acknowledge the right of gay persons to their sexual preference; who does not know how to separate sexual myth from sexual reality; who cannot discuss sexual anatomy and the response cycle in an accurate and comfortable way; who tries to impose false standards of sexual behavior on clients, such as extolling the superiority of vaginal, multiple, or simultaneous orgasms; who prescribes long-term, dynamic therapy to resolve problems of anorgasmia, premature ejaculation, or erectile dysfunction; who reacts to clients' sexual issues with disgust or withdrawal; or who uses the power of his or her authority to attain sexual gratification from clients or students is just as incompetent as is a psychotherapist who cannot recognize florid psychotic symptoms or who fails to assess suicidal symptoms in a severely depressed client.

Some will say that these standards are overly rigorous. Others may disagree with these values about sexuality. Our current training, however, will remain inadequate as long as we are unwilling to acknowledge our deficiencies in dealing with clients' sexual issues, and as long as we fail to use the results of empirical research to improve our repertoire of clinical skills. Based on the results of the studies cited in this chapter, this author thinks it is fair to say that there is significant bias in therapists' current practices regarding sexuality. Whether our societal attitudes and training programs will make as much progress in eradicating this bias as we have made so far in dealing with sex-role bias remains to be seen.

NOTES

[1]Although these problems would not be diagnosed as dysfunctions by many sex therapists, they were chosen as very common, mild sexual complaints. The two resulting tapes were labeled the "dysfunction" condition for the sake of having a convenient name.

REFERENCE NOTES

1. Levenson, H. Data from a national survey. In B. Kalis (Chair), *Sexual conduct between psychology educators and students.* Symposium presented at the meeting of the American Psychological Association, New York, August 1979.

2. Schover, L. R. First-person accounts of seduction in psychology graduate training. In B. Kalis (Chair), *Sexual conduct between psychology educators and students.* Symposium presented at the meeting of the American Psychological Association, New York, August 1979.

REFERENCES

Abramowitz, S. I., Abramowitz, C. V., Roback, H. B., Corney, R. T., & McKee, E. Sex-role-related countertransference in psychotherapy. *Archives of General Psychiatry*, 1976, *33*, 71–73.

Abramson, P. R., Goldberg, P. A., Mosher, D. L., Abramson, L. M., & Gottesdiener, L. Experimenter effects on responses to explicitly sexual stimuli. *Journal of Research in Personality*, 1975, *9*, 136–146.

Abramson, P. R., & Handschumacher, I. W. Experimenter effects on responses to double-entendre words. *Journal of Personality Assessment*, 1978, *42*, 592–596.

Bandura, A., Lipsher, D. H., & Miller, P. E. Psychotherapists' approach-avoidance reactions to patients' expressions of hostility. *Journal of Consulting Psychology*, 1960, *21*, 96–100.

Belote, B. *Sexual intimacy between female clients and male psychotherapists: Masochistic sabotage*. Unpublished doctoral dissertation, California School of Professional Psychology, San Francisco, 1974.

Benedek, E. P. Training the woman resident to be a psychiatrist. *American Journal of Psychiatry*, 1973, *130*, 1131–1135.

Benedek, E. P., Barton, G., & Bieniek, C. Problems for women in psychiatric residency. *American Journal of Psychiatry*, 1977, *134*, 1244–1248.

Berman, L. Countertransference and attitudes of the analyst in the therapeutic process. *Psychiatry*, 1949, *12*, 159–166.

Brodsky, A. M. Countertransference issues and the woman therapist: Sex and the student therapist. *Clinical Psychologist*, 1977, *30*, 12–14.

Butler, S., & Zelen, S. L. Sexual intimacies between therapists and patients. *Psychotherapy: Theory, Research, and Practice*, 1977, *14*, 139–145.

Byrne, D. Social psychology and the study of sexual behavior. *Personality and Social Psychology Bulletin*, 1977, *3*, 3–30.

Caracena, P. F. Elicitation of dependency expressions in the initial stage of psychotherapy. *Journal of Counseling Psychology*, 1965, *12*, 268–274.

Cinnamon, K. M., & Morris, K. T. (Eds.). *Controversial issues in human relations training groups*. Springfield, Ill.: Charles C Thomas, 1976.

Cohen, M. B. Countertransference and anxiety. *Psychiatry*, 1952, *15*, 231–244.

Dahlberg, C. C. Sexual contact between patient and therapist. *Contemporary Psychoanalysis*, 1970, *6*, 107–124.

Davidson, V. Psychiatry's problem with no name: Therapist-patient sex. *American Journal of Psychoanalysis*, 1977, *37*, 43–50.

Dickes, R., & Strauss, D. Countertransference as a factor in premature termination of apparently successful cases. *Journal of Sex and Marital Therapy*, 1979, *5*, 22–27.

Dunn, M. E., & Dickes, R. Erotic issues in cotherapy. *Journal of Sex and Marital Therapy*, 1977, *3*, 205–211.

Flescher, J. On different types of countertransference. *International Journal of Group Psychotherapy*, 1953, *3*, 357–372.

Freud, S. Further recommendations on the technique of psychoanalysis: Observations on transference love. In J. Strachey (Ed.), *Collected Papers* (Vol. 2). London: Hogarth Press, 1949. (Originally published, 1915.)

Golden, J. S., & Golden, M. A. You know who and what's her name: The woman's role in sex therapy. *Journal of Sex and Marital Therapy*, 1976, *2*, 6–16.

Harris, S., & Masling, J. Examiner sex, subject sex, and Rorschach productivity. *Journal of Consulting and Clinical Psychology*, 1970, *34*, 60–63.

Hartman, W. A., & Fithian, M. A. *Treatment of sexual dysfunction*. Long Beach, Calif.: Center for Marital and Sexual Studies, 1972.

Heiman, J. A psychophysiological exploration of sexual arousal patterns in females and males. *Psychophysiology*, 1977, *14*, 266–274.

Helms, J. S. Counselor reactions to female clients: Generalizing from analogue research to a counseling setting. *Journal of Counseling Psychology*, 1978, *25*, 193–199.

Hersen, M. Sexual aspects of TAT administration: A failure at replication with an inpatient population. *Journal of Consulting and Clinical Psychology*, 1971, *36*, 20–22.

Holroyd, J. C., & Brodsky, A. M. Psychologists' attitudes and practices regarding erotic and nonerotic physical contact with patients. *American Psychologist*, 1977, *32*, 843–849.

Howard, K. I., Orlinsky, D. E., & Hill, J. A. The therapist's feelings in the therapeutic process. *Journal of Clinical Psychology*, 1969, *25*, 83–93.

Kaplan, H. S. Training of sex therapists. In W. H. Masters, V. E. Johnson, & R. C. Kolodny (Eds.), *Ethical issues in sex therapy and research*. Boston: Little, Brown, 1977.

Kardener, S. H., Fuller, M., & Mensh, I. N. A survey of physicians' attitudes and practices regarding erotic and nonerotic contact with patients. *American Journal of Psychiatry*, 1973, *10*, 1077–1081.

Kirshner, L. A., Genack, A., & Hauser, S. T. Effects of gender on short-term psychotherapy. *Psychotherapy: Theory, Practice, and Research*, 1978, *15*, 158–167.

Levay, A. N., Kagle, A., & Weissberg, J. H. Issues of transference in sex therapy. *Journal of Sex and Marital Therapy*, 1979, *5*, 15–21.

Lief, H. I. Sexual survey #7: Current thinking on seductive patients. *Medical Aspects of Human Sexuality*, February 1978, pp. 46–47.

Lief, H. I., & Reed, D. M. *Sex knowledge and attitude test* (2nd ed.). Philadelphia: Center for the Study of Sex Education in Medicine, Department of Psychiatry, University of Pennsylvania School of Medicine, 1972.

LoPiccolo, J. The professionalization of sex therapy: Issues and problems. In J. LoPiccolo & L. LoPiccolo (Eds.), *Handbook of sex therapy*. New York: Plenum Press, 1978.

Maher, B. A. Stimulus sampling in clinical research: Representative design reviewed. *Journal of Consulting and Clinical Psychology*, 1978, *46*, 643–647.

Marmor, J. The seductive psychotherapist. *Psychiatry Digest*, 1970, *31*(10), 10–16.

Marmor, J. Some psychodynamic aspects of the seduction of patients in psychotherapy. *American Journal of Psychoanalysis*, 1976, *36*, 319–326.

Masling, J., & Harris, S. Sexual aspects of TAT administration. *Journal of Consulting and Clinical Psychology*, 1969, *33*, 166–169.

Masters, W. H., & Johnson, V. E. Principles of the new sex therapy. *American Journal of Psychiatry*, 1976, *133*, 548–554.

Masters, W. H., Johnson, V. E., & Kolodny, R. C. (Eds.). *Ethical issues in sex therapy and research*. Boston: Little, Brown, 1977.

McCartney, J. L. Overt transference. *Journal of Sex Research*, 1966, *2*, 227–237.

Miller, A. H. On being a divorced female therapist. *Voices*, 1976, *12*, 72–75.

Milner, T. S., & Moses, T. H. Effects of administrator's gender on sexual content and productivity in the Rorschach. *Journal of Clinical Psychology*, 1974, *30*, 159–161.

Morokoff, P. Determinants of female orgasm. In J. LoPiccolo & L. LoPiccolo (Eds.), *Handbook of sex therapy*. New York: Plenum Press, 1978.

Mosher, D. L. The development and multitrait-multimethod matrix analysis of three measures of three aspects of guilt. *Journal of Consulting Psychology*, 1966, *30*, 25–29.

Mosher, D. L. Measurement of guilt in females by self-report inventories. *Journal of Consulting and Clinical Psychology*, 1968, *32*, 690–695.

Mosher, D. L., & Abramson, P. R. Subjective sexual arousal to films of masturbation. *Journal of Consulting and Clinical Psychology*, 1977, *45*, 796–807.

Perry, J. A. Physicians' erotic and nonerotic physical involvement with patients. *American Journal of Psychiatry*, 1976, *33*, 838–840.

Pope, K. S., Levenson, H., & Schover, L. R. Sexual intimacy in psychology training: Results and implications of a national survey. *American Psychologist*, 1979, *34*, 682–689.

Quinn, R. E. Coping with Cupid: The formation, impact, and management of romantic relationships in organizations. *Administrative Science Quarterly*, 1977, *22*, 30–45.

Reich, A. On counter-transference. *International Journal of Psychoanalysis*, 1951, *32*, 25–31.

Russell, D., Peplau, A. L., & Ferguson, M. A. Developing a measure of loneliness. *Journal of Personality Assessment*, 1978, *42*, 290–294.

Safer, J. Effects of sex of patient and therapist on length of therapy. *International Mental Health Research Newsletter*, 1975, *17*, 12–13.

Saretsky, L. Sex related countertransference issues of a female therapist. *Clinical Psychologist*, 1977, *30*, 11–12.

Scheflen, A. E. Quasi-courtship behavior in psychotherapy. *Psychiatry*, 1965, *28*, 245–257.

Schofield, W. *Psychotherapy: The purchase of friendship*. Englewood Cliffs, N.J.: Prentice-Hall, 1964.

Schuldt, W. J. Psychotherapists' approach-avoidance responses and clients' expressions of dependency. *Journal of Counseling Psychology*, 1966, *13*, 178–184.

Searles, H. F. Oedipal love in the countertransference. *International Journal of Psychoanalysis*, 1959, *40*, 180–190.

Siskind, G. Sexual aspects of TAT administration: A note on "mature clinicians." *Journal of Consulting and Clinical Psychology*, 1973, *40*, 20–21.

Varble, D. L. Relationship between the therapist's approach-avoidance reactions to hostility and client behavior in therapy. *Journal of Consulting and Clinical Psychology*, 1968, *32*, 237–242.

Whalen, C. K., & Flowers, J. V. Effects of role and gender mix on verbal communication modes. *Journal of Counseling Psychology*, 1977, *24*, 281–287.

Wilder, D. H., Hoyt, A. E., Zettle, R. D., & Hauck, W. E. Client personality and preferred sex of counselor. *Psychotherapy: Theory, Research, and Practice*, 1978, *15*, 135–139.

Winder, C. L., Ahmad, F. Z., Bandura, A., & Rau, L. C. Dependency of patients, psychotherapists' responses, and aspects of psychotherapy. *Journal of Consulting Psychology*, 1962, *26*, 129–134.

Zentner, E. B., & Pouyat, S. B. The erotic factor as a complication in the dual-sex therapy team's effective functioning. *Journal of Sex and Marital Therapy*, 1978, *7*, 114–121.

Zilbergeld, B. *Male sexuality*. Boston: Little, Brown, 1978.

11 Erotic Contact as an Instance of Sex-Biased Therapy

JEAN C. HOLROYD

Sexual contact between therapist and patient is perhaps the quintessence of sex-biased therapeutic practice. It occurs more often for female than male patients (Holroyd & Brodsky, 1977), and there is no therapeutic rationale for the differential treatment. Rather, women patients have had sexual contact with their therapists in part because of social attitudes and expectancies about gender-related role behavior, and in part because of psychopathology in therapists. While there are many other examples of sex-biased therapy, erotic contact is a particularly salient one.

Evidence from several sources consistently suggests that erotic contact is prevalent for male therapists with female patients (Holroyd & Brodsky, 1977; Kardener, Fuller, & Mensh, 1973; Perry, 1976; Pope, Levenson, & Schover, 1979). Conservative estimates indicate that one in 20 male therapists and one in 200 female therapists have had intercourse with patients during treatment. A much higher percentage have had erotic contact with patients, and again it is primarily female patients who are involved. Therefore, this chapter is concerned with *differential* treatment of female patients and its implications for the therapeutic process.

Differential treatment of male and female patients does not in and of itself imply gender bias. A number of well-established treatments are associated more often with one gender or the other, yet are not considered sex-biased.

Grateful appreciation is extended to Barbara Malarek for her editorial advice; Ruth Buteyn for library research; and RuthAnn Parvin, J.D., for her critical comments.

These treatments may be referred to as *gender-specific* treatments and *gender-related* treatments. Gender-specific treatments are for problems associated only with one sex. An example of gender-specific treatment is guided instruction in masturbation for preorgasmic women. Men who have problems associated with orgasms may complain of premature ejaculation or a delayed orgasm, but it is the rare man who has had no orgasm. Gender-related treatments, on the other hand, may be appropriate for the opposite sex, but the treatments have been applied more often either to men and women because of differential needs in the population—for example, assertion training for women who have been socialized to a passive role, and sensitivity training for men who have been socialized for suppression of emotions. Men, of course, may also benefit from assertion training, and women may benefit from sensitivity training. Both gender-specific and gender-related treatments have some therapeutic rationale for differential treatment of the sexes. Neither are predicated upon sex-role stereotypes.

Therapy practices that differ for men and women, that have no therapeutic rationale, and that relate to sex-role stereotypes are *sex-biased* practices. Examples of sex-biased treatment are found in a publication of the American Psychological Association, which groups such practices into four categories: (1) fostering traditional sex roles; (2) bias in expectations and devaluation of women; (3) sexist use of psychoanalytic concepts; and (4) responding to women as sex objects, *including seduction of female clients* (American Psychological Association, 1975, italics added). The American Psychological Association's Task Force on the subject has published "Guidelines for Therapy with Women" in order to assure that female clients or patients are treated first of all as human beings, without reference to preconceptions about "how women are or ought to be" (American Psychological Association Task Force on Sex Bias and Sex-Role Stereotyping in Psychotherapeutic Practice, 1978). Preconceptions about gender role invariably lead to sex-biased treatment.

Therapists have violated the "Guidelines for Therapy with Women" whenever they have responded to women as sex objects or seduced female clients (American Psychological Association, 1975). In the words of one respondent to the Task Force survey, "This is the ultimate of sex-role bias: the rationalization of the therapist that his exploitation of the doctor-patient relationship for his gratification could be construed as therapeutic 'for a woman'" (American Psychological Association, 1975, p. 1173). The subject of this chapter, erotic contact, falls generally within the limits of responding to women as sex objects. Of course, erotic contact includes much more than seduction of clients. Erotic contact also includes instances in which the client actively seeks a sexual relationship with the therapist and instances in which both therapist and patient collude in acting out their mutual attraction. The sexual relationship may be unidirectional or mutual, and it includes intercourse as well as a great variety of other sexual activities. Problems of definition, which are significant and are to be addressed later, need not obfuscate the most salient issue: Sexual relationships imply sexist treatment of the female patient.

Historically, sexual *contact* between therapist and patient has not until recently been a subject of inquiry in the professional literature, whereas erotic *attraction* between therapist and patient has been recognized since the earliest days of psychotherapy. In the 18th century, the father of dynamic psychiatry, Franz Anton Mesmer, may have become romantically involved with a young patient who lived in his home (Ellenberger, 1970). A century later, both Freud and Breuer had to deal with blatant and ubiquitous sexuality in the treatment hour (Jones, 1963). Freud focused on the patient's erotic feelings toward the therapist, which he labeled *transference,* and the patient's romantic feelings for the therapist were viewed as an important element in therapy. As sexual feelings emerged, the psychoanalyst was able to trace a neurosis to its presumed sexual origins. Freud clearly proscribed the therapist's permitting any sexual contact with the patient, but mostly he and his followers wrote about analysis of the patient's transference *feelings,* rather than the therapist's activities.

Despite general awareness within the professions of heightened romantic and sexual feelings between therapist and patient, as reflected in extensive literature on the transference phenomenon, sexual *activity* with women patients has been largely ignored (Davidson, 1977; Taylor & Wagner, 1976). An objective observer might even say that the facts of sexual activities have been hidden. We now know that sexual relationships occur frequently, to the detriment of patients, and they probably did not begin yesterday. Sexual activities of therapists with patients have been obscured in primarily three related ways: by writers who focus on dynamic issues of transference and countertransference in therapy; by therapists who shift attention to motivations of the woman patient; and by lack of research on the occurrence and effects of such activities.

Psychoanalytic writers who have focused attention on transference and countertransference issues in psychotherapy have developed fascinating theories about intrapsychic phenomena and interpersonal dynamics. At the same time, they seem to have avoided writing about therapist-patient sexual behavior—about standards of care, ethics, and the self-serving aspects of such therapist behavior. Furthermore, the psychoanalytic language applied to sex in psychotherapy has effectively muted the impact of this emotion-charged topic: *Transference* and *countertransference* are intellectualized terms that provide distance from the anxiety-provoking sexual feelings they are intended to describe. The cloak of protective language has been removed recently, largely as a result of the research and publications of psychologists and psychiatrists who consider erotic contact in therapy an abuse of women patients (Butler & Zelen, 1977; Chesler, 1972; D'Addario, 1977; Kardener et al., 1973; Marmor, 1972; Taylor & Wagner, 1976).

Psychotherapists who attributed sexual attraction in therapy to the female patient's errant libido generally overlooked the therapist's sexual motivations. Only recently have the therapists themselves come under scrutiny. In 1972, Marmor drew attention to that other significant part of reality: "The psychoanalyst or psychotherapist is himself beset by deeply rooted, often unconscious, needs that tend to foster or stimulate impulses toward physical closeness towards his patient" (p. 3). However, even today the literature is scant regarding the sexual thoughts and feelings of therapists.

Davidson (1977) suggested that general sex bias within the profession has supported the sexual exploitation of female patients. She raised a number of questions along that line:

> Is this particular form of patient exploitation related to sexism within the profession? Does it represent the covert sanctioning by male practitioners of behavior which degrades all women? . . . Do male therapists, who themselves do not engage in sexual activity with patients, lend subtle support to the practice by protecting their errant male colleagues with silence or with treatment? Do they allow facile notions to go unchallenged which place the blame for seductive psychotherapy on the woman patient? Is therapist-patient sex a form of rape? Do women victims of seductive therapy need special forms of therapeutic intervention when they decide to reveal to a friend, family, or another therapist that prior therapy has included sex? (p. 48)

Davidson's treatise reflected a sense of urgency not apparent in earlier theoretical discourse about transference and countertransference. That sense of urgency has propelled the various mental health professions toward a more active involvement in the problems of patient-therapist sexuality.

DEFINING EROTIC CONTACT

Several questions require clarification before the issue of erotic contact as an instance of sex-biased therapy can be explored. What is erotic contact? How does it differ from nonerotic contact? What is sexual intimacy? What is the difference between a sex therapist and a therapist having sex? Can a therapist also function as a sexual surrogate in the treatment of sexual dysfunction? Can a male therapist help the sexually dysfunctional female patient by becoming her lover?

Definitions of *erotic contact* and *sexual intimacy* reflect an intrinsic difficulty in discriminating between a therapist's intention and the ultimate effect of his or her behavior on the patient. To give an example, a touch on the arm may be erotic or not, depending on a number of factors: the situation, the motivations of the therapist, how it is done, and the attitudes and feelings of the patient. The American Psychological Association, preferring not to get into "above or below the belt" issues, avoided the problem of definitions. Its ethics code simply reads, "Sexual intimacies with clients are unethical" (American Psychological Association, 1977, p. 23). The analogous section of the American Psychiatric Association's principles of ethics reads, "Sexual activity with a patient is unethical" (American Psychiatric Association, 1973, p. 1061). The California State Psychological Association (CSPA) Ethics Committee has defined *sexual intimacy* to include genital or erotic contact of any kind (Franklyn, 1978). However, in what could become an infinite regress, *erotic contact* is not defined. *Erotic contact* has been somewhat vaguely defined in survey research as "that which is primarily intended to arouse or satisfy sexual desire" (Holroyd & Brodsky, 1977; Kardener *et al.*, 1973; Perry, 1976). Other researchers have defined *sexual intimacy* in terms of "erotic contact . . . which leads to petting or intercourse" (Butler & Zelen, 1977). A succinct definition of *erotic contact* and/or *sexual intimacy* in objective behavioral terms appears to be impossible, because so much depends on context and circumstances (Keith-Spiegel, Note 1).

Some writers have tried to clarify issues by distinguishing between *erotic contact* and *nonerotic contact*. Distinguishing erotic contact from nonerotic physical contact is important because the latter is considered by many to be a legitimate part of therapy (Holroyd & Brodsky, 1977). Therapists use nonerotic contact for socially or emotionally immature patients (children, schizophrenics, patients with a history of maternal deprivation); for periods of acute distress (grief, trauma, or severe depression); for general support (reassurance, personal contact, expression of warmth); for greeting; and at termination of treatment. Female therapists and those who categorize themselves as humanistic rather than psychodynamic, behavior modification, rational-emotive, or eclectic therapists are particularly inclined to use nonerotic contact for both male and female patients (Holroyd & Brodsky, 1977).

The distinction therapists make between nonerotic contact and erotic contact may be artifical or spurious, for what is nonerotic to one person may be erotic to another. Several surveys which inquire about "nonerotic hugging, kissing, (and) affectionate touching of patients" (Holroyd & Brodsky, 1977; Kardener et al., 1973; Perry, 1976) rely on the therapist's personal definition of what is nonerotic. It is not at all clear what the patient may have felt. Some patients may sexualize virtually all contacts (Cavenar, Sullivan, & Maltbie, 1979). Also, some therapists may be unaware or disregardful of their own romantic or sexual arousal during such "nonerotic" contacts, and thereby may communicate to the patients a different message from what they consciously intended.

The boundary between "nonerotic hugging, kissing, and affectionate touching" and erotic contact has been found to be particularly unclear for those therapists who have had intercourse with patients (Holroyd & Brodsky, 1980). Those therapists advocated and used *nonerotic* contact more than did other therapists, but they used nonerotic contact exclusively with opposite-sex patients. In other words, male therapists who had intercourse with their patients were more inclined than other therapists were to use nonerotic contact in therapy, but only with their female patients, not their male patients. Why would male therapists touch *only* female patients? Are they being paternalistic? Do they regard female patients as more socially or emotionally immature than their male patients? Do they think females are more accepting of touch? Or does physical touching between men arouse some erotic thoughts and feelings that they and their male clients would find unacceptable? Whatever the reasons, a willingness to touch *only* opposite-sex patients signals the potential for sexual involvement with those patients.

WHAT ABOUT SEX THERAPISTS?

Just as nonerotic contact must be distinguished from erotic contact, so sex therapists must be clearly differentiated from therapists having sex. There has been some confusion about the therapist's proper role in the treatment of sexual disorders. Confusion regarding roles may have occurred because the Masters and Johnson *in vivo* sexual dysfunction treatments using surrogate partners developed at the same time as did contemporary humanistic psychotherapies that permit therapists to reveal themselves to their patients as human beings. Would it be possible for a therapist also to function as a sexual partner with patients? Only one psychotherapist has openly advocated the combination of roles (McCartney, 1966), and he was subsequently expelled from the American Psychiatric Association because of his own involvement with patients (Riskin, 1979).

The Masters and Johnson treatment program has always kept the roles of sex therapist and sexual surrogate distinct. While use of surrogates entails its own problems (Elias, 1977; Humo, 1975; Jacobs, Thompson, & Truxaw, 1975; Len & Fischer, 1978), it does not imply either self-serving behavior on the part of the psychotherapist or lack of therapeutic rationale for the treatment. The mental health profession has been fairly clear about the inadvisability of combining the roles of therapist and sexual surrogate. Maguire (Note 2) has elucidated the reasons for this separation:

1. The therapist must be able to deal with psychopathology as it emerges, and assumption of the lover role significantly reduces degrees of freedom for intervention.
2. It is impossible for a therapist-lover to compartmentalize sufficiently to prevent functions of one role from spilling over into the other role. The "therapist" part may become an objective spectator watching the patient during sexual sessions, or the "lover" part may react personally

with either strong positive or negative feelings, which in turn affect clinical judgment about the patient and treatment.

3. The therapist-patient relationship is educational rather than egalitarian, and the patient may attribute sexual success to the helpfulness of the all-knowing therapist, thereby not generalizing learning to other situations.

The very idea of a therapist presuming to "help" sexually needy clients by engaging with them in sex has been viewed as farcical by some.

(a) Ought one to charge the patient for the hour (50 minutes) of intercourse? That is, is this therapy for the patient and thus within the rubric of professional handling, or is this "pleasure" and thus a nonprofessional interaction? (b) Ought one to have intercourse with every patient who "needs" him whether or not they "turn him on"? (c) How does the heterosexual therapist deal with the homosexual patient, whose sexual desire for the same-sex therapist is just as strong as in a cross-sexed relationship, and for whom the reasons adduced in support of a therapist-patient sexual relationship are just as valid? Ought a therapist become bisexual for his patient's sake? (d) How would one deal with a young adolescent? Ought not the initiation of the youngster be through a skillful, practiced sexual partner? While the issue of sexual exploitation is universally condemned, what of the pubescent youngster who has had prior sexual experience? (e) Are patients who are seduced kept on indefinitely? This would mean that within a year or two, thirty, forty, or fifty patients are being serviced by one therapist. (Seagull, Note 3)

The ridicule directed at therapists who might seek to justify their behavior reflects almost unanimous condemnation by psychotherapists who have taken rather strong stands on the impropriety of patient-therapist sex (Holroyd & Brodsky, 1977). Yet the question of whether it need be forbidden is sometimes raised by other sources. Recently a law professor (Riskin, 1979) advocated prospective research on the effects of therapists' having sexual relations with their patients. He recommended stringent experimental controls, including all the usual constraints of project review by a human subjects protection committee and informed consent given by patients. Therapists would have sexual intercourse with patients who would be informed in advance that sexual intercourse might be a part of the treatment. Riskin's proposal would circumvent some of the sources of bias found in post hoc research, but it fails to respect the collective opinions of mental health professionals whose clinical experience suggests that sexual contact would be harmful. Some scientific experiments cannot be undertaken, because the potential for harm is too significant. At any rate, the fact that such a proposal could be published in a respected law journal indicates that the issue of role confusion has not been fully resolved.

WHY DO THERAPISTS HAVE SEX WITH PATIENTS?

From the foregoing analysis, we see that the roles of psychotherapist and sexual partner cannot coexist. Furthermore, most therapists interpret sexual contact as an abrogation of the therapist's responsibility (Holroyd & Brodsky, 1977). Why, then, do some mental health professionals have sexual relations with their patients? And why does that occur more often for female than for male patients?

The reasons for a transgression of therapy boundaries are emotional and social or political. The emotional and social/political causes can be analyzed separately, though they interact in complex ways for any therapist-patient pair. Emotionally, the patient and therapist often experience the psychotherapy process as a loving experience with sexual overtones. Sociopolitically, the patriarchal structure of our society supports men in ascendent positions choosing women of lower status as sexual partners. The interaction of love and patriarchal power in a therapy situation appears to create prerequisite conditions for sexual congress to occur in therapy. However, other factors specific to the individual therapists involved may act as catalysts.

Passionate love and erotic attraction in psychotherapy have at least three sources: the ongoing intense and intimate interpersonal relationship between therapist and client; the perception of other emotions aroused in therapy (e.g., anxiety) as sexual arousal; and unresolved or conflicted sexualized relationships with people in the past (transference and countertransference). With respect to the first source, when two people spend a considerable amount of time communicating about deeply intimate feelings, thoughts, and experiences, they will inevitably grow fond of each other. The intimacy may be pleasurable on both sides, and seductive to the point of becoming an end in itself for some therapists and patients (Schofield, 1964). The intensity of the feelings involved may then shade over into pleasurable erotic experience. Hence, the first source of sexual attraction in an opposite-sex therapist-client dyad is the contemporaneous relationship between a man and a woman who are attractive in their own rights.

The second source of sexual attraction derives from a variety of emotions that may be misperceived and mislabeled by the patient as sexuality. In a somewhat indirect or convoluted fashion, less pleasurable but intense emotions such as anxiety or anger may increase the general arousal state and be experienced as erotic impulses (Gross, Note 4). For example, not uncommonly, people may masturbate to reduce a general state of arousal that is created by anxiety rather than by erotic stimulation. At a greater extreme, men who rape are seen as motivated by anger more than by sexuality (Walker & Brodsky, 1976). One of the tasks of psychotherapy is to help patients identify and label emotions they are experiencing. Failure to address the question of the genesis of the patient's sexual impulses may be a collusion with the patient's psychopathology.

Finally, a female patient may become infatuated and sexually attracted to her male therapist because he represents a meaningful parent figure with whom sex could not be consummated. Defined as *transference*, this source of sexual attraction is most frequently referred to in the early literature. Emphasis on transference feelings has been at the cost of attention to the nonneurotic sources of sexual attraction that are also important contributors to the therapist-patient sexual dilemma.

More is understood about the dynamics of erotic attraction in therapy than about why it is primarily women who are involved sexually with their therapists. It cannot be because there are more male therapists than female therapists, because the *rate* is 10 times higher for male therapists. And common sense suggests that male patients are just as inclined toward passionate love and erotic attraction as female patients. Male-female pairs face the same conditions for experiencing intense emotions, intimacy, and transference in therapy, regardless of the gender identity of the therapist and the patient. But the normative conditions for sexual liaison in our patriarchal society are reproduced only when the therapist is male and the patient is female.

The differential rate of sexual involvement with male and female patients probably relates more to our patriarchal social structure and power distribution than to differences in erotic attraction. The status difference between males and females in society at large is reproduced in the male therapist–female client relationship. Not only does the (male) therapist have more power by virtue of education, training, social status, and being defined as the "healthy" member of the dyad, but he also has power because of his detailed knowledge of the patient. In a study of therapists who had erotic contact with patients, 70% of the therapists said they had a more dominant and/or paternalistic role than that of their client/lover, and 15% described themselves as in fact domineering and controlling (Butler & Zelen, 1977). Therefore it is the natural order of things in our society for a male therapist to pair off with a woman who is his inferior in terms of social adjustment.

In contrast to the synergistic relationship between sexual attraction and power distribution that exists for male therapists and female clients, female therapist–male client pairs are discordant with societal expectations for power distribution. The female therapist holds the power associated with educational and vocational status, as well as her intimate knowledge of the patient's life history. But she would be disinclined to pair up with one who is her social inferior. Therefore, feelings of intensity and intimacy may be modulated so that erotic feelings are diverted or suppressed. Whereas additional power accruing to a therapist by virtue of the professional role complements the sexuality of a male therapist, it interferes with sexual experiencing and display for female therapists. The socially nonnormative power distribution between female therapist and male patient may partially explain why there are many fewer sexual liaisons between such pairs.

Obviously, not all male therapists who are attracted to their female patients and are in the ascendant position engage in intercourse or other sexual practices with them. What accounts for those who do? Though information about the idiosyncratic characteristics of involved therapists is sketchy, data from different sources using different research methods present a consistent picture. Generally, the therapists are significantly older than the patients involved—usually averaging 16 years more senior (D'Addario, 1977; Taylor & Wagner, Note 5; California State Psychological Association Task Force on Sexual Intimacy between Patient and Therapist, Note 6). Most commonly, therapists in their 40s or 50s have sex with women in their 20s or 30s. (Perhaps "ageism" could be added to the charge of sexism!) Butler and Zelen (1977) interviewed 20 therapists who admitted to sexual intimacy (petting or intercourse) with patients. Those therapists reported that they felt vulnerable, needy, or lonely at the time the sexual relationship began. Usually the therapist brought up the issue of sexual feelings experienced for the patient, and intercourse ensued. In view of the fact that some people have assumed that a sexually involved therapist was simply carrying an intimate therapy relationship to the degree of ultimate intimacy (Holroyd & Brodsky, 1977), it is interesting that most therapists in the Butler and Zelen research described themselves as frightened of intimacy. D'Addario (1977), who interviewed involved female patients, found that the therapists were all facing a personal or professional crisis (e.g., loss of job or demotion, fear of aging, threat of surgery, unsatisfactory marriage, or alienation from their children). The involved patients also reported that there had been a significant amount of sexual dysfunction among the therapists: impotence, priapism, and premature ejaculation. In the opinion of a psychologist with extensive experience on the American Psychological Association's Committee on Scientific and Professional Ethics and Conduct, "there is nothing in the contemporary image of the seductive psychologist that anyone would want to stand in line for" (Keith-Spiegel, Note 1, p. 3).

There is also evidence that the sexualizing therapists have acted impulsively and irrationally. The CSPA Task Force on Sexual Intimacy between Patient and Therapist (Note 6), relying on information provided by therapists of patients who had sex with *previous* therapists, found that the therapist was usually the one to initiate sexual activity, and that sexual contact most often occurred in the therapist's office. Sexual contact began in the first 3 months of therapy for one-third of the cases, and in the first 6 months for half of the cases. Therapy payments continued after sex began for most of the cases. Hence the patients were paying psychotherapists for sex that their therapists initiated!

The occurrence of sexual relationships within psychotherapy appears to involve the following causal factors: erotic attraction between a male therapist and female client who are recapitulating the socially normative power relationship (dominance-submission); and a therapist characterized as vulnerable, needy, in crisis, and possibly socially or sexually inadequate. Mere existence of erotic attraction and the socially sanctioned male-female power structure are probably insufficient to account for erotic contact, as they inhere in most occurrences of male therapist–female patient dyads. To those conditioning factors must be added the apparently maladjusted characters of the therapists. Also, mere existence of erotic attraction and maladjustment of the therapist do not account for patient-therapist sexual intercourse, as these two conditions presumably would occur for many women therapists. Apparently female therapists who are vulnerable and needy do not have sex with clients. Sexual contact occurs when a therapist is vulnerable, *and* erotic attraction exists, *and* the socially normative pattern of dominance-submission is replicated in the therapist-patient pair. Sexual contact is sex-biased therapy because it is a product of sex-role stereotypes.

WHAT ARE THE EFFECTS ON THE PATIENTS?

Given that women are the recipients of sex-biased treatment in the form of erotic contact, the next significant question is "What are the effects?" Most mental health professionals regard erotic contact and intercourse to be very harmful to patients. A total of 96% of psychologists and 97% of psychiatrists (Holroyd & Brodsky, 1977; Kardener et al., 1973) answered "Rarely" or "Never" when asked "Do you believe erotic contact with patients may be beneficial to their treatment?" Comments on their questionnaires indicated that they thought erotic contact was exploitative, unethical, unprofessional, and antitherapeutic.

Prior to the past few years, there has been little other than anecdotal information or case studies on which to base opinion about effects. Among published case studies, approximately half found negative effects for either the patient or therapist or both; one-third found mixed positive-negative effects; and approximately one-fifth of the cases were characterized as having positive effects (Taylor & Wagner, 1976). Recently more direct data from larger samples have begun to appear: interviews with involved therapists (Butler & Zelen, 1977); and questionnaires from therapists of patients who had sexual contact with previous therapists (CSPA Task Force, Note 6). Data on the effects of sexual contact would be expected to differ for research samples with such disparate points of view.

Therapists who saw such clients later (CSPA Task Force, Note 6) reported the effects mainly to be negative, ranging from impaired social and sexual adjustment to hospitalization and suicide. Patients were reported to feel angry, devastated, betrayed, ripped off, victimized, abandoned, anxious and fearful. Their personality organization was affected negatively in general, and they no longer trusted therapists or men. Very frequently the therapy ended abruptly, or if it continued it was affected adversely. Many patients had difficulty resuming therapy with a new therapist. (Nevertheless, a few patients reported positive outcomes such as improved self-concept or growth, and some reported "no effects.")

Therapists who themselves were involved sexually (Butler & Zelen, 1977) reported growthful relationships as well as conflict experienced by both parties. These involved therapists noted the "anger, hurt and damage experienced by the patient when the relationship was over," yet probably underestimated the psychological damage accruing to their patients.[1] Data collected by the CSPA Task Force (Note 6) suggest that therapy ended within the first month after sex began for over one-third of the cases and within 3 months for 60% of the cases surveyed. Thus therapy ended precipitously for most cases. In Keith-Spiegel's observations (Note 1) of cases reviewed by the American Psychological Association Ethics Committee, "To most of these clients, sex includes 'love' or something like it, and the clients' views of the relationship vastly expanded, to encompass extratherapeutic situations and longer-term commitment— often with a perhaps not fully conscious goal of totality and exclusivity. Or, put another way, clients do not use their therapists as 'one-night stands'" (p. 7). The fact that *neither* the sexual relationship nor the therapy relationship is likely to continue speaks to the aversive consequences of therapist-patient sex. The preponderance of evidence is that sexual contact yields a very high rate of negative fallout for patients.

Rarely is sexual contact between men and women viewed as having such dire consequences as it seems to have in the case of sexual contact between male therapists and female patients. Why should sex between two consenting adults, two people who probably are attracted to each other, be so disorganizing? Some writers have theorized that it is harmful because it bears many similarities to incest and to rape. Therapists function as parents because of their power and their position as guides or counselors. In order for parents (therapists) to carry out guidance and protective functions, they assume the right to intimacy and power while eschewing opportunities for sexuality. Incest is harmful not so much because sex occurs between relatives, but because the protective role of parent is abrogated. "The child involved in incest is denied this vitally needed person (parent), and this denial contributes to the emotional trauma of incest. In an exactly parallel way the physician, as a source of healing, support, and succor, becomes lost to his patient when he changes roles and becomes lover" (Kardener, 1974, p. 1135). Siassi and Thomas (1973) note that it is the physician's responsibility to assure that sexual contact does not occur even if the patient is an aggressive initiator, just as it is the parent's responsibility to avoid incest with a seductive child.

The similarity of therapist-patient sex to rape is largely due to the manner in which the female (victim) has been regarded and treated.[2] As a group and as individuals, female victims of rape and of therapist seduction have been punished: Their credibility is doubted, their sexual history is investigated, and their motivations are questioned. The subsequent investigation of rape by the judicial system and of therapist sex by the professional ethics system has been very damaging to complainants. In the recent past, the judicial system has modified laws and procedures to protect rape victims. Counselors have been introduced into police departments; advocates have accompanied victims as they proceed through the maze of the judicial system; and rape crisis centers have been established. Women whose therapists have abused them sexually should have similar people to whom they can turn if they need help.

The dramatic analogies of rape and incest must not detract from the most obvious and immediate effects: In almost two-thirds of the cases, the therapist and patient who became sexually involved quickly said goodbye. As mentioned earlier, the therapeutic relationship ended within a month for 35% of the cases and in another two months for 24% of the cases. Two-thirds of patients who had sex with their therapists took the initiative in ending therapy, and another one-sixth ended it by mutual agreement with the therapist (CSPA Task Force, Note 6). This reflects the loss of power a therapist has for effective intervention with a patient by virtue of changing his position as "healer" to "lover" (Gross, Note 4). The therapist loses credibility *qua* therapist. Of course, the extreme case of a therapist's losing therapeutic effectiveness is when the patient quits therapy.

Even if therapy continues, the work of therapy comes to a grinding halt when sex is introduced, according to psychoanalytic writers. Acting out the sexual impulses prevents the discovery of whatever unconscious conflicts lead to sexual feelings. Strong feelings of anger or sexuality directed toward the therapist must be blocked from direct expression, so that free associations can lead to memories of early childhood experiences that cause the contemporary feelings. To participate in acting out sexual feelings is an abrogation of the analytic task, and the female patient is no longer receiving therapy (Moldawsky, Note 7). Furthermore, the dominant male–subservient female relationship found for most therapist-client lovers recapitulates stereotypic authority-dependency relationships in our society. Such reinforcement of a patriarchal model is contrary to development of autonomy in the female client (American Psychological Association Task Force, 1978).

WHAT SHOULD BE DONE TO PREVENT OCCURRENCE?

The highly negative character of what happens to patients—from personality disorganization to hospitalization and suicide—plus the high rate at which therapy is prematurely terminated suggest that the mental health profession must find ways to prevent occurrences of therapist-patient sex. It has not proven sufficient to prohibit sexual activity in ethics codes, and severe punishments have not served as much of a deterrent (Riskin, 1979). Educating and training therapists to function in spite of their own erotic excitement and the attractiveness of their patients is essential. The profession's educational system is responsible for assuring that therapists can work effectively with patients without indulging wishes for sexual contact. The American Psychological Association has recommended workshops, conferences, and the development of training material to counteract sexism in the mental health professions (American Psychological Association, 1975). Professional training programs might help by requiring that *all* mental health courses include a discussion of sexuality and sex roles as they may apply to the subject matter at hand.

Teaching therapists to handle patients' erotic material therapeutically while at the same time recognizing and using their own sexual feelings should be no more difficult than teaching other essential therapy skills should be. Therapists are taught how to respond to suicidality and paranoia, as well as to many other kinds of powerful therapist-patient emotional interactions. They can just as easily be trained to respond effectively and therapeutically to sexual vibrancy between themselves and patients. Forer (1969) has stated, "Both therapist and client need to learn tolerance for their own (erotic) excitement and realize that fantasies need not lead to action" (p. 231). Gross extended that statement by underlining the therapist's responsibility for learning to confront the sexual feelings and emotions flowing between patient and therapist directly.

> It is absolutely necessary for therapists to not only "tolerate their own excitement," but they should learn to experience the whole range of their affective intensities, without having to do anything. This is particularly true of the loving intensities which are most frequently transformed into sexual arousal, and which naturally occur when personal growth is a product of psychotherapy . . . irresponsibility has not only to do with sexual acting-out, but with therapists avoiding the work of the emotionality of the person. . . . I have come to the conclusion [that] the major source of damage that ensues, when it ensues, is not from the sex act, but from the confusion, blindness, guilt, and avoidance of the therapist. Both acting-out and/or the avoidance of emotional issues that arise between therapist and person have the same technical result. The work of therapy comes to an end. (Gross, Note 4)

WHAT SHOULD BE DONE ONCE SEX OCCURS?

The sanctions against erotic contact are professional (i.e., involving standards of care), ethical, and legal. It follows that the problem of patient-therapist sex can therefore be addressed by professional, ethical, and legal means. Since the three domains have very different implications, they are considered separately here.

Professional Remedies

Professional standards of care are very explicit. The article "Guidelines for Therapy with Women," developed by the American Psychological Association Task Force on Sex Bias and Sex-Role Stereotyping in Psychotherapeutic Practice (1978), specifies. "The psychologist should not have sexual relations with a woman client nor treat her as a sex object." Siassi and Thomas (1973) stress that the prohibition against sexual contact is a pragmatic concern rather than simply a moral issue. The therapist's objectivity is at stake; each patient should be offered a relationship with an empathic, dispassionate therapist in a safe, protected situation. To fail in meeting this standard is to provide inadequate treatment for women.

Taylor and Wagner (1976) recommend that a therapist and a patient who experience erotic attraction discuss the situation, clarify their fantasies and expectations, and decide openly either to rule out sex or to terminate therapy. They state that it would be optimal to recognize the feelings of both parties and integrate them into the therapy, with the therapist both providing controls and reassuring the patient. For example, the therapist might say, "There is no way that we are going to have a sexual relationship—for me that is just not ethically acceptable—but I want you to know I find you very attractive" (Taylor & Wagner, 1976, p. 599). If therapy must be terminated, Taylor and Wagner suggest that the patient be referred to another therapist, with the expectation that the sexualized involvement will be discussed with the new therapist. Keith-Spiegel (Note 1) has suggested that both involved parties go to a new therapist together in order to evaluate the psychodynamics of their mutual attraction. Most psychotherapists who have engaged in intercourse or petting with patients favor referral of the patient elsewhere for treatment, but few of them actually make referrals. Those therapists who did terminate therapy with their patients were less conflicted about the patients' welfare than were those who attempted to continue therapy, whether sexual contacts continued or had ended (Butler & Zelen, 1977).

Probably the best course of action for a therapist to take when he or she has difficulty dealing with sexual attraction for a patient, or when a patient's sexual desire becomes difficult to manage, is to seek consultation from another therapist. Simply seeking consultation can provide a type of external control as a temporary expedient. (Of course the consultation relationship *also* should be free of dual-role constraints; i.e., it should not be with a friend or relative.) A consultant can be of great assistance in helping the therapist deal with sexuality constructively, in which case probably very few patients would have to be referred elsewhere for treatment.

Ethical Remedies

The ethics of a profession go beyond standards of care to incorporate the moral values of its members and of society at large. Ethics codes are derived from actual events that members of a profession do not wish to recur. Sexual contact with patients is specifically proscribed by the ethics codes of both the American Psychiatric Association (1973) and the American Psychological Association (1977, 1979). The American Psychological Association's code (1979) states:

> Psychologists are continually cognizant of their own needs and of their inherently powerful position vis-a-vis clients, in order to avoid exploiting their trust and dependency. Psychologists make every effort to avoid dual relationships with clients and/or relationships which might impair their professional judgment or increase the risk of client exploitation. Examples of such dual relationships include treating employees, students, supervisees, close friends, or relatives. Sexual intimacies with clients are unethical. (Principle 6a)[3]

Furthermore, Hare-Mustin (1974) has noted that sexual intercourse with clients is precluded by several other principles of the *Ethical Standards of Psychologists*. In the current revision (American Psychological Association, 1979) those principles are as follows:

> As practitioners, psychologists know that they bear a heavy social responsibility because their recommendations and professional actions may alter the lives of others. They are alert to personal . . . pressures that might lead to misuse of their influence. (Principle 1e)
>
> Psychologists recognize the boundaries of their competence and the limitations of their techniques and only provide services and use techniques that meet recognized standards for which they are qualified by training and experience. In those areas in which recognized standards do not yet exist, psychologists take whatever precautions are necessary to protect the welfare of their clients. (Principle 2)
>
> Psychologists recognize that personal problems and conflicts may interfere with professional effectiveness. Accordingly, they refrain from undertaking activities in which a personal problem may lead to inadequate professional services or harm to a client. If psychologists become aware of such a personal problem, they seek competent professional assistance to determine whether they should suspend, terminate, or limit the scope of their professional and/or scientific activities. (Principle 2e)
>
> Regarding their own personal behavior, psychologists are sensitive to the prevailing community standards and of the possible impact upon the quality of professional services provided by their conformity to or deviation from these standards. (Principle 3)
>
> Psychologists fully inform consumers as to the purpose and nature of an evaluative, treatment, educational, or training procedure. . . . (Principle 6)

If a member of a professional organization transgresses a principle of an ethics code, charges of unethical behavior may be brought against that person. The mental health professions are sufficiently concerned about controlling the behavior of members in these areas of agreement that they have established structures within their organizations for reviewing members against whom accusations are made. Local, state, and national ethics committees hear evidence and sit in judgment on their peers. A negative evaluation by an ethics committee may result in loss of membership in the professional organization.

Women rarely bring charges against a therapist to an ethics committee, for a number of reasons (CSPA Task Force, Note 6; Grunebaum, Nadelson, & Macht, Note 8; Keith-Spiegel, Note 1). First of all, some women may not know that sexual contact is unethical until they are so informed by another therapist. Secondly, a therapist who learns of possible sexual involvement by a mental health professional is forbidden by ethics and laws governing confidentiality from simply telephoning the ethics committee or the state licensing board. The patient must give permission for the therapist who learns of such unethical or illegal behavior to contact the previous therapist, or to notify an ethics committee or a licensing board. A patient may decide not to grant such permission because she fears the consequences of disclosure. She may prefer that the sexual affair remain unknown to her spouse or lover. She may feel protective toward the earlier therapist, not wanting to jeopardize his career even if she is deeply disturbed by what transpired. Patient refusal to have the information about sexual contact disclosed frequently impedes investigation. Finally, therapists frequently are reluctant to become involved because they do not know how to assess the patient's credibility,[4] how to prove the patient's charges, and how to report the event to the responsible authority. In the past, these factors have resulted in underreporting, with very few complaints filed.[5]

Now that both patients and therapists are becoming educated to the issues and more charges are likely to be filed, the therapist who learns of sexual involvement by another therapist must carefully consider the patient's welfare. A hearing before the Ethics Committee may be emotionally draining, particularly for a person whose psychological resources were taxed to the point of requiring therapy in the first place. There may be a problem of proving the patient's allegations if the events occurred a long time ago or in a distant state, or if it comes down to "his word against hers." Psychotherapy is carried out under the most private circumstances, behind closed doors and sound-deadened walls. Many therapists do not even have a secretary in an outer office. An ethics charge usually is not sustained "*if* there are no witnesses, and *if* there is only one complainant within a reasonable time frame,[6] and *if* the psychologist chooses to categorically deny the charges and makes no slip-ups" (Keith-Spiegel, Note 1). For all these reasons, some therapists who are concerned primarily about the welfare of their patients may judge that it would not be in the best interests of the patients to report the event.

If a patient does notify an ethics committee about sexual exploitation by her therapist, she may learn how handicapped those committees are in investigating cases and imposing restrictions or punishments on offenders (Grunebaum et al., Note 8). Ethics committees are hampered by small budgets, do not have a legal mandate for investigating the circumstances which led to the patient's accusation, and may in fact be sued by the therapist they are attempting to investigate. The only "punishment" that can be meted out is cancelation of membership in the professional organization. Cancelation of membership is not a very frightening prospect to many therapists. There are virtually no financial consequences in loss of membership, and the social consequences are limited, inasmuch as many mental health professionals do not even bother to join a professional organization to begin with.

Legal Remedies

Perhaps because of the relative impotence of ethics procedures, more and more complainants are seeking redress through legal channels. Few states have laws specifically prohibiting psychotherapists from having sex with patients.[7] However, Stone (1976) and Riskin (1979) list three other routes for legal redress: criminal prosecution (e.g., for rape), civil actions (e.g., malpractice suits), and revocation of license to practice by the state licensing board.

Legal redress by *criminal prosecution* is the least likely to be undertaken. Masters and Johnson, pioneers in the sex therapy field, have taken the position that

> the therapist should initially be sued for rape rather than for malpractice, i.e., the legal process should be criminal rather than civil. Few psychotherapists would be willing to appear in court on behalf of a colleague and testify that the sexually dysfunctional patient's facility for decision making could be considered normally objective when he or she accepts sexual submission after developing extreme emotional dependence on the therapist. (Quoted in Stone, 1976, p. 1138)

In reviewing the legal literature, Stone (1976) and Riskin (1979) found that rape charges are generally filed only for cases involving physical coercion (e.g., having intercourse after administering drugs or electroshock therapy). Psychological coercion, in which therapists exploited the patient's transference or "prescribed" sexual intercourse as therapy, is not sufficient for a rape charge. For psychological coercion to be proven, it would have to be demonstrated that the adult patient was incompetent to consent to intercourse; the victim would have to be placed in an unfavorable light to prove there was no consent.

Civil suits claiming malpractice or professional negligence are more frequent than are criminal suits, though the number of cases tried for malpractice is estimated to be very low compared to the incidence of sexual contact (Hogan, 1979). Malpractice suits against psychotherapists are rare to begin with, and among those cases charges of sexual contact are infrequent. Of 300 reported cases of malpractice suits against psychotherapists, only 12 (4%) involved sexual contact (Hogan, 1979). Malpractice suits in surgery or general medicine are much more readily undertaken.

One reason why few malpractice suits are filed is uncertainty about exactly what constitutes malpractice when there has been sexual contact. The grounds for determining malpractice vary from state to state. "Some courts have stated that a practice is negligent unless 'supported by a respectable minority.' Others have held that 'any variance from the accepted mode of treatment renders the physician liable,' and still others allow no more than 'what a reasonable and prudent doctor would have done under the circumstances'" (Riskin, 1979). How those general malpractice laws may be interpreted in the case of sexuality specifically depends on the results of cases that are appealed to a higher court. As mentioned above, only 12 cases dealing with sexual relationships were located by Hogan (1979) in his review of appealed malpractice suits in the United States. Because of the paucity of these cases, strong legal precedent that would establish adequate cause for malpractice when therapists have been sexually involved with clients is still lacking. With interstate variability in laws and the absence of sufficient numbers of appealed cases to establish "adequate cause," there appear to be no clearcut criteria for judging whether a malpractice suit should be brought.

Psychotherapist sexual behavior that is considered unprofessional, unethical, or even reprehensible by the profession may not in fact be illegal, depending on state laws and their interpretation. According to Stone (1976), a therapist may be judged to be less culpable if the affair is separate from the treatment; if the state has a "heart balm" statute that bars civil liability for such things as seduction or alienation of affections; if the patient freely has consented to the affair and knew it was not therapy; or if the therapist informed the patient before therapy began that sexual activity would be part of the therapy. Therapists may be judged to be more culpable if sexual activity is prescribed as treatment or if legal precedent establishes the therapist-patient relationship as analogous to the guardian-ward relationship. The number of civil suits may increase as states pass laws that specifically prohibit sex between therapist and client, rather than relying on loosely interpreted malpractice laws.

Although the number of cases presently brought to civil trial may be few, the number is increasing exponentially, and the attendant publicity may have deterrent effects. The media have publicized large settlements granted in successful suits, and has also increased public awareness of the problem with educational programs on public issues. In the past, insurance companies have been in the position of having to pay hundreds of thousands of dollars to complainants. Now many professional insurance carriers specifically exclude liability for sexual activity. Thus, while insurance attorneys may defend subscribers so charged, the insurance company will not accept liability for damages if the charges are proven. Therapists charged with sexual activity must pay damages to the plaintiffs out of their own pockets.

The third type of legal action is to bring a *complaint to the state licensing board*, which has the power to revoke licenses. Without licenses to practice, therapists may not provide services for fees in the private sector (though they could still work for some agencies or as a teacher or a researcher). In some cases, the licensing board may choose to revoke a license temporarily or place limits on the conditions of practice (e.g., requiring practice under supervision), rather than revoke the license permanently and irrevocably.

Bringing a case to the state licensing board has its advantages and disadvantages. Licensing boards are authorized to carry out investigations, including questioning other clients and sending an undercover investigator to the therapist as a client. The evidence uncovered at state expense as a result of licensing board investigation activity could be useful in a later civil suit. Many state licensing boards are often underbudgeted for carrying out investigations, however. Also, licensing boards are organized quite differently in each state, so this approach has the disadvantages of civil procedures that are variable from state to state, with none of the advantages of financial compensation for damages sustained. It is not uncommon for a client to seek both a malpractice decision in a civil court and a licensing board's revocation of the license to practice.

With all the shortcomings of licensing boards and civil law, there nevertheless is more redress for grievance against licensed mental health professionals than there is against those who offer "therapy" but who do not come under the auspices of state licensing laws. Many untrained and poorly educated people attempt to do psychotherapy under the guise of other pseudoscientific titles—"personal counselor," "hypnotist," and so on. In many states these titles may be listed in the yellow pages, with no warning to consumers that the title does not require special training in psychotherapy. Such quasitherapists may have sexual relations with clients with impunity. The professional negligence or malpractice laws that apply to psychologists, psychiatrists, and social workers do not apply to people functioning as therapists outside the mainstream mental health professions.

Summary

Therapists who are asked for advice regarding charges against other therapists accused of sexual contact with patients should be aware of the consequences that might ensue.

1. Ethics committees of professional organizations can hold hearings, censure the professionals in question, and cancel their membership in the organization. However, they often are powerless to pursue extensive investigations, and generally they rely upon statements given by the complainants and the accused professionals. Revocation of membership in the organization is not a formidable punishment. After a client goes through all the process of an ethics committee hearing and the charges are proven, an offender can nevertheless continue to practice.

2. Civil laws governing malpractice and professional negligence differ from state to state. In general, they are not as restrictive as the ethics codes of professional societies. For example, in some states sexual contact might be considered "between consenting adults." However, a successful malpractice suit can result in considerable financial compensation being awarded to the patient, particularly if it is determined that the patient was harmed by the practice. Some states are now passing laws that specifically prohibit sex between therapist and patient.

3. State licensing boards may have police powers to investigate a case, including sending in an undercover agent posing as an unsuspecting patient. They can hold judicial (administrative) hearings and impose penalties up to and including complete revocation of the license to practice. However, frequently they are significantly handicapped by limited budgets and resources.

In considering courses of action to be taken, the welfare of clients is to be served above all. Before *any* action is taken, the clients must be willing to disclose not only names but circumstances and intimate details. The clients' psychiatric history may become an issue, as well as their sexual history and credibility. The stress to be expected in a full-scale investigation and subsequent hearings may be judged to be excessive for the benefits that would accrue to a particular patient. Frustration and anger aroused by this type of sex-biased treatment can be directed at promoting changes in professional practice, and can become a constructive force in the training of the members of the profession and the education of the public.

CONCLUSION

Most instances of sex between male therapists and female patients occur because of sexist values that make it "natural" for men to pair with women in less powerful, or even weak, positions. The emotional problems of therapists are also contributory, but probably are not sufficient in and of themselves. Even the most healthy therapists may experience loneliness and unmet sexual needs at some time in their long careers, but usually they do not have sex with patients. *Patient-therapist sex occurs when therapists who have mental and emotional problems also have sexist values.*

The problem of sex between therapists and patients, recognized only yesterday, will not disappear tomorrow. For one thing, the sexism that supports the practice is not likely to go away. The incidence of sexual exploitation may be lowered by educational programs for professionals and the public and by increased support for women who protest, but the most effective approach may be protective legislation that directly prohibits sex between mental health professionals and their clients.

NOTES

[1]Though Butler and Zelen (1977) and Keith-Spiegel (Note 1) imply that the therapists ended the relationship and the patient was hurt by that action, data from the CSPA Task Force survey (Note 6) suggest the therapist independently initiated the ending in only 15% of the cases, and mutually with the client in another 18% of the cases. For the majority of cases, the client initiated ending the sexual relationship. Taylor and Wagner (1976) observed that patients sometimes tried to avoid hurting their therapists' egos by either declining or removing themselves from the situation, thereby playing the role of "good patient."

[2]However, instances of rape in the office are also known to occur (CSPA Task Force, Note 6).

[3]The issue of who initiates the sexual activity is held to be irrelevant by the American Psychological Association Committee on Scientific and Professional Ethics (Keith-Spiegel, Note 1).

[4]The issue of false charges is similar to the issue of false rape charges. However, bringing ethics or legal charges results in months or years of expensive litigation, which most people do not undertake lightly. Falsely charging a "respected member of one of the learned professions" with sexual misconduct is perhaps more stupid or daring than is falsely charging a male acquaintance with rape. The male professional is surrounded by a phalanx of other professionals, his professional organization(s), and malpractice insurance company attorneys who specialize in defense against such charges. Any therapist who is responsibly managing a difficult erotic component in therapy and fears false charges can be somewhat self-protective by reviewing therapy transactions with a consultant and keeping careful records.

[5]Again, a comparison to rape cases may be interesting. In Denver, only 4% of reported rape cases were brought to trial in 1971–1972 (Walker & Brodsky, 1976).

[6]*Author's Note:* Grunebaum et al. (Note 9) have recommended that ethics committees maintain records over a period of years, so that a later complaint about the same therapist might receive substantiation by the existence of an earlier complaint.

[7]However, a law enacted in 1980 in California (*West's Annotated California Codes*, 1964) reads: 'The commission of any act of sexual abuse, misconduct, or relations with a patient . . . constitutes unprofessional conduct and grounds for disciplinary action for any person licensed under this division." The California Licensing Board may deny, revoke, or suspend a license for "any act of sexual abuse, or sexual relations with a patient, or sexual misconduct which is substantially related to the qualifications, functions, or duties of a psychologist or psychological assistant." (Article 10.5)

REFERENCE NOTES

1. Keith-Spiegel, P. *Sex with clients: Ten reasons why it is a very stupid thing to do.* Paper presented at the annual meeting of the American Psychological Association, New York, September 1979.

2. Maguire, L. *A sex therapist's view of sexual contacts.* Paper presented at the annual meeting of the American Psychological Association, San Francisco, August 1977.

3. Seagull, A. A. *Should a therapist have intercourse with patients?* Paper presented at the annual meeting of the American Psychological Association, Honolulu, 1972.

4. Gross, Z. *Erotic contact as a source of emotional learning in psychotherapy.* Paper presented at the annual meeting of the American Psychological Association, San Francisco, August 1977.

5. Taylor, B. J., & Wagner, N. N. *Sex between therapists and clients: A review and analysis.* Unpublished manuscript, 1975.

6. California State Psychological Association Task Force on Sexual Intimacy between Patient and Therapist (Jacqueline Bouhoutsos, Chairperson). Unpublished data, 1980.

7. Moldawsky, S. *Some theoretical and clinical issues in therapist-patient contact, or everybody gets screwed and nobody gets helped.* Paper presented at the annual meeting of the American Psychological Association, San Francisco, August 1977.

8. Grunebaum, H., Nadelson, C., & Macht, L. *Sexual activity with the psychiatrist: A district branch dilemma.* Paper presented at the annual meeting of the American Psychiatric Association, Washington, D.C., May 1976.

REFERENCES

American Psychiatric Association. The principles of medical ethics with annotations especially applicable to psychiatry. *American Journal of Psychiatry, 1973, 130,* 1057–1064.

American Psychological Association. Report of the Task Force on Sex Bias and Sex-Role Stereotyping in Psychotherapeutic Practice. *American Psychologist, 1975, 30,* 1169–1175.

American Psychological Association. Ethical standards of psychologists. *APA Monitor,* March 1977, pp. 22–23.

American Psychological Association. Latest changes in the ethics code. *APA Monitor,* November 1979, pp. 16–17.

American Psychological Association Task Force on Sex Bias and Sex-Role Stereotyping in Psychotherapeutic Practice. Guidelines for therapy with women. *American Psychologist, 1978, 33,* 1122–1123.

Butler, S., & Zelen, S. Sexual intimacies between psychotherapists and their patients. *Psychotherapy: Theory, Research, and Practice, 1977, 139,* 143–144.

Cavenar, J. O., Sullivan, J. L., & Maltbie, A. A. A clinical note on hysterical psychosis. *American Journal of Psychiatry, 1979, 136,* 830–832.

Chesler, P. *Women and madness.* New York: Doubleday, 1972.

D'Addario, L. *Sexual relationships between female clients and male therapists.* Unpublished doctoral dissertation, California School of Professional Psychology, Los Angeles, 1977.

Davidson, V. Psychiatry's problem with no name: Therapist-patient sex. *American Journal of Psychoanalysis, 1977, 37,* 43–50.

Elias, M. Stand-in for errors. *Human Behavior,* March 1977, pp. 17–23.

Ellenberger, H. *The discovery of the unconscious.* New York: Basic Books, 1970.

Forer, B. The taboo against touching in psychotherapy. *Psychotherapy: Theory, Research, and Practice, 1969, 6,* 229–231.

Franklyn, T. Sexual transgressions against patients. *The California State Psychologist,* June 1978, pp. 7–8.

Hare-Mustin, R. T. Ethical considerations in the use of sexual contact in psychotherapy. *Psychotherapy: Theory, Research, and Practice, 1974, 11,* 308–310.

Hogan, D. B. *The regulation of psychotherapists* (Vol. 3, *A review of malpractice suits in the United States*). Cambridge, Mass.: Ballinger, 1979.

Holroyd, J., & Brodsky, A. M. Psychologists' attitudes and practices regarding erotic and non-erotic physical contact with patients. *American Psychologist*, 1977, *32*, 843–849.

Holroyd, J., & Brodsky, A. Does touching patients lead to sexual intercourse? *Professional Psychology*, 1980, *11*, 807–811.

Humo, T. Counselors prescribe surrogate sex partners. *Clinical Psychiatry News*, 1975, *3*, 2, 21.

Jacobs, M., Thompson, L. A., & Truxaw, P. The use of sexual surrogates in counseling. *The Counseling Psychologist*, 1975, *5*, 73–77.

Jones, E. *The life and work of Sigmund Freud* (L. Trilling & S. Marcus, Eds.). New York: Anchor, 1963.

Kardener, S. H. Sex and the physician-patient relationship. *American Journal of Psychiatry*, 1974, *131*, 1134–1136.

Kardener, S., Fuller, M., & Mensh, I. A survey of physicians' attitudes and practices regarding erotic and nonerotic contact with patients. *American Journal of Psychiatry*, 1973, *130*, 1077–1081.

Len, M., & Fischer, J. Clinicians' attitudes toward and use of four body contact or sexual techniques with clients. *Journal of Sex Research*, 1978, *14*, 40–49.

Marmor, J. Sexual acting-out in psychotherapy. *American Journal of Psychoanalysis*, 1972, *22*, 3–8.

Masters, W. H., & Johnson, V. E. Principles of the new sex therapy. *American Journal of Psychiatry*, 1976, *133*, 548–554.

McCartney, J. Overt transference. *Journal of Sex Research*, 1966, *2*, 227–237.

Perry, J. A. Physicians' erotic and nonerotic physical involvement with patients. *American Journal of Psychiatry*, 1976, *133*, 838–840.

Pope, K. S., Levenson, H., & Schover, L. R. Sexual intimacy in psychology training: Results and implications of a national survey. *American Psychologist*, 1979, *34*, 682–689.

Riskin, L. Sexual relations between psychotherapists and their patients: Toward research or restraint. *California Law Review*, 1979, *67*, 1000–1027.

Schofield, W. *Psychotherapy: The purchase of friendship*. Englewood Cliffs, N.J.: Prentice-Hall, 1964.

Siassi, I., & Thomas, M. Physicians and the new sexual freedom. *American Journal of Psychiatry*, 1973, *130*, 1256–1257.

Stone, A. A. The legal implications of sexual activity between psychiatrist and patient. *American Journal of Psychiatry*, 1976, *133*, 1138–1141.

Taylor, B. J., & Wagner, N. N. Sex between therapists and clients: A review and analysis. *Professional Psychology*, 1976, *7*, 593–601.

Walker, M. J., & Brodsky, S. L. (Eds.). *Sexual assault: The victim and the rapist*. Lexington, Mass.: Lexington Books, 1976.

West's annotated California codes: Business and Professions Code. St. Paul: West Publishing, 1964.

12 Heterosexual Bias in Psychotherapy

STEPHEN F. MORIN AND
KENNETH A. CHARLES

The nature of the psychotherapeutic process is generally conceived to be a most powerful one, with the therapist having the power to influence the client in both direct and indirect ways (Haley, 1969). This chapter focuses on how heterosexual bias on the part of a psychotherapist adversely affects the quality of the therapeutic intervention with a lesbian or gay male client. *Heterosexual bias* is defined as a belief system that values heterosexuality as superior to and/or more "natural" than homosexuality (Morin, 1977).

This chapter addresses both the obvious forms of heterosexual bias (i.e., therapies that focus on the origins of homosexuality as a form of psychopathology) and the more subtle forms of heterosexual bias deeply ingrained in the language of psychotherapy. If the reader is not a lesbian or gay man seeking psychotherapeutic services, it might be interesting to take that perspective and attempt to imagine strategies for coping with the various forms of heterosexual bias that are discussed. If the reader is a psychotherapist, he or she might pay attention to the possible ways in which heterosexual bias is currently influencing interventions and to specific ways in which this bias can be eliminated.

This discussion of heterosexual bias in psychotherapy begins with a story that the authors recently heard from a friend who has been in psychotherapy

The authors would like to acknowledge their appreciation to Fred Jandt, Kathy Grady, Joan Murray, Virginia O'Leary, Mary-Perry Miller, Gary McDonald, and Ellen Garfinkle for conceptual input on early drafts. The authors also wish to express their appreciation to Tom Coughlin for his skill and dedication in the preparation of this manuscript.

with the same therapist for the past 10 years. This friend, a 44-year-old man, has enjoyed an active social and sexual gay lifestyle for the past 22 years. He leads a productive yet highly complex life. Some of these complexities were what originally brought him into therapy. Over the course of therapy, he has reported developing a good rapport with his therapist, whose advice and consent he covets. He has also casually mentioned that on his doctor's desk is a photograph of the doctor proudly embracing his wife and children. The photograph is inadvertently a display of the therapist's value system; some of these values his patient surely will not model. That an adult heterosexual developmental stage, according to his doctor's school of thought, has not been reached by his patient can be interpreted as a measure of the patient's failure.

The patient told the authors that his therapist encourages him to entertain thoughts of having sexual relations with women, irrespective of the patient's reports to the doctor that sexual relations with women do not interest him as a goal of therapy. Advice to do so causes him considerable discomfort. However, his therapist remains undaunted and changes his therapeutic suggestions as little as he has changed the photograph that graces his desk.

This story serves to illustrate a case of heterosexual bias operative in a psychotherapeutic relationship. It also serves to point out that well-informed consumers need not choose the services of those who wish to change them in ways *in which the consumer does not wish to change.*

Heterosexual bias, pervasive in psychological interventions, needs to be examined on ethical and professional levels. This bias has manifold unfortunate consequences for the individual in treatment, as well as for the practice of psychotherapy. When psychology accepts heterosexual behavior as ideal, it propagates an unbalanced system of judging human behavior with a heavy thumb on the scales, giving increased weight and validity to heterosexual behavior while shortchanging those whose sexual orientations are otherwise.

This chapter focuses on how heterosexual bias has become an insidious ingression into the microcosm of psychological theory, practice, and therapeutic interventions. By raising the level of awareness of the origins of heterosexual bias and how it functions, the authors hope to facilitate the evolution of suggestions for ultimately altering this destructive bias. The authors outline the beginnings of new conceptual frames of reference for psychotherapy, which are defined as *lesbian/gay-affirmative psychotherapies.*

VALUES IN PSYCHOTHERAPY

A truly value-free psychological intervention does not exist. It may be hoped that interventions follow from carefully prepared treatment plans. The values of client, therapist, and society all interact in formulating treatment outcome goals. *Bias in psychological interventions becomes a ma-*

jor issue when the therapist's values, rather than the client's, directly or indi-rectly dictate the goals of treatment. The therapeutic relationship involves a heightened vulnerability on the part of the client to the therapist's influences and thus demands responsibility on the part of the therapist to be aware of and clear with regard to the ways in which the therapist's value system may influence the course of the client's therapy.

To put the authors' position in perspective, the reader should understand that they believe that the choice of an adult lesbian or gay identity and life-style is a positive, normal, and healthy choice for many individuals. In addi-tion, they believe that there are both important similarities and important differences among lesbian, gay, and heterosexual identities and lifestyles. *The authors value the diversity and the right to be different.* These values form the cornerstone of lesbian/gay-affirmative psychotherapies.

Lesbian-affirmative psychotherapy is by its very nature a form of feminist psychotherapy. Lesbians share in common those issues and concerns that are common to all women (Abbott & Love, 1977; Johnston, 1973; Klaich, 1969; Martin & Lyon, 1972). In addition, lesbians need to learn strategies for cop-ing with heterosexual bias, particularly as it manifests itself in psychotherapy (Riddle & Sang, 1978; Sang, 1977). In lesbian-affirmative psychotherapy, the stresses of lesbian life may be placed in a social/political context so that the lesbian client has a clearer understanding of the multiple sources of stress under which she functions. Many lesbian feminists support and encourage ways of interacting that presuppose two equal partners, both active, yet neither imposing herself on the other. Lesbian-affirmative psychotherapy typically focuses on relationships, with particular value on egalitarian rela-tionships. The man-woman power structure is frequently seen by feminists to presuppose a more active and more powerful agent in interaction with a more passive and less powerful agent. Lesbian relationships are viewed as an op-portunity to overcome this power issue and fully validate the power of women in loving relationships with women.

Gay-affirmative psychotherapy is parallel to lesbian affirmative psycho-therapy from a male perspective.[1] Basic to gay-affirmative psychotherapy is an appreciation of the way in which male sex-role stereotypes limit options and deprive men of the potentially rewarding experiences of learning from and being close to one another. In addition, there is a recognition of the ways in which the male role, as defined by the culture as sex-role-appropriate be-havior, interferes with the development of intimacy between and among men (Morin & Garfinkle, 1978). As such, gay-affirmative psychotherapy has its underpinnings in an understanding of the male experience (Lewis, 1981; Pleck & Brannon, 1978; Pleck & Sawyer, 1974). Gay-affirmative psychotherapy values gay male intimacy and attempts to counteract the pathogenic cultural attitudes, such as competitiveness, that adversely affect male psychological development (D. Clark, 1977, 1979; Malyon, Note 1). Gay-affirmative psychotherapy is unique in that it values the violation of traditional male role expectations and attempts to foster positive self-concepts among those who violate these sex-role stereotypes. This violation of traditional male role expectations is essential to the development of intimacy between and among men. We believe that men can be men with men in new, different, and fulfilling ways.

Lesbian/gay-affirmative psychotherapies share a goal of deprogramming the negative conditioning associated with lesbian and gay stereotypes (D. Clark, 1977). In addition, these psychotherapies share a common concern with the interaction between sex role stereotypes and lesbian/gay identity. Lesbian- and gay-affirmative psychotherapies are likely to embody a principle of working toward a peer relationship with the lesbian or gay male client. The message of such a relationship is that the lesbian or gay male client is not a second-class or inferior person. For those lesbian or gay readers considering being consumers of psychological services, it is recommended that the issue of the values of the possible psychotherapist be discussed before the provider of psychological services is selected. Lesbian and gay consumers need not tolerate heterosexually biased interventions.

BIAS IN PSYCHOLOGICAL THEORY

Psychological interventions are typically made in the context of theories of personality and human development. Each perspective of development has some notion with regard to how an adult sexual orientation is achieved. Therapeutic interventions based on different theories vary greatly as a result, in part, of the degree to which the individual's history is seen as the focus in resolving the presenting problems in therapy. The following discussion divides psychological theories into the following three categories: (1) theories that are inherently heterosexually biased; (2) theories that are essentially value-free, but have generally been applied in a heterosexually biased manner; and (3) theories that are neither heterosexually biased nor applied in a heterosexually biased fashion.

Heterosexually Biased Theories

Any psychological theory of development is inherently heterosexually biased if the assumption is made that the development of a lesbian or gay identity in adulthood is "pathological." Perhaps the best examples of inherently heterosexually biased theories are the traditional and some contemporary psychoanalytic writings. For example, Bieber and colleagues tell us that "All psychoanalytic theories assume that adult homosexuality is psychopathologic" (Bieber, Dain, Dince, Drellich, Grand, Gundlach, Kremer, Rifkin, Wilber, & Bieber, 1962).

Psychoanalytic writings and case studies on the "treatment of homosexuality" reflect a colorful variety of idiosyncratic approaches. Most of these theoretical elaborations are based on analysts' interpretations of their patients' reconstructions of childhood memories. These early writings, a foundation for a variety of psychological thought, perpetuate a 19th-century tendency to take what the analyst found aesthetically unpleasant and to reframe it from the prevailing religious perspective of "sinfulness" to the medical perspective of a form of "deep-rooted psychopathology."

Despite prevailing Victorian attitudes, Freud's letter to an American mother requesting treatment for her son is a sympathetic statement:

> Homosexuality is assuredly no advantage but it is nothing to be ashamed of, no vice, degradation, it cannot be classified as an illness; consider it to be a variation of the sexual function produced by a certain arrest of sexual development. Many highly respectable individuals of ancient and modern times have been homosexuals, several of the greatest men among them (Plato, Michelangelo, Leonardo da Vinci, etc.). It is a great injustice to persecute homosexuality as a crime and cruelty too. If you do not believe me, read the books of Havelock Ellis. (Freud, 1935/1951, p. 786)

Freud wrote this positive statement as part of a letter designed to comfort a mother concerned about her son, and therefore the statement appears far more positive than Freud's actual position on the matter. His use of the phrase "arrest of development" does indicate that he viewed homosexual orientation as "less mature" and less healthy than heterosexual orientation. That homosexual outcome is inherently pathological has been exaggerated in later psychoanalytic writing both on women (Caprio, 1954; Kaye, Berl, Clare, Eleston, Gershwin, Gershwin, Kogan, Torda, & Wilber, 1967)[2] and on men (Bieber et al., 1962; Hadden, 1971; Socarides, 1970). The assumption of pathology continues to be found in even some of the more contemporary psychoanalytic writings (Hendin, 1975).

The psychoanalytic tradition continues to exert a major influence on psychological research on lesbianism and male homosexuality. Morin (1977) found that approximately 30% of psychological studies on lesbians and gay men between 1967 and 1974 focused on the etiology of homosexuality. The majority of these studies followed directly from a psychoanalytic model, which concentrates on parental background and parenting styles (R. B. Evans, 1972; Kenyon, 1968), family constellation (Siegelman, 1973), or other idiosyncratic psychoanalytic notions (e.g., "flight from incest") (Silverman, Kwawer, Wolitzky, & Coron, 1973).

Many current practitioners of psychoanalytically oriented psychotherapy view homosexuality as "pathological." Nonetheless, some contemporary psychoanalytic writers have questioned the assumption that the development of a lesbian or gay identity is in any way pathological (Marmor, 1980); it is perhaps unfair to attack psychoanalytic theory as a whole. However, the present authors assert that any theory that has the inherent assumption of "arrested development" and speaks of the "etiology of homosexuality" is heterosexually biased.[3]

Biased Application of Theories

A second group of theories can be defined on the basis of their not being inherently heterosexually biased, in that the theory does not make any assumptions that lesbian or gay outcome is pathological by its very nature. Yet this second category of theories is noteworthy, because unbiased theory has been applied in a heterosexually biased manner. Perhaps the best example of this type of theoretical approach is learning theory.

Learning theory focuses on the process by which behaviors are acquired. Behaviors are not considered inherently good or bad, healthy or pathological. These value judgments are made by observers of the behavior. From a developmental perspective, learning theorists have focused on the socialization process, including notions of direct reinforcement of behaviors, as well as more complicated second-order learning through imitation. Although social learning theorists have paid considerable attention to the process of sex-role acquistion, they have paid relatively little attention to the development of sexual orientation and/or identities.

Learning theorists who have considered homosexual orientations pathological have sought to explain homosexual behavior in men on the basis of a learned aversion to women. Treatment strategies based on this assumption have attempted to punish sexual arousal directed toward males. McConaghy (1967) went so far as to devise a concrete behavioral measure of sexual arousal in men, and consequently a behavioral measure of change in therapy.

In this research, an instrument called the "phallometer" was developed to measure penile volume changes in response to viewing pictures of male and female nudes. The biased assumption underlying this research and treatment was that homosexual preference in men was a maladaptive aversion to women, rather than a healthy, conditioned attraction to men. Contrary to the predicted results, the researchers found no evidence of aversion to women among androphilic men.[4] On the basis of penile volume measures, androphilic men were found to have no aversion to (1) pictures of nude adult females (Freund, Langevin, Gibiri, & Zajac, 1973); (2) auditory or written descriptions of heterosexual intercourse (Freund, Langevin, Chamberlayne, Deosoron, & Zajac, 1974); or (3) pictures of the vulva, the face, or the breasts of a mature female (Freund, Langevin, & Zajac, 1974).

Undaunted by the lack of evidence for their assumptions of pathology, McConaghy and others proceeded to describe the "therapeutic" use of aversive conditioning procedures to eradicate homoerotic responses (e.g., electric shock to the genital area) (Bancroft, 1969; Barr & McConaghy, 1971). Although in some cases behavior therapy has used appetitive conditioning to increase heterosexual arousal, in other cases the only intervention has been to eliminate homoerotic response without substituting new sources of erotic attraction. The implications that are easily drawn are that being asexual is the goal of treatment (i.e., no pleasure is better than homosexual pleasure).

Another study demonstrating a heterosexually biased application of learning theory is found in the work of T. Clark and Epstein (1972). These researchers hypothesized that androphilic men would demonstrate a greater expectancy of negative reinforcement from female figures than from male figures. Using a technique of guessing at the frequency of smiling and angry faces, the study found that the tendency to overestimate and underestimate the number of smiling and angry faces was contingent upon self-concept and not upon the sex of the faces. The study failed to find any evidence that androphilic men have an erotic preference for other men due to a high expectancy of rejection from women. Although this study concluded that "male homosexuality" cannot be usefully considered a homogeneous or unitary grouping, it reflects a heterosexual bias by virtue of the assumption that led to the research questions (i.e., men are gay because of histories of rejection from women).

Learning theory, unlike psychoanalytic theory, is value-neutral in that it does *not* start with an assumption that lesbian/gay outcome is "less mature" and therefore "less healthy" than is heterosexual outcome. That some learning theorists have attempted to answer empirical questions of learned aversion as an explanation of lesbian/gay outcome reflects the bias of the researchers and therapists rather than an inherent assumption of pathology within the learning model.

Nonbiased Theories, Nonbiased Approaches

A third group of psychological theories makes no assumption about pathology regarding the development of lesbian/gay outcome and has not been used in a heterosexually biased manner. Perhaps the clearest example of this type of theory is ethology.

Ethological methods and theory have become increasingly popular as a means of studying and understanding the social behavior of humans (Jones, 1972). The ethological perspective has its roots in the methods used to study animal behavior (Lorenz, 1966; Tinbergen, 1953). As a theoretical perspective, ethology reflects a new emphasis on the natural evolution of human behaviors (e.g., attachment behavior in infants) (Ainsworth, 1973). When naturally evolving behaviors are disrupted, severe psychopathology and even death can result (Bowlby, 1969).

Ethological approaches to the study of human behavior have been remarkably free of heterosexual bias. For example, Ford and Beach (1951) found that some form of homosexual behavior occurs *naturally* in almost all species. Furthermore, homosexual behavior was found in almost all the human societies studied, even in those that, like the United States, maintain strict cultural injunctions against such behavior. Later ethological studies have simply observed the ways in which homosexual behavior develops naturally in non-human primates (Chevalier-Skolnikoff, 1974). This comparative and cross-cultural study of homosexual behavior has strongly challenged the beliefs that homosexual behavior is "unnatural."

From an ethological perspective, homosexual outcome is not only natural; it is also seen as adaptive. Konrad Lorenz offered a refreshingly honest observation in a 1974 interview:

> There can be no moral objection to homosexuality. Many people have an aesthetic, emotional aversion to homosexual behavior. I once saw two boys embrace in a bathroom. The sight was slightly repulsive to me, but in moral terms, why shouldn't they kiss? In an overpopulated world, it would be a good thing if there were more homosexuality. (R. I. Evans, 1974, p. 84)

Lorenz reported the same aesthetic repulsion as did the early psychoanalysts, yet his description of homosexual behavior as natural and adaptive demonstrates the ability to transcend a personal aesthetic reaction and report a theory without heterosexual bias. For the ethologist, neither homosexual or heterosexual outcome is pictured as being more "natural" or superior. Therefore, the issue of psychopathology is not raised. Perhaps because of the lack of inference regarding psychopathology, the ethological perspective is generally given little attention in the training of psychotherapists whose job it is to diagnose, assess, and treat psychopathology. However, as psychotherapists or as consumers or psychological services, we would be well advised to pay attention to the value-neutral position on sexuality displayed in this model.

THE EVOLUTION OF LESBIAN/ GAY-AFFIRMATIVE THEORY

The development of lesbian/gay-affirmative theory with regard to human development is a relatively recent trend. These models of human development pay particular attention to lesbian and gay identity formation (Berzon, 1979; Cass, 1979; D. Clark, 1977, 1979; Kimmel, 1978; Morin & Miller, Note 2; Morin & Schultz, 1978). Each of these models has adopted a perspective of "stages" in order to understand the process of people coming to be positive about their lesbian or gay identity.

This evolving lesbian/gay-affirmative theory can be placed in the context of cognitive-developmental approaches to socialization (Kohlberg, 1969; Piaget, 1967). Although cognitive-developmental theory has focused very little on the development of sexual orientation, these theorists have paid considerable attention to the development of sex roles.

Unlike neopsychoanalytic theory, which places heavy emphasis on identification with the same-sex parent, or learning theory, which places heavy emphasis upon reinforcement for sex-role-appropriate behavior, cognitive-developmental theory explains the acquisition of sex roles on the basis of cognitive structures. Cognitive-developmental theory argues that the child learns to sex-type himself or herself and to conform activities to this concept at an early age. For example, once the concept of being a "boy" is formed, it becomes more satisfying to do "boy things." Thus, the concept of the self that develops very early in life and continually undergoes changes throughout life defines what behaviors will be consistent with that self-concept. As cognitive abilities develop through various stages, the concept of self also evolves.

Several writers who have analyzed the development of lesbian/gay identity have emphasized the importance of cognitive aspects of development, as well as the stages and sequence of this development (Cass, 1979; Dank, 1971; McDonald, in press; Morin & Schultz, 1978; Troiden, 1979). This focus on the stages and sequence of developing a positive lesbian or gay identity is often referred to as the "coming-out" process (de Monteflores & Schultz, 1978; Morin & Schultz, 1978).

A number of milestone events have been identified in the coming-out process that could conceivably unfold in a stage-sequential pattern. Such a pattern became evident in a recent study of lesbian and gay members of the American Psychological Association (Riddle & Morin, 1977), as described in Table 1. In this particular study, it was found that first awareness of homosexual feelings occurred at approximately age 13 or 14. The first same-sex sexual experience occurred at approximately age 20 for the lesbians and approximately age 15 for the gay men. This discrepancy can be explained on the basis of gay males' tending to be early maturers (Tripp, 1975). This is the only point at which there was a wide discrepancy between the experiences of lesbians and gay men in the coming-out process. In terms of understanding in a cognitive sense what the term *homosexual* meant, lesbians developed this understanding at approximately age 16, and gay men at approximately age 17. First homosexual relationships were maintained for lesbians at an average age of 23 and for gay men at an average age of 22. At approximately the same time, both groups tended to consider or label themselves "homosexual" for the first time.

These data indicate an 8- or 9-year gap between the first awareness of homosexual feelings and the first labeling of the self as "homosexual." These would appear to be the years of maximum conflict for lesbians and gay men as they struggle with developing positive identities. Woodman and Lenna

TABLE 1

Mean Ages of "Coming Out" Experiences for Lesbian and Gay Male Respondents

EXPERIENCE	LESBIAN ($n=63$)	GAY MALE ($n=138$)
Aware of homosexual feelings	13.8	12.8
Had first same-sex experience	19.9	14.9
Understood what term *homosexual* meant	15.6	17.2
Had first homosexual relationship	22.8	21.9
Considered self "homosexual"	23.2	21.1
Acquired positive "gay" identity	29.7	28.5

Note. Based on data from Riddle & Morin (1977). For a more complete analysis of the data, the reader is referred to the final report of the Task Force on the Status of Lesbian and Gay Male Psychologists (1980).

(1980) describe this as the "denial phase." Psychotherapeutic interventions may be the most critical during this time.

The vast majority of respondents in this study reported acquiring a "positive gay identity"; for lesbians, the mean age was 30, and for gay men, the mean age was 29. On the average, this development of a positive gay identity occurred from six to seven years after the individuals first considered themselves to be "homosexual." This data on coming out finds a 16-year gap between the first awareness of homosexual feelings and the development of a positive gay identity. A recent replication of this study with a sample of gay men more representative of the general population than a group of psychologists would be yielded very similar results, with the only major difference being the development of a positive gay identity approximately 4 years earlier than in the professional sample (McDonald, in press). Nonetheless, the present authors assert that the very existence of this gap between the development of a "homosexual" identity and the development of a positive gay identity is an indictment of the extent to which social pressures operate to prevent lesbians or gay men from feeling good about their sexual selves.

The concern for stage and sequence has been expanded to more sophisticated developmental models of lesbian and gay male adult development by Kimmel (1978). This analysis has attempted to put in perspective both the historical and lifestyle events for lesbians and gay males born in particular decades and the developmental stage that those of each decade have attained. As Kimmel (1978) notes, "A young person dealing with being gay in the 1970s has an entirely different set of historical-cultural conditions to ease the development of a positive gay identity from that of a person who grew up in the early 1900s" (p. 124). Consistent with this perspective, McDonald (in press) found that younger age groups understood the meaning of the term *homosexual*, labeled themselves as such, and became involved in same-sex relationships at significantly earlier ages than did men in older age groups.

Although stage and sequence are apparent in a number of recent studies of the coming-out process, more recent research suggests that the individual differences found among lesbians and gay men in their coming out may not support a strict stage-sequential model, at least as defined in terms of the most frequently mentioned milestone experiences (McDonald, in press). This is to say that individuals may go through these experiences in a different order than is found in the group data, making these stages descriptive of typical development of lesbian or gay identity but not defining an invariant progression. Nonetheless, the stage-sequential progression suggested by cognitive-developmental theory may be present in defining a sequence where the understanding of the meaning of the concept *homosexual* must proceed the meaningful application of the concept to the self, which in turn must precede the beginnings of integrating that concept of the self into a positive lesbian or gay identity.

These approaches are lesbian- or gay-affirmative in that they have attempted to place into a theoretical context the issues of the development of lesbian or gay male identity as part of the more general theoretical perspectives of human development. There is no connotation of pathology, and the issues are discussed in the context of the development of lesbian and gay identity as a valid option for at least some individuals. Although clearly in their beginning stages, lesbian/gay-affirmative theories of human development are evolving, relying heavily on the importance of how people think of themselves in cognitive terms. Altering cognitive structures and their parallel affective responses is a critical part of the psychotherapeutic process, and it results in people both thinking and feeling positively about themselves. It is for these positive thoughts and feelings that the client has enlisted the aid of the psychotherapist, who must, in service to the client, facilitate these cognitive and affective changes. The consumer has the right to demand this.

INTERVENTIONS

It has already been asserted that a truly value-free psychological intervention does not exist. Within the therapeutic context, the specific techniques of intervention selected by a therapist are less important than is the value system within which the decisions regarding therapeutic change are made. The mere existence of a technology for behavioral affective or cognitive change does not mean that this technology must be used. In this context, the medium is *not* the message.

Let us consider the case of a client presenting himself or herself for treatment and requesting a change of sexual orientation or sexual arousal pattern (i.e., conversion or reversion therapy) (Masters & Johnson, 1979). The case involved a 27-year-old male with an exclusively androphilic history who presented himself to Masters and Johnson's institute for conversion therapy. The crisis situation that brought him to therapy involved his making an inappropriate sexual advance toward a male member of his firm. The indiscretion was reported, and his employment situation was threatened. Apparently in an attempt to prove his heterosexual interests, he attempted to engage in erotic activity with a woman from the same company. This resulted in what was described by the client as a severe anxiety attack. The client's presenting problem was that he felt that he needed to function heterosexually in order to survive socially and professionally.

This man's presenting problems and requests for change or conversion raised value issues that Masters and Johnson (1979) discuss at some length. On the one hand, the therapists could have applied the technology of sex therapy toward a goal of heterosexual functioning. On the other hand, the therapists could have proceeded toward a goal of decreasing this man's distress in his work situation. Making these decisions is a critical point in the therapeutic process. The goals of treatment must be determined from the outset for this type of therapy to be successful. This is a strategic point for the interception of bias and a careful examination of the therapist's own value system.

Masters and Johnson present themselves as being value-neutral in regard to homosexual orientation; however, their advice to this young man was that homosexual men without female partners were not treated at the Institute. In all fairness to Masters and Johnson, this requirement of being in a committed couple appears to be applied equally to both heterosexual and lesbian/gay candidates for sex therapy.

At any rate, after hearing this advice, the client spent the next year avoiding homosexual experiences and attempting to find an appropriate female partner. At the end of the year, he presented himself with his appropriate female partner at the Institute to begin treatment. After 1 week of intensive treatment, during which the client experienced intense anxiety, the treatment was declared a failure.

The failure of the treatment was discussed with the client, and short-term psychotherapy was offered for the psychosocial insecurities that developed as a result of his failure to convert to heterosexuality. Following treatment, this client returned to his former homosexual activities and his anxieties disappeared. He was counseled to be less overt in his sexual solicitation, to keep his sexual life separate from his professional life, and to restrict his heterosexual social commitments to business demands only. With these modest alterations in his lifestyle, the client reported no further difficulties at the time of follow-up.

In this case, the therapists mapped out the direction of this man's therapy according to their policy of not treating androphilic men wishing to convert to heterosexual orientation unless they had female partners. The assumption of and validation for a heterosexual outcome are implicit in the very rules of the Institute. Heterosexual bias became the revolving door that this client circulated through at the Institute.

The treatment literature is replete with examples of programs specifically designed to stamp out homosexuality. Some of these "therapies" include drug therapy (Litkey & Feniczy, 1967; Pondelickova & Nedoma, 1970); electroconvulsive shock therapy (Sachs & Titievsky, 1967); testicular pulpectomy (i.e., surgical removal of the sex glands) (Roboch & Nedoma, 1970); study of "aesthetic realism" with Eli Siegel (Kranz, 1971)[5]; LSD therapy (Alpert, 1969); therapy that includes becoming a born-again Pentecostal Christian (Pattison & Pattison, 1980); and last, but not least, brain surgery: "A distinct reduction was noted after surgery, with the complete abolition of homosexual tendencies in two of the patients and sufficient reduction in the third to enable them to be controlled" (Anonymous, 1969).[6]

Although these efforts to change sexual orientation regularly fail (Tripp, 1975), their poor success rates do not mean that these efforts are harmless. On the contrary, the failure has a much more insidious impact than would success. Davidson (1976), in his presidential address to the Association for the Advancement of Behavior Therapy, points out that the very existence of such intervention programs conveys a very powerful message to gay people: "You are sick and ought to be cured." The failure of these interventions may even compound the damage, implying: "You are so bad off, you can't get better despite what we do for you."

People typically enter treatment feeling the need to change. The therapist agrees that they need to change. When they are then declared treatment failures, they are left with a monumental amount of frustration: "I need to change but I can't." Such an untherapeutic set-up constitutes psychological abuse.

Coming from a psychodynamic perspective, Weinberg (1972) has reached a similar conclusion to that offered by Davidson. In discussing a client with homosexual feelings who presented himself for treatment to increase his sexual interest in women in general and his wife in particular, Weinberg states:

> Such an assignment is more than any psychologist, living or dead, could have handled. However, it is not a stigma on psychotherapists that we have failed. The real stigma would be on us if we had succeeded. For then we would have been stamping out one aspect of human variety, one facet of human possibility —merely because it distressed us to think about that possibility. (p. 138)

It is important once again to assert that the *techniques* of intervention are not the problem. Let us consider a second case example reported by Masters and Johnson (1979). In this case, a lesbian couple presented themselves for sex therapy.[7] One woman complained of primary anorgasmia, and her partner complained of situational and occasional sexual anxiety. Using such intervention techniques as the sensate-focus approach, both women left treatment confident and satisfied with their sexual responsivity. Similar outcomes are reported with sexually dissatisfied gay men.

The techniques discussed above have been primarily behaviorally based interventions. That the bias is not in the technique but in the values of the therapist also applies to more analytically oriented psychodynamic therapies, which place greater emphasis on insight and interpretation than on behavior or action. In the psychoanalytic approach as outlined by Socarides (1978) and Hatterer (1972), emphasis is placed on having the patient understand and gain insight into the origins of what these therapists consider to be inappropriate object choices. That the "object choice" is inappropriate is assumed by the therapist and is never raised in therapy as an issue for discussion.

Other therapists using insight techniques might choose to focus on why the client is defining the homosexual orientation as a problem. For example, Weinberg (1972) suggests offering interpretations to such clients about their internalizing society's negative attitudes regarding homosexuality. Rather than making interpretations regarding the possible childhood origins of the homosexual orientations, insight into the possible origins of the clients' "homophobia" are explored. For Weinberg, *homophobia* is an irrational fear or hatred of homosexuals. For homosexuals, homophobia is expressed in self-hatred. Within Weinberg's value system, no patient, heterosexual or homosexual, is considered healthy unless prejudice against homosexuality is overcome.

More contemporary and positive psychoanalytic writers express optimism for the value of a psychoanalytic model in helping people to attain their desired sexual identities (Herron, Kinter, Sollinger, & Trubowitz, 1980). Thus, psychodynamic therapy may be used from a heterosexually biased perspective to uncover the roots of the assumed pathology or from a lesbian/gay-affirmative perspective, to explore the roots of homophobia. In certain cases it may be appropriate to explore the roots of *heterophobia*, the irrational fear or hatred of heterosexual people. The maintaining of homophobia or heterophobia that interferes with social functioning is not adaptive. The value system of the therapist clearly directs the course of therapy.

HETEROSEXUAL BIAS IN LANGUAGE

The stigma long associated with homosexual orientation has been reinforced by the language of psychotherapy as well as the language of the culture. In order for an intervention to be truly lesbian/gay-affirmative, the language of that intervention must suggest health rather than illness. Lesbian/gay-affirmative psychotherapies require that language that would lead the lesbian or the gay male client to feel sick, bad, crazy, stupid, guilty, or invisible be altered.

Heterosexual bias is reflected in language in at least four ways: connotation, inference, contiguity, and omission. The most pervasive form of heterosexual bias in language is found in what the authors call "the sin of *omission*." This particular problem is so pervasive that it is difficult even to begin to discuss its implications. So much of psychological literature and so much of psychotherapeutic interventions begins with heterosexual assumption. The inappropriate use of words such as *husband, wife,* or even *spouse,* rather than *friend* or *partner,* gives a powerful message to lesbian or gay male listeners. The message is that they are different and that they do not fit within the language structure of psychotherapy or of everyday life.

The bias of omission is present each time the context or linguistic structure is such that a lesbian or gay male listener or reader cannot readily identify with the meaning of the sentence. As such, it is analogous to those criteria used to assess sexist language (Henley, Tennov, Grady, Parlee, & Brannon, Note 4). The experience of reading a passage in which one is excluded by the linguistic structure is consistent with a lesbian/gay experience called the "pain of invisibility."[8]

The feeling of being on the outside looking in or simply not being there at all can be extended to include the idea that one's sexual orientation is too bad even to mention. Homosexuality has often been called "the love that dare not speak its name." Young lesbian or gay developing children's exposure to the media underlines the feeling of invisibility, as they rarely, if ever, see a coherent gay male or lesbian role model. Gay- or lesbian-identified people who grew up in the 1950s with television were never able to find themselves on *The Donna Reed Show* or *My Little Margie.* The sin of omission during these years was so great that the *New York Times* did not mention the word *homosexual* until 1963 (Morin & Miller, Note 2). In a recent study, McDonald (1981) found that in the 48 most commonly used introductory psychology textbooks, eight made no reference to homosexuality. Discussion of lesbianism was more notably absent; only 14 of the 48 introductory textbooks mentioned lesbians. When lesbians have been mentioned, the general tendency has been to assume similarities to gay males when such similarities may not exist. The invisibility of lesbians in psychological literature has been so great that it has led many lesbians to insist that the generic use of *gay* referring to both men and women be replaced by a linguistic pattern that would make "lesbian" and "gay" distinctly different and give increased visibility to lesbians and their separate issues.

The bias of omission persists in the more advanced field of psychotherapy and its concurrent literature. For example, omission occurs in Erikson's discussion of the adult developmental task of establishing intimacy versus isolation (Erikson, 1963). The "utopia of genitality" is described as requiring "mutuality of orgasm with a loved partner of the other sex." If this intimacy is not achieved, psychopathology in the form of severe "character problems" can develop. As intimacy and the next Eriksonian developmental task (*generativity*, or making a contribution to the next generation) are not specific to heterosexual people, the inclusion of the phrase "of the other sex" is painfully unnecessary. This is the pain of invisibility. It is easy to observe how this type of omission supports old stereotypic notions regarding the lack of validity of same-sex intimate relationships. Readers who are not lesbian or gay might try to imagine their reaction to this omission if they were lesbian or gay.[9]

The problem of omission and heterosexual assumption is enormous. Consider the way in which histories are taken from clients when they first present themselves for psychotherapy. Consider the questions that are asked on typical insurance forms. Consider the inferior treatment that lesbians and gay men may receive due to heterosexual assumption and inappropriate history taking in the context of medical evaluations (Dardick & Grady, 1980). This problem of invisibility appears to be greater for lesbian women than for gay men, in that on insurance forms and in history taking, lesbians are more likely to indicate having been married and having children. Thus, the heterosexual assumption is more likely to be made (Riddle & Morin, 1977). For example, with the absence of a sexual history, a physician may treat a lesbian woman for vaginitis and may neglect to treat an available partner concurrently.

Although the problem of omission and invisibility may seem overwhelming, as the chapter goes on to describe the other ways in which language is heterosexually biased, it may lead some readers to appreciate omission as the lesser of two available evils: Being ignored may be preferable to being humiliated.

The use of words with negative *connotation* in the psychological literature on lesbian women and gay men is the most blatant form of heterosexual bias in language. In order to investigate what is known about lesbian women or gay men, a reader would have to research psychological citations under the heading of "Lesbianism" or "Male Homosexuality." In that both these terms have the strong pathological connotation of clinical entities, this investigation starts with a powerful message. The message for the reader, especially the lesbian or gay reader, clearly is that persons or behaviors described under these titles are sick.

Once the curious reader unearths the research and treatment literature, he or she would find a variety of unfortunate words used in these writings to describe those with same-sex sexual attraction or preference (i.e., *pervert, degenerate, invert, sexual deviate*, etc.). What these terms have in common is the connotation of pathology. McDonald's analysis of introductory psychology textbooks found that for every one source of relevant information on lesbians or gay men, there were more than four sources that reflected either misleading information or heterosexual bias (McDonald, 1981). In approximately 60% of those textbooks containing material on lesbians and gay men, the material was included in chapters or subheadings connoting pathology (e.g., "Sexual Deviations," "Sexual Dysfunction," etc.). As one explores the rather hostile territory of the psychological literature on lesbians and gay men, one could unwittingly be pulled into the quicksand of pathological connotations and thinking.

The more recent use of such terms as *lesbian-identified* or *gay-male-identified* reflects a movement away from pathological connotations toward self-affirming identification. Although the term *homosexual* may have started out as a neutral term, it has acquired a strongly negative connotation. The distinction between being homosexual and being lesbian- or gay-identified is psychological as well as political. The term *gay* or *lesbian*, like *black*, *Chicano*, and *woman*, connotes a value system as well as designates group membership. These terms, which have been chosen by the various groups themselves in an affirmation of their feeling positive about themselves, are distinctly different from the terms that the larger society and the psychological establishment have imposed upon them.

Lesbian or *gay* connotes an identity that is proud, angry, open, visible, political, and healthy—all of the positive things that *homosexual* does not connote (Morin & Miller, Note 2). Pointing to the importance of such considerations in psychotherapy, Weinberg (1972) began to differentiate between a *homosexual*, one with an erotic preference for a member of the same gender, and a *gay person*, one with an erotic preference for the same gender who has managed to reject a negative societal stereotype associated with this preference. Within Weinberg's frame of reference, one can begin to appreciate the importance of the language of psychotherapy: Working with a client toward facilitating a "lesbian" or "gay" identity may be hoped to result in a feeling of psychological health, whereas accepting and imposing a "homosexual" identity may result in feelings of inferior social and psychological status. This distinction between identity labels has been confirmed by a recent investigation by McDonald (in press). Respondents in this study identified themselves as having developed either a "homosexual" identity or a "gay" identity. Those men with "homosexual" identity had significantly more negative attitudes toward male homosexuality; participated less in the gay subculture; were less likely to disclose their sexual/affectional preference to others; and were more likely to report feeling guilty, anxious, and ashamed than were those men describing themselves as having a "gay" identity. Lesbian/gay-affirmative psychotherapists must attempt to work with the language of the client to shape that language in such a way as to impart a message of psychological health and psychological wealth.

Yet another way in which language is heterosexually biased is seen in the use of negative *inferences*. Small and seemingly subtle alterations in the structure and content of a passage of writing or speech can, by inference, alter the entire meaning of that passage. The following excerpt from the *Casebook on Ethical Standards of Psychologists* (American Psychological Association, 1970) provides a vivid example. The left column is the original statement, and the right is a version that the present authors have edited.

A psychologist with homosexual tendencies formed a close relationship with a male patient in the hospital where he worked. When the patient, a minor, was discharged from the hospital, the psychologist arranged for the boy to live with him and when the psychologist was dropped from the staff, he took the boy with him and moved to another city.

Opinion. The psychologist was unethical and unprofessional in his conduct and his resignation from APA was requested. The action was not taken on the basis of homosexuality, for the APA does not presume to supervise the private lives of its members, but because he had betrayed his responsibility for the welfare of patients, and his notorious conduct had injured the reputation of the profession. (p. 34)

A psychologist formed a close relationship with a patient in a hospital setting where the psychologist worked. When the patient, a minor, was discharged from the hospital, the psychologist entered into an intimate relationship with the former patient and both moved to another city.

Opinion. The psychologist was unethical and unprofessional in conduct, and resignation from APA was requested. Although APA does not presume to supervise the private lives of its members, the psychologist had betrayed professional responsibility for the welfare of patients, and this conduct had injured the reputation of the profession.

In the left column, the phrase "with homosexual tendencies" is used to make the inference that the relationship was unethical because it was homosexual. The reader must infer that the relationship was sexual, in that this is never clearly stated. How does the reader know that the ethical standard of avoiding dual relationships has been violated? When the phrase "with homosexual tendencies" is removed, what it was that made the relationship "notorious" is unclear. It is not even clear in this case example that the patient was ever involved in a therapeutic contract with the psychologist. All the reader learns from the case example is that the psychologist worked at the same hospital where the patient was hospitalized.

It should also be noted that in the edited version, the authors have removed reference to both the sex of the psychologist and the sex of the patient, in that neither are relevant factors. In that this case example was presented in order to illustrate an ethical violation involving dual relationships between therapist and client, the same-sex character of the interaction is not a relevant factor. By altering the language of this case to eliminate the same-sex nature of the interaction, the point regarding a dual relationship becomes clear. The unethical quality of the relationship in the original version requires that the reader make certain pejorative inferences based on stereotypes with regard to how people with "homosexual tendencies" are likely to act. The power of a few words in a particular arrangement to deliver a vigorous and dynamic message is not to be underestimated.

A fourth way in which heterosexual bias is reflected in language involves the concept of *contiguity* (i.e., guilt by syntactic association). For example, Wolfgang and Wolfgang (1971) studied attitudes toward "homosexuals" and other "marginal figures." Using methodology of interpersonal space, they found that people were likely to position themselves significantly further away from "marijuana users," "drug addicts," "obese persons," and "homosexuals" than from "normal peers." For those readers who are not lesbians or gay men, it should not be difficult to appreciate what a Herculean task it is to feel positive about oneself in reading a psychological literature that uses language to make unjust moral, psychological, and social indictments.

Heterosexual bias through linguistic continuity is common in the treatment literature. For example, Glasser (1965) states the following in discussing the treatment of those with "sexual deviations": "Regardless of how they manifest their problem—Peeping Tom, Exhibitionist, Fetishist, Transvestite, or Homosexual—they do not feel themselves to be the sex that nature has given them" (p. 150). This one sentence demonstrates heterosexual bias through connotation (i.e., use of "sexual deviation"), through negative inference (i.e., unnaturalness is inferred by the use of the phrase "the sex that nature has given them"), and through contiguity, (i.e., being placed in a list with "Peeping Toms").[10]

Language that is heterosexually biased to this extreme is not at all uncommon. An even more recent book on forensic medicine by Rupp (1980) states that "Homosexuality is a sexual perversion, not an alternate lifestyle. It must be placed in the same group of perversions which relate to other than normal sexual preference, such as bestiality (a sexual preference for animals), pedophilia (a sexual preference for children), gerontophilia (a sexual preference for the old), and necrophilia (a sexual preference for the dead)" (p. 582). Given this barrage of bare insults in the psychological literature, one can appreciate how many lesbians and gay men develop mistrust or outright hostility toward the helping professions (Morin, 1978).

In December 1973, the Board of Trustees of the American Psychiatric Association voted to eliminate "homosexuality" per se as a mental disorder and to substitute a new category, "sexual orientation disturbance," reserved for those homosexuals who are "disturbed by, in conflict with, or wish to change their sexual orientation." Prior to 1973, homosexuality was included with fetishism, pedophilia, transvestism, exhibitionism, voyeurism, sadism, and masochism. Thus, the historical context for many writers including homosexual interest as a paraphilia is quite clear.

In the latest classification of mental disorders (American Psychiatric Association, 1980), "sexual orientation disturbance" has been replaced by a new category, "egodystonic homosexuality," classified under "other psychosexual disorders." This specifically refers to individuals who are uncomfortable with a homosexual orientation and wish to become heterosexual. John Money has pointed out that this classification was inserted to appease more traditional psychiatrists as a guarantee of insurance payments for those who decree treatment for "homosexual men and women" (Mass, 1980). Underlying many "moral" arguments are economic motives, which certainly appear operative in this case. Money further contends that intellectually, as a matter of logic of classification, this diagnostic category cannot be defended without also having "egodystonic masturbation," "egodystonic heterosexuality," and so on.

Even with all the debate regarding the nomenclature, a reader of the current classification system would still encounter "homosexuality," even if qualified by "egodystonic," in the list of mental disorders. Although the justification for the inclusion of homosexuality in such lists has become more convoluted and more sophisticated over the years, the result is the same. As long as these lists include homosexuality, the heterosexually biased assumption of guilt by syntactic association will continue.

To a large extent, language shapes thinking, and thinking in turn shapes behavior. The continued use of heterosexually biased language will perpetuate results like those obtained in the aforementioned study by Wolfgang and Wolfgang (1971), where people place "homosexuals" further away from themselves than they do "normal peers." Lesbian women and gay men are, in fact, different. The language used to describe this difference can deliver either a message of pathology or a message of health. Researchers, writers, and therapists need to be aware of the powerful impact of language that can either point a condemning finger or lend a supportive and uplifting hand.

A TALE OF TWO THERAPIES

Examples of heterosexual bias in intervention strategies are numerous. Glasser (1965) provides us with a particularly vivid case study as he describes a client whose present problem was anxiety stemming from his having gay feelings. The client, Fred, expressed a great deal of ambivalence about wanting to pursue a gay lifestyle and also maintain an ongoing heterosexual marriage. Fred explained that he had not led an openly gay lifestyle for fear that it would hurt his wife, ruin his career, and have a disastrous effect upon his children. The intervention outlined by Glasser demonstrates how a pro-family bias on the part of the therapist can lead to an intervention such as the following:

> From the beginning I laid my cards openly on the table. I told him, as he already knew, that his kind of case was very difficult to treat. If he came, he must understand some conditions of treatment. He was told that he was to come once a week indefinitely; as an added emphasis I added, in a half-serious, half-joking way, that he might have to come for the rest of his life. In stressing the time, the all-important point was made that I would not give up on him. No matter how difficult the treatment became, I would stick with him.
>
> The final condition was that I did not want Fred to dwell on his problem during the therapy hour. No matter how much he told me about his homosexual feelings, I had no magic words to banish homosexuality. I was willing to discuss anything else. Heterosexuality was fine, as well as business, jokes, books, movies, the world situation, politics, and sports. Only in a crisis, such as his wanting to leave his work and family, would we discuss his problem, and then only to arrive at some way in which he could gain temporary relief. I credited him with being the expert on homosexuality because he had read almost every reputable book on the subject. (pp. 151–152)

Whereas Glasser says, "From the beginning I laid my cards openly on the table," the present authors suggest that he was playing with a marked deck. Glasser's underlying assumption in this intervention, as underscored in further descriptions of this same case, is that homosexual men are not real men. Therapy consists of establishing a relationship with a "real man" (i.e., the therapist). Although Fred was distressed by his gay feelings, it would appear that the therapist was even more distressed by these gay feelings, to the point that he would not even permit the client to discuss them.

The therapist in this case study was blatant in the belief that the client's exploration of his gay feelings was wrong. Glasser used the therapeutic relationship to make these specific value decisions for the client. The following excerpt demonstrates how the therapeutic relationship may be used to impose a heterosexual outcome:

> We now have enough involvement so that during a crisis, when he wants to run into the homosexual world, I can coldly confront him with his responsibility to his children, which wrenches him emotionally and serves to prevent him from giving up. Even though it may seem cruel to put Fred through such an emotional ordeal, there is no other choice; if I did not do so, he would lose respect for me. In years to come I hope to be able to report a successful conclusion to this case that so vitally affects the future of a family. (p. 153)

Fred's "homosexual desires" were viewed by the therapist as a direct antagonist to his family system, which the therapist believed must be preserved at all costs. The possible options that these desires and the family unit could co-exist, or the option that this particular family might disband in the best interest of the client and the family, do not appear even to have been considered in the course of therapy. It is unfortunate for Fred, and many others like him, that their therapists' heterosexual bias and its associated narrow view of the world and its options have turned therapy into a "cruel . . . emotional ordeal" dictating only one path to salvation (i.e., having and maintaining a family). While there may be nothing intrinsically wrong with the confrontational techniques used in this intervention, it is difficult to justify the imposition of heterosexual dogma upon this client as being therapeutic.

This anatomy of an intervention demonstrates how the therapist's values can become insidious darts hitting the target of the patient's self-image, which in part is derived from his or her sexuality. In this context, the biased therapist's office never acquires the attribute of safety for the patient, as the therapist mirrors the menace of a sexually moralistic society.

Examples of lesbian/gay-affirmative psychotherapeutic strategies are less numerous. Nonetheless, D. Clark (1979) presents a striking case study of a client with a presenting problem similar to that described by Fred. The client, Jim, was married, with children almost old enough to be on their own. He and his wife had a marriage that was reported to be the envy of all their friends. Jim's presenting problem was depression and suicidal ideation, stemming from his beginning to explore gay feelings and his recently having met a man for whom he had developed a strong attraction. Like Fred, Jim was experiencing the ambivalence of wanting to explore a gay lifestyle and also wanting to maintain an ongoing marriage and keep his family intact. The following excerpt shows how a gay-affirmative perspective values gay feelings and also demonstrates the creative violation of traditional male roles:

> We worked together for several months. Then he felt he was moving too fast and needed time out to take stock. During our time together, I could see his integrity and strength building. He found parts of himself that he had only glimpsed at times when he was drunk. He took pleasure in the sight and feel of his body. It was no longer a display of manly muscle to mislead other people. He learned that he needed to cry and feel tenderness in the arms of a man. He learned that it was safe to be a peer instead of a competitor with another man. He found his anger, which had been unacceptable to him when he was trying to have everyone like him. He found his greed and resentment connected with stored-up need for love with another man. And he found many other parts of himself revealed in dreams and defenseless love making. Slowly the pieces fitted together. Suicide was no longer tempting. There was too much to live for. True, the present agonies and those that lay ahead were frightening. But fright and timidity were newly discovered parts of his self that had to be accommodated to make it whole and strong. (p. 123)

In this intervention, we can note the ways in which the client and therapist explored how the male role interfered with Jim's ability to explore his gay feelings. In particular, it is important to note the way in which anger was uncovered and interpreted as good for the client. Previously, it had been "unacceptable to him when he was trying to have everyone like him." In addition, Jim learned to relate to another man as "a peer instead of a competitor." The therapist's approach—valuing this client's exploration of gay feelings and assisting him in uncovering ways in which the male role was interfering with his developing intimacy with other men—is typical of a gay-affirmative perspective.

In marked contrast to the profamily bias demonstrated in Glasser's therapeutic intervention, consider the way in which Clark dealt with the client's profamily bias:

> He was looking ahead to the probable end of a marriage, the shattering of his reputation, and possible rejection by his children because of false values he had helped them to build when he was a pretend person, and to a career that was already ending. The last time we met he cried through half of the session. As he was leaving the office, he said, "It's odd. I know I don't see things clearly because this is a time of change. There was a time when if I had cried I would have thought myself a weakling. Now, it's *because* I am crying that I know I am going to make it. Without the tears I could have been broken. The tears make me strong. I can heal myself and let some other people help. I don't have to be strong on the outside and hollow inside." (p. 123)

Jim's gay feelings and his right to explore them were seen by the therapist as part of the development of both integrity and dignity on the part of the client. Clearly, Jim's evolution through therapy was difficult for him. Like Fred in the previous intervention, Jim had gone through an emotional ordeal; however, the therapist's values in his interaction with Jim did not dictate a particular outcome as the only possible option. The decisions and choices that Jim had to make were his own; part of his suffering came from having to make troublesome choices and suffer consequences for those choices. The decisions were coming from Jim and not imposed by the therapist or a moralistic society. This is illustrative of a gay-affirmative intervention, in that the further exploration of gay feelings was valued as a possible choice, and the traditionally held male sex role that had led to many of Jim's problems was questioned and discussed, *while the decisions were left to the client.* Jim did not have to fear retribution from a frowning therapist. In this context, the gay-affirmative therapist's office acquired the safety necessary for the client's exploration and development of a sense of integrity and a definition of direction.

It would not be difficult for readers to visualize parallel case examples involving a married woman with lesbian feelings presenting herself for psychotherapy. The distinctions between a heterosexually biased intervention and a lesbian-affirmative intervention would be just as striking.

THE POWER POLITICS OF PSYCHOTHERAPY

Psychotherapists maintain an extremely powerful position in the lives of the people with whom they work. An awareness of just how this power relationship operates is essential to working with lesbian and gay male clients. Lesbian/gay-affirmative psychotherapy is not a technique; rather, it is more clearly a "frame of reference" (Malyon, Note 1). Materials specifically designed to facilitate lesbian/gay-affirmative psychotherapies are becoming available (Babuscio, 1977; Berzon & Leighton, 1979; D. Clark, 1977; Woodman & Lenna, 1980). With this "frame of reference" notion in mind, the present authors would like to consider some suggested guidelines for mental health professionals working with lesbian and gay male clients that have been developed by Betty Berzon and Don Clark (Clark, 1977). Although 12 guidelines are elaborated upon in Berzon and Clark's work, the present authors focus on the following four as they apply to lesbian/gay-affirmative psychotherapy.

1. *Therapists should use the weight of their authority to approve homosexual thoughts, behavior, and feelings, in general, when reported by clients.* This recommendation recognizes the power relationship of therapist and client. Heterosexual bias in psychotherapy can give the lesbian or gay male client the direct message, "You are sick." It is important that the weight of the therapist's role be used especially in the beginning stages of therapy to counteract past experiences of disapproval that may have been imparted by any number of agents of socialization. It is important to note that heterosexual thoughts and feelings are not discouraged. Lesbian/gay-affirmative therapies value the integrity of individuals in their life choices.

2. *Therapists should encourage clients to question basic assumptions about being gay and to develop personally relevant value systems as a basis for self-assessment. They should also point out the dangers of relying on society's value system for self-validation.* This recommendation acknowledges that lesbian or gay persons have grown up in a society where many of their thoughts and feelings have been considered "bad." The gradual process of becoming positive about their lesbian/gay identification requires that many of their previously held values be reexamined and redefined. Although redefining personal values rather than accepting external guidelines is undoubtably part of all persons' growth, this process takes on new and especially significant meaning for lesbian or gay clients.

3. *Therapists should desensitize shame and guilt surrounding homosexual thoughts, feelings, and behavior, in general, by pleasantly encouraging graphic descriptions of gay experiences and, when appropriate, sharing their own.*

This recommendation recognizes the sheer delight that many people experience when they are able to talk to nonjudgmental listeners. So often lesbian or gay male clients have not been able to talk about many of their feelings or fantasies about sexuality or relationships. This recommendation also recognizes that the lesbian or gay male therapist working with a lesbian or gay male client is involved in an interaction where therapist-client similarity can lead to less of a power differential. The use of one's own experience in a therapeutic setting can do much to reduce the power discrepancy between the therapist and client. This is equally true if the therapist is not a lesbian or gay man.

4. *Therapists should work toward a peer relationship with their clients. The message: "You are not a second-class or inferior person."* The lesbian or gay person may well have had the experience of growing up feeling sick, bad, crazy, stupid, and/or inferior. Psychotherapy is an opportunity to help undo this learning. This goal of trying to undo the therapist-client power structure as part of the therapy is totally consistent with the philosophy of feminist therapy, as well as an integral part of lesbian- and gay-affirmative psychotherapies.

The power inherent in the role of the mental health professional needs to be carefully examined because of the responsibilities of the potential misuse of that power. The ethical and moral issues that therapists need to address about this power structure are basic to the question of whether or not a given therapist can be of assistance to a lesbian or a gay man. The therapist must be continually asking the question, "What message am I giving to this client?"

The training of therapists who intend to work with lesbians and gay men should include specific training with regard to lesbian/and gay issues. Graduate training including personal interactions with lesbian women and gay men outside a clinical setting has proved beneficial in the desensitization of therapists' fears and in the alleviation of misconceptions regarding lesbian and gay male lifestyles (Garfinkle & Morin, 1978; Morin & Garfinkle, 1978). The lessening of stereotypes and education regarding misconceptions about lesbians and gay men has been shown to result in a significant increase in therapists' own feelings of competency (Morin, 1974). Knowledge, competency, and the developing of techniques to avoid all forms of bias are thought to be essential to improving the quality of interventions offered to all consumers of psychological services.

CONCLUSION

This chapter has attempted to review the background knowledge used as a basis for psychologoical interventions with lesbian women and gay men from a lesbian/gay-affirmative perspective (i.e., a perspective that values an adult same-sex relationship style as a positive outcome for some people). The psychological literature has been reviewed in order to determine the extent to which it reflects a heterosexual bias (i.e., the valuing of heterosexual outcome as superior to and/or more natural than homosexual outcome). Lesbian/gay-affirmative psychotherapies are in part defined as an absence of heterosexual bias; however, lesbian/gay affirmative psychotherapies are not based on a homosexual bias (i.e., a belief that homosexual outcome is superior to and/or more natural than heterosexual outcome). *Lesbian/gay-affirmative psychotherapies value diversity and the integrity of each individual.*

A review of the literature on psychotherapy clearly reveals the extent of heterosexual bias in the theory and research upon which psychological interventions are based. This bias is found in theory, in case studies of interventions, and in the language of psychotherapy; it is believed to have an adverse effect on the therapeutic outcome of interventions with lesbian women and gay men. Although no definitive answers have been made for the problem of heterosexual bias in psychotherapy, it is hoped that by raising the level of awareness of the existence of this problem, that mental health professionals will explore options that better serve lesbian or gay male clients.

Lesbian/and gay sexual orientations have long suffered from the stigma of being labeled mental illness. In order for truly lesbian- and/or gay-affirmative therapy to evolve, future interventions must suggest mental health rather than mental illness. Optimistic lesbian- or gay-affirmative options and possibilities must be on the menu that is offered to the lesbian woman or gay male client in order to facilitate a well-integrated, healthy concept of self. It is the responsibility of mental health professionals to clear the roadblock of heterosexual bias so that there can be free access to explore all of the avenues of human potential. It is the responsibility of consumers of psychological services to insist that these options be made available.

NOTES

[1]For the purposes of this chapter, *gay* is used as synonymous with *gay male*, and not in the generic sense to refer both to women and men.

[2]For a more detailed review of the theory and research, as well as an elaboration on the possibilities of a feminist redirection of theory and research on lesbians, the reader is directed to Mannion (1976).

[3]The authors' objection to theories of "etiology" is the connotation of pathology that they entail. The authors do not object to a developmental perspective, which they believe to be an essential part of lesbian/gay-affirmative psychotherapies. For a more comprehensive and contemporary perspective on theories of sexual orientation, see Storms (1980).

[4]The authors prefer the term *androphilic,* meaning erotosexual pairing with a man either by a woman (androphilic woman) or by another man (androphilic man), to the term *homosexual.* The parallel term for erotosexual pairing with a woman is *gynophilic.* Both terms include falling in love. See Money (1980).

[5]For those readers unfamiliar with aesthetic realism, it is a brainwashing or cult-like approach to

converting people from same-sex attraction to opposite-sex attraction. These groups are similar to Alcoholics Anonymous groups and are sometimes called "H Persuasion" groups.

[6]The authors wish to acknowledge Steve Berman, who uncovered most of these references (Berman, Note 3), and who greatly influenced the authors' thinking on these issues.

[7]Unlike the previous example, these women were part of a committed couple and were therefore eligible to be accepted by the Institute.

[8]The authors would like to acknowledge Dorothy Riddle and Barbara Love, both of whom have spoken eloquently on this issue.

[9]This particular recommendation, which serves as a model for avoiding heterosexual assumption, has been suggested by Nancy Henley's book on power, sex, and nonverbal communication (Henley, 1977).

[10]Besides illustrating three ways in which language can be biased, the sentance is also confused and nonsensical. In what way do "Peeping Toms" not "feel themselves to be the sex that nature has given them"?

REFERENCE NOTES

1. Malyon, A. *Toward a definition of gay-affirmative psychotherapy.* Paper presented at the annual convention of the American Psychological Association, Montreal, September 1980.

2. Morin, S. F., & Miller, J. S. *On fostering positive identity in gay men: The implications of gender identity research and treatment.* Paper presented at the annual meeting of the American Orthopsychiatric Association, San Francisco, March 1978.

3. Berman, S. *Psychotherapy with gay people: A review of the literature published and unpublished.* Unpublished manuscript, 1974.

4. Henley, N., Tennov, D., Grady, K., Parlee, M., & Brannon, R. *Eliminating sexist language: The can, should, and how to.* Paper presented at the Open Forum, annual meeting of the American Psychological Association, Chicago, August 1975.

REFERENCES

Abbott, F., & Love, B. *Sappho was a right-on woman: A liberated view of lesbianism.* New York: Stein & Day, 1977.

Ainsworth, M. S. The development of infant-mother attachment. In B. M. Caldwell & H. N. Ricciuti (Eds.), *Review of child development research* (Vol. 3). Chicago: University of Chicago Press, 1973.

Alpert, R. LSD and sexuality. *Psychedelic Review,* 1969, *10,* 21–24.

American Psychiatric Association. *Diagnostic and statistical manual of mental disorders* (3rd ed.). Washington, D.C.: Author, 1980.

American Psychological Association. *Casebook on ethical standards of psychologists.* Washington, D.C.: Author, 1970.

Anonymous. Brain surgery for sexual disorders. *British Medical Journal,* 1969, *4*(5678), 250–251.

Babuscio, J. *We speak for ourselves: Experiences in homosexual counseling.* Philadelphia: Fortress Press, 1977.

Bancroft, J. Aversion therapy of homosexuality. *British Journal of Psychiatry,* 1969, *115*(529), 1417–1431.

Barr, R. F., & McConaghy, N. Penile responses to appetitive and aversive stimuli in relation to sexual orientation and conditioning performance. *British Journal of Psychiatry*, 1971, *119*(551), 377–383.

Berzon, B. Developing a positive gay identity. In B. Berzon & R. Leighton (Eds.), *Positively gay*. Milbrae, Calif.: Celestial Arts, 1979.

Berzon, B., & Leighton, R. (Eds.). *Positively gay*. Milbrae, Calif.: Celestial Arts, 1979.

Bieber, I., Dain, H. J., Dince, P. R., Drellich, M. G., Grand, H. G., Gundlach, R. H., Kremer, M. W., Rifkin, A. H., Wilber, C. B., & Bieber, T. B. *Homosexuality: A psychoanalytic study*. New York: Basic Books, 1962.

Bowlby, J. *Attachment and loss* (Vol. 1, *Attachment*). New York: Basic Books, 1969.

Caprio, F. *Female homosexuality: A psychodynamic study of lesbianism*. New York: Citadel, 1954.

Cass, V. Homosexual identity formation: A theoretical model. *Journal of Homosexuality*, 1979, *4*, 219–235.

Chevalier-Skolnikoff, S. Male-female, female-female, and male-male behavior in the stumptail monkey. *Archives of Sexual Behavior*, 1974, *3*, 95–116.

Clark, D. *Loving someone gay*. Milbrae, Calif.: Celestial Press, 1977.

Clark, D. *Living gay*. Milbrae, Calif.: Celestial Press, 1979.

Clark, T., & Epstein, R. Self-concept and expectancy for social reinforcement in noninstitutionalized male homosexuals. *Journal of Consulting and Clinical Psychology*, 1972, *38*, 174–180.

Dank, B. Coming out in the gay world. *Psychiatry*, 1971, *34*, 180–197.

Dardick, L., & Grady, K. E. Openness between gay persons and health professionals. *Annals of Internal Medicine*, 1980, *93*,(1), 115–119.

Davidson, G. C. Homosexuality: The ethical challenge. *Journal of Consulting and Clinical Psychology*, 1976, *44*(2), 157–162.

de Monteflores, C., & Schultz, S. J. Coming out: Similarities and differences for lesbians and gay men. *Journal of Social Issues*, 1978, *34*(3), 59–72.

Erickson, E. *Childhood and society*. New York: Norton, 1963.

Evans, R. B. Physical and biochemical characteristics of homosexual men. *Journal of Consulting and Clinical Psychology*, 1972, *39*, 140–147.

Evans, R. I. A conversation with Konrad Lorenz. *Psychology Today*, November 1974, pp. 83–93.

Ford, C., & Beach, F. *Patterns of sexual behavior*. New York: Harper & Row, 1951.

Freud, S. A letter from Freud (April 9, 1935). *American Journal of Psychiatry*, 1951, *107*, 786–787.

Freund, K., Langevin, R., Chamberlayne, R., Deosoran, A., & Zajac, Y. The phobic theory of male homosexuality. *Archives of General Psychiatry*, 1974, *31*, 496–499.

Freund, K., Langevin, R., Gibiri, S., & Zajac, Y. Heterosexual aversion to homosexual males. *British Journal of Psychiatry*, 1973, *122*, 163–169.

Freund, K., Langevin, R., & Zajac, Y. Heterosexual aversion in homosexual males: A second experiment. *British Journal of Psychiatry*, 1974, *125*, 177–180.

Garfinkle, E. M., & Morin, S. F. Psychologists' attitudes toward homosexual clients. *Journal of Social Issues*, 1978, *34*(3), 101–112.

Glasser, W. *Reality therapy*. New York: Harper & Row, 1965.

Hadden, S. B. Group therapy for homosexuals. *Medical Aspects of Human Sexuality*, 1971, *5*, 116–126.

Haley, J. *The power tactics of Jesus Christ and other essays*. New York: Avon, 1969.

Hatterer, L. J. A critique of Green's "Homosexuality as a mental illness." *American Journal of Psychiatry*, 1972, *10*(1), 103–104.

Hendin, H. *The age of sensation*. New York: Norton, 1975.

Henley, N. *Body politics*. Englewood Cliffs, N.J.: Prentice-Hall, 1977.

Herron, W., Kinter, T., Sollinger, I., & Trubowitz, J. New psychoanalytic perspectives on the treatment of a homosexual male. *Journal of Homosexuality*, 1980, *5*(4), 393–403.

Johnston, J. *Lesbian nation: The feminist solution.* New York: Simon & Schuster, 1973.

Jones, N. B. *Ethological studies of child behavior.* Cambridge, England: Cambridge University Press, 1972.

Kaye, H., Berl, S., Clare, J., Eleston, M., Gershwin, B., Gershwin, P., Kogan, L., Torda, C., & Wilber, C. Homosexuality in women. *Archives of General Psychiatry*, 1967, *17*, 626–634.

Kenyon, F. E. Studies of female homosexuality: IV. Social and psychiatric aspects. *British Journal of Psychiatry*, 1968, *114*, 1337–1350.

Kimmel, D. C. Adult development and aging: A gay perspective. *Journal of Social Issues*, 1978, *34*(3), 113–130.

Klaich, D. *Woman plus woman: Attitudes toward lesbianism.* New York: Avon, 1969.

Kohlberg, L. Stage and sequence: The cognitive developmental approach to socialization. In D. A. Goslin (Ed.), *Handbook of socialization theory and research.* Chicago: Rand McNally, 1969.

Kranz, S. (Ed.). *The H persuasion: How persons have permanently changed from homosexuality through the study of aesthetic realism with Eli Siegel.* New York: Definition Press, 1971.

Lewis, R. *Men in difficult times.* Englewood Cliffs, N.J.: Prentice-Hall, 1981.

Litkey, L. J., & Feniczy, P. An approach to the control of homosexual practices. *International Journal of Neuropsychiatry*, 1967, *3*(1), 20–23.

Lorenz, K. *On aggression.* London: Methuen, 1966.

Mannion, K. Female homosexuality: A comprehensive review of theory and research. *JSAS Catalog of Selected Documents in Psychology*, 1976, *6*(1), 44. (Ms. No. 1247)

Marmor, J. *Homosexual behavior: A modern reappraisal.* New York: Basic Books, 1980.

Martin, D., & Lyon, P. *Lesbian/woman.* New York: Bantam, 1972. .

Mass, L. The birds, the bees, and John Money. *Christopher Street*, September 1980, pp. 24–30.

Masters, W. H., & Johnson, V. E. *Homosexuality in perspective.* Boston: Little, Brown, 1979.

McConaghy, N. Penile volume changes to moving pictures of male and female nudes in heterosexual and homosexual males. *Behaviour Research and Therapy*, 1967, *5*, 43–48.

McDonald, G. J. Misrepresentation, liberalism and heterosexual bias in introductory psychology textbooks. *Journal of Homosexuality*, 1981, *6*(3), 45–60.

McDonald, G. J. Individual differences in the coming out process for gay men: Implications for theoretical models. *Journal of Homosexuality*, in press.

Money, J. *Love and love sickness: The science of sex, gender difference, and pair bonding.* Baltimore: Johns Hopkins University Press, 1980.

Morin, S. F. Educational programs as a means of changing attitudes toward gay people. *Homosexual Counseling Journal*, 1974, *1*, 160–165.

Morin, S. F. Heterosexual bias in psychological research on lesbianism and male homosexuality. *American Psychologist*, 1977, *32*(8), 629–637.

Morin, S. F. Psychology in the gay community: An overview. *Journal of Social Issues*, 1978, *34* (3), 1–6.

Morin, S. F., & Garfinkle, E. P. Male homophobia. *Journal of Social Issues*, 1978, *34*(1), 29–47.

Morin, S. F., & Schultz, S. J. The gay movement and the rights of children. *Journal of Social Issues*, 1978, *34*(2), 137–148.

Pattison, E. M., & Pattison, L. M. Ex-gays: Religiously mediated change in homosexuals. *American Journal of Psychiatry*, 1980, *137*(12), 1552–1562.

Piaget, J. *Six psychological studies.* New York: Random House, 1967.

Pleck, J. H., & Brannon, R. (Eds.). Male roles and the male experience. *Journal of Social Issues*, 1978, *34*(1) (whole issue).

Pleck, J. H., & Sawyer, J. (Eds.). *Men and masculinity*. Englewood Cliffs, N.J.: Prentice-Hall, 1974.

Pondelickova, J., & Nedoma, K. Experience with outpatient treatment of sexual deviants. *Ceskoslovenska Psychiatris*, 1970, *66*(1), 23–26.

Riddle, D. I., & Morin, S. F. Removing the stigma: Data from individuals. *APA Monitor*, November 1977, pp. 16, 28.

Riddle, D. I., & Sang, B. Psychotherapy with lesbians. *Journal of Social Issues*, 1978, *34*(3), 84–100.

Roboch, J., & Nedoma, K. Indications of testicular pulpectomy in sexual delinquents. *Ceskoslovenska Psychiatris*, 1970, *66*(3), 152–157.

Rupp, J. *Modern legal medicine, psychiatry, and forensic science*. Philadelphia: F. A. Davis, 1980.

Sachs, L. J., & Titievsky, J. Electroconvulsive treatment and the homosexual aspect of schizophrenia: A psychodynamic consideration. *Journal of the Hillside Hospital*, 1967, *16*(3–4), 205–218.

Sang, B. Psychotherapy with lesbians: Some observations and tentative generalizations. In D. K. Carter & E. I. Rollins (Eds.), *Psychotherapy for women: Treatment toward equality*. Springfield, Ill.: Charles C Thomas, 1977.

Siegelman, M. Birth order and family size of homosexual men and women. *Journal of Consulting and Clinical Psychology*, 1973, *41*, 164.

Silverman, L. H., Kwawer, J. S., Wolitzky, C., & Coron, M. An experimental study of the psychoanalytic theory of male homosexuality. *Journal of Abnormal Psychology*, 1973, *82*, 178–188.

Socarides, C. W. Homosexuality and medicine. *Journal of the American Medical Association*, 1970, *212*, 1199–1202.

Socarides, C. W. *Homosexuality*. New York: Jason Aronson, 1978.

Storms, M. D. Theories of sexual orientation. *Journal of Personality and Social Psychology*, 1980, *38*(5), 783–792.

Task Force on the Status of Lesbian and Gay Male Psychologists. Removing the stigma: Final report of the Board of Social and Ethical Responsibility for Psychology's Task Force on the Status of Lesbian and Gay Male Psychologists. JSAS *Catalogue of Selected Documents in Psychology*, 1980, *10*, 81. (Ms. No. 2121)

Tinbergen, N. *Social behavior in animals*. London: Methuen, 1953.

Tripp, C. A. *The homosexual matrix*. New York: New American Library, 1975.

Troiden, R. R. Becoming homosexual: A model of gay identity acquisition. *Psychiatry*, 1979, *42*(4), 362–373.

Weinberg, G. *Society and the healthy homosexual*. New York: St. Martin's Press, 1972.

Wolfgang, A., & Wolfgang, J. Exploration of attitudes via physical interpersonal distance toward the obese, drug users, homosexuals, police, and other marginal figures. *Journal of Clinical Psychology*, 1971, *27*, 510–512.

Woodman, N. J., & Lenna, H. R. *Counseling with gay men and women*. San Francisco: Jossey-Bass, 1980.

IV Reducing Bias in Therapy

Clearly, the evidence is not yet in on whether sex bias exists in psychotherapy. Even though a number of studies have reported negative results, recent advances in research methods have led to findings of definite sex bias. Consequently, it seems appropriate to consider what can be done to minimize sex bias in clinical practice.

In the next chapter, Cooley and Murray discuss what can be done about gender bias in psychotherapy. Many of their suggestions can be applied to other forms of bias also.

13 What Can Be Done about Bias in Therapy?

ELIZABETH COOLEY AND JOAN MURRAY

The question of what can be done to reduce bias in therapy must be broken down into two separate questions—where to intervene, and how. It would seem that the most effective place to try to make changes is in the training of new therapists. Accordingly, how to do so is discussed here at length. But what about therapists who are already practicing? How do we reach them? Some suggestions are offered on how to reach them, not only directly, but also indirectly through raising the consciousness of clients and prospective clients—what might be called consumer education.

This chapter focuses on the case of women in therapy. A similar case can be made for gays in therapy, for blacks in therapy, or for any other group that experiences bias. The same principles for change apply, but the content of the information conveyed to the therapist or consumer is different.

THERAPIST TRAINING

In any of the settings where therapists are trained—psychology departments in universities, social work departments in universities, professional schools, or medical settings—the following suggestions could be applied toward the end of reducing bias in therapy. No matter what the setting is, any program to diminish bias in therapy must have *institutional support*— that is, those who run the institution (university, professional school, etc.) must believe that women's issues are real and need to be dealt with in training. These issues include the position of women in society.

341

The Position of Women

An unbiased view of women in our society must acknowledge the realistic position of women psychologically, socially, economically, and politically. A woman's psychological problems cannot be viewed as totally the result of individual pathology. Social, economic, and political factors must be considered. For instance, consider the case of a woman raising two children alone. Her income is the sole source of financial support for herself and her family, and she is concerned about what she will do if inflation continues unchecked. She comes up for a promotion at work, but is passed over; the promotion is given to a man less qualified than herself. Shortly afterward, she develops anxiety attacks and seeks the help of a psychotherapist (assuming, of course, that she could get such help on her income). Now, in this situation, the authors believe that it would be insensitive to attribute the entire "cause" of the psychological malady to intrapsychic factors. The therapist must address the economic and social causes too, and must make them part of the psychotherapeutic process. Here the economic cause is the contribution of recent events at work to her realistic fear that she will not be able to support her family on her present income, and the social cause is the gender bias in our society that permits a woman to be denied a promotion in favor of a less qualified man. These considerations are not trivial, and to avoid them would be a great injustice to the client.

In many cases of women in therapy, social, economic, and/or political factors are involved. *Social factors* can include cases where a woman is hampered by the constraints of the female role (often combined with pressure to conform to that role), ranging from situations where a woman's husband expects her to do all of the housework even though they both work full-time, to situations involving spouse abuse and rape. These last two instances involve political and economic factors as well. *Political factors* include such questions as these: Is it legal for a husband to force a wife to have sex when she doesn't want to? How does the law treat a man who beats his wife? *Economic factors* could also apply in both cases: perhaps the woman is fed up with the way her husband treats her and would like to leave him. But she has no job and no salable skills. So where can she go? What will she do for money?

Another issue that may need to be addressed in therapy with female clients is pressure to conform to the female role. Women are often told that their dissatisfaction with the restrictions of the female role (e.g., being a wife and mother to the exclusion of all other endeavors) is neurotic or unfeminine. Moreover, they are often encouraged by friends, family, and even some therapists to accept the restrictions and be happy living within them. When a woman in therapy is experiencing such pressure, it is important for the therapist to help her clarify her feelings about her role, and to develop a strategy to mediate the pressure.

Whenever a woman is confronted with constraints of the female role and/or pressure to conform to this role, or sex discrimination in the economic and/or political spheres, in addition to any presenting problems, she is likely to be angry. If she is angry, it is important for the therapist to acknowledge this anger and its appropriateness.

Also in working with women in therapy, it is essential for the therapist to acknowledge that the pressure on women to conform is not always external. Many women have been socialized to believe that the female role encompasses all the possible behaviors that are normal for them. When a woman seeks to step outside the female role, she may experience *internal* conflict with all her unconscious expectations. In addition, it may be difficult for her to institute change, since she is used to being rewarded when she conforms to the female role and punished when she does not. Any or all of this must be addressed in psychotherapy, with the intent being to support behaviors that are within the female role as well as behaviors outside of it.

Specifics of a Training Program

In all aspects of a training program for therapists, women's issues need to be recognized. The chapter now elaborates on how this can be done in various facets of therapist training—courses, supervision, case discussions, and others.

Courses

In every therapy course, the unique position and experiences of women should be addressed and brought up in all possible connections. The potential for sex bias should be illustrated and discussed; situations where sex bias is likely to occur should also be mentioned. In addition, special classes can be offered dealing with women's issues, the development of women in our society, and/or political and economic factors affecting women.[1]

Theory. A theory course should include literature that focuses specifically on women. As we have seen, some psychoanalytic theories present women in a negative perspective, with normality conceived as conformity to the female sex role.[2] This topic obviously needs to be discussed. It is also important to include newer theories that link psychopathology in women to the female sex role, such as Joanna Bunker Rohrbaugh's conceptualization in *Women: Psychology's Puzzle* (1979).

Rohrbaugh suggests that male-female relationships may be significant in the etiology of depression in women. Her approach focuses on the social role for women and on "the personality characteristics which that role fosters" (p. 406). One theory holds that women "have learned to respond to adverse circumstances with depression rather than with positive action (Weissman & Klerman, 1977)" (p. 403). This view is based on Seligman's animal model of depression, called *learned helplessness.* The basic idea is that animals (or people) who have been exposed to unavoidable trauma—*trauma that they can do nothing about*—later react passively when faced with new trauma. Apparently, they have learned that there is nothing they can do to avoid or lessen the trauma, so they develop the response of passively "taking it": "Seligman (1974) believes that learned helplessness in animals may parallel the lack of initiative and the hopeless attitude about the effectiveness of one's actions that are typical of depression in humans." The process conceptualized for women is this:

> Childhood experiences teach girls to think of themselves as powerless, helpless, and ineffective, and . . . therefore as women they respond to stress and trauma with passivity and the hopelessness of depression. As Aaron Beck and Ruth Greenberg explain it:
>
>> According to Seligman, it was not trauma *per se* "that produced failure to escape, but having learned that no response at all can control trauma." Many female children are taught that their personal worth and survival depend not on effective responding to life situations but on physical beauty and appeal to men—that is, that they have no *direct* control over the circumstances of their lives. Throughout adolescence they are subjected not to physical shock [the unavoidable trauma to which the animals were subjected], but to parental and institutional supervision that both restricts their alternatives and shelters them from the consequences of any disapproved alternatives they do choose to pursue. Perhaps women, like dogs who have learned that their own behavior is unrelated to their subsequent welfare [dogs were the animals used in the original helplessness experiments], lose their ability to respond effectively and to learn that responding produces relief. (1974, pp. 120–121) (Rohrbaugh, 1979, p. 404)

A related theory, the *social status hypothesis,* "suggests that sexual discrimination and inequality lead to economic and legal helplessness and dependence on others—qualities that are accompanied by low self-esteem, low aspirations, and eventually depression" (Rohrbaugh, 1979, p. 407). Scarf (1979) has developed a model that incorporates learned helplessness and the social status hypothesis. Her reasoning goes as follows: Women are encouraged to be dependent on others and not to be self-sufficient (this amounts to being helpless). They are encouraged to invest strongly in a small number of intensely important relationships and to define themselves in terms of (usually) their husbands. So, if the relationship with the husband is disrupted, the woman feels she has failed completely, and depression occurs.

Arieti and Bemporad (1978) have offered a theory that addresses depression in men and women. Depression in men is seen as associated with disappointments in the man's career, whereas in women it is associated with loss of attachments. A female is brought up to serve the needs of others, be submissive to her husband, and accept her subordinate position in life. As an adult, the woman often represses the sorrow, anger, and frustration that accompany her subordinate position. This repression, at best, leads to neurotic defenses; at worst, it facilitates serious mental disorders, especially depression. To make matters worse, once a woman has become dependent, she is criticized for being dependent but given no way to assert her independence. In addition, her primary function of homemaking is increasingly devalued in modern society (Rohrbaugh, 1979).

Therapy. Such courses should consider the implications of therapy for women. They should note the differential frequencies of occurrence of certain emotional disorders in men and women (depression and anorexia nervosa are more common in women) and discuss causal factors. One possible area of focus might be the suggestion that "female illnesses" have clear themes. Rohrbaugh offers an interpretation of how such themes manifest themselves in depression, anorexia nervosa, hysteria, and phobias (especially agoraphobia):

> Women suffering from them [female illnesses] are likely to be extremely dependent, passive, and helpless and to derive a sense of identity only through others—primarily men but also children. In a frantic attempt to please others, some of these women become conventional, martyred caretakers who are then vulnerable to the depression that can accompany the empty-nest syndrome. Some become depressed trying to conform to the expectations of their Dominant Other [usually the husband]. Some women starve themselves in response to demands for autonomy or in a vain attempt to attain a distorted image of physical beauty that they see as the path to happiness and fulfillment through male attentions. And still other women rely on superficial social charm and emotional appeals to manipulate the men in their lives.
>
> As a group these women tend to shun traditionally masculine behavior involving self-assertion, competition, and mastery. They are especially loath to express their anger: They turn it on themselves in depression or self-starvation; they try to deny and block it out, and hence develop pervasive phobias; or they turn it on others through the subtle manipulations of superficial charm.
>
> The striking thing about all of these women is their extreme—and conflicted —expression of traditionally feminine characteristics. While Freudians interpret their distressing symptoms as a *denial* of femininity stemming from unresolved Oedipal conflicts, feminists interpret them as a *caricature* of femininity stemming from socialization pressures and resulting social role conflicts. The Freudians and the feminists appear, however, to agree on one central point: *Femininity may be harmful to a woman's health.* (1979, pp. 421–422)

Sex-related concepts for health are another important area for consideration in a therapy course. Such a course could include discussion of which characteristics and qualities are seen as healthy for men, and which are seen as healthy for women. The Broverman group's research (Broverman, Broverman, Clarkson, Rosenkrantz, & Vogel, 1970) suggested that a healthy man was described as having characteristics different from those of a healthy woman, and that the characteristics considered healthy for a male were seen as *healthier* than the characteristics seen as healthy for a female. Such sex-related differences are especially important when setting *goals* for the therapy.

Lastly, a course in therapy could also include exposure to nonsexist therapies. In most cases, nonsexist therapy involves using a wide array of existing therapeutic techniques, with attention to eliminating the sexist aspects. Feminist therapy, in addition, brings in political values, including the belief that the inferior status of women "is due to their having less political and economic power than men"; the belief that the "primary source of women's pathology is social, not personal: external, not internal"; and the goal of social and political change—feminist therapy is opposed to personal adjustment to existing social conditions (Rohrbaugh, 1979, p. 444).

Development of women. Whether in a separate course or as part of an existing course, attention must be given to the unique features of psychosocial development in women. These include sex-role socialization, as well as the special problems that women encounter—the empty-nest syndrome, role conflicts, and dealing with aging. *The empty-nest syndrome* (Bart, 1971) refers to depression that occurs in the woman who has made raising her children the main focus of her life after those children grow up and leave home. When a woman defines her purpose in life as raising her children, what does she have left when her children are gone?

At the present time, role conflicts are common among women because of the changing role of women in society. When women are brought up with traditional values and then exposed to the values of women's liberation, serious conflicts can result. A woman may not know what to do or what to expect from herself. One area that has received a great deal of attention is conflict over achievement—the "fear of success," especially well described by Horner (1970). Whatever conflicts a woman has, these need to be addressed in therapy, along with any attendant guilt, fear, and so on.

Another experience that is unique to women is that of being devalued as one gets older. While a man is often viewed as more successful and more valuable as he ages, a woman is more likely to be viewed as less successful and less valuable. The reason has to do with sex-role-related concepts of success. A man is more successful, valuable, and desirable as he gets a better job, makes more money, and so forth. On the other hand, a woman is often viewed as successful and desirable only if she is physically attractive. Consequently, as a man gets older, he is likely to be further advanced in his career and therefore to be viewed as *more* successful and more desirable; but as a woman gets older, she is likely to be viewed as *less* successful and less desirable because she is seen as becoming less physically attractive. Consequently, aging in women is likely to be a major issue in therapy, especially for those women who believe that they are valuable and desirable only because of their physical beauty.

Courses outside psychology. Students should be encouraged to take courses and/or to read in areas other than psychology in order to better understand the social, economic, and political position of women. The disciplines of sociology, economics, and political science are possible sources of appropriate courses and material, and fiction often offers considerable insight into the position of women (e.g., Tillie Olsen's "Tell Me a Riddle," 1961; Marilyn French's *The Women's Room,* 1977).

Case Discussions

Women's issues should also be addressed during case discussions or presentations. These include social, political, and economic factors, as well as developmental problems faced by women. An individual case can be analyzed from sexist, nonsexist, and feminist viewpoints to clarify the differences among them. Similarly, diagnostic bias can be illustrated and areas where diagnostic bias is likely should be noted.

To familiarize students with how diagnoses vary between men and women, they could be assigned a project where they go through all the diagnoses given to men clients and to women clients at their setting (clinic, hospital, etc.) in the last year; then they might tabulate these and discuss how the diagnoses given to male clients differ from those given to female clients.

Demonstrations and/or films can also be used in this context. For instance, a nonbiased therapist and a sex-biased therapist could interview the same client (live or on film) and talk about their impressions, theoretical considerations, conclusions, diagnosis, and treatment plans. Then the students could discuss how the two therapists differ. This could be very useful in pointing up the variety of differences between the sex-biased and non-sex-biased approaches.

Supervision

Students should obviously have supervisors who are not sex-biased. This is of major import because how students learn to do therapy is greatly influenced by the direction of their supervisors. These supervisors need to be able to discuss sex bias in the actual therapy session, and to provide alternative non-biased interventions.

This is a good place to reiterate the necessity of having institutional support. That is, the school must be committed to training students to be nonbiased. In the case of supervision, the institution has a very direct influence because it (in the form of some committee, say) hires the actual supervisors. Care must be taken to hire supervisors who are not sex-biased.

Women's Resources

As part of their training, students need to learn about what resources are available for women in their neighborhood, town, and/or city.

These include resources providing medical care free or at low cost, specialized care for women addicted to alcohol or drugs, child care, shelter and assistance for battered women, legal aid, and educational/career counseling.

Research

An effort should be made to eliminate sex bias from research and to encourage research on women's issues. Research on women's issues must be viewed as valid and valuable. Faculty members should not be penalized for concentrating their research on women. In tenure decisions, research on women's issues should obviously not be devalued. On the positive side, the school could set up research projects on various topics related to women and could provide the resources and funding to allow students to work on them.

Admissions

In deciding who will be admitted to a training program, committees should be careful not to discriminate against feminists, and an effort should be made to include a number of feminists among those admitted.

Overview

In order to train therapists who are sensitive to sex bias, a concern with women's issues has to be built into the training program. This requires that the training institution recognize women's issues and want to make an effort to teach students about them. In practice, there have to be people in the training program—faculty and students—who understand women's issues and can raise and discuss them in various aspects of the program. It is desirable to include a number of feminists among the faculty and/or supervision staff and among the students so that they can expose trainees to the feminist perspective. For therapists who have already been trained, a different approach is required.

PRACTICING THERAPISTS

Practicing therapists are admittedly much more difficult to reach and influence. For therapists working in institutional settings—hospitals, clinics, universities, etc.—the administration could offer (require?) short courses aimed at reducing sex bias in the practice of therapy in that particular setting. Such courses should cover the same areas discussed in regard to therapists in training. The institution could also provide case conferences in which outside therapists sit in and bring up sex bias and women's issues. In addition, the institution and its staff should be open to the contributions of trainees and newer therapists who have an understanding of women's issues. Again, in regard to hiring, a concern for women needs to enter into consideration of applicants. Those who show obvious sex bias should not be hired. And there must be no discrimination against feminists.

Therapists in private practice are even more difficult to reach. One way to influence them is through continuing education courses (required in many states). Here, therapists could learn about sex bias and how to avoid it. It might also be possible for women's groups to set up files of nonsexist therapists for women to consult when selecting a therapist.

THE PUBLIC

Consumers (clients) can have a great impact on therapists, especially those in private practice. If a woman goes to a therapist and finds that he or she is sex-biased, the client can change therapists, preferably telling the first therapist why she is doing so. Once consumers know that they have discretion with biased therapists, they may provide an impetus for biased therapists to change. What is required for this to happen is consumer education. Just as consumers have become more careful in purchasing goods, they can learn to be more selective in purchasing the service of psychotherapy. Consumer education can be accomplished through college courses, books, television, newspapers, magazines, and any other method that will reach the public.

MINORITY GROUPS

The present chapter has focused on reducing *sex* bias in therapy. However, the methods offered can easily be applied to other groups that may experience therapeutic bias—blacks, Hispanics, gays, and others. The modalities stay the same; only the content changes. In fact, any or all of the interventions mentioned—courses, supervision, and so forth—could be utilized to reduce *all* types of bias through programs that address not only the issues and problems of women, but those of all minority groups.

CONCLUSION

It is clear that any effort to reduce bias in therapy requires support. In the case of training, the support must come from the training institution. In the case of practicing therapists, the support must come from state licensing boards, governent consumer agencies, consumer groups, and the public. In the case of the public, the support can come from a variety of sources, including government, the media, schools, and professional associations. Without commitment to change, no change will occur.

NOTES

[1]Similar considerations apply to blacks, gays, and other groups.
[2]For a discussion of views of women in theory, see Chapter 2.

REFERENCES

Arieti, S., & Bemporad, J. *Severe and mild depression*. New York: Basic Books, 1978.

Bart, P. B. Depression in middle-aged women. In V. Gornick & B. K. Moran (Eds.), *Woman in sexist society*. New York: Basic Books, 1971.

Beck, A. T., & Greenberg, R. L. Cognitive therapy with depressed women. In V. Franks & V. Burtle (Eds.), *Women in therapy: New psychotherapies for a changing society*. New York: Brunner/Mazel, 1974.

Broverman, I. K., Broverman, D. M., Clarkson, F. E., Rosenkrantz, P. S., & Vogel, S. R. Sex-role stereotypes and clinical judgments of mental health. *Journal of Consulting and Clinical Psychology*, 1970, *34*, 1–7.

French, M. *The women's room*. New York: Summit Books, 1977.

Horner, M. S. Femininity and successful achievement: A basic inconsistency. In J. M. Bardwick, E. Douvan, M. S. Horner, & D. Gutmann (Eds.), *Feminine personality and conflict*. Belmont, Calif.: Brooks/Cole, 1970.

Olsen, T. Tell me a riddle. In T. Olsen, *Tell me a riddle and other stories*. New York: Dell, 1961.

Rohrbaugh, J. B. *Women: Psychology's puzzle*. New York: Basic Books, 1979.

Scarf, M. The more sorrowful sex. *Psychology Today*, April 1979, pp. 44–45, 47–48.

Seligman, M. E. P. Depression and learned helplessness. In R. J. Friedman & M. M. Katz (Eds.), *The psychology of depression: Contemporary theory and research*. Washington, D.C.: Winston-Wiley, 1974.

Weissman, M. S., & Klerman, L. Sex differences and the epidemiology of depression. *Archives of General Psychiatry*, 1977, *34*, 98–111.

V Conclusions and Future Directions

A number of types of bias have been found in psychotherapy. Hatfield and Perlmutter (Chapter 3), as well as Murray and Abramson (Chapter 6), report findings of gender and attractiveness bias, plus bias in interactions of gender with attractiveness; Abramowitz and Murray (Chapter 9) report evidence of circumscribed racial bias; Schover (Chapter 10) finds bias relating to therapist gender and client gender when client sexual material is involved; Holroyd (Chapter 11) presents definitive evidence of erotic contact between therapist and patient, the "quintessence of sex bias"; and Morin and Charles (Chapter 12) discuss heterosexual bias. Moreover, the operation of social-psychological processes such as expectancy effects (Chapter 4) and effects on attributions and memory (Chapter 5) make it unlikely that a therapist could function totally objectively.

Looking over all the chapters in this book, it seems that we are just learning how to study bias in therapy. As more specific measures and additional variables such as attractiveness have been included in research designs, more bias appears. As Stricker and Shafran say in Chapter 8, bias is not "monolithic." It occurs when researchers pinpoint appropriate combinations of therapist characteristics and/or client characteristics and specific areas (measures or problems). Schover, and Hatfield and Perlmutter, found clear biases when employing open-ended responses. So, type of response may be a factor. Realism also seems important—Schover used audiotapes, and Hatfield and Perlmutter did not rely on questionnaires either.

In the last chapter of the volume, López presents a useful integration of the chapters in this book and some very interesting suggestions for future research. He organizes the present material into the areas of historical roots, the scope of psychotherapy bias research, the interface with social psychology, and clinical guidelines. Concluding that general bias is not likely to exist but

351

that specific biases probably do, he offers some thought-provoking proposals, including the following: (1) expanding the definition of bias to include minimizing bias; (2) investigating specific presenting problems that clinicians perceive as related to gender, race, age, or social class; and (3) grounding studies of clinical judgment bias in a theoretical base in order to facilitate identification of when biases occur and to increase our understanding of the process through which biased clinical judgments come about. As one possibility for a theoretical framework, López suggests causal attribution theory, particularly its concept of stable and unstable cases of behavior.

14 The Study of Psychotherapy Bias: Some Conceptual Issues and Some Concluding Remarks

STEVEN LÓPEZ

Most research examining bias in psychotherapy has concerned itself with the study of clinical judgment. Recent reviews of the effects of client gender and race on clinical judgment conclude that there is little evidence of bias (Abramowitz & Murray, Chapter 9; Davidson & Abramowitz, 1980; Smith, 1980). Some researchers interpret these findings as reflecting the inability of the research methodologies to document gender or race bias in psychotherapy (Abramowitz & Murray, Chapter 9; Davidson & Abramowitz, 1980). Others argue that symptomatology, personal history, and other case-related variables are more important than the client's gender is (Billingsley, 1977; Stearns, Penner, & Kimmel, 1980). Before we can reject methodologies or conclude that client variables such as gender and race or physical attractiveness are of minimal significance, we must first consider conceptual factors. As previously noted by Zeldow (1978) and Davidson (Chapter 7), past research contains no conceptual framework. One purpose of this chapter is to address significant conceptual issues in the study of clinical judgment bias and to suggest one conceptual framework for this area of study.

Given the rather negative air of the literature on clinical judgment bias, the

The author wishes to thank Joan Murray and Bernard Weiner for their helpful comments on earlier drafts.

contributions in this book are particularly timely. They provide researchers and clinicians with an opportunity to reexamine significant research and clinical literature in order to reassess their views about therapists' prejudices and the effect these attitudes might have on treatment process and outcome. Before addressing the conceptual issues in the study of clinical judgment bias, let us review the contributions in this book with an eye toward identifying the directions that the emerging field of psychotherapy bias may take.

RESEARCH ON PSYCHOTHERAPY BIAS

Historical Roots

In any developing field of study, it is important to be cognizant of the field's history. Several authors in this volume discuss the historical roots of the study of sex bias. The most comprehensive review is that of Murray (Chapter 1). She reviews historically significant psychological theories and their reviews of women. In addition, she considers research pertaining to sex roles, stereotypes, and therapist-related studies of bias toward women. Stricker and Shafran (Chapter 8) also review this empirical research, as well as the research of patients' preferences for the gender of their therapist. Davidson (Chapter 7) and Schover (Chapter 10) contribute further to the examination of the historical roots of sex bias. Davidson summarizes the development of the countertransference concept, and Schover notes past and present views of countertransference related specifically to sexual feelings. Finally, the summary of Chesler's book (Chapter 2) represents the political fervor of the 1960s, when issues of equality and civil rights were especially significant. This period contributed greatly to the development of the study of psychotherapy bias in general.

The consideration of past efforts may contribute to new insights and new research strategies for the future. For the study of sex bias in psychotherapy, the present volume allows the reader to reflect on some of the historical roots. For the study of race bias, the reader might read Thomas and Sillen's historical account of racism and psychiatry (1972) in combination with Abramowitz and Murray's account (Chapter 9) to become familiar with significant issues in the study of racism and psychotherapy.

The Scope of Psychotherapy Bias Research

The methods used in the study of psychotherapy bias research have extended beyond the analogue study or the clinical judgment paradigm. This is not to say that analogue studies are no longer useful, as Davidson (Chapter 7) and Bloch, Weitz, and Abramowitz (1980) have suggested. On the contrary, studies by both Schover (Chapter 10) and Murray and Abramson (Chapter 6) indicate that analogue methods can provide meaningful data. Other methods—such as survey research, as reported by Holroyd (Chapter 11) and by Schover (Chapter 10); treatment studies, as suggested by Abramowitz and Murray (Chapter 6); and observational and process studies, as recommended by Davidson (Chapter 7)—will serve to broaden the research base of this field.

In addition to an increase in the number of research methods, there has been a parallel increase in the number of content areas considered as part of the psychotherapy bias literature. Other content areas identified in this book besides the traditional sex and race biases include physical attractiveness of clients (Hatfield & Perlmutter, Chapter 3; Murray & Abramson, Chapter 6); therapists' theoretical orientation and/or discipline (Murray & Abramson, Chapter 6; Schover, Chapter 10); therapists' level of experience (Stricker & Shafran, Chapter 8); the sexual orientation of clients (Morin & Charles, Chapter 12); sexual attraction/erotic contact (Schover, Chapter 10; Holroyd, Chapter 11); and patient preferences in regard to therapist gender (Stricker & Shafran, Chapter 8). Although these areas have been previously identified in the research literature, their inclusion in this volume serves to underscore their importance. Other significant biases in psychotherapy not addressed in this volume involve patients' age (Ford & Sbordone, 1980), language (Marcos, Urcuyo, Kesselman, & Alpert, 1973), and social class (C. V. Abramowitz & Dokecki, 1977).

The growth in the number of research methodologies and content areas is encouraging. The sociopolitical aspects of psychotherapy are finally beginning to be openly examined. In order for research findings to have any impact on training and services, however, it is important that the research represent systematic efforts in the study of psychotherapy biases. Scattered, loosely related findings of psychotherapy bias do not provide convincing evidence for the need to educate therapists about gender, race, and other sociopolitical issues. Furthermore, without systematic findings, our knowledge about bias is deficient, as are our efforts to prevent and minimize its occurrence. The systematic documentation and examination of these biases may lead to improved pre- and postgraduate training of psychotherapists. In turn, as systematic biases are minimized, the quality of services to those segments of society that are most underserved or most inappropriately served may then improve.

The Interface of Social Psychology with Psychotherapy Bias

The inclusion of chapters by such recognized social psychologists as Hatfield and Perlmutter (Chapter 3), Rosenthal (Chapter 4), and Hamilton (Chapter 5) provides the reader an opportunity to review social-psychological research relevant to the study of psychotherapy bias. Clinical researchers might be able to gain some insights from their methodological approaches, and, most importantly, from their conceptualizations. Biases toward women or black patients could very well be conceptualized, as Rosenthal suggests, in terms of expectancies, such as the therapist's expectancies for the patient's treatment compliance and outcome. A similar conceptualization, related to Hamilton's review, might pertain to therapists' stereotypes about specific patient groups and the influence that these stereotypes have on therapists' judgments and behavior. And drawing from Hatfield and Perlmutter's research, physical attractiveness can play a significant role in therapist's interaction with the patient.

The study of bias in psychotherapy represents a combination of the study of psychotherapy and prejudice. Although social-psychological research has made significant advances in the study of prejudice, researchers of clinical bias have demonstrated little awareness of this body of research. A better understanding of psychotherapy bias will result from an interface with social psychology, particularly its conceptualizations of prejudice and stereotyping.

Clinical Guidelines

In addition to addressing significant research issues in the study of psychotherapy bias, several contributors also provide straightforward guidelines that practitioners can consider in dealing with their own biases and that of their colleagues. Both Schover (Chapter 10) and Holroyd (Chapter 11) examine reasons why therapists are sexually attracted to clients and become sexually involved with them. They suggest ways in which the therapist can deal with feelings of sexual attraction. Holroyd also carefully addresses the issues that practitioners should consider in assisting a client who has been sexually involved with a former therapist. Her recommendations show considerable insight into significant therapeutic issues and the ethics codes and sections of the legal system pertinent to psychotherapists. Finally, both authors underscore the importance of training mental health professionals to learn how to deal appropriately with sexual issues in the therapy setting.

Morin and Charles (Chapter 12) point out clear examples of heterosexually biased therapy and gay/lesbian-affirmative therapy. They provide specific clinical guidelines that therapists should consider in the provision of psychotherapy for gay and lesbian clients. Last, Cooley and Murray (Chapter 13) present recommendations for addressing prejudices and biases in the therapy context and in the training of therapists. In sum, practitioners and researchers would do well to give careful attention to these guidelines. Practitioners can become familiar with ways to identify and potentially minimize their own biases, while researchers can learn what issues in psychotherapy bias are deemed important by others.

CONCEPTUAL ISSUES

Although bias research now extends beyond studies of clinical judgment to considerations of social-psychological and other phenomena, the clinical judgment research deserves special attention, since it has been the primary research focus in the past. Contrary to the conclusions of Abramowitz and Murray (Chapter 9) and Davidson (Chapter 7), even the analogue paradigm is still quite useful. What has restricted past efforts from successfully documenting bias is not so much the methodology, but the way in which the methodology has been used. Specifically, no conceptual framework has been applied in the research using analogue methodology. The purpose of this section is to consider key conceptual issues that can be applied to the study of clinical judgment bias. These issues include (1) the definition of bias in clinical judgment; (2) the consideration of a second type of bias; (3) the identification of when bias occurs; and (4) causal attributions and clinical judgment bias. Research recommendations are then offered based on these conceptual factors.

Definition of Bias

The term *bias* has been used in the study of clinical judgment to imply a prejudgment or prejudice. Specifically, it has been used to refer to error or inaccuracy in the clinical judgments of women and minority patients. For example, gender bias is reported in analogue research when a woman patient is judged to be significantly more disturbed than a male patient with the identical presenting problem is judged to be (e.g., S. I. Abramowitz, Abramowitz, Jackson, & Gomes, 1973). Similarly, in treatment studies, bias is identified when treatment differences are found between male and female patients when the level of psychopathology has been shown to be equivalent for both groups (e.g., Stein, Del Gaudio, & Ansley, 1976). In both types of research, bias has generally been reported when the women or minority-group patient is perceived as more disturbed or as requiring more treatment. This might best be termed an *overpathologizing bias*. It is important to note that a major assumption underlying this bias is that these differences are not due to actual normative differences between genders or between races, but to error on the part of clinicians.

A Second Type of Bias

Lewis and her associates recently presented data that suggest a second type of bias—one that is here identified as a *minimizing bias* (Lewis, Balla, & Shanok, 1979; Lewis, Shanok, Cohen, Kligfeld, & Frisone, 1980).

They reported several findings indicating that mental health and health personnel tend to dismiss signs of psychotic and/or organic disorders in adolescent black delinquents as culturally appropriate and not amenable to psychiatric treatment, while white adolescents with the same symptomatology are appropriately referred for mental health treatment. Although some of the statistical results are rather weak, the presentation of case studies combined with the statistically reliable findings provide evidence in support of the minimizing bias. This type of bias has consequences that may be as damaging to the patient as the overpathologizing bias may be; services are not rendered, even though there is a significant need for them.

Prior to the studies of Lewis and her colleagues, other researchers had not considered a minimizing bias. Bias was identified when a patient representing one group was judged to be more pathological than a patient representing the contrasting group was judged to be. There are, however, some findings from previous studies that are consistent with the minimizing bias. In the literature on social class bias, Koscherak and Masling (1972), Norman and Martinez (1978), and Routh and King (1972) found that lower-class patients were judged to be less disturbed or in less need of treatment than middle-class patients were judged to be. Similarly, in the literature on gender bias, there are several isolated findings consistent with the minimizing bias. Feinblatt and Gold (1976) found that the female, in a condition stereotypic for females, was judged to need mental health treatment less than the male in that condition was judged to need it (the reader is referred to Chapter 1 for a more detailed account of this study). In a study of social workers, female clients seeking help for marital problems were judged to be more emotionally mature and intelligent (and perhaps perceived as needing *less* care) than their male counterparts were judged to be (Fischer, Dulaney, Fazio, Hudak, & Zivotofsky, 1976). Also, Kelly and Kiersky (Note 1) found that male clinicians rated the depressed female client as less disturbed than they did the depressed male client. Unlike the findings of Lewis and her associates, it is unclear whether these findings represent instances where the problems of the lower-class and women patients were actually minimized. Only further research will be able to clarify this issue. Nonetheless, in at least the study of the treatment of black and white adolescent delinquents, there is some support for a minimizing bias. It seems plausible that there might also be specific presenting problems that are perceived to be more normative for women, the elderly, and members of lower social classes. As a result, patients in need of treatment may not be given the necessary treatment.

There is certainly much research that has failed to find any gender or race bias, and there is much research that supports the overpathologizing bias as it relates to social class. However, the acceptance of these findings need not exclude the existence of a minimizing bias. Some presenting problems may lead to a minimizing bias; others may result in an overpathologizing bias; and still others may lead to no bias whatsoever. The specific presenting problem along with the identity (race, gender, etc.) of the client appears to be important in the identification of the specific type of bias.

When Does Bias Occur?

The findings of Broverman, Broverman, Clarkson, Rosenkrantz, and Vogel (1970) have been most frequently cited as indicating that therapists perceive sex differences in normative behavior. These findings, however, may have misled researchers to search only for an overpathologizing bias and for a double standard that pertains to all presenting problems. To date, the majority of studies have found no bias. Smith (1980) and Stricker (1977) have argued that because of the limited support, there is no evidence for bias. Although there is no evidence for the double standard that pertains to *all* presenting problems, there is evidence of bias pertaining to *specific* presenting problems. In this section, those studies that found bias in clinical judgment are contrasted to those that found no bias. This research suggests that bias occurs for some presenting problems, but not for others.

The treatment studies of Del Gaudio and associates most clearly point out the importance of the presenting problem in gender bias research. They found that female patients given the diagnosis of neurotic depression were seen for more treatment sessions and were administered some form of antidepressant drugs more than males with the same diagnosis were (Stein et al., 1976).[1] In contrast, a larger clinic sample representing a broad spectrum of diagnoses revealed no treatment differences (Del Gaudio, Carpenter, & Morrow, 1978). These findings suggest that treatment biases occur for specific presenting problems only. Similarly, Feinblatt and Gold (1976) presented findings indicating that sex-role-deviant boys and girls comprise a significant proportion of a clinical sample, and they were rated in an analogue study as in greater need of treatment than children with congruent sex role behavior. Zeldow (1976) and Kelly and Kiersky (Note 1) present further data that sex-role-deviant behavior is judged to be more disturbed than sex-role-congruent behavior is. Fischer et al. (1976) and Stearns et al., (1980) are two studies that did *not* find differences attributable to sex-role-related symptoms or behavior.

With respect to the race of the patient, bias has been found in clinical studies of juvenile delinquency (Lewis et al., 1979; Lewis et al., 1980). Analogue studies have provided no support for bias using the following presenting problems: (1) multiple symptomatology, including "depression, somatic complaints, sexual conflicts, and overdriven perfectionism" (Schwartz & Abramowitz, 1975); (2) a passive-dependent, unassertive, and self-doubting male who was also experiencing unsatisfactory sexual relations with his partner (Benefee, Abramowitz, Weitz, & Armstrong, 1976; Bloch et al., 1980);

and (3) actual cases of psychosis, alcoholism, personality disorder, neurosis, and situational disturbance (Bamgbose, Edwards, & Johnson, 1980). The specific presenting problem of delinquency may elicit more biased judgments than multiple symptom problems and general problems may.

Age bias has been found in the prognosis ratings of depression and alcohol abuse cases, but not for agoraphobia or mania (Ford & Sbordone, 1980). And in regard to social class bias, it is difficult to say what specific presenting problems resulted in biased clinical judgments, since many of the studies were based on projective test protocols or on several vignettes of which only one was presented in the published report.

The cases that tapped biased judgments may have been perceived by the subjects as gender-, race-, or age-linked. That is, clinicians may have perceived these problems to have different norms for the specific groups under study. For instance, clinicians may have perceived psychopathological symptoms as more normative for black adolescents than for white adolescents (minimizing bias). Also, clinicians may have viewed alcohol abuse or depression as related to age, such that elderly patients presenting these problems would be perceived as more disturbed than younger patients (overpathologizing bias). These findings suggest that the clinicians' perceptions of the relationship between the specific presenting problem and the specific client variable under study is critical to the identification of minimizing and overpathologizing biases. This includes in-role and out-of-role behavior, as well as behavior or symptoms that are stereotypically perceived to be related to the gender, age, race, or social class of the patient.

One possible reason why there have been few findings of biased judgments is that researchers have been looking for main effects of the client variables independent of the presenting problems. This selective review suggests that *interactions of the type of presenting problem and the specific client variable under study* will prove fruitful in the study of bias in clinical judgment.

An Attributional Analysis of Clinical Judgment Bias

To date, the study of clinical bias has been rather atheoretical in nature. Past studies have been limited to demonstrating whether biases exist. A number of these support the existence of clinical judgment bias. However, the degree of support varies with the specific client variable under study; moreover, many studies find no bias. Accordingly, the application of a theoretical framework to this area of study is viewed as necessary (1) to help identify *when* biases occur and (2) to help understand the *process* through which biased clinical judgments come about.

Weiner's attributional theory (1979, 1980) has the potential to contribute significantly to this area of research, because it is conceptually related to the clinical judgment process and to stereotyping and prejudice. Research has demonstrated the important role that attributions play in clinical judgment (Batson & Marz, 1979; Snyder, 1977) and in stereotyping and prejudice (Hamilton, Chapter 5; Pettigrew, 1979; Taylor & Jaggi, 1974).

A major focus of causal attribution theory and research is the identification of ways in which people make sense of their own behavior and the behavior of others—that is, what people perceive as the causes of behavior. Systematic research has identified and documented three basic perceptions of causes or causal dimensions: locus, stability, and controllability. The *locus* dimension considers whether the causes are perceived to be internal events (person variables) or external events (situation variables). *Stability* refers to the perceived variability (unstable) or permanency (stable) of the causes of behavior. And the *controllability* dimension considers the degree to which the causes are perceived to be under the control of the individual. Each of these causal dimensions has been found to be related to specific consequences. The consequences of the stability dimension are probably the most applicable to clinical judgment, for stability has been shown to be clearly linked to the expectancy of behavior change—or, in clinical terms, to prognosis. If the causes of the presenting problem are thought to be stable, then the patient's prognosis is generally considered poor. On the other hand, if the causes are perceived as unstable, the prognosis is usually considered much better. The consequences of the other dimensions are not dealt with here.

Let us consider the findings of Lewis et al.'s study of racial bias (1980) to illustrate the significance of causal dimensions in clinical judgment and to point out how attributional theory can contribute to the understanding of bias. Lewis and her associates found that race accounted for the most variance in the referral of violent adolescents to either an inpatient psychiatric unit or to a correctional facility in the state of Connecticut. Blacks were significantly overrepresented in the correctional facility, while whites were overrepresented in the inpatient unit, even though the psychiatric symptomatology was judged to be equivalent in the two groups. The authors interpreted these results as "a tendency for white psychiatrists to overlook or rationalize as normal the signs and symptoms of psychopathology in black individuals" (p. 1215).

Assuming that white psychiatrists viewed the symptoms as more normative for black adolescents than for white adolescents, it is plausible that the causes of these symptoms also were perceived differently by race. Clinicians may have perceived the causes of black adolescents' violent behavior as being more related to environmental stressors such as poverty, limited educational opportunities, and culture. These causes are generally stable for the low-income population. In contrast, personal adjustment problems or specific intrapsychic conflicts might have been more salient in the therapists' attributions about the white adolescents. These causes may be classified as less stable than external stressors may be. Problems that are perceived to be caused by less stable factors would appear to be more amenable to mental health interventions than problems caused by more stable factors would seem to be. Therefore, when therapists attribute violent behavior to stable environmental stressors, the individual may be viewed as having a poor prognosis. As a result, the patient would be less likely to be accepted for treatment and more likely to be referred to a correctional institution.

There are other possible interpretations of the Lewis et al. (1980) study based on Weiner's theory. This interpretation serves only to illustrate the applicability of the theory to the study of clinical bias. Empirical studies could identify the specific attributional patterns that lead to clinical judgment bias. Knowledge of these patterns would greatly assist those attempting to ameliorate and prevent clinical bias. Training could then be directed at not only pointing out the presenting problems that are most likely to evoke bias, but also the therapists' attributional patterns that lead to biased and nonbiased judgments.

Recommendations for Future Research

The first recommendation is that the definition of bias be expanded to include the minimizing bias in addition to the traditional overpathologizing bias. If clinicians are less inclined to perceive a need for treatment for female and minority patients when it is clear that treatment is needed, then this is clearly an injustice to these patients.

Second, the type of presenting problem should be considered in the study of clinical judgment bias. The notion that bias occurs across all presenting problems has clearly not been supported. Bias is most likely to occur in the diagnosis of those presenting problems that clinicians perceive to be related to gender, race, age, or social class. Therefore, empirical research is recommended that investigates clinicians' perceptions of *specific presenting problems* (not bipolar adjectives) as they relate to the important client variables. That is, do clinicians perceive certain presenting problems to be more likely representative of males or females, blacks or whites, and so on? Several researchers have examined presumed sex-role-congruent and deviant behaviors as symptoms without first establishing whether clinicians perceive those behaviors or symptoms as sex-role-related. Given the more limited findings of replications and/or extensions of the Broverman et al. (1970) study (i.e., Aslin, 1977; Cowan, 1976; Maslin & Davis, 1975), clinicians may not have the same sex-role stereotypes that the general population has.

Last, it is recommended that researchers include a theoretical base in their studies of clinical judgment bias. Descriptive accounts of when and under what conditions bias might occur are helpful. However, the application of theory may contribute to a better understanding of this phenomenon, which, in turn, may significantly contribute to efforts to prevent or ameliorate any such biases. Weiner's attributional theory has been offered as one theoretical base that might prove fruitful.

Conclusion

A major assumption underlying this chapter is that the biases related to client variables share a common social-psychological process. For instance, even though it is likely that there are quantitative and qualitative differences between age and gender bias, it appears that the same social-psychological process occurs for all clinical judgment biases. Clinicians have preconceived ideas about the appropriateness of a specific presenting problem to the person's age, sex, race, or social class. Through a process similar to the one described by Hamilton (Chapter 5), the adherence to this stereotype increases the likelihood that clinicians will either overlook and/or dismiss pathological symptomatology (the minimizing bias), or will overlook and/or dismiss normative behavior and emphasize the pathological behavior (the overpathologizing bias). A promising direction for future reserach is to begin systematically identifying those specific presenting problems that lead to overpathologizing and minimizing biases in clinical judgment and to begin identifying the attributional patterns that are involved in these biases.

NOTES

[1]These findings appear to contradict the study of Kelly and Kiersky (Note 1), which found that the depressed female was rated as less disturbed than the depressed male was. It should be noted, however, that the patients in the Stein et al. study were diagnosed as having depressive neurosis, while the patient/actors in the Kelly and Kiersky study were described as depressed. Clinical judgments may differ for clients diagnosed as having depressive neurosis and for clients who are depressed.

REFERENCE NOTES

1. Kelly, K., & Kiersky, S. *Psychotherapists and sexual stereotypes: A study of bias in diagnostic interviews employing videotape simulations.* Paper presented at the annual meeting of the New York State Psychological Association, Saratoga, New York, 1979.

REFERENCES

Abramowitz, C. V., & Dokecki, P. R. The politics of clinical judgment. *Psychological Bulletin,* 1977, *84,* 460–476.
Abramowitz, S. I., Abramowitz, C. V., Jackson, C., & Gomes, B. The politics of clinical judgment: What nonliberal examiners infer about women who do not stifle themselves. *Jour-*

nal of Consulting and Clinical Psychology, 1973, *41*, 385–391.

Aslin, A. L. Feminist and community mental health center psychotherapists' expectations for women. *Sex Roles*, 1977, *3*, 537–544.

Bamgbose, O., Edwards, D., & Johnson, S. The effects of race and social class on clinical judgment. *Journal of Clinical Psychology*, 1980, *36*, 605–609.

Batson, C. D., & Marz, B. Dispositional bias in trained therapists' diagnoses: Does it exist? *Journal of Applied Social Psychology*, 1979, *9*, 476–489.

Benefee, L M., Abramowitz, S. I., Weitz, L. J., & Armstrong, S. H. Effects of patient racial attribution on black clinicians' inferences. *American Journal of Community Psychology*, 1976, *4*, 263–273.

Billingsley, D. Sex bias in psychotherapy: An examination of the effects of client sex, client pathology, and therapist sex on treatment planning. *Journal of Consulting and Clinical Psychology*, 1977, *45*, 250–256.

Bloch, P. M., Weitz, L. J., & Abramowitz, S. I. Racial attribution effects on clinical judgment: A failure to replicate among white clinicians. *American Journal of Community Psychology*, 1980, *8*, 484–493.

Broverman, I. K., Broverman, D. M., Clarkson, F. E., Rosenkrantz, P. S., & Vogel, S. R. Sex-role stereotypes and clinical judgments of mental health. *Journal of Consulting and Clinical Psychology*, 1970, *34*, 1–7.

Cowan, G. Therapist judgments of clients' sex-role problems. *Psychology of Women Quarterly*, 1976, *1*, 115–124.

Davidson, C. V., & Abramowitz, S. I. Sex bias in clinical judgment: Later empirical returns. *Psychology of Women Quarterly*, 1980, *4*, 377–395.

Del Gaudio, A. C., Carpenter, P. J., & Morrow, G. R. Male and female treatment differences: Can they be generalized? *Journal of Consulting and Clinical Psychology*, 1978, *46*, 1577–1578.

Feinblatt, J. A., & Gold, A. R. Sex roles and the psychiatric referral process. *Sex Roles*, 1976, *2*, 109–122.

Fischer, J., Dulaney, D. D., Fazio, R. T., Hudak, M. T., & Zivotofsky, E. Are social workers sexists? *Social Work*, 1976, *21*, 428–433.

Ford, C. V., & Sbordone, R. J. Attitudes of psychiatrists toward elderly patients. *American Journal of Psychiatry*, 1980, *137*, 679–682.

Koscherak, S., & Masling, J. Noblesse oblige effect: The interpretation of rorschach responses as a function of ascribed social class. *Journal of Consulting and Clinical Psychology*, 1972, *39*, 415–419.

Lewis, D. O., Balla, D. A., & Shanok, S. S. Some evidence of race bias in the diagnosis and treatment of the juvenile offender. *American Journal of Orthopsychiatry*, 1979, *49*, 53–61.

Lewis, D. O., Shanok, S. S., Cohen, R. J., Kligfeld, M., & Frisone, G. Race bias in the diagnosis and disposition of violent adolescents. *American Journal of Psychiatry*, 1980, *137*, 1211–1216.

Marcos, L. R., Urcuyo, L., Kesselman, M., & Alpert, M. The language barrier in evaluating Spanish-American patients. *Archives of General Psychiatry*, 1973, *29*, 655–659.

Maslin, A., & Davis, J. L. Sex-role stereotyping as a factor in mental health standards among counselors-in-training. *Journal of Counseling Psychology*, 1975, *22*, 87–91.

Norman, R. D., & Martinez, R. Social class and ethnicity effects on clinical judgments. *Psychological Reports*, 1978, *43*, 91–98.

Pettigrew, T. F. The ultimate attribution error: Extending Allport's cognitive analysis of prejudice. *Personality and Social Psychology Bulletin*, 1979, *4*, 461–476.

Routh, D. K., & King, K. W. Social class bias and clinical judgment. *Journal of Consulting and Clinical Psychology*, 1972, *38*, 202–207.

Schwartz, J. M., & Abramowitz, S. I. Value-related effects on psychiatric judgment. *Archives* of *General Psychiatry*, 1975, *32*, 1525–1529.

Smith, M. L. Sex bias in counseling and psychotherapy. *Psychological Bulletin*, 1980, *87*, 392–407.

Snyder, C. R. "A patient by any other name" revisited: Maladjustment or attributional locus of problem? *Journal of Consulting and Clinical Psychology*, 1977, *45*, 101–103.

Stearns, B. C., Penner, L. A., & Kimmel, E. Sexism among psychotherapists: A case not yet proven. *Journal of Consulting and Clinical Psychology*, 1980, *48*, 548–550.

Stein, L., Del Gaudio, A., & Ansley, M. A comparison of female and male neurotic depressives. *Journal of Clinical Psychology*, 1976, *32*, 19–21.

Stricker, G. Implications of research for psychotherapeutic treatment of women. *American Psychologist*, 1977, *32*, 14–22.

Taylor, D. M., & Jaggi, U. Ethnocentrism and causal attribution in a South Indian context. *Journal of Cross-Cultural Psychology*, 1974, *5*, 162–170.

Thomas, A., & Sillen, S. *Racism and psychiatry*. Secaucus, N.J.: The Citadel Press, 1972.

Weiner, B. A theory of motivation for some classroom experiences. *Journal of Educational Psychology*, 1979, *71*, 3–25.

Weiner, B. *Human motivation*. New York: Holt, Rinehart & Winston, 1980.

Zeldow, P. Effects of nonpathological sex-role stereotypes on evaluations of psychiatric patients. *Journal of Consulting and Clinical Psychology*, 1976, *44*, 304.

Zeldow, P. Sex differences in psychiatric evaluation and treatment: An empirical review. *Archives of General Psychiatry*, 1978, *35*, 89–93.

Name Index

Subject Index

Abnormality. *See* Normality

Adjustment. *See* Therapist's judgment of client adjustment

Aggression, 5

Analogue research, 32, 126–127, 171–173, 217–218, 222, 223, 224, 262, 264, 355, 357; advantages of, 218, 241, 245, 263–264; generalizability of, 275–276; problems with, 192–193, 218, 222, 264; support for, 200–201

Anatomical determinism, 9, 10, 11, 12, 13, 41–42, 43

Approach/avoidance responses by therapists, 266

Archival method, 126, 217–218, 219, 224, 226

Attractiveness effects, 34, 53–83, 133–134, 351; characteristics of attractive/unattractive people, 65–72, 78–79 [happiness, 69; mental illness, 70–72, 79; origin of differences, 67; personality, 67–68; popularity, 68; self-concept, 67; sociability, 68–69]; differences in behavior toward the attractive/unattractive, 63–66, 79 [in help seeking behavior, 66; in helping behavior, 65–66; in intimate settings, 64–65; summary, 66]; expectations about attractive people, 57–64, 79 [among clients, 60; among psychotherapists, 59–60; and transgressions, 60–62; are positive, 57–59, 60–63; conclusion, 63–64; in children, 57–58; sex by attractiveness interactions, 63; victims, 62]; future research, 72–73; in psychotherapists, 53, 54, 72–73, 74–77; in psychotherapy, 34, 125, 129, 133, 134–135, 144, 146, 147, 151, 351 [attractiveness and bias in diagnosis, 73; attractiveness and length of therapy, 74; attractiveness and outcome, 76–77]; review of research on, 53; stereotypes of attractive people, 57–

64, 79; who is attractive, 54–57, 78–79 [agreement on, 54, 56–57, 79; cross-cultural data, 55, 78; in our society, 55–57, 78]

Attribution: influence of stereotypes on causal attributions, 105–108, 120–121 [sex stereotypes, 106–107; race stereotypes, 107]. *See also* Cognitive processes

Beauty, 5

Biased attitudes/biased behavior distinction, 126, 194, 199, 208–209, 351

Bias in psychotherapy: attribution theory and, 352, 360–362; clinical guidelines regarding, 356; cognitive processes and, 103–121; conceptual factors, 353, 356; conceptualization, 356, 357, 360; conclusions, 351; content areas in, 355; definition of bias, 357; historical roots, 354; minimizing bias, 352, 357–359, 360, 362, 363; overpathologizing bias, 357, 358, 360, 362, 363; presenting problem and, 358–360, 362, 363; recommendations for research, 351, 362–363; remedies for, 339–350 [in consumers, 349; in practicing therapists, 348–349; in therapist training, 341–348]; research methodology, 351, 353, 354–355, 356, 357, 360, 362–363 [open-ended responses, 351; realism, 351; specificity, 359–360, 362]; scope of research on, 351; social psychology and, 355–356, 363; theoretical base, 352, 362; training of therapists and, 356; types of, 351, when it occurs, 359. *See also* Attractiveness effects; Gender bias in evaluation; Gender bias in hiring; Gender bias in psychotherapy; Heterosexual bias in psychotherapy; Race bias in psychological testing; Race bias in psychotherapy

About the Editors
and the Contributors

JOAN MURRAY is actively doing consulting and teaching in the Los Angeles area. Until 1982 she was Research Co-ordinator for Project STEP, a large-scale study of stepfamily interaction and child adjustment.

Dr. Murray has published in varied areas in psychology. Her articles have appeared in the *Journal of Personality and Social Psychology*, the *Journal of Personality*, and *Developmental Psychology*.

Dr. Murray holds a B.A. degree from the University of Pennsylvania, and an M.A. and Ph.D. in clinical psychology from the University of California, Los Angeles.

PAUL R. ABRAMSON is Associate Professor of Psychology at the University of California, Los Angeles.

Dr. Abramson has published widely in the areas of personality and human sexuality. His articles have appeared in the *Journal of Consulting and Clinical Psychology*, the *Journal of Personality and Social Psychology*, the *Journal of Research in Personality*, the *Journal of Social Issues*, *Archives of Sexual Behavior*, and *American Psychologist*, and he has published a textbook entitled *Personality*.

STEPHEN I. ABRAMOWITZ, School of Medicine, University of California at Davis, has written numerous articles on bias in psychotherapy.

KENNETH A. CHARLES is a free-lance writer in San Francisco. He currently works as a psychotherapist at Operation Concern, a lesbian/gay mental health agency.

PHYLLIS CHESLER is the author of the groundbreaking works *Women and Madness, About Men*, and *With Child*. She is an Associate Professor of Psychology at the College of Staten Island, lectures frequently, and is completing a book on *Women and Custody*.

ELIZABETH COOLEY, one of the founders of the Wright Institute in Los Angeles, is now in private practice in that city.

CHRISTINE V. DAVIDSON, Department of Psychiatry, Cook County Hospital, Chicago, has written numerous articles on gender bias in psychotherapy and the politics of therapy.

DAVID L. HAMILTON, Professor of Psychology, University of California at Santa Barbara, has written broadly on social perception and recently edited a volume entitled *Cognitive Processes in Stereotyping and Intergroup Behavior.*

ELAINE HATFIELD, Chair, Psychology Department, University of Hawaii at Manoa, has published numerous articles in experimental social psychology. She is an author of *A New Look at Love, Mirror Mirror on the Wall, Interpersonal Attraction,* and *Equity: Theory and Research.* She is a family therapist at King Kalakaua Clinic in Honolulu, Hawaii.

JEAN C. HOLROYD, Psychiatry Department, UCLA, was co-chairperson of the American Psychological Association Task Force on Sex Bias and Sex-Role Stereotyping in Psychotherapeutic Practice.

STEVEN LÓPEZ, Assistant Professor of Psychology, University of Southern California, has done work on clinical issues related to Chicanos and on psychotherapeutic bias.

STEPHEN S. MORIN is a licensed clinical psychologist in private practice in San Francisco. He was co-founder and first chairperson of the Association of Gay Psychologists. He has written extensively on lesbian and gay issues.

MORTON S. PERLMUTTER, Professor, School of Social Work, University of Wisconsin at Madison, is Education and Training Consultant to the Wisconsin Family Studies Institute and is engaged in private practice there.

ROBERT ROSENTHAL, Professor, Department of Psychology and Social Relations, Harvard University, is widely known for his work on experimenter effects, including the classic *Pygmalion in the Classroom* (1968).

LESLIE R. SCHOVER, Section of Sexual Rehabilitation, Department of Urology, M. D. Anderson Hospital and Tumor Institute, Texas Medical Center, Houston, has done research on sexual dysfunction, sexual intimacy in psychological training, and therapists' responses to patients' sexual material.

ROBIN SHAFRAN is a psychologist in independent practice in New York City. Her doctoral dissertation and current research interests are in the area of stereotyping and psychotherapy.

GEORGE STRICKER, Assistant Dean and Professor of Psychology, Institute of Advanced Psychological Studies, Adelphi University, is the author of the controversial 1977 *American Psychologist* review article on sex bias in psychotherapy.